THE HISTORY AND ARCHAEOLOGY OF
Fort Ouiatenon

300 Years in the Making

The History and Archaeology of
Fort Ouiatenon

300 Years in the Making

Edited by:
Misty M. Jackson, H. Kory Cooper,
and David M. Hovde

Purdue University Press • West Lafayette, Indiana

Copyright 2024 by Purdue University. All rights reserved.
Printed in the United States of America.

Cataloging-in-Publication Data is available from the Library of Congress.
978-1-61249-876-8 (hardback)
978-1-61249-877-5 (paperback)
978-1-61249-878-2 (epub)
978-1-61249-879-9 (epdf)

Cover image: Layout by Purdue University Press using the following assets: Carte Du Cours De L'Ohio Ou De La Belle Riviere/British Library Images Online; Possible signet ring from Fort Ouiatenon in the TCHA collection/Misty M. Jackson/ Tippecanoe County Historical Association; Trade silver brooch/Brooke Sauter/Tippecanoe County Historical Association; German Westerwold mug fragment/Brooke Sauter/Tippecanoe County Historical Association; Paste glass sleeve buttons/Brooke Sauter/Tippecanoe County Historical Association; Trade silver brooch/Brooke Sauter/Tippecanoe County Historical Association;

CONTENTS

Preface   *vii*
VERGIL E. NOBLE

Introduction   *xi*
MISTY M. JACKSON, ARBRE CROCHE CULTURAL RESOURCES, LLC,
AND H. KORY COOPER, ASSOCIATE PROFESSOR, DEPARTMENT OF ANTHROPOLOGY

Part I: History and Archaeology

1   Fort Ouiatenon: Three Hundred Years from the Founding, Loss, Rediscovery, and Archaeology   3
DAVID M. HOVDE, PROFESSOR EMERITUS, PURDUE UNIVERSITY

2   The History of the Archaeology of Ouiatenon   35
KELSEY NOACK MYERS, US ARMY CORPS OF ENGINEERS

3   Outside the Fort: Completing the Picture of the Ouiatenon Landscape   57
MICHAEL STREZEWSKI, UNIVERSITY OF SOUTHERN INDIANA

4   French Colonial History and Archaeology at Fort Miamis and Vincennes   81
MICHAEL STREZEWSKI, UNIVERSITY OF SOUTHERN INDIANA

Part II: Artifact Studies

5   Use of Animals at Fort Ouiatenon   105
TERRANCE J. MARTIN, CURATOR EMERITUS OF ANTHROPOLOGY,
ILLINOIS STATE MUSEUM

6   Symbolism, Nationality, Identity, and Gender as Interpreted from an Eighteenth-Century Ring from Fort Ouiatenon   151
MISTY M. JACKSON, ARBRE CROCHE CULTURAL RESOURCES LLC,
AND H. KORY COOPER, ASSOCIATE PROFESSOR, DEPARTMENT OF ANTHROPOLOGY

7   Buckles from Fort Ouiatenon: Searching for Interpretive Clues in the
    Documents and Testing for Their Composition   173
    MISTY M. JACKSON, ARBRE CROCHE CULTURAL RESOURCES LLC, LINA C. PATINO,
    NATIONAL SCIENCE FOUNDATION, AND DAVID W. SZYMANSKI, DEPARTMENT OF
    NATURAL AND APPLIED SCIENCES, BENTLEY UNIVERSITY

8   Flintlocks on the Frontier: A Case Study of Fort St. Joseph (20BE23),
    Niles, Michigan   193
    KEVIN P. JONES

PART III: COMMUNITY, STAKEHOLDERS, AND PRESERVATION

9   Myaamiaki (Miami People): A Living People with a Past   217
    DIANE HUNTER, TRIBAL HISTORIC PRESERVATION OFFICER (RET.), MIAMI TRIBE
    OF OKLAHOMA

10 The Feast of the Hunters' Moon: A Commemoration of the
    History of Indiana's First European Settlement   233
    DAVID M. HOVDE, PROFESSOR EMERITUS, PURDUE UNIVERSITY

11 Connecting the Song to the Artifact at the Feast of the Hunters' Moon   261
    RONALD V. MORRIS, BALL STATE UNIVERSITY, AND LESLIE MARTIN CONWELL,
    TIPPECANOE COUNTY HISTORICAL ASSOCIATION

12 Preserving the Past for the Future: Sustainable and Responsible Curation
    of Colonial Archaeological Collections in the Midwest   283
    ERIKA K. HARTLEY, FORT ST. JOSEPH CURATORIAL FELLOW, CHRISTINA H.
    ARSENEAU, DIRECTOR, NILES HISTORY CENTER, AND MICHAEL S. NASSANEY,
    PROFESSOR EMERITUS, WESTERN MICHIGAN UNIVERSITY

13 At the Edge of Forever: Preserving Fort Ouiatenon and the Creation
    of the Ouiatenon Preserve, a Roy Whistler Foundation Project   311
    J. COLBY BARTLETT, DIRECTOR, OUIATENON PRESERVE INC.

Acknowledgments   *323*

Contributors   *325*

Index   *331*

PREFACE

VERGIL E. NOBLE

UNTIL THE SPRING OF 1974 I HAD NEVER HEARD OF FORT OUIATENON. I was then approaching the end of my senior year at Michigan State University (MSU), and I was looking forward to another summer of archaeological fieldwork conducted under the auspices of the MSU Museum. During the summer of 1973, I had enjoyed my first field experience working at a place that came to be known as the Mill Creek site, an eighteenth-century milling complex located at the Straits of Mackinac east of the site of Fort Michilimackinac in what is now northern Michigan. My interest in historical archaeology had been piqued at Mill Creek, and I was excited about further honing my excavation skills and knowledge of the period at a roughly contemporary site in Indiana.

This opportunity all began when earlier in the year the Tippecanoe County Historical Association (TCHA) contacted Dr. Charles E. Cleland, professor of anthropology and curator of anthropology at the MSU Museum, Dr. Charles E. Cleland. They knew of MSU's cooperative investigations at the site of Michilimackinac since 1959 and hoped that MSU would agree to expand on preliminary work performed by Dr. James Kellar of Indiana University in 1968 and 1969. Kellar was not trained in historical archaeology, as few were of his generation, but his large block excavation confirming the location of Fort Ouiatenon was sufficient to get the site listed on the National Register of Historic Places in 1970. A deal was struck, and senior graduate student Judith D. Tordoff, who had previously dug at such sites as Michilimackinac, was assigned to direct the field excavations under the general direction of Principal Investigator Cleland.

Tordoff's primary goal was to define the limits of Ouiatenon by digging end-to-end units, ten by five feet, on the cardinal directions to form trenches that might intersect evidence of the stockade walls. We also hosted a team of physicists from Purdue University, directed by graduate student Ralph R. B. von Frese as his master's thesis project, who were experimenting with the use of various geophysical prospection techniques on an archaeological site. The devices were extremely primitive by modern standards yet effective in pinpointing cultural anomalies.

My 1974 field season at Ouiatenon was an edifying and exciting experience, convincing me to pursue historical archaeology as a career. But I wasn't quite ready for graduate school, and I instead took to the road, shovel-bumming from one project to another until I had had my fill of fieldwork and headed back to East Lansing in hopes of earning some real money. Early in 1975, I approached Chuck Cleland about applying for grad school at MSU. At the time there really were only two schools that specialized in historical archaeology. You could go to MSU and study under Cleland or go to Brown University and study under Dr. James Deetz. I chose MSU, and Chuck encouraged me to apply.

In the spring I was accepted into the graduate program at MSU for the fall quarter, which led to an offer to serve as assistant director under Judy Tordoff at Ouiatenon that summer. I took the offer, of course, and the field crew delved deeper into physical remains of the trading post, including several excavations inspired by geophysical anomalies that resulted in the excavation of a small forge and a semisubterranean trade goods storehouse. A well was also found and excavated to the water table, where ancient cribbing was found.

For the summer of 1976 in order to broaden my experience, I embarked on a largely precontact project surveying a state park near the city of Charlevoix in northern Michigan. But I was also well aware that 1976 would be Tordoff's third and final season of collecting data for her dissertation on Fort Ouiatenon. Accordingly, a decent interval after I began graduate studies, I made an appointment with Cleland to discuss my future prospects. I asked if the TCHA planned to continue supporting MSU's research efforts and if so would he consider putting me forward as the new field director. Within a few months he was able to tell me that the program would indeed continue, thanks to TCHA's generosity, and that I would have the assignment of leading field investigations at Ouiatenon for the next three summers.

During the years 1977–1979, I instituted a sampling program that would provide broad coverage of what had been determined to be the north half of the fort site. It was my thought that statistical analyses of artifact frequencies gathered from test units dispersed across the area might help reveal discrete activity areas within and immediately surrounding the stockade delineated by Tordoff's work. In the end, those analytical efforts did not prove as fruitful as I would have hoped, but the sampling design itself was quite successful in disclosing the locations of a wide variety of cultural features, including evidence of numerous interior structures, a second well, and the post cemetery. Four burials were encountered in test units, and Ralph von Frese's reanalysis of his data showed indications of the burial ground, though we had not known how to interpret those linear anomalies when the geophysical data were first plotted on maps.

More intriguing perhaps was evidence of a smaller stockade perimeter that doubtless represented the first Fort Ouiatenon before its apparent expansion.

Despite several interruptions that impeded my progress, I ultimately completed analysis of the data, described the collections, and wrote my dissertation, which I defended successfully in 1983. In the years following, several other students at MSU and other universities completed master's and doctoral projects using data from the site. It has now been over forty years since I worked at Fort Ouiatenon, and I have stood only once on the site in the intervening years. But I am pleased that other researchers with new perspectives and new techniques have continued to explore the site and its environs, particularly the numerous Native village sites that lie to the north of the fort. Indeed, during the last decade renewed interest in the site and its environs has grown considerably.

The chapters compiled in this volume ably summarize the history of Fort Ouiatenon, its varied excavations, and much of the recent archaeological and geophysical research conducted at and near the site. Some chapters also summarize work done at contemporary fur trade–era sites for its comparative value. Therefore, I am delighted that the editors have labored to pull this volume together. The book serves to bring me up to date on this site I used to know so well, and I hope that it will similarly inform other readers about this important place on the banks of the Wabash. Ouiatenon is a special place in the history of America and especially of Indiana. Moreover, as researchers continue to delve into its cultural remains, the archaeological preserve has the ability to enhance our understanding of the eighteenth-century fur trade and interactions between Native peoples and Europeans. For that, I am truly gratified.

INTRODUCTION

MISTY M. JACKSON, ARBRE CROCHE CULTURAL RESOURCES, LLC, AND H. KORY COOPER, ASSOCIATE PROFESSOR, DEPARTMENT OF ANTHROPOLOGY

IN 1955 THE INDIANA HISTORICAL SOCIETY PUBLISHED *OUIATANON Documents*, a collection of many of the primary documents referencing Fort Ouiatenon and translated from French by editor Frances Krauskopf. Though Krauskopf's dissertation and a few publications predated it (Craig 1893; Dunn 1894; Krauskopf 1953), the volume remained the main source published on the fort until archaeological investigations began at the location of the fort in the 1960s. James Kellar (1970) published a brief summary of Indiana University's excavations, and eventually six dissertations (Noble 1983; Tordoff 1983; Martin 1986; Jones 1988; Jackson 2005; Noack Myers 2017) resulted from the excavations conducted by Michigan State University and Indiana University. One master's thesis focused on remote sensing conducted at the site (von Frese 1978). A number of other publications primarily in the form of chapters, reports, and articles also appeared over time (Johnson 2000; Jones 1984; McGroarty 1982; Noack Myers 2019; Noble 1979, 1991; Strezewski and McCullough 2010; Strezewski 2014; Trubowitz 1992).

Historic documents and twentieth-century literature reveal a variety of spellings for the fort's name, a common one being that used in the title of Krauskopf's volume. The Tippecanoe County Historical Association's use of the spelling "Ouiatenon" appears to have become the most widely accepted and therefore has been adopted for this volume. It is also noteworthy that the term "Ouiatenon" as used by Krauskopf and other writers refers to the fort and its environs as well as the Wea people for whom the fort was named, depending on context.

The Midwest Historical Archaeology Conference was held in Lafayette, Indiana, in 2017 to commemorate the three hundredth anniversary of the founding of Fort Ouiatenon, papers from which as well as additional invited chapters have resulted in this volume. *The History and Archaeology of Fort Ouiatenon: 300 Years in the Making* brings together a variety of themes and research objectives offering a look at where the archaeological and historical study of Fort Ouiatenon has been and where it is heading as well as past and present developments in community involvement and preservation of the fort's site and surrounding area.

Readers will note that each of the three sections into which this volume is divided includes chapters on other forts in addition to Ouiatenon (chapters 4, 8, and 12), including Fort Miamis, Post Vincennes, and Fort St. Joseph, with one chapter also bringing in Fort Michilimackinac for comparison (chapter 12) (figure I.1). Fort Ouiatenon along with the other forts stood within the Pays d'en Haut (Upper Country), as the French referred to the land upriver from Montreal and all the Great Lakes region during the eighteenth century (see White 1991, x–xi). As such, they shared many connections. One of the obvious connections was that of waterways, portages, and overland trails. The portage between the St. Marys and Wabash Rivers connected Forts Miamis and Ouiatenon (figure I.2).

Thomas Hutchins's 1762 map records the northern three posts and their connecting rivers and trails. Hutchins traversed what he referred to as the road between Fort St. Joseph and Fort Miamis from August 9 to 12, 1762 (Bond 1942, 79, 82, 85; figure I.3). On a map dated 1778 Hutchins recorded a road between Forts Ouiatenon and St. Joseph (figure I.4). His notes on this latter map are the same as that dated 1762. The road between Ouiatenon and St. Joseph may have existed at the time Hutchins made his visit to the region resulting in the earlier map, but he did not record traversing it and therefore may have chosen to exclude it on the earlier map (Tucker 1942, plate 29).

Three of the posts were also similar in the size of their populations, at least at the beginning of the British period, according to Hutchins. During his visits in 1762 to Forts Michilimackinac, St. Joseph, and Ouiatenon he recorded families numbering one dozen at the first two posts and fifteen at Ouiatenon. In his 1778 account he indicated a dozen families at Fort Ouiatenon (Bond 1942, 81–82; Hutchins 1904, 101).

Other connections between the four southernmost posts included shared commandants, missionaries, and aid in times of conflict as recorded in Krauskopf's *Ouiatanon Documents* (1955). For example, Jacques-Charles Renaud Dubuisson was sent to command at the new post among the Miami, Fort St. Philip (present-day Fort Wayne), where he resided while also commanding at Ouiatenon. François-Marie Vincennes, whose father was respected by the Miami and also had acquired influence among the Native Americans of the area around Ouiatenon, was sent to the latter and the Wea in lieu of Dubuisson's presence. Vincennes later established the post that bore his name and served there until his death in 1736. The Potawatomi from Fort St. Joseph aided the French in their war against the English and the Miami at Pickawillany in 1752 in an effort to bring the Miami back under French influence. The interrelated nature of Fort Ouiatenon with the other three posts provides a basis for their inclusion and allows for

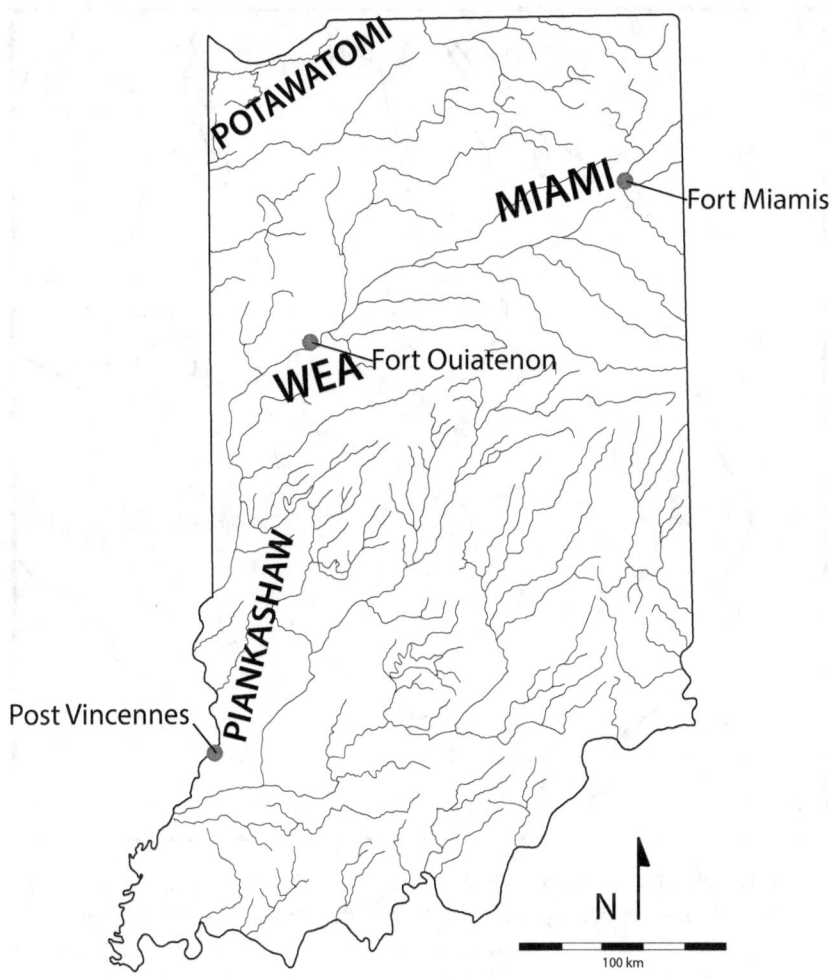

Figure I.1. Circa 1760 locations of major historic period Native American tribes and French Colonial establishments in the present state of Indiana. Map by Michael Strezewski.

their contextualization within the larger Native American and French worlds of the eighteenth-century Pays d'en Haut.

Over the last sixty years researchers have incorporated many theoretical frameworks, reflecting the shift in focus and continuity in the methods used to explore the site over that time. During the early 1980s Tordorf's (1983) dissertation situated the fort at the colonial periphery of the European core, as it provided the supplies of furs for production of goods. Jones (1984, 1988) examined European artifacts from Native American contexts including the Wea village (12T6) associated with Fort Ouiatenon (12T9)

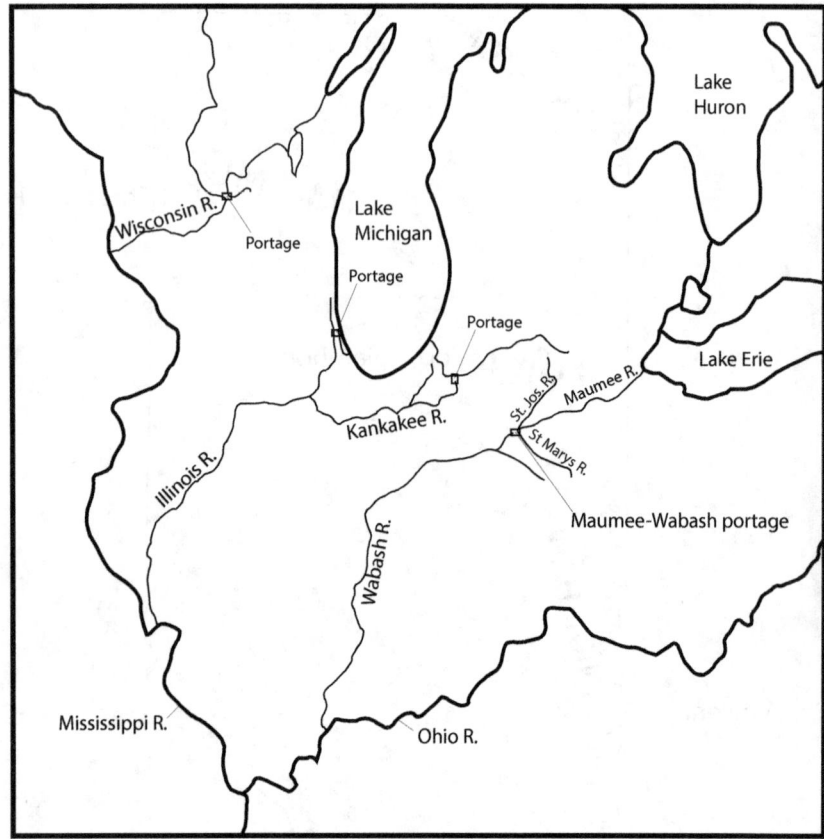

Figure I.2. Detail of Thomas Hutchins's *A Tour from Fort Cumberland North Westward Round Part of the Lakes Erie, Huron, and Michigan, Including Part of the Rivers St. Joseph, the Wabach, and Miamis, with a Sketch of the Road from Thence to the Lower Shawnoe Town to Fort Pitt* (1762) recording forts Ouiatenon, Miamis, and St. Joseph, and their connecting rivers and trails. Map by Michael Strezewski.

within the framework of acculturation. However, theoretical shifts occurring in the 1980s and 1990s began movement away from Eurocentric world systems theory and acculturation models for understanding change in Native American societies. Richard White's (1991) notion of a metaphorical "middle ground" gained attention as he argued that interaction between Europeans and Native Americans in the Pays d'en Haut was dominated not by Europeans or Native Americans but instead by way of negotiation between cultures, encompassing both. Yet, this was also a time of Native American power and control of events within the region, a time of "entanglement" rather than passive adoption of European material culture or European supremacy (DeCorse and Beier 2018). Acculturation models gave way to those emphasizing adoption and

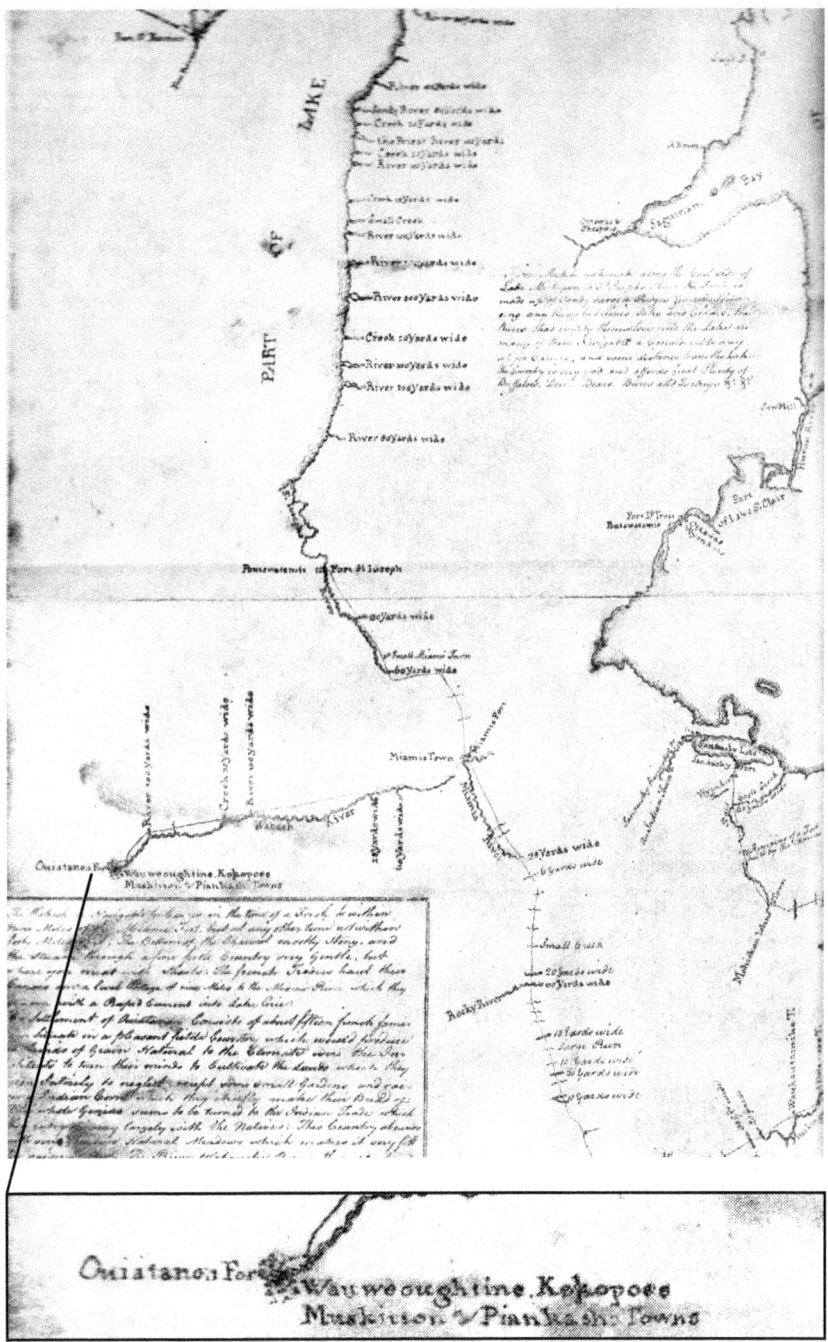

Figure I.3. Detail of Thomas Hutchins's *A Tour from Fort Cumberland North Westward Round Part of the Lakes Erie, Huron, and Michigan, Including Part of the Rivers St. Joseph, the Wabach, and Miamis, with a Sketch of the Road from Thence to the Lower Shawnoe Town to Fort Pitt* (1762) recording Forts Ouiatenon, Miamis, and St. Joseph, and their connecting rivers and trails. Bond 1942; mssHM 1091, The Huntington Library, San Marino, California.

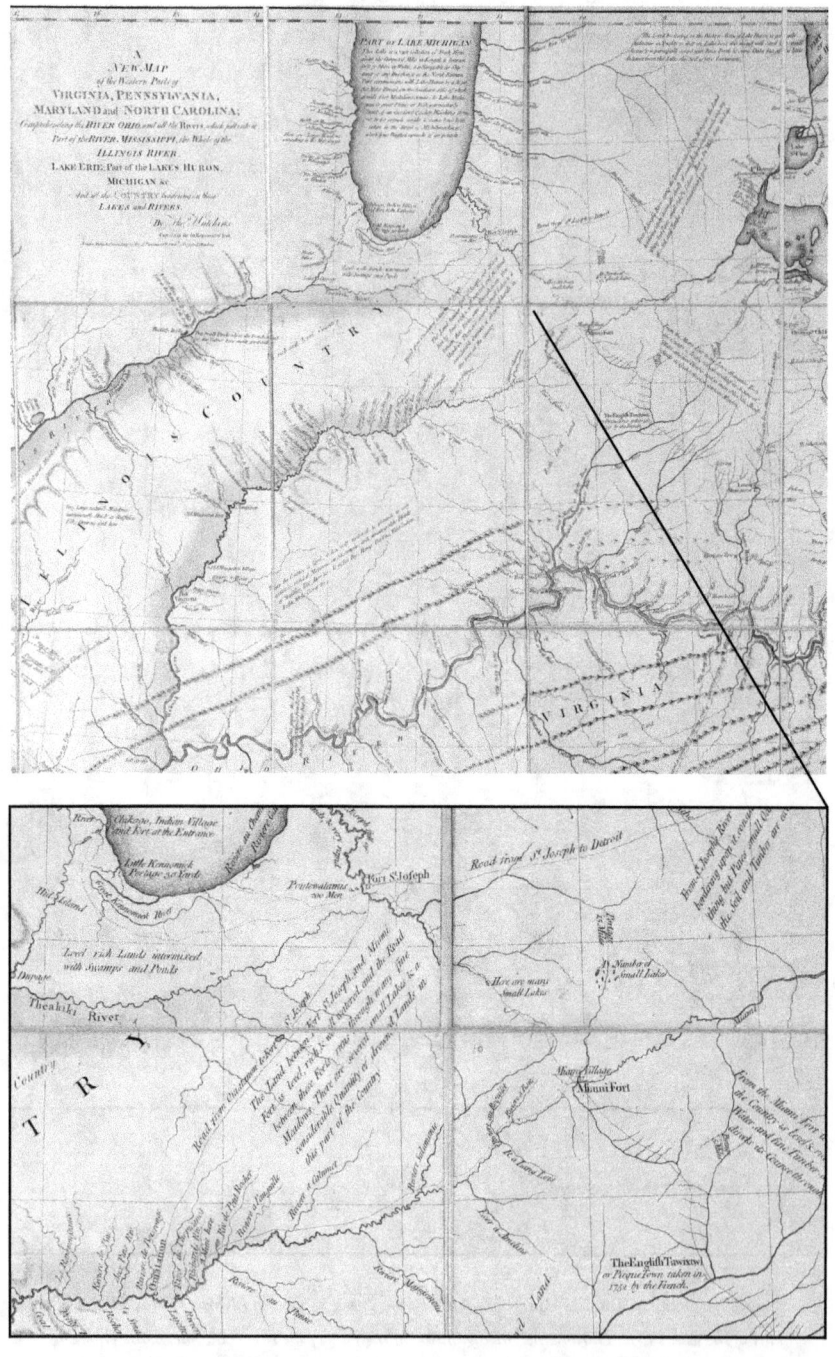

Figure I.4. Detail of Thomas Hutchins's 1778 *A New Map of the Western Parts of Virginia, Pennsylvania, Maryland and North Carolina* recording the trail between forts Ouiatenon and St. Joseph. RB 152923, The Huntington Library, San Marino, California.

alteration of European material culture in ways that suited Native American lifeways. European goods were added to those available to Indigenous people, and changing material culture did not equate with loss of Native American culture (Branstner 1992; Trubowitz 1992). Similarly, cultural adaptations occurred, with the French adopting aspects of Native American culture. The notion of cultural adoptions on both sides of the European/Native American dichotomy has continued to influence research into the twenty-first century (White 2012). The shift in focus from the fort and the French to inclusion of the Native American communities outside the fort continues the movement from the Eurocentric world systems theory to a more Native American–centered approach (Strezewski 2014; Strezewski and McCullough 2010, 2017, 2019; Noack Myers 2017).

Readers might also note the variety of writing styles reflecting the broad range of contributors. Their backgrounds influence their approach whether they come from academia, education, public outreach, or a community with a connection to Fort Ouiatenon. The variation is also part of the movement toward more reflexive writing that allows authors to insert themselves into the narrative, using "I" in place of more distanced third-person terms.

The chapters in the volume are organized into three thematic sections. In Part I: History and Archaeology, the authors provide summaries of research conducted to date. David Hovde (chapter 1) provides a history of the fort, including the search for and relocation of it using documents and archaeological exploration. He provides details on the search to relocate the fort beginning in the nineteenth century. The chapter makes evident that artifacts recovered from locations that ultimately proved to not be that of the fort, including kettles, trade silver ornaments, cloth, and copper with hair, are those recovered almost exclusively from burials, whether in cemeteries or as single features. Most of these would have been those of Native Americans. Today professional researchers must treat such discoveries differently and must involve the descendants, to whom the human remains and artifacts are returned. Chapter 1 includes the history of practices that are not acceptable today but regardless form part of the Fort Ouiatenon story. Noack Myers (chapter 2) provides an in-depth and much-needed summary of the history of archaeology at the fort, focusing on the early work by Kellar for which little has been written. Michael Strezewski (chapter 3) offers a look at the archaeology conducted outside of the fort in the areas occupied by Native Americans, filling a crucial research gap because previous excavations focused on Europeans. He also reviews the search for and the archaeology conducted in efforts to relocate Fort Miami and Post Vincennes (chapter 4), thereby contextualizing Ouiatenon among the other French establishments along the Wabash River with which it held relationships.

To date no one has undertaken a comprehensive treatment of all artifacts from Fort Ouiatenon, though Tordoff's and Noble's dissertations describe the artifacts recovered by Michigan State University's excavations in the 1970s. Part II: Artifact Studies includes four contributions focusing on a limited number of artifact types. During the 1970s use of new field methods, particularly remote sensing, aided in locating features for excavation and site interpretation (Noble 1983; von Frese 1978). Use of remote sensing has continued, including in the areas outside of the fort (Strezewski 2014; Strezewski and McCullough 2010, 2017, 2019). Martin's (1986) dissertation analyzed the artifact category of faunal remains from the fort, and his contribution provides a summary of those findings in chapter 5 for a clearer understanding of foodways and fur trading at the fort and how the local environment influenced the trade. Tordorf's and Noble's dissertations classified artifacts based on form and function to describe and group artifact types and varieties. A comparison of archaeologists' classifications of artifacts with the manner in which eighteenth-century merchants and military personnel described and recorded them has also been previously conducted with a focus on the Ouiatenon collections (Jackson 2005). Included in this volume are studies employing methods for analyzing the composition of artifacts to aid in understanding how they were manufactured and what this can reveal about users and wearers. Chapter 6 presents a study of a ring from the fort using X-ray fluorescence. Chapter 7 provides at look at the social information that becomes available when subjecting buckles to the analysis technique of laser ablation–inductively coupled plasma–mass spectrometry in combination with data from historic documents that reveal the categories used by eighteenth-century merchants and military personnel to classify goods. Chapter 8 examines flintlocks at Fort St. Joseph, a study with implications for that artifact type in the Ouiatenon collections given the ties between the two posts.

Part III: Community, Stakeholders, and Preservation brings together chapters on the contributions made by the community associated with Fort Ouiatenon to its preservation and celebration. They serve to educate the public and honor those who lived together at the site and in the surrounding area. Community involvement in historic preservation and archaeology in general has grown over the last two decades, but the community supporting Fort Ouiatenon has a much longer history. Involvement of the descendant community is a particularly welcome contribution, with representation in Diane Hunter's chapter. In chapter 9, she tells of the origin of the Myaamia (Miami) people and the bands of the Tribe, including the Waayaahtanookis (Wea), who comprised the main group of Native Americans living at the confluence of the Waapaahšiki Siipiiwi (Wabash River) and Wea Creek. The Waayaahtanooki compelled the French to construct Fort Ouiatenon near their village in order to trade with them when the French could not convince them to return to the village at Fort St. Joseph, revealing another connection between the two forts. Hunter contextualizes the Tribe by providing an overview of its history through to the present day. In doing so, she details the hardships endured but also demonstrates the continuing importance of and affection for their homeland held by the Myaamia and the connection that persists to their former village of Waayaahtanonki.

Chapters 10 and 11 focus on aspects of the annual public celebration Feast of the Hunters' Moon hosted by the Tippecanoe County Historical Association. David Hovde's chapter chronicles the Feast of the Hunters' Moon, noting that the earliest recorded reenactment at the Fort Ouiatenon park site may have occurred in 1929. Ronald Morris and Leslie Martin Conwell explore the connection between the period music and instruments as lived and performed at Fort Ouiatenon and the feast and its representations in the documents and artifacts from the site.

As legacy collections continue to offer opportunities for research in historical archaeology in general, those from Fort Ouiatenon especially provide untapped data, since a complete and systematic study of artifacts held at Indiana University's Glenn Black Laboratory of Archaeology has yet to be conducted. In chapter 12, Erika Hartley, Christina Arseneau, and Michael Nassaney review and compare the curation practices for collections from Fort Ouiatenon with those of Forts Michilimackinac and St. Joseph. If research is to continue on extant collections, their future preservation for all stakeholders depends on current disposition and care and presents an issue of utmost importance for consideration and action.

The final chapter brings the reader to the latest developments resulting from community advocacy for the site: the creation of the 230-acre Ouiatenon Preserve in 2016. Along with this important action of preservation, on January 13, 2021, the US secretary of the interior designated the known archaeological sites within the Ouiatenon Preserve as a National Historic Landmark archaeological district. Colby Bartlett details the journey to this important point in the history of Fort Ouiatenon and surrounding archaeological sites and describes future plans.

Future directions for research at Fort Ouiatenon can continue, with explorations of Indigenous agency and the relationship between the Myaamiaki bands and the Waayaahtanooki on whose land the French lived and with whom the French sought political, economic, and social relations. Public outreach and ongoing community involvement in the site's interpretation and protection are also planned as part of the mission of the Ouiatenon Preserve. The editors hope that this volume serves to inspire continuing interest and future research into the history and archaeology of Fort Ouiatenon and the surrounding Native American sites and that it promotes within readers a desire to support the work of preservation initiated by the community and stakeholders devoted to the site of Ouiatenon, the surrounding Native American sites, and the Ouiatenon Preserve.

REFERENCES

Bond, Beverly W., Jr. ed. 1942. *The Courses of the Ohio River Taken by Lt. T. Hutchins Anno 1766 and Two Accompanying Maps.* Cincinnati: Historical and Philosophical Society of Ohio.

Branstner, Susan M. 1992. "Tionontate Huron Occupation at the Marquette Mission." In *Calumet and Fleur-de-Lys: Archaeology of Indian and French Contact in the Midcontinent,* ed. John A. Walthall and Thomas E. Emerson, 177–201. Washington, DC: Smithsonian Institution Press.

Craig, Oscar. 1893. "Ouiatanon: A Study in Indiana History." *Indiana Historical Society Publications* 2, no. 8: 317–48.

DeCorse, Christopher, and Zachary J. M. Beier. 2018. "Introduction: Forts, Communities, and Their Entanglements." In *British Forts and Their Communities: Archaeological and Historical Perspectives,* ed. Christopher DeCorse and Zachary Beier, 1–30. Gainesville: University Press of Florida.

Dunn, Jacob P. 1894. "Documents Relating to the French Settlements on the Wabash." *Indiana Historical Society Publications* 2, no. 2: 404–42.

Hutchins, Thomas. 1778. "A New Map of the Western Parts of Virginia, Pennsylvania, Maryland, and North Carolina." Huntington Rare Book Maps. https://hdl.huntington.org/digital/iiif/p15150coll4/1940/full/full/0/default.jpg.

———. 1904. *A Topographical Description of Virginia, Pennsylvania, Maryland, and North Carolina, Reprinted from the Original Edition of 1778,* ed. Frederick Charles Hicks. Cleveland: Burrows Brothers.

Jackson, Misty May. 2005. "Classifications by Historical Archaeologists and Eighteenth Century Montreal Merchants and Military Personnel in New France: Emic and Etic Approaches." PhD diss., Michigan State University.

Johnson, Mary M. 2000. *Ouiatenon: The French Post among the Ouia.* West Lafayette, IN: Ouabache Press.

Jones, James R., III. 1984. *Eighteenth and Early Nineteenth Century Aboriginal and Euroamerican Occupations in the Vicinity of Lafayette, Tippecanoe County, Indiana.* Indiana Department of Natural Resources, Division of Historic Preservation and Archaeology. Glenn A. Black Laboratory of Archaeology, Indiana University, Bloomington.

———. 1988. "Degrees of Acculturation at Two 18th Century Aboriginal Villages Near Lafayette, Tippecanoe County, Indiana: Ethnohistoric and Archaeological Perspectives." PhD diss., Indiana University, Bloomington.

Kellar, James H. 1970. "The Search for Ouiatanon." *Indiana History Bulletin* 47, no. 11: 123–33.

Krauskopf, Frances. 1953. "The French in Indiana, 1700–1760: A Political History." PhD diss., Indiana University, Bloomington.

———, ed. and trans. 1955. *Ouiatanon Documents.* Indiana Historical Society Publications 18.

Martin, Terrance J. 1986. "A Faunal Analysis of Fort Ouiatenon, an Eighteenth-Century Trading Post in the Wabash Valley of Indiana." PhD diss., Michigan State University.

McGroarty, Jean. 1982. "Ouiatenon and the Establishment of the Northwest." *Tippecanoe Tales* 8. Lafayette, IN: Tippecanoe County Historical Association.

Noack Myers, Kelsey. 2017. "Indigenous Landscapes and Legacy Archaeology at Ouiatenon, Indiana." PhD diss., Indiana University, Bloomington.

———. 2019. "Reconstructing Site Provenience at Ouiatenon, Indiana." In *New Life for Archaeological Collections*, ed. Rebecca Allen and Ben Ford, 272–88. Lincoln: University of Nebraska Press.

Noble, Vergil E., Jr. "Discovering Fort Ouiatenon: Its History and Archaeology." *Tippecanoe Tales*, no. 6. Lafayette, IN: Tippecanoe County Historical Association.

———. 1979. 1983. "Functional Classification and Intra-site Analysis in Historical Archaeology: A Case Study from Fort Ouiatenon." PhD diss., Michigan State University.

———. 1991. "Ouiatenon on the Ouabache: Archaeological Investigations at a Fur Trading Post on the Wabash River." In *French Colonial Archaeology*, ed. John H. Walthall, 65–77. Urbana: University of Illinois Press.

Strezewski, Michael. 2014. *Fur Trade Archaeology in the Fort Ouiatenon Vicinity: The 2012/2013 Investigations*. University of Southern Indiana Archaeological Laboratory Reports of Investigations 13-03.

Strezewski, Michael, and Robert G. McCullough. 2010. *Report of the 2009 Archaeological Investigations at Three Fur Trade-Era Sites in Tippecanoe County, Indiana: Kethtippecanunk (12-T-59), Fort Ouiatenon (12-T-9), and a Kickapoo-Mascouten Village (12-T-335)*. Indiana University–Purdue University Fort Wayne Archaeological Survey Reports of Investigations 903.

———. 2017. *Fur Trade Archaeology at the Ouiatenon Preserve: The 2016/2017 Geophysical Investigations*. University of Southern Indiana Archaeology Laboratory Reports of Investigations 16-03.

———. 2019. "Fort Ouiatenon, 1717–2019: 300+ Years of Indiana History." *Indiana Archaeology* 14, no. 1: 54–88. Indianapolis: Indiana Department of Natural Resources Division of Historic Preservation and Archaeology.

Tordoff, Judith D. 1983. "An Archaeological Perspective on the Organization of the Fur Trade in Eighteenth Century New France." PhD diss., Michigan State University.

Trubowitz, Neal L. 1992. "Native Americans and French on the Central Wabash." In *Calumet and Fleur-de-Lys: Archaeology of Indian and French Contact in the Midcontinent*, ed. John A. Walthall and Thomas E. Emerson, 241–64. Washington, DC: Smithsonian Institution Press.

Tucker, Sara Jones, ed. 1942. *Indian Villages of the Illinois Country*. Illinois State Museum Scientific Papers, Vol. 2, Part 1. Springfield: Illinois State Museum.

von Frese, Ralph R. B. 1978. "Magnetic Exploration of Historical Midwestern Archaeological Sites as Exemplified by a Survey of Fort Ouiatenon." Master's thesis, Purdue University.

White, Richard. 1991. *The Middle Ground: Indians, Empires, and Republics in the Great Lakes Region, 1650–1815*. New York: Cambridge University Press.

White, Sophie. 2012. *Wild Frenchmen and Frenchified Indians: Material Culture and Race in Colonial Louisiana*. Philadelphia: University of Pennsylvania Press.

PART I

HISTORY AND ARCHAEOLOGY

I

FORT OUIATENON

Three Hundred Years from the Founding, Loss, Rediscovery, and Archaeology

DAVID M. HOVDE, PROFESSOR EMERITUS,
PURDUE UNIVERSITY

MANY YEARS HAVE PASSED SINCE THE DESTRUCTION OF THE REMAINS of Fort Ouiatenon in 1791. What was left slowly washed away in the flooding of the Wabash River and covered by river silt. However, maps of what became Indiana, produced in Europe and the United States and dating into the first three decades of the nineteenth century, continued to note its location. Spelled in various ways including Ouiatenon, Ouatinon, Ouiatanon, or Ouatenon, at times shown with the accompanying Native villages, the site remained on maps of Indiana until the region's counties and communities were platted and current life became more important than the historical past. As the land was being purchased and occupied by Anglo-American settlers, stories of the fort and the surrounding villages became part of local lore.[1]

THE FRENCH PERIOD AND THE ESTABLISHMENT OF FORT OUIATENON

Several hundred years ago, New France was a vast riverine empire. The inland waterways of North America served as highways for exploration, commerce, and settlement. The two colonies of New France included Canada (1534–1760) and Louisiane (1682–1803).

The administration of New France was split into the two territories in 1715, with the boundary somewhere between Fort Ouiatenon and Vincennes. For Canada, the St. Lawrence River and the Great Lakes that fed it served as its highway, and for Louisiane, the Mississippi, Ohio, and Missouri River systems provided access.

From the beginning, the way the French viewed what is now Indiana differed from how we view it today. The passage along the Maumee and Wabash Rivers provided an artery of commerce and communication between the Great Lakes and the Mississippi River Valley. In fact, the French looked upon the Ohio River as a tributary of the Wabash (Brodhead 1855, 891; Pease and Jenison 1940, 266; Michigan Pioneer and Historical Society 1904, 481).

In a period document sent to the governor of Louisiane concerning the efforts of Francois-Marie Bissot, Sieur de Vincennes, observing the actions of the English, the French geographical knowledge is clearly shown:

> About 120 miles above the Arkansas there flows into the Mississippi the Ouabache river formed of four other rivers, one of which rises near Lake Erie and is called the St. Jerome or the Ouabache, the other called the Ohio rises among the Iroquois, and the two others called Tennessee and Cumberland rise near Virginia. The country which these rivers water abounds in wild cattle and is not yet occupied by any European nation (Roy 1918, 87–88; see also Pease and Jenison 1940, 97).

The water route from the north began at the mouth of the Maumee River on Lake Erie and ran through modern-day Toledo, Ohio, to the portage between the Maumee and Wabash drainages at present-day Fort Wayne, Indiana. Period sources note the portage as being nine miles long (Alvord and Carter 1916, 35). Once on the Wabash, depending on the source, one or more rapids on either side of Fort Ouiatenon hindered traffic. A beautiful map of the region created by John Cary and published in 1805 combined the geographical knowledge of both the French and the British (figure 1.1). It describes the Ouiatanon-Wabash as "Nav. to here for Batteaux & to Miami carrying place for large Boats" (Cary 1805).[2] The rapids near the site of Fort Ouiatenon did present a barrier of sorts during this period, as mentioned in nineteenth- and early twentieth-century historical literature (Burroughs 1907, 1; Craig 1893, 11–12; DeHart 1909, 147; Hassam 1872, 15; Mavity 1925). Oscar J. Craig (figure 1.2) states that lighter craft were used north of the barrier and heavier craft south of the barrier. (The city of Lafayette, established in 1825 just upriver from the fort, was located at the highest point up the Wabash, as it turned out, that could handle nineteenth-century steamboat navigation.) From the fort, river traffic continued into the Ohio River and on to the Mississippi River. Period maps also show trails between Forts St. Joseph, Miami, and Ouiatenon (see figure I.4). From Fort St. Joseph, the trail also led to Detroit.

Figure 1.1. A close-up of John Cary's 1805 map using French and British sources showing the Fort, Native villages, and references to rivercraft used on the Wabash. *A new map of part of the United States of North America: exhibiting the Western Territory, Kentucky, Pennsylvania, Maryland, Virginia &c., also, the Lakes Superior, Michigan, Huron, Ontario & Erie, with Upper and Lower Canada &c.* J. Cary. London by John Cary, 1805. Courtesy of the Indiana Historical Society.

Figure 1.2. Purdue University professor Oscar J. Craig, professor of political economy and history, wrote an early history of Fort Ouiatenon and the French presence in Indiana. He also engaged in archaeological investigations during his search for the site. Courtesy of the Purdue University Archives and Special Collections.

Fort Ouiatenon existed from 1717 to 1791. It was under the control of the colonial government of New France until 1760. The fort's existence and its location were neither an accident nor random. The fort was a piece in the chess game being played by the French and the British in the eastern part of North America to control the land and resources. For the French, the fort's location was strategic. As Phillipe de Rigaud, Marquis de Vaudreuil, the governor and lieutenant general of New France, notes in a communique written in the third person and dated December 12, 1717:

> Because the Ouiatenon are too close to the English of Carolina and exposed to their practices, and the latter spare neither solicitations nor presents to detach these savages from our interests and to attract them to their side, he had contemplated sending a captain, a subaltern, sergeant, and ten soldiers among them to establish a post there [at Ouiatenon] to disrupt these practices and to keep them at peace with the Illinois. But since the region where they are at present is too far from the colony to take there easily what is necessary to support a post and a garrison, he believed that it was more appropriate to begin by urging them to return to Chicago or else to the upper Kankakee, where they formerly lived and where they would no longer be tempted to have connections with the English.
>
> From this viewpoint and in order to satisfy the eagerness of this nation, which for a long time has been asking for an officer to govern them, a missionary to instruct them, and a blacksmith, he sent them the Sieur de Bellestre, ensign, with four soldiers and three other Frenchmen whom he permitted him to take, and the Sieur de Sabrevois sent a blacksmith from Detroit. (Krauskopf 1955, 160).

On the map *Carte du Cours de l'Ohio ou de la Belle Riviere: Depuis sa Source jusqu'à sa Jonction avec celle d'Ouabache, avec les pays les plus voisins* by Jacques Nicolas Bellin dated 1755, Ouiatenon located on the north side of the "R. Ouabache ou de St. Jerome" has three symbols designating the site as a village, a mission, and a fort (figure 1.3) (Bellin, 1755). In its time, it was the home of twelve to fifteen French families who may have been métis, traders, blacksmiths, priests, servants, members of the Compagnies Franches de la Marine, and perhaps voyageurs overwintering. The fort was surrounded by Native American villages and farmsteads on either side of the river.

The seventeenth- and early eighteenth-century interactions in North America were complex and fluid. The French economic relationship with the Native American populations centered on the fur trade. Because of a distinct manpower shortage and the technologies of the day, including that the spring trap had yet to be invented, trapping was left to Indigenous people. Government and church policies as well as individual action affected French expansion into the Great Lakes and the Ohio and Mississippi Valleys. At times, the governor of New France and the government in Paris were not

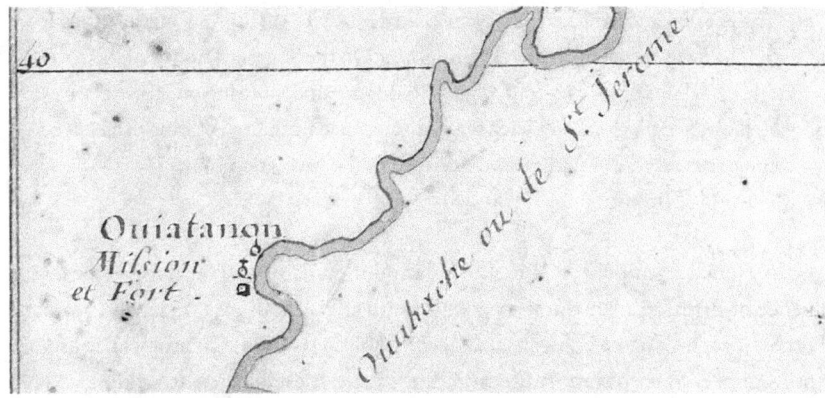

Figure 1.3. Fort Ouiatenon is shown with three symbols of a village, a mission, and a fort. *Carte du Cours de l'Ohio ou de la Belle Riviere: Depuis sa Source jusqu'a sa Jonction avec celle d'Ouabache, avec les pays les plus voisins* by Jacques Nicolas Bellin, 1755. Courtesy of the British Library Board/MS 57714.

fully committed to an expansionist policy and reduced its territorial footprint by the closing of forts on the frontier. During the latter half of the seventeenth century, the fur trade exploded; however, due to royal policy restricting this trade to one company, and controlling prices, corruption, and smuggling also exploded. Additionally, France faced conflicts with the English and their Native American allies.

By 1698 a serious oversupply of furs led the king to order the fur trade closed, and western posts were evacuated (Skinner 2008, 90), leading to an increased British influence in the region. In 1701 the War of Spanish Succession began, and the conflict continued into 1713. With peace, the English continued to expand their influence even into the Mississippi Valley, and armed conflicts with various tribes continued. In 1715, the French returned to the issuing of licenses for the fur trade. Enforcement was impossible, and the system was abandoned in 1719 to be replaced by a new system of licenses, leasing by auction, and the subleasing of posts. Direct royal control was established in 1728. At times, French authorities regulated the number of canoes, the number of men in the canoes, the boundaries of the trade, etc. The 1715 line that had split New France into two territories, Canada and Louisiane, caused problems with attempts to restrict trade across the boundary. The French continued to modify the system over time. The British, on the other hand, embraced free enterprise and could sell their goods at lower rates and undercut their French competitors (Krauskopf 1955, 140).

The British continued their encroachment. In January 1717, Governor-General Philippe Rigaud de Vaudreuil received the following instructions from the Council of Marine concerning English incursions into French territory:

Monsieur de Vaudreuil... will pay special attention to garrisoning all the posts. It is of the Utmost importance to establish those On the Southern frontier, where the English of Pennsylvania, Carolina, and Virginia are anxious to introduce themselves, which would ruin the Commerce not only of Canada, but even of Louisiana, on account of the easy Communication furnished by the Rivers that empty into the great Mississippi. (Thwaites 1902, 345–346)

The French attempted to move the Wea and the Miami westward to reduce the influence of British traders but were unsuccessful (Krauskopf 1955, 142). To the north, Fort St. Joseph (Niles, Michigan) had been established in 1691. To protect the important Maumee-Wabash trade route, a trading post was established at Kekionga (Fort Wayne, Indiana), the Miami capital, in 1715. It was later upgraded to a fort in 1722. Fort Ouiatenon, established in 1717, was part of a line of these forts intended to be a barrier to British expansion. Vincennes, the most southern post on the route, was established in 1722 (Skinner 2008, 101).

At the time, Fort Ouiatenon would be the closest post to the British expansion. It was named for a branch of the Miami nation. The first Frenchmen to establish the fort were Ensign François Picoté de Bellestre, four soldiers, a blacksmith, and three others (Krauskopf 1955, 160). The highly respected Sieur de Jean-Baptiste Bissot Vincennes, who had worked tirelessly to maintain the French influence in the region and served as the agent among the Miami died in 1719. His son, François-Marie Vincennes, arrived at Fort Ouiatenon in 1721. In 1725 after being promised for years, Governor Vaudreuil sent a Jesuit priest to the Ouiatenon and Miamis posts. In the eyes of the leadership in Quebec, the priest was a control mechanism to keep the Wea and the Miami pacified and within the French sphere of influence.

During this period, the French experienced continued concern over British encroachment and active conflict with Native American nations. The Maumee-Wabash corridor between the two territories became increasingly important due to conflicts with the Fox and their allies. They had all but closed the two other main waterways, the Fox-Wisconsin and the Chicago-Illinois portages, to the French (Kellogg 1925, 340). This put the main communication link, the Maumee-Wabash corridor, within reach of British influence.

The Fox Wars from 1712 to 1733 not only caused death among the Fox and the French and disruption to trade but also heightened tensions with other Native American populations. In the early 1730s, the French were still trying to concentrate tribes for ease of trade and control. They persuaded the Piankashaw Tribe, a branch of the Miami to move to Ouiatenon and later tried to move the Shawnee closer to the fort. In 1733 the area villages were hit with an epidemic. Hundreds died. The French blamed it on poisoned British brandy. Tensions continued in 1734, with Fort Ouiatenon being ransacked after a fight between a Native American and a Frenchman. Notified of the event, authorities assembled a force of over three hundred French and Native Americans to punish the offenders; however, before the force started out, word arrived that everything had been returned and peace was restored (Krauskopf 1955, 181–84).

These conflicts cost the French a great deal of money, and in 1743 forts such as Ouiatenon were sold to the highest bidder, and prices of goods were raised.[3] Then in 1744, the War of Austrian Succession, or King George's War, once again put France and England into direct conflict. The war resulted in the capture of Fortress Louisbourg (Nova Scotia, Canada) in 1745 and a closing of supply routes from the Atlantic through the St. Lawrence River. To maintain relationships, the French distributed gifts to their allies. From September 1746 to May 1747, 6,245 livres of goods including tobacco, gunpowder, blankets, vermillion, brandy, and meat were given out at Fort Ouiatenon (Krauskopf 1955, 195–205). Because of the loss of Fortress Louisbourg, by 1747 no merchandise was available to distribute to forts on the frontier, and open hostilities began. Voyageurs were attacked, and five were killed by the Miami while en route to Fort Ouiatenon (Skinner 2008, 159). In 1748 Fortress Louisbourg was restored to France, and soon after French trading vessels returned; the warring Native American populations returned to the French fold except for the Miami.

In 1749, the new governor of Canada sent a large force of French and Indigenous warriors south to convince the Miami to return. On September 25 near the end of the expedition, the French commander met with the Miami at Kiskakon (Kekionga), the Miami capital, on their way to Detroit. Little resolution came from the council or the expedition (Thwaites 1908a, 55).[4] A 1752 letter between governor of Canada Charles Le Moyne, Baron de Longueuil, and the minister of marine and colonies reported continued conflict and killings and noted the Native Americans of the Ohio were fully within the influence of the British. Further, the governor stated that the commandant of Fort Ouiatenon was warned to protect himself from the storm that was coming to all Frenchmen in the Ohio Country (Brodhead 1852, 245–51).

The storm came in the form of George Washington. To counter British advances in the Ohio Valley, the French built Fort Duquesne in 1754 at the confluence of the Allegheny and Monongahela Rivers (in Pennsylvania) after capturing a small British force stationed there. Colonel Washington, having been sent to build a post at the site, encountered a small party of French sent to give the British notice they were trespassing. Washington's forces ambushed the French, killing ten, and some of the survivors who had surrendered were killed by Native American allies of the British. This incident led to the French and Indian War that was the killing blow to French Canada. The war ended with the signing of the Treaty of Paris in February 1763. France ceded to Britain Canada and the part of the Louisiane territory east of the Mississippi River except for New Orleans and the Mississippi delta. This treaty marked a dramatic change in the nature of the French empire in North America, leading to the British occupation of the area surrounding Fort Ouiatenon.

THE BRITISH PERIOD AND THE DECLINE OF FORT OUIATENON

This vast new territory would prove to be an economic and logistical burden for the British, whose colonial interests lay elsewhere in the world (Horsman 1976, 100–109). When the British began occupying Canada and the Illinois Country, their policies differed from those of the French, causing dissension among the Native Americans. To the British, they were a conquered people, not economic partners. Further, the British did not appreciate the importance of the economic relationships built by the French who intermarried with their trading partners. Beginning in May 1763, forces under Pontiac besieged Fort Detroit. Word spread, and warriors attacked other forts and communities. Hundreds were either killed or captured, and a number of forts were destroyed. Fort Ouiatenon was one of the forts taken during Pontiac's Rebellion. Lieutenant Edward Jenkins, who commanded the fort at the time, was warned of impending troubles. He and his men were soon captured. However, the remaining French settlers protected them, and none of the garrison was killed (Alvord and Carter 1915, 11–13).

Soon after, two British military expeditions and treaties ended most of the conflicts in the East. However, in the West some Indigenous leaders continued to advocate resistance. Fort Des Chartres (Illinois), the most significant fortification in the region, remained unoccupied by British forces. A small British party was sent to the Illinois Country under the command of Captain Thomas Morris via the Maumee and Wabash Rivers. Along the way Morris encountered Pontiac and his followers and was saved by two Frenchmen in the party, and they proceeded to Fort Miamis, where Morris was again threatened and where he turned back. In May 1765, George Croghan was sent to treat with tribes in the Wabash and Illinois Countries. His party was attacked, and several members were killed near the mouth of the Wabash. The rest were captured and taken to Vincennes. Croghan was then taken to Ouiatenon, where he conferred with representatives of the local tribes. Near the fort Croghan encountered Pontiac, who promised no further conflict with the British. Another council, with Pontiac in attendance, at Fort Ontario on July 25, 1766, ended the widespread hostilities with the Native peoples.

Oddly, although the British recognized that the Maumee-Wabash corridor was critically important for communication between Canada and the Illinois Country, they did not reoccupy Fort Ouiatenon or Fort Miamis. Fort Ouiatenon continued to be a small settlement (Barnhart and Riker 1971, 156–58); however, the visitors clearly saw it in decline.

In 1765 George Croghan, without mentioning conditions of the fort, noted that this Place is situated on the Cuabache; about 14 French Families are living in the Fort which Stands on the North Side of the River: The Kicapoos & Musquatimes whose Warriors had taken us live nigh the Fort on the Same Side of the River where they have two Villages and the Cauatanons have a Village on the South Side of the River. (Alvord and Carter 1916, 33–34)

In 1766, Lieutenant Alexander Fraser wrote that "two Forts on Ouabach the one called the great Ouiachtonon was dependant on Canada & the other at little Ouiachtonon or St Vincent—dependant on Orleans all those excepting fort Charters are entirely in ruins, some of them that you can scarce see any appearance of they did not seem to me of any great consequence were they even on a better footing as they were situated" (Alvord and Carter 1916, 230).

Edward Cole, commissioner for Indian affairs in the Illinois Country, purchased sundries from Joseph Pallier at Ouiatenon during the summer of 1766 on his way to Fort Des Chartres. By this time, however, Ouiatenon was no longer a commissioned trading post, and no blacksmiths were located at Fort Ouiatenon or Fort Miamis. During this period, the Native Americans of the Wabash country complained that no trading post existed between Detroit and Fort Des Chartres. What trade did occur came mainly from St. Louis by way of French and Spanish traders, much to the chagrin of British traders. The British made no attempt to reestablish posts in the upper Wabash, and the most significant military garrison in the region, Fort Des Chartres, was withdrawn in 1772. The last of the forces in the area left Kaskaskia in 1776 (Barnhart and Riker 1971, 167, 175).

When Lieutenant Governor Edward Abbott traveled down the Wabash on the way to Vincennes in the spring of 1777, he mentioned the Wea but made no mention of the fort:

The Wabache is perhaps one of the finest rivers in the world, on its banks are several Indian Towns, the most considerable is the Ouija, where it is said there are 1000 men capable to bear arms, I found them so numerous, and needy, I could not pass without great expense; The presents though very large, were in a manner despised, saying their antient [sic] Father (the french) never spoke to them without a barnfull of goods. (Dunn 1894, 440–441)

With the American Revolution well under way, British lieutenant governor Henry Hamilton of Detroit began sending raiding parties against the western settlements in 1777 and 1778. His nemesis, Major George Rogers Clark of the Kentucky County Militia, was responsible for organizing the defense of the western country under

Virginia's control. Clark's plan for defense was a good offense by capturing western British outposts, a plan approved by the Virginia government. He successfully secured Kaskaskia, Cahokia, and Vincennes in July 1778. Hearing of this victory, Hamilton mounted an ill-fated expedition to defeat Clark and took the Maumee-Wabash route to achieve that goal. On November 30, 1778, he described Fort Ouiatenon:

> 30th. The Men were exercised in firing at a Mark—Went to the Fort which is formed of a double range of houses enclosed with a Stockade 10 feet high, and very poorly defensive against small arms. The Indian Cabins of this settlement are about 90, the families may be estimated at 10 to a cabin. (Indiana Historical Bureau 1778)

THE AMERICAN PERIOD AND THE DESTRUCTION OF FORT OUIATENON

After the Revolutionary War concluded, the United States and Great Britain signed the treaty in which Great Britain recognized the existence of the United States and defined its boundaries on September 3, 1783, and Congress ratified it on January 14, 1784. The American government, like the French and British before them, began attempts to control the Ohio Country and the Illinois Country. However, the British were not evacuating the forts within the American territories and encouraged the various tribes to believe that the Americans would honor earlier treaties signed by the British. Treaties established during these early years, such as the Treaty of Stanwix, were largely ignored by the Native Americans of the region, and a movement toward the establishment of an Indigenous confederation was under way (Winkler 2011, 11). French families began abandoning Fort Ouiatenon in 1780. With no military protection available and no government representatives in the vicinity, the Wabash had become unsafe even for the French inhabitants (Thwaites 1908b, 429).

In Vincennes during the spring of 1786, new American inhabitants were disrupting the culture and the economy of the village and the surrounding countryside. American farmers were distilling their corn into whiskey and selling it to the Native Americans. With tensions on the rise, the French and American inhabitants of Vincennes asked for protection, and both Ouiatenon and Miamis Town (later Fort Wayne) were evacuated due to rising hostilities toward the new American pressures (Helderman 1938, 458–59). Inhabitants of Fort Ouiatenon moved to Vincennes or Kethtippekenunck, ending the French presence permanently. Attempts were made to request both US Army troops and militia forces, and expeditions of militia were mounted with mixed results. The US Congress authorized Colonel Josiah Harmar with a force of some three hundred troops to move on Vincennes to control the militia under George Rogers Clark and protect the settlement (Barnhart and Riker 1971, 262–65). Harmar set up a military post and held talks with the Wea and Piankashaw

Back in Washington, the Northwest Ordinance of 1787 was ratified, thus opening the territory from the Appalachians to the Mississippi north of the Ohio to the Great Lakes for the creation of new states. The Fort Harmar treaties of 1789 did little to change tribal attitudes toward American expansion, and because Native Americans along the Wabash were not involved, they did not accept its authority. Raiding parties from above the Ohio River and below continued (Thornbrough 1957, 37, 119, 174, 199).

An attempt by Northwest Territory governor Arthur St. Clair to make peace with the Miami, Delaware, and Shawnee using the Treaty of Fort Harmar was unsuccessful. St. Clair called for a military campaign against the tribes. This expedition, led by Harmar and made of regulars and untrained and ill-equipped militia, was one of the least prepared and ill-conceived expeditions in American military history. Starting out on September 30, 1790, they reached the Miami settlements in mid-October around present-day Fort Wayne, Indiana. Part of the force engaged in two battles that ended in Miami victories. A second expedition, led by Major John Hamtramck of Fort Knox (Vincennes) and made up of regulars and French and Kentucky militia, moved up the Wabash. Due to poor planning, lack of supplies, and desertions, the expedition returned to Vincennes (Metcalf 1913, 81–85; Stewart 2009, 117–18; Winkler 2011, 14–15).

With raids continuing along the Ohio River, Virginia governor Beverley, at George Washington's recommendation, appointed Randolph Charles Scott to the rank of brigadier general in the Virginia militia. In late May 1791, his force of 850 militia crossed the Ohio River, and their targets were Ouiatenon, Kethtippecanuck, and other settlements along the Wabash. Arriving on June 1, the force began its assault with actions such as killing all the occupants in five canoes trying to flee across the river.[5] Scott and Colonel James Wilkinson took prisoners and destroyed the towns, stores, and fields. No mention was made of a fort ruined or otherwise, which may indicate that the bastion was no longer present. A second expedition in August led by the now General Wilkinson returned to Ouiatenon and other villages, destroying houses and the replanted fields (Metcalf 1913, 85–98). If there had been any occupation on the site of the fort in 1791, it was now at an end.

FORT OUIATENON DISAPPEARS

Fort Ouiatenon after 1791 continued to be shown on maps and gazetteers into the 1820s. Some of these maps, along with French and British colonial documents, would be used by late nineteenth-century researchers in their search for the site. After the British defeated the French in 1760, British observers made a few important references to the fort. For instance, Major Robert Rogers was under orders to relieve the French garrisons of several forts including Forts Miamis and Ouiatenon. In December 1761, he ordered Lieutenant John Butler to take possession of them. After occupying Fort Miamis, Butler headed downriver and found a sergeant, seven privates, and nineteen Canadians whom he required to take an oath of allegiance to the British crown. He described the stockade (which was probably Fort Ouiatenon) as being 100 by 150 feet in size, with fourteen houses belonging to the merchant except one. The fort, according to Butler, was on low land and had been flooded in the spring to the depth of 4 feet. He also noted that the Wabash was too low during the summer to allow river traffic (Widder 2013, 65).

Lieutenant Thomas Hutchins of the British Army was one of several officers charged with traveling into the newly acquired territory. The mission was to undertake land surveying and recording of Native American and French populations, transportation routes, economic value of the region, French installations, and settlements (McCord 1970, 11). Hutchins noted the economic importance of Fort Ouiatenon, stating that 8,000 British pound sterling's worth of skins and furs shipped from the post annually. This would translate into 2023 US dollars as $1,910,809.48 (Hutchins 1904, 101; The Money Converter 2023; Webster 2023).

German-born British engineering officer Lieutenant Detrich Brehm visited Fort Ouiatenon, along with a corporal and four privates, on an exploratory mission in 1762. In his report he wrote:

> The Fort Viattanow is old and decay'd and several Stokados fallen down, it Stands on a low Rich Soil, and is every Spring more or less inundated, the water is some times 6 or 7 feet. There are no Buildings belonging to the King but a large guard Room; the houses are all built like in the other Forts, the Banquets or Platforms are also wanting. (Brehm 1762; Widder 2013, 93)

Whether the condition of the fort was due to the flood, as noted by Brehm, or due to neglect remains unclear. However, in 1766 Lieutenant Alexander Fraser noted that the fort was in ruin (Alvord and Carter 1916, 230). During the attack and destruction of Ouiatenon and the surrounding settlements by Scott and Wilkinson in 1791, there is no mention of any sort of fortification wall. It can be assumed, then, that the fort had all but disappeared by that time and that the French abandoned that area after the destruction of Kethtippekenunck.

In 1795 two of General Anthony Wayne's officers, Ensign Thomas Bodley and Lieutenant John Wade, made trips up and down the Wabash. In this endeavor they seem to have used Thomas Hutchins's 1778 map (see figure I.4) and described in some detail the width and depth of the river, the topography, the environment, and the length, weight, and type of rivercraft that could be used on the Wabash (Bodley 1795; Hutchins 1778; Smith 1954; Wade 1795). Bodley, in his report dated June 12, 1795, notes:

> The old village on the S.E. side stood on low ground on the verge of the river—about 300 yd. back is a high Hill on the Top of which is an extensive Prairie about 10 miles in length & three in breadth. On the N.W. side was the Old French Village it stood in a large Prairie part of which overflow's at times, the soil is fertile—here about 300 acres has been Cultivated by the Indian's—About one mile above the Old Village on the N.W. side, is high ground & some beautiful Springs, this would be an eligible situation for a Fort. (Bodley 1795)

Nothing could be more ironic than the last two lines of this quotation for the researchers looking for the fort one hundred years later. It seems that this was one document they did not consult. His "eligible location" is the site of the Fort Ouiatenon park and blockhouse.

In 1817, Samuel R. Brown published *The Western Gazetteer; or Emigrant's Directory containing a Geographical Description of the Western States and Territories*. In this work, clearly drawn from a variety of sources, Ouiatenon is mentioned several times with two different spellings, Ouitanon and Ouitanan. In it, the author mentions trails, the rapids in the vicinity of the site, and the fact that different rivercraft operate on the upstream and downstream side of it, with the distance from the mouth of the Wabash to Ouiatenon being four hundred miles (Brown 1817, 39).

David Thomas, a horticulturalist, self-taught geologist, author, and explorer, traveled to Indiana in 1816. In 1819, he published his journal of his expedition and made two references related to settlements in Indiana relevant to this story. As he moved up the Wabash to what is now Terre Haute, he noted that "we were then six to eight miles beyond the limits of the civilized world; and no white settlers of any description, are known above Fort Harrison." Later in the text where he discusses his journey from Fort Harrison to Fort Wayne, he only mentions three Native American villages: Miami, Massasinaway, and an Indian town. Two are on the Eel River, and one is on Pipe Creek where they drain into the Wabash. The Eel River joins the Wabash at Logansport in Cass County between Lafayette and Fort Wayne, and Pipe Creek is farther east along the Wabash River in Cass County (Thomas 1970, 183, 240). Thomas makes no mention of former French occupations along the Wabash.

THE AMERICAN SETTLEMENT PERIOD

The Battle of Fallen Timbers (Maumee, Ohio) in August 1794 was the last conflict between Indigenous peoples and the United States for control of the Northwest Territory. The victory of the forces led by General Anthony Wayne set the stage for Native American removal from much of the state of Ohio. The subsequent Treaty of Greenville of 1795 foreshadowed future treaties, annual annuity payments, and removals. Next came the St. Marys treaties with the Delaware, Miami, Ottawa, Potawatomi, Seneca, Shawnee, Wea, and Wyandot tribes during September and October 1818. The two treaties that directly affected the Wabash tribal groups and the site of Fort Ouiatenon were the cession by the Pottawatomi on October 2, 1818, and the cession by the Miami on October 6, 1818 (Royce 1881). The first involved a strip of land along the north side of the Wabash bordered to the east by the Tippecanoe River. The second treaty addressed the center of the state of Indiana south of the Wabash River. Both treaties led to the area that makes up present-day Tippecanoe County opening for settlement by people of Euro-American descent.

Euro-American travelers continued to move through the Wabash area despite the hostility of local Tribes. One, a surveyor, Henry P. Benton, traveled down the Wabash in the spring of 1820. He mentions only the remains of the Battle of Tippecanoe (in current-day Battle Ground, Indiana), which he toured on April 10 with a Native American guide who had fought in the battle (Ricker 1941, 384–95). In 1821, Henry R. Schoolcraft traveled down the Wabash and visited the Native American villages of Mississinewa and Winemac. The only ruins he mentions are those of Prophetstown (Schoolcraft 1825, 128) near Battle Ground.

Township and range lines in this part of Tippecanoe County were laid in 1822 by John Milroy and his deputy B. Bently. During his survey of the fort site along the line between sections 27 and 28 on December 27 and 28, he recorded that the bottomland prairie was level and rich, while the rolling uplands were "2nd rate." The trees were a scattering of oaks and black jack with small hickory. Other tree species included honey locust, willow, cottonwood, bur oak, sugar maple, and red oak. The simple fact that trees were present in the grassland and that no structures were noted demonstrates the changes that had taken place. The map in his report shows the mouth of Wea Creek to the east of the French descriptions of its location just west of the line separating Sections 27 and 26 (Indiana Archives and Records Administration n.d.).

By 1866, the mouth of the creek had continued its eastward migration to the section line (Warner 1866). By 1878, the Wea Creek mouth was roughly in its current location as of 2020 (Kingman Brothers 1878, 55). Interestingly, a remnant channel can be seen directly south of the boat ramp and blockhouse in Fort Ouiatenon Park today.

Richard Patten DeHart credits Peter Weaver as being the earliest settler in Tippecanoe County, who in the fall of 1822 or early spring of 1823 built a cabin on the south side of the Wabash at the lower end of the Wea Plain. In an uncited footnote, DeHart mentions another possible candidate by the name of Elijah Moore who settled in Wayne Township in the fall of 1822 (DeHart 1909, 147).

As late as 1826, the fort remained marked in gazetteers.

This post is situated on the north bank of the Wabash river a short distance below the mouth of the Eel river, and 262 miles from the mouth of the Wabash. It was established, according to Cramer's account, in 1775, it is a small stockade fort. A silver mine has been discovered a short distance from the fort.

This work was reprinted into the 1850s. The Eel River flows into the Wabash in present-day Logansport in Cass County, forty-five miles northeast of where the fort lies (Scott 1826, 95–96).[6]

The parents of Sanford C. Cox purchased sixty-five acres in the southeast portion of the west half of section 29 on the south side of the Wabash River in 1826. In his book *Recollections of the Early Settlement of the Wabash Valley*, first published in 1860, he recalls his boyhood memories of the remains of the earlier French and Native American occupations:

> My father's farm was on the ground once covered with this Indian town. In the Fall, after the grass was burnt on the prairie, the boys of the neighborhood used to amuse themselves with hunting up the blades of butcher knives, tomahawks, brass kettles, gun barrels, etc., and the little girls in picking up beads, which in many places were strewn over the face of the ground, and had been washed by the rains into gulches along the hillside. I remember that one day my little sister and a neighbor girl came running into the cabin, exclaiming, "Is not this a rich country, when even the grass and weeds bear beads?" (Cox 1972, 34–35)

One of the earliest Fort Ouiatenon researchers was Professor John Collett, who later became the Indiana state geologist. In 1873 using period documents, he erroneously worked out the location of the fort to be Black Rock, south in Warren County. Visiting the site, he found evidence of fires, chimneys, etc., and that settled the question in his mind (*Indianapolis Journal* 1887a).

THE TIPPECANOE COUNTY HISTORICAL ASSOCIATION AND THE SEARCH FOR FORT OUIATENON

What follows is a review of the efforts by many individuals to find the remains of Fort Ouiatenon up to the mid to late twentieth-century excavations of the actual fort site. This will be the first time some of these individuals and their work have found their way into such a study. Some of the descriptions may be unsettling, but in order to provide a complete history, the works of early efforts are included. Much of what is described was not unusual methodologies for their time. Certainly, methodologies, justifications for the research, and sensitivities toward human remains have advanced considerably. As a student and then as a professional archaeologist, I witnessed and participated in the repatriation and reburial of remains recovered from pot hunters, museums, and academic collections. I also participated in meetings with traditional religious leaders, at times one on one, concerning these issues. With the passage of the Native American Graves Protection and Repatriation Act in 1990, human remains and grave goods are now treated much differently than what was done in the past.

As noted in the earlier Sanford Cox quotation, collecting of artifacts began in the first phase of Anglo-American settlement along the Wabash. From the 1870s and well into the twentieth century, the study of and search for Fort Ouiatenon has involved archival research, field surveys, collecting, pot hunting, and excavations. These were undertaken by a variety of individuals, both amateur and academic. Unfortunately, a good deal of the material collected has been lost. Only a handful of these efforts were reported. If field notes were taken and reports were written up, these have also been lost. The excavations undertaken were not by any standards of today considered ethical. Again, the descriptions of the desecration of graves are certainly disturbing but are necessary for understanding the history of the discovery of the fort and how the process evolved. Further, they reflect the history of archaeological practices during that period.

Statements such as these below appeared often in Indiana newspapers in the late nineteenth and early twentieth centuries:

> Modern authorities have this little stockade fort strung all along the Wabash, on both sides of the stream, from Terre Haute to Logansport. (*Indianapolis Journal* 1887b)
>
> A portion of the skeleton of a white man, evidently a Catholic priest, was found by workmen in a gravel-pit, four miles from Lafayette. A number of buttons and a silver cross were also found. It is thought the gravel-pit is a portion of the original site of the old French post, Ouiatenon, established about two hundred years ago, when the French were in possession of this State. (*Indianapolis Journal* 1889)

Richard B. Wetherill (figure 1.4) credits the founding of the Historical Society of Tippecanoe County (1923–1928) to a discovery (figures 1.5, 1.6, and 1.7) of "several silver crosses and a silver disc inscribed with arms of France" (Wetherill 1929; Waters n.d.). The first of three countywide historical societies in Tippecanoe County, the Tippecanoe Historical Society, was also inspired by these artifacts. It was founded by Benjamin Wilson Smith, Robert Hatcher, and Richard B. Wetherill in 1888, but it did not survive for long. The artifacts, which for Wetherill revealed the location of Fort

Ouiatenon, were apparently found by Robert Hatcher. Others involved in the discovery included Dr. Arvill Wayne Bitting, Dr. Oscar J. Craig, the Honorable Benjamin Wilson Smith, Colonel John Levering, and Judge Richard P. DeHart. In that year, gravel haulers dug into a ravine between the ridge and the cemetery of the Sand Ridge Church, which was located uphill and across the road from the later Fort Ouiatenon Park. The Sand Ridge Cemetery remains, but the church was demolished in 1930. A good deal of skeletal material and artifacts including various sized "double crosses" were collected by several individuals (*Lafayette Leader* 1921).

Ruby Burroughs (figure 1.8), in her 1907 Purdue University thesis, outlines the history of the research on Fort Ouiatenon up to that date and includes the names Judge Beckwith, Jacob Piatt Dunn, and John B. Dillon as others looking for the site. Burroughs in fact credits Smith as the person who first identified the site, now the Fort Ouiatenon Park, where the fort was incorrectly thought to be located (Burroughs 1907, 1). Smith served as a state representative at the time. The history of Smith's research, findings, and admitted mistakes are described in an unpublished paper titled "How I Found Ouiatenon" (Smith n.d.). Smith mentioned a talk he gave at the Sand Ridge Church discussing finds such as crosses, brooches, beads, arrowheads, and Indian implements on the old Cuppy farm, and he also referred to a Mrs. Sunderland. Farms were owned by Cuppy and Sunderland families in the area, particularly on the north half of sections 26 and 27 of Wabash Township, Tippecanoe County, with Francis Sunderland's holdings occupying the Fort Ouiatenon Park blockhouse location (Boyd 2007, 100–101). After Smith's talk, a young man affirmed that he had often heard his grandmother Sunderland say she had seen the logs of the blockhouse in 1818, and her family had set out their orchard on the spot. The young man's statement was generally dismissed, and no evidence of such a structure was ever recorded.

In 1887 Jacob Piatt Dunn, the secretary of the Indiana Historical Society, outlined his research on the location of the fort in great detail. He used a variety of early maps and written descriptions by Thomas Hutchins, methodically eliminating various tributaries of the Wabash. At the same time, Dunn attacked Judge Beckwith, who placed the fort on a hill in the vicinity of Black Rock, Indiana, south of the actual fort

Figure 1.4. Richard B. Wetherill, 1934. Courtesy of the Tippecanoe County Historical Association.

Figure 1.5. This trade silver disc is one of the artifacts that inspired Richard Wetherill to create the Historical Society of Tippecanoe County. Courtesy of the Eiteljorg Museum of American Indians and Western Art.

site. Dunn placed the fort on the north side of the river somewhere between Indian Creek and Wea Creek (*Indianapolis Journal* 1887b). His conclusion proved true.

B. Wilson Smith, a local familiar with the area acting on a request from Dunn, mounted a search for the fort beginning in 1887–1888. Smith used "General Haldimand's documents" from what was described as the "Canadian Archives." These documents give an account of the location of the fort including the distance from the riverbank. Smith was one of the many researchers of the day who recognized that the Wea Creek had changed course since the time when the fort was occupied. He noted that the mouth had moved a full half mile from the great flood of 1875. He placed the fort site fifty to seventy rods north of the Sand Ridge Church. He referred to local lore about the site and associated villages as "dumb" (Smith n.d.). With the help of General R. P. DeHart, another local historian and a prominent local judge, the two men located what was believed to be the original mouth of the Wea. This abandoned channel still exists and enters the south side of the Wabash almost directly across from the

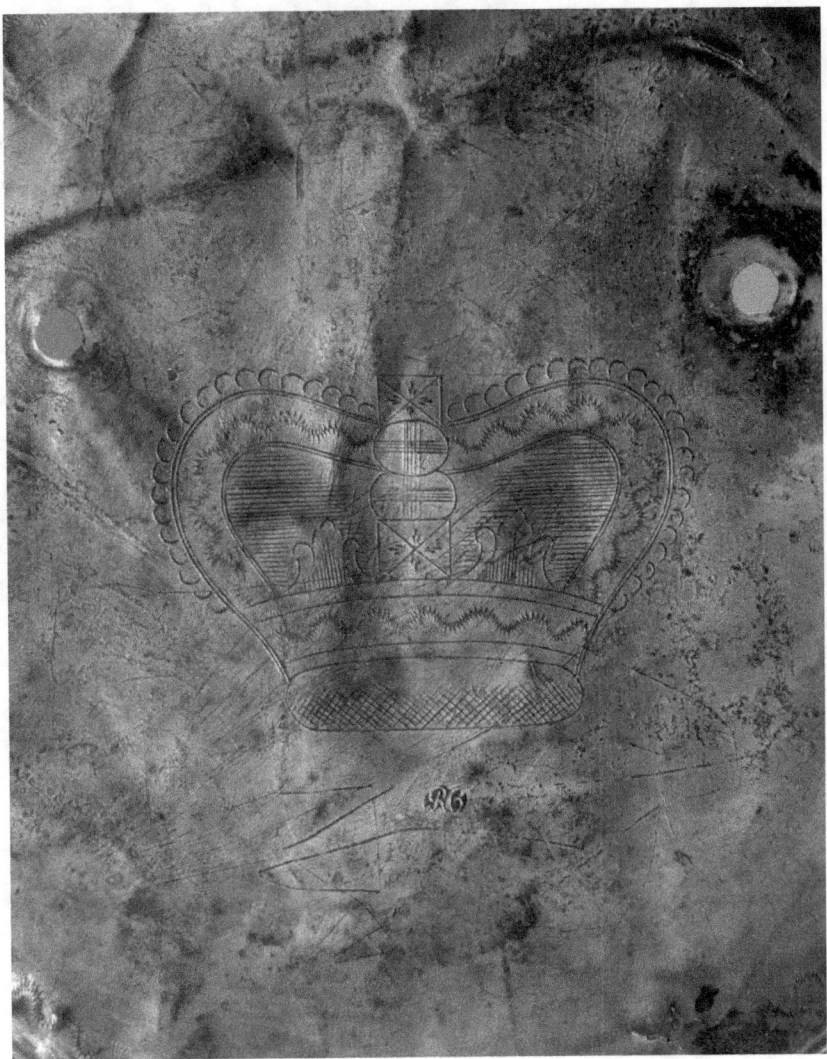

Figure 1.6. Close-up of the engraved imagery on the trade silver disc. Courtesy of the Eiteljorg Museum of American Indians and Western Art.

present-day park boat ramp and blockhouse on the north bank.[7] Smith then paced off measurements until they located what they believed to be the site where an old stable was then standing. This was all done with DeHart, Thomas Lonergan, and a couple of fishermen in a boat. According to Smith, where the blockhouse now stands DeHart exclaimed after they had surveyed the site, "A surveyor could find a corner from that description. It is right here—here is the site" (Smith n.d.). As stated earlier,

Figure 1.7. One of the crosses that inspired Richard Wetherill to create the Historical Society of Tippecanoe County. Courtesy of the Eiteljorg Museum of American Indians and Western Art.

this was the same site that Ensign Bodley in 1795 viewed as "an eligible situation for a Fort" (Bodley 1795).

Interestingly, in a letter written by Dr. Arvill Bitting to Amos W. Butler dated June 14, 1910, Bitting noted an event that took place after 1890:

> From the information which Mr. Hatcher had, we located the Fort as being on the west side of the creek that passes the Sand Ridge church. We [Bitting and Professor Oscar J. Craig of Purdue University] made some diggings in the hill and opened several graves. We recovered four or five good skeletons or parts of them, obtained cloth and decorations of soldiers clothes. Most important of all in locating the fort, was the outline by rotting timber in the ground as posts of what we believed to be a palisade. This was about 90 by possibly 150 feet. (Bitting 1910)[8]

Bitting did not give much in the way of specifics other than noting a hill, but the creek in question is Indian Creek, which empties into the Wabash halfway between the actual fort site and the current blockhouse. However, it appears that Bitting and Craig may have been the first known discoverers of the actual fort site. Bitting continued to champion the discovery as time went on. Some of the material recovered by Craig, Bitting, and Hatcher ended up in one of the Purdue University museums. Various departments at Purdue from its earliest days developed museums and cabinets as teaching aids. Most disappeared before World War I. Only the Locomotive Museum survived into the mid-twentieth century. The whereabouts of the artifacts and specimens from these early collections are largely unknown. No archival records of their disbursement exist. According to an article from the January 1, 1891, Purdue University student newspaper the *Purdue Exponent*:

Figure 1.8. Ruby Burroughs, an early local author, wrote her Purdue University thesis on the search for and history of Fort Ouiatenon in 1907. Courtesy of the Purdue University Archives and Special Collections.

There is in the museum a very fine collection of remains from Fort Ouiatenon that were deposited by Mr. Hatcher. They consist of a skull and an iron band that surrounded it, two large earrings about two inches across and made like wheels, three parts of an epaulet that are silver and have engraved upon them the form of a swan, and pigeon, two silver armlets about three and a half inches broad also engraved, silver wristlets, one plain and one engraved, nails, knives that have completely oxidized, a cup, parts of two bowls and two spoons. All these articles showed long exposure to dampness as they were oxidized in whatever part that was susceptible to such action. Some Indian relics were also found, two red sandstone pipes, some war paint, flint strikes, tomahawks, a large number of small copper ornaments in which small bunches of hair still remained. A remarkable part of the find was that of small pieces of cloth. Microscopic examination will be made to determine the fiber. All these articles have a peculiar odor which will scent anything with which they come in contact. The perfume is of such durable character that it will remain fixed for a number of days. This is probably the best find ever made in the State. The department of History is doing original work in trying to find further evidence as to the first settlement in this State. Vincennes is no doubt the oldest town in the State and claims the honor of being the first settlement. The facts already possessed seems [*sic*] to prove very clearly that the honor should go to Ouiatanon and the search now is for things that will further confirm the facts already in hand.... On Jan. 6, the ... party went to the old fort Ouiatanon and made some excavations. Two skeletons were unearthed one of an adult very probably French and judging from appearances of the teeth it was about twenty-two or three. The other skeleton was of a child and probably Indian. Vermillion was found in the grave with it. A French copper coin bearing the date 1674, was procured from one of the residents also a silver bracelet. Further work will be done in the Spring. (*Purdue Exponent* 1891)

At one point the artifacts were displayed in the basement of University Hall (Waters n.d.).

The Ouiatenon Club of Crawfordsville, a group never mentioned by Tippecanoe County historians, was also actively interested in locating the fort. The club was a literary society consisting of male faculty at Wabash College and men from the local community. The lectures given at the club's meetings were wide-ranging. However, in an 1897 meeting the club examined an 1824 map of Indiana that "showed the location of the Village of Ouiatenon—on the Wabash River" (Ouiatenon Club 1897). In that same year, the *Crawfordsville Journal* noted the discovery of a skeleton clothed in the remnants of a French uniform associated with military equipment, silver crosses, and other items on the north bank of the Wabash River near the mouth of Wea Creek (*Crawfordsville Journal* 1897).

In 1897, the Indiana Academy of Science annual meeting at Purdue University toured various sites within the county, one being the future Fort Ouiatenon Park site (Indiana Academy of Science 1898, 33). However, a reminiscence of Amos Butler indicates that the group visited what we now understand to be the actual site of the fort. In this account, Butler relates various theories about the fort's location. Colonel John Levering, one of the members of the tour, rejected all these locations based on his understanding of the historical record. Levering was a banker and a member of the Indiana State Board of Agriculture and had been an officer in the American Civil War. Dr. Bitting showed some kettles recovered from "a ridge in the low bottoms almost opposite the Sand Ridge Church." The group walked to a low sandy ridge not far from the river and found beads. Walking farther west and nearer the river, the group found a wide area of building debris of stone, brick, mortar, nails, and glass. Other material included gun parts, copper objects, a spoon with a coat of arms, and a fine silver bracelet (Butler n.d.). Sadly, the manuscript is undated. However, this may be the same location where Craig and Bitting undertook their earlier excavations.

Two separate investigations using "General Haldimand's documents" from the "Canadian Archives" noted above were used to locate the site before 1907 (Burroughs 1907, 1). The first investigation was by B. Wilson Smith, and a later survey was undertaken by Hatcher and DeHart. One source states that Hatcher visited Paris to examine period French maps (*Purdue Exponent* 1890). Both investigations placed the fort at the site of the blockhouse. DeHart believed that he confirmed his findings by local lore, which included the Sunderland family's recollection of a blockhouse on the knoll and another's memory of the Wea Creek emptying into the Wabash opposite that knoll. Just upstream in those days, rapids were present that could still impede boaters. In 1905, Smith and DeHart hosted an assemblage of interested parties to formally establish the location of the fort. By 1907, many who were researching the topic agreed about the fort's location at the future Fort Ouiatenon Park site. Artifacts found on the knoll, according to Ruby M. Burroughs, included Jesuit crosses, flint, and other items. Another source reported a significant amount of trade silver trinkets worth "hundreds of dollars" that were regularly uncovered by the plow at this location on land owned by Darius Frazer. Many were sold to an unnamed Lafayette jeweler (Historian's Records 1894–1912, 222; *Indianapolis News* 1903). Burroughs believed that a spring behind the site and its commanding view of the area supported the archaeological and archival evidence (Smith n.d.; Burroughs 1907, 1).

On a statewide level, the state legislature attempted in 1903 to pass a bill for the erection of a monument at the future park site. Nothing came of the effort (Herschell 1903). In 1907, the General de La Fayette Chapter of the Daughters of the American Revolution, much to the dismay of Arvill Bitting, placed a monument along the road north of the knoll, and it remains there today (Bitting 1910). For the Daughters of the American Revolution, belief in the original fort's location was clear. The statement on the monument reads "Fort Ouiatenon stood 200 feet south of this spot." Bitting knew better but seems to have been ignored.

By 1920, there were calls for the site to become a national or state park. In 1921, the Indiana Historical Society made efforts to locate the actual site so a monument could be erected. However, apparently there was no satisfactory agreement by all concerned as to its correct location (*Herald-Democrat* 1921).

In addition, the Ouiatenon Club of Crawfordsville worked independently to find the fort's actual location. On October 11, 1922, the men along with their wives made a pilgrimage to the future park site. Dr. J. N. Taylor, an early member of the club, was a driving force in the decades-long research about the fort and its history. He collected documents from Montreal, Quebec, and Paris. As part of the event he traveled by boat, "arriving at the identical time of year and time of the day, for all the world just as the first commandant, Sieur du Buisson, had done two hundred and three years before" (*Lafayette Journal and Courier* 1920; Ouiatenon Club 1923, 39–40).

The Historical Society of Tippecanoe County organized in 1923 and then reorganized in 1928 to become the Tippecanoe County Historical Association (TCHA). The 1925 centennial celebrations of the founding of Lafayette, Indiana, helped generate further interest in Tippecanoe County history, and with it came renewed interest in Fort

Ouiatenon. The principal driver in this effort was Richard B. Wetherill, future president of the TCHA. Wetherill grew up in the city and became a successful physician. After retirement, he became a philanthropist and world traveler.

On September 29, 1928, a reception was held at Eliza Fowler Hall on the Purdue University campus. First came the celebration of the opening of the new county museum and art gallery in the Ross Building on Seventh and Main Streets. Second, Wetherill presented the deed for 8.91 acres of land that he had purchased from the landowner Darius Frazer, the area where many researchers believed Fort Ouiatenon was located. Wetherill was fearful that the site would be covered in riverside cottages, so he gave the deed to TCHA in hopes that the site would be preserved from development and opened to the public (*Lafayette Journal and Courier* 1928; McCollough 1982–1983). One of his goals was to reconstruct "the old blockhouse and palisades." In November, Wetherill visited Old Fort Harrod at the Kentucky Pioneer Memorial State Park to study costs and construction methods of log buildings and fortifications.

To further support Wetherill's belief that he had purchased the site of the fort, physics professor Raymond Barrington Abbott of Purdue University surveyed the future park site with a metal detector he had built originally to find meteorites. He was accompanied by Wetherill. Abbott recovered "Indian Relics," which he donated to the TCHA (*Lafayette Journal and Courier* 1929a, 1929b). This was the first attempt to locate the fort using remote sensing technology. However, research later in the century revealed that the land purchased was not the actual fort site.

DOUBTS AND REDISCOVERY

The work of Craig and Bitting had always cast doubt on the pervasive beliefs of the location of Fort Ouiatenon. According to Alameda McCollough, by the 1960s it was becoming clear that the blockhouse site was not the actual location of the fort (McCollough 1982–1983). Professor Robert Raymond Mulvey of Purdue University had become increasingly familiar with artifacts coming from a site less than a mile to the west of the blockhouse. McCollough and Dr. Bill Sholty, the TCHA board president at the time, became concerned that the site might be compromised if it continued to be ignored. In the early 1960s Del Bartlett, a Wabash College student and area resident, became increasingly interested in local history and studied sites and artifact collections from the area. Bartlett, Larry Chowning, and John Henry independently examined the site and shared their findings with Dr. Mulvey and Dr. Sholty. Bartlett used the Amos Butler account of the 1897 Indiana Academy of Science visit as a guide for his field walking. Bartlett took an additional step of taking an aerial photograph of the site. Following a meeting attended by Dr. James Kellar (state archaeologist and

Figure 1.9. Dr. Wetherill using Professor Abbott's meteorite detector.
Courtesy of the Tippecanoe County Historical Association.

director of the Glenn Black Laboratory at Indiana University, Bloomington), Del Bartlett, Alameda McCullough, Hubert Hawkins (secretary of the Indiana Historical Society), and other interested parties, the decision was made to undertake archaeological excavations of the site during the summer of 1968 (Bartlett 2017). If you accept Bitting's claims, these excavations and subsequent work confirmed the location that Craig and Bitting had discovered as the actual site of Fort Ouiatenon, approximately one mile west of the blockhouse.

Since the rediscovery of Fort Ouiatenon in the late 1960s, several archaeological excavations have been undertaken, and these will be discussed in remaining chapters. Archaeological investigations over the years have been undertaken by teams from Purdue University, Indiana University, Michigan State University, and the University of Southern Indiana.

Much of what is in this volume came from papers given at the 2017 Midwest Historical Archaeology Conference under the theme "Reconstructing, Representing and Reenacting: Historical Archaeology and Public Education." This conference could not have happened without the leadership of Dr. Harold Kory Cooper of Purdue University. The papers focused on the fur trade, Fort Ouiatenon, and the Feast of the Hunters' Moon. The conference was part of a series of monthly events, coordinated by the author of this chapter, leading up to the 2017 Feast of the Hunters' Moon. The Feast is a commemoration of the founding of the fort, and 2017 marked three hundred years since that founding. It had also been fifty years since the first public weekend Feast of the Hunter's Moon had occurred. Further, one year earlier the 230-acre Ouiatenon Preserve had been established thanks to the generosity of the Roy Whistler Foundation. It is co-owned by the Tippecanoe County Historical Association and the Archaeological Conservancy and managed by the Ouiatenon Preserve Inc. The preserve will be discussed in detail in chapter 13.

CONCLUSION

For three hundred years, the site of Fort Ouiatenon moved through phases that reflected the transitions of the region. Activities of the early years were driven by economic and political forces that created alliances between Europeans and Native American tribes. As political changes came about, the fort declined, and the site was eventually lost to history. Over the later years, dedicated researchers used what knowledge they could gather to ascertain the location. Despite erroneously maintaining for several decades that the site occupied the current Fort Ouiatenon Park, advanced methods and the ongoing interest of historians and archaeologists have clarified the actual location, allowing us to understand more about this unique place, the first European settlement in what is now Indiana and one that has never been affected by urbanization.

NOTES

1. The site of one of the outlying native villages was reoccupied by the Anglo-American village of Granville, established in 1834; it is now a collection of houses. What remains of the village cemetery may be the last remaining undisturbed remnant of the Wea Prairie.
2. For a period eyewitness account, see Alvord and Carter (1916, 35). George Croghan also mentions the type of craft used on the Wabash River.
3. For an English translation of the 1743 Regulations for Leasing the Ouiatenon Post, see Peyser 1996, 63–66.
4. Kiskakon, also known as Pacan's Village, was located at the confluence of the Maumee, St. Joseph, and St. Marys Rivers in what is now northeastern Indiana.
5. Kethtippecanuck, spelled variously Keth Tippecanuck, Kethlipecanuck, Kathtippacanunck, Kathtippacanunk, Kehtipaquowonk, and Kithtippecanuck, was a large European and Native American village that had been established on the north side of the Wabash River at the mouth of the Tippecanoe River. The site is currently within the Prophetstown State Park. "This town, which contained about 120 houses, 80 of which were shingle roofed,... the best houses belonged to French traders, whose gardens and improvements round the town were truly delightful, and, everything considered, not a little wonderful; there was a tavern, with cellars, bar, public, and private rooms; and the whole marked a considerable share of order, and no small degree of civilization" (Lindley 1916, 12). This village is one of the locations where residents of Fort Ouiatenon retreated after 1780.
6. Another reason the French were interested in settling the Wabash Valley was the rumors of coal, copper, and silver deposits. Mine locations can be seen on period maps. However, no geological strata containing such deposits exist in the Ouiatenon area or north of it. Some peat deposits have been found along Indian Creek. Coal beds do exist south of Ouiatenon in Fountain and Warren Counties. Reports of lead, copper, and silver during the French regime and into the nineteenth century were undoubtedly occasional finds in glacial deposits (Gorby 1886, 96; Erd and Greenberg 1960, 24, 29, 49).
7. At present, the mouth of Wea Creek enters the Wabash near the east-west center point of section 35 directly south of section 26 (Cory & Sons 1888; Tippecanoe County Surveyor 1998; United States Geological Survey 2020; Warner 1866).
8. Professor Oscar J. Craig started his career at Purdue University in 1883. In 1886, he became the chair of the Department of History and Political Science. He wrote a number of historical works including "Ouiatenon: A Study in Indiana History" for *Indiana Historical Society Publications*. Craig left Purdue University in 1895 to become the first president of the University of Montana. Dr. Arvill Wayne Bitting was born in Tippecanoe County and graduated from Purdue University in 1891. He received his doctorate of veterinary medicine from Iowa State College in 1895 and a doctor of medicine degree from the Medical College of Indiana University in 1900. Between 1893 and 1907 he worked for the Purdue University Agricultural Experiment Station. He then worked for the US Bureau of Chemistry.

REFERENCES

Alvord, Clarence Walworth, and Clarence Edwin Carter, eds. 1915. "Jenkins to Gladwin, March 28, 1763." In *British Series, Vol 1: The New Regime 1765–1767*. Collections of the Illinois State Historical Library, Vol. 10. Trustees of the Illinois State Historical Library, Springfield.

———. 1916. "George Croghan's Journals, February 28, 1765, to October 8, 1765." In *British Series, Vol. 2: The New Regime 1765–1767*. Collections of the Illinois State Historical Library, Vol. 11. Trustees of the Illinois State Historical Library, Springfield.

Barnhart, John D., and Dorothy L. Riker. 1971. *Indiana to 1816: The Colonial Period*. Indiana Historical Bureau & Indiana Historical Society, Indianapolis.

Bartlett, Joseph D. 2017. Email to author. July 18, 2017.

Bellin, Jacques Nicolas. 1755. *CARTE DU COURS DE L'OHIO OU DE LA BELLE RIVIERE: Depuis sa Source jusqu'a sa jonction avec celle d'Ouabache, avec les pays les plus voisins*. Norman B. Leventhal Map & Education Center, Boston Public Library. https://collections.leventhalmap.org/search/commonwealth:hx11z213x.

Bitting, A.W. 1910. "A. W. Bitting letter to Amos W. Butler, June 14, 1910." Correspondence, Fort Ouiatenon Research Files, box 1. Tippecanoe County Historical Association, Lafayette.

Bodley, Thomas. 1795. "Observations on the Navigation, Soil, Water & Villages of the Wabash, from Port Vincennes to Portage Nine Miles from Fort Wayne." June 12, 1795. Anthony Wayne Papers, Collection# 0699. Historical Society of Pennsylvania, Philadelphia.

Boyd, Gregory A. 2007. *Family Maps of Tippecanoe County, Indiana, Deluxe Edition with Homesteads, Roads, Waterways, Towns, Cemeteries, Railroads, and More*. Norman: Arphax Publishing.

Brehm, Detrich. 1762. "Report to His Excellency Sir Jeffery Amherst Commander in Chieff of His Majestys Forces in North America etc: etc: etc: of the Lakes, Creeks, and Roads, seen in going round the Frontier Posts of Canada, with a Detachment, first Commanded by Major Gladwin and latest by Cap Henry Balfourt." Jeffery Amherst Papers, War Office 34/102 f.20–23. The National Archives of the United Kingdom, Kew.

Brodhead, John Romeyn. 1852. "M. de Longueuil to M. de Rouillé." April 21, 1752. *Documents relative to the Colonial History of the State of New York; Holland, England, and France, 10*. Albany, NY: Weed, Parsons and Co.

———. 1855. "Memoir on the Indians of Canada as far as the River Mississippi, with remarks on their manners and trade, 1718." In *Documents Relative to the Colonial History of the State of New-York; Holland, England, and France*, Vol. 9. Weed, Parsons and Company, Albany.

Brown, Samuel R. 1817. *The western gazetteer; or emigrant's directory, containing a geographical description of the western states and territories, viz. the states of Kentucky, Indiana, Louisiana, Ohio, Tennessee i.e. Tennessee and Mississippi: and the territories of Illinois, Missouri, Alabama, Michigan, and North-Western. With an Appendix, containing sketches of some of the western counties of New-York, Pennsylvania, and Virginia; a description of the great northern lakes; Indian annuities, and directions to emigrants*. Auburn, NY: H. C. Southwick.

Burroughs, Ruby M. 1907. "Fort Ouiatenon History." Master's thesis. Purdue University, West Lafayette.

Butler, Amos W. n.d. "Old Post Ouiatenon." 8.1 Butler, Amos W. file, Fort Ouiatenon Research Files, box 2 of 2. Tippecanoe County Historical Association, Lafayette.

Cary, John. 1805. *A new map of part of the United States of North America: exhibiting the Western Territory, Kentucky, Pennsylvania, Maryland, Virginia &c., also, the Lakes Superior, Michigan, Huron, Ontario & Erie, with Upper and Lower Canada &c.* London: J. Cary. Indiana Historical Society, Indianapolis. http://images.indianahistory.org/cdm/ref/collection/dc035/id/133.

Cory & Sons. 1888. *Atlas of Tippecanoe County, Ind.* Lafayette, IN: Cory & Sons, Civil and Mechanical Engineers.

Cox, Sanford C. 1972. *Recollections of the Early Settlement of the Wabash Valley.* Chaska, MN: Buckskin.

Craig, Oscar J. 1893. "Ouiatanon: A Study in Indiana History." *Indiana Historical Society Publications* 2, no. 8.

Crawfordsville Journal. 1897. "Fort Ouiatenon." August 6, 1897, 1.

DeHart, Richard Patten. 1909. *Past and Present of Tippecanoe County Indiana*, Vol. 1. Indianapolis: B. F. Bowen.

Dunn, Jacob Piatt. 1894. "Documents Relating to the French Settlements on the Wabash." *Indiana Historical Society Publications* 2. no. 2. Indianapolis: Bowen-Merrill.

Erd, Richard C., and Seymour S. Greenberg. 1960. *Minerals of Indiana.* Geological Survey. Bloomington: Indiana Department of Conservation.

Gorby, S. S. 1886. "Geology of Tippecanoe County." In *Fifteenth Annual Report Indiana Department of Geology and Natural History.* Indianapolis: William R. Burford, Contractor for State Printing and Binding.

Hassam, Loren. 1872. *A Historical Sketch of Lafayette, Indiana: Its Attractions as a Home and Advantages for Business.* Lafayette, IN: S. Vater, Journal Job Printing Establishment.

Helderman, Leonard C. 1938. "Danger on the Wabash." *Indiana Magazine of History* 34, no. 4: 455–67.

Herald-Democrat. 1921. "Local Men Assist in Locating Famous Old French Fort." October 14, 1.

Herschell, W. M. 1903. "Movement for Monument to Mark the Site of Historic Fort Ouiatenon That Fell When the Treacherous Pontiac Marched on English Posts." *Indianapolis News*, September 26, 15.

Historian's Records. n.d. *1894–1912 Historian's Records, General De Lafayette Chapter. Daughters of the American Revolution.* Lafayette: Tippecanoe County Historical Association.

Horsman, Reginald. 1976. "Great Britain and the Illinois Country in the Era of the American Revolution." *Journal of the Illinois State Historical Society* 69, no. 2: 100–109.

Hutchins, Thomas. 1778. *A new map of the western parts of Virginia, Pennsylvania, Maryland and North Carolina; comprehending the river Ohio, and all the rivers, which fall into it; part of the river Mississippi, the whole of the Illinois River, Lake Erie; part of the lakes Huron, Michigan &c. and all the country bordering on these lakes and rivers.* London: Thomas Hutchins. Indiana Historical Association, Indianapolis. http://hdl.loc.gov/loc.gmd/g3707o.ar078900.

———. 1904. *A topographical description of Virginia, Pennsylvania, Maryland, and North Carolina; reprinted from the original ed. of 1778;* ed. by Frederick Charles Hicks. Cleveland, OH: Burrows Brothers.

Indiana Academy of Science. 1898. "The Field Meeting of 1897." *Proceedings of the Indiana Academy of Science.* Indianapolis: William B. Burford.

Indiana Archives and Records Administration. n.d. "Lands North and West of the 2nd Meridian." Series, 15, roll #1746. State Land Office Collection. Indiana Archives and Records Administration, Indianapolis.

Indiana Historical Bureau. 1778. "Ouiatenon to Vincennes, Hamilton Takes Vincennes, November 29 to December 17, 1778." *Henry Hamilton's Journal.* https://www.in.gov/history/for-educators/all-resources-for-educators/resources/george-rogers-clark/henry-hamiltons-journal/ouiatenon-to-vincennes-hamilton-takes-vincennes-november-29-to-december-17-1778/.

Indianapolis Journal. 1887a. "Site of Fort Ouiatenon." March 25, 4.

———. 1887b. "The Site of Ouiatenon." March 26, 4.

———. 1889. "Indiana and Illinois News." February 14, 2.

Indianapolis News. 1903. "Movement for Monument to Mark the Site of Historic Fort Ouiatenon That Fell When the Treacherous Pontiac Marched on English Posts." September 26, 15.

Kellogg, Louise Phelps. 1925. *The French Régime in Wisconsin and the Northwest.* Macison: State Historical Society of Wisconsin.

Kingman Brothers. 1878. *Historical Atlas Tippecanoe County Indiana.* Chicago: Kingman Brothers.

Krauskopf, Frances. 1955. *Ouiatenton Documents.* Indianapolis: Indiana Historical Society.

Lafayette Journal and Courier. 1920. "Monument and Park Proposed for Ouiatenon." *Lafayette Journal and Courier,* November 16, 12.

———. 1928. "Historic Fort Ouiatenon Site Presented to Local Society." *Lafayette Journal and Courier.* October 1, 1, 12.

———. 1929a. "History Society Governors Will Meet Saturday," *Lafayette Journal and Courier.* April 24, 1.

———. 1929b. "History Society Board Luncheon." *Lafayette Journal and Courier.* April 27, 13.

Lafayette Leader. 1921. "An Interesting Paper." *Lafayette Leader.* December 7, page unknown. No known copies of this newspaper from 1921 exist. Forts-Fort Ouiatenon-General. Vertical File. Tippecanoe County Historical Association, Lafayette.

Lindley, Harlow. 1916. *Indiana as Seen by Early Travelers.* Indiana Historical Commission, Indianapolis.

Mavity, Paul W. 1925. *The Centennial Book: Official Program of the Ceremonies and the Pageant in Celebration of the Centennial of Lafayette and Tippecanoe County, Indiana.* Lafayette: Haywood Publishing

McCollough, Alameda. 1982–1983. *Oral History Interview, Alameda McCollough, September 1982 and June 1983.* Accession 83.018. Lafayette: Tippecanoe County Historical Association.

McCord, Shirley S. 1970. *Travel Accounts of Indiana: A Collection of Observations by Wayfaring Foreigners, Itinerants, and Peripatetic Hoosiers.* Indianapolis: Indiana Historical Bureau, Indianapolis.

Metcalf, Samuel L. 1913. *A Collection of Some of the Most Interesting Narratives of Indian Warfare in the West.* New York: William Abbatt.

Michigan Pioneer and Historical Society. 1904. "Necessity for Re-establishing Mackinac. Endorsed—Colonies. M. de Vaudreuil 3rd Septr. 1710." *Collections and Researches*, 33. Landing: Michigan Pioneer and Historical Society.

The Money Converter. 2023. "Convert from British Pound Sterling (GBP) to United States Dollar (USD)." https://themoneyconverter.com/GBP/USD.

Ouiatenon Club. 1897. Book 1: Minutes of the Ouiatenon Club; The Ouiatenon Club. Crawfordsville, Indiana, Papers, 1883–1897, Marian Morrison Local History Collection. Crawfordsville District Public Library.

———. 1923. Summarized Record, November 1923: The Ouiatenon Club, Crawfordsville, Marian Morrison Local History Collection. Crawfordsville District Public Library.

Pease, Theodore Calvin, and Ernestine Jenison. 1940. *Illinois on the Eve of the Seven Years War 1747–1755, French Series III.* Collections of the Illinois State Historical Library, Vol. 29. The Trustees of the Illinois State Historical Library, Springfield.

Peyser, Joseph L. 1996. *Jacques Legardeur De Saint-Pierre: Officer, Gentleman, Entrepeneur.* East Landing: Michigan State University Press.

Purdue Exponent. 1890. "Fort Ouiatanon: An Historical Sketch." *Purdue Exponent.* December, 50.

———. 1891. "Department Notes." *Purdue Exponent.* January 1, 81.

Ricker, Dorothy. 1941. "Two Accounts of the Upper Wabash Country 1819–1820." *Indiana Magazine of History* 37, no. 4.

Roy, Pierre-Georges. 1918. "Sieur de Vincennes Identified." *Indiana Historical Society Publications*, 7.

Royce, C. C. 1881. "Cessions of Land by Indian Tribes to the United States: Illustrated by Those in the State of Indiana." *First Annual Report of the Bureau of Ethnology to the Secretary of the Smithsonian Institution, 1879–80*, 247–62. Washington, DC: US Government Printing Office.

Schoolcraft, Henry R. 1825. *Travels in the Central Portions of the Mississippi Valley: Comprising Observations on Its Mineral Geography, Internal Resources, and Aboriginal Population.* New York: Collins and Hannay.

Scott, John. 1826. *The Indiana gazetteer: or, Topographical dictionary: containing a description of the several counties, towns, villages, settlements, roads, lakes, rivers, creeks, and springs, in the state of Indiana.* Centreville, IN: J. Scott & W. M. Doughty.

SD Bullion. 2020. https://sdbullion.com/silver-prices-2020.

Skinner, Claiborne A. 2008. *The Upper Country: French Enterprise in the Colonial Great Lakes.* Baltimore: Johns Hopkins University Press.

Smith, B. Wilson. n.d. "How I Found Ouiatenon." Ouiatenon Research Files 8.1, box 2 of 2. Tippecanoe County Historical Association, Lafayette.

Smith, Dwight L. 1954. "Notes on the Wabash River in 1795." *Indiana Magazine of History* 50, no. 3: 277–90.

Stewart, Richard W. 2009. *American Military History*, Vol. 1, *The United States Army and the Forging of a Nation, 1775–1917*. Washington, DC: Center for Military History United States Army.

Thomas, David. 1970. *Travels through the Western Country in the Summer of 1816*. Darien, CT: Hafner Publishing.

Thornbrough, Gayle. 1957. "Outpost on the Wabash, 1787–1791; letters of Brigadier General Josiah Harmar and Major John Francis Hamtramck, and other letters and documents selected from the Harmar papers in the William L. Clements Library." *Indiana Historical Society Publications* 19. Indiana Historical Society, Indianapolis.

Thwaites, Reuben Gold. 1902. "L.A. de Bourbon. Proceedings of the Council of Marine. January 6, 1717." In *The French Regime in Wisconsin-1 1634–1727*. Collections of the State Historical Society of Wisconsin, 16. State Historical Society of Wisconsin, Madison.

———. 1908a. "Célerons Expedition Down the Ohio." In *The French Regime in Wisconsin*, Vol. 1 *1743–1760*. Collections of the State Historical Society of Wisconsin, 18. State Historical Society of Wisconsin, Madison.

———. 1908b. "Instructions for Spanish Governor of St. Louis." In *The British Regime in Wisconsin 1760–1800*. Collections of the State Historical Society of Wisconsin, 18. State Historical Society of Wisconsin, Madison.

Tippecanoe County Surveyor. 1998. *Tippecanoe County, Indiana, Highway and Drainage Map*. Lafayette: Tippecanoe County Surveyor.

United States Geological Survey. 2020. *USGS Topographic, Indiana Map, Indiana Geological & Water Survey*. Bloomington: Indiana University. https://igws.indiana.edu/maps/recent (accessed August 31, 2020).

Wade, John. 1795. "No.1," June 12, 1795, Anthony Wayne Papers, Collection # 0699. Historical Society of Pennsylvania, Philadelphia.

Warner, A. 1866. *Map of Tippecanoe County Indiana from Actual Surveys*. Philadelphia: C. O. Titus.

Waters, Elmer R. n.d. "Quiatenon Crosses." *Tippecanoe County Historical Association Photographic Archive: Fort Ouiatenon: Artifacts*. Lafayette: Tippecanoe County Historical Association.

Webster, Ian. 2023. "£8,000 in 1778→2023 | UK Inflation Calculator." Official Inflation Data, Alioth Finance, October 24, 2023. https://www.officialdata.org/uk/inflation/1778?amount=8000.

Wetherill, Richard B. 1929. "Letter to Nellie Colfax Smith from Richard B. Wetherill. August 10, 1929." Folder 1, box 1, Series 3, Richard Benbridge Wetherill Collection. Tippecanoe County Historical Association, Lafayette.

Widder, Keith R. 2013. *Beyond Potiac's Shadow: Michilimackinac and the Anglo-Indian War of 1763*. East Lansing: Michigan State University Press.

Wikipedia. 2022. "French Livre." https://en.wikipedia.org/wiki/French_livre. 08/07/2022.

Winkler, John F. 2011. *Wabash 1791: St. Clair's Defeat*. London: Osprey.

2

THE HISTORY OF THE ARCHAEOLOGY OF OUIATENON

KELSEY NOACK MYERS, US ARMY CORPS OF ENGINEERS

Ouiatenon has been the subject of intensive archaeological research over the past fifty years. However, data from the first excavations conducted at the site were never completely analyzed to provide an informational basis and contextual key for later work. Although the site was successfully nominated to the National Register of Historic Places in 1970, annual excavations conducted over the following decade were undertaken without being informed by Indiana University archaeologist James Kellar's initial work at the site. Through synthesis of student journals written during the 1969 field school at Fort Ouiatenon, Kellar's handwritten notes, and modern geospatial and remote sensing data, it was possible to complete a summary report nearly fifty years after the data had been collected (Myers 2017, 2019). This report, which is the subject of this chapter, links contexts for all of the archaeological data collected from the site to inform current and future research using the legacy collections that represent this complex site of cultural contact and deep Indigenous history.

Following the statehood of Indiana in 1816, the Indian Removal Act of 1830, and the Treaty of Tippecanoe in 1832, the federal government facilitated removal of Native American groups from the region by offering lands west of the Mississippi in exchange for previously designated reservation lands in the Midwest. This plan disregarded earlier promises made under treaty by the US government to Native Americans regarding the preservation of traditional tribal lands (Miller 2006) and appealed to tribal representatives' concern over dwindling access to traditional lands and resources. For example, half a million acres of land that had been established as Myaamia (Miami) reservation land between 1795 and 1830 in Indiana were reclaimed by the federal government through promise of annuity and cash payments, individual land grants, and new reservation lands in Kansas. Similarly, more than four million acres of Potawatomi land in northeastern Indiana were ceded by treaty in the 1830s, including the site of the post at Ouiatenon.

In both cases, the Tribes had agreed to relocate to their new reservation lands within a few years of signing. From 1836 to 1846 several Potawatomi removals occurred, with smaller groups moving to Kansas and Canada, including the Potawatomi Trail of Death in 1838 (Madison 2014, 122). In October 1846, about half of the Miami people living on original reservation lands were made to board three canal boats near Peru, Indiana, to begin a twenty-seven-year journey westward. The group lived for a time in Kansas before being removed westward once again and were eventually settled in what is now Miami, Oklahoma (Ironstrack 2013). Soon after the removals occurred, the many villages and camps once occupied by the Native people of Indiana became farmland and empty spaces between the towns and homesteads created by American settlers.

Early residents of these towns, including Lafayette, were entertained with a history of Indiana that began with the first settlements in the area made by American citizens rather than any of the Native or French colonial inhabitants who had come before. Relating to the Crawfordsville area specifically in adjacent Montgomery County, a written history was available via the journal of the Black Creek School master, Sandford C. Cox (1859). Cox himself had come to Indiana in 1824 at the age of fourteen, had witnessed the end of the residency of Native American groups and the removal period firsthand, and published a summary of his early memories in a columnar series titled "Old Settlers" in the *Lafayette Daily Courier*. While tangible evidence of the trading post of Ouiatenon no longer existed, by the early twentieth century the community of Lafayette had not only maintained an awareness of its colonial history but also developed a sentimental fondness for narratives of "the pioneer days."

The series of newspaper articles written by Cox (1859) and several other nineteenth-century works (Brodhead, Fernow, and O'Callaghan 1853; Ontario 1878; Smith 1903; Craig 1893) recount the temporal span between the post's abandonment and its first use as historical interpretive material by local history enthusiasts on the guided tour, with the "Tri-County Historical Itinerary" serving as the first pamphlet for this purpose (Barce and Whicker 1925). The first collection of articles written by Cox (1859), which was later revised and edited into a volume including stories by additional authors, begins in 1823 and sets the stage of early historic Indiana as "almost an entire wilderness. Its wide and tangled forests, and undisturbed prairies were the haunts of wild beasts, and the home of the wandering Indian." Cox goes on to refer to the Miamis and other Native people as "native forest lords, whose hostile incursions were yet dreaded by the almost defenceless inhabitants." Surely it is not difficult for a contemporary audience to read between the lines of Cox's text to identify the underlying assumptions and worldview associated with his vernacular tone and vocabulary. This was the type of writing that contributed to the mindsets and education of those who would go on to conduct the first archaeological projects at Ouiatenon. The Native American history of Indiana known to residents of the area consisted of little more than vague references to Native people "wandering" through the region, undermining the deep history of Indigenous occupation in the Wabash River valley.

As the bicentennial of Ouiatenon's establishment approached in 1917, members of the Daughters of the American Revolution formed a small local interest group called the Fort Ouiatenon Society. In 1906, informed by "an old Jesuit's journal, recently discovered in Paris," this group gathered for the purpose of raising money to place a marker commemorating the site of the trading post (Daughters of the American Revolution 1906, 200). However, the group was unable to definitively determine the exact location where the post had once stood and instead decided to use the gathered funds to place the marker at a suitable location somewhere within the approximate area. Land thought to have possibly been the site of the post was later purchased by local avocational historian Dr. Richard B. Whetherhill in 1928. Whetherhill intended to use this land to create a park and reconstructed blockhouse to commemorate the post's existence. Much of the effort put forth to locate the site on this parcel was made by local avocational historians and surface collectors as well as the Tippecanoe County Historical Association (TCHA), of which Whetherhill was the first president. But again, no satisfactory location could be determined on this purchased parcel that could be pronounced confidently as the place where the post once stood.

In 1957, the TCHA held a special event dinner for its members named "The Feast of the Hunters' Moon." It was after this first feast event that the land around the blockhouse was transferred to the care of the Tippecanoe County Park Department. The now annual event has evolved into a large-scale two-day historical reenactment that occupies more than twenty-two acres of campground (and nearly fifty acres of parking) and is attended by many more people than ever would have been present at the historic trading post during the height of its operation (Allison 1986, 26). This event took place annually for fifty-two years, with an interruption during its fifty-third year as the event was canceled in 2020 based on Centers for Disease Control and Prevention guidelines during the novel coronavirus pandemic. However, even with the interruption, the event has occurred annually for a decade longer than the entire French colonial period of the post, a testament to the significance of Ouiatenon in local collective memory.

A set of aerial photographs produced in 1968 by a local artifact collector and college senior, Del Bartlett (who later became a president of the TCHA), demonstrated promising evidence of an archaeological site in an agricultural field near the Ouiatenon county park. According to the recollection of Bartlett, the farmer who cultivated this property had recently purchased a new plow and tractor, and the increased capabilities of the new equipment added approximately four inches of depth to the existing plow zone. This created a discoloration in the soil as seen from the air that indicated to Bartlett, and eventually to archaeologist James Kellar, the potential outline of the original palisade line of the trading post at Ouiatenon. It is possible that Kellar may have already been aware of the potential existence of the archaeological site in this location after conducting research with local avocational historians, soil scientist Robert Mulvey, and medical doctor William Sholty (Strezewski 2014, 29). In the summer of 1968 after being approached formally by the TCHA, Kellar taught the first archaeological field school on the site sponsored jointly by Indiana University at Bloomington and the Indiana Historical Society (Noble 1991, 69). At the time, the property was under private ownership and used for agricultural purposes. The following year a field school student reported that the 1968 excavations "uncovered 30 feet of [stockade] trench, minor trenches (e.g., 'outhouse trenches'), pits, and many artifacts" (Neff 1969, 4). No documents related to the fieldwork in 1968 can be located today. Only the field specimen logs and artifact catalogs remain in the archives of the Glenn A. Black Laboratory of Archaeology (GBL).

Encouraged by his findings the year before, in 1969 Kellar again led a field school on the site, which commenced in mid-June and lasted for eight weeks. While no records of daily field activities or a journal of any kind written by Kellar himself from this year have come to light, four field school students' (Lucianne Neff, Alphonso Stadler, Vivianne Heacox, and Michael Whalen) journals from 1969 are archived at the GBL. Three of these students submitted to Kellar summary papers in addition to their field journals and maps for grading purposes. Two of the journal copies maintained in the archive include not only the handwritten and typed texts by the students but also the handwritten comments of Kellar. In addition to undergraduate students who participated in the field school for academic credit, several community members participated for the experience but did not leave behind journals or notes. The journal kept by field school student Neff makes mention of both "Junior Historical Society girls," or junior members of the Indiana Historical Society, accompanied by a chaperone and "Members (assumed to be TCHA members)" on the site as volunteer field crew.

Based on the 1968 and 1969 excavations, the site was nominated and accepted to the National Register of Historic Places in 1970 (Noble 1991, 69). Kellar himself never reported on the material from the field schools aside from a short article published by the Indiana Historical Society under the title "The Search for Post Ouiatanon." With this article it seems that Kellar's interest in the site waned, and he ended his short foray into historical archaeology. He then returned to his previous research on the Mississippian period site of Angel Mounds in southern Indiana and other "Indians of the Wabash Valley" (Drury to Kellar, pers. comm., 1971). Ouiatenon was a rare project in the region at that time, and few professionals in the field focused on historical archaeological research. No one involved with the project during the 1968–1969 field seasons had possessed more than "a passing familiarity with eighteenth-century material culture and colonial fortifications," and little comparative literature existed against which to compare the results or to drive analysis beyond identification of the site (Noble 1991, 70). In a letter only four sentences long written in 1973 addressed "To Whom It May Concern," Kellar concluded that Ouiatenon had been found. This letter was likely meant for inclusion in a grant application or research proposal, but it speaks to the scant amount of publishable information that was produced after two years of field research. According to the TCHA, no parties with professional archaeological experience were willing or able to conduct additional research following the National Register designation of the site in 1970. With no formal plans to continue research at the site and with a lack of professional community or venue in which to discuss the data, Ouiatenon was again left to revert to farmland.

COMMUNITY-BASED ARCHAEOLOGY

To maintain local interest in Ouiatenon, the TCHA approached Purdue undergraduate students in anthropology in search of someone who would lead volunteer field crews to excavate sections of the plow zone during the summer. A letter archived at the GBL to James Kellar from Clark Dobbs, program director of the TCHA, was written during this time to request information regarding the previous field seasons. The intention of Dobbs's request had been to provide the new excavators with background information about the site and a sense of direction in planning their summer work. Specifically, he had asked for information on the original grid system and a sketch map of the site, brief information on the system of cataloging used by Kellar, and any slides that could be used in a two-day orientation that was planned for the field-workers. Kellar discussed in his June 1971 response that the field where the site was located had been plowed earlier that spring and that any of his wooden datum stakes would have been buried by the plow. Reestablishment of the grid required that the metal rods placed near the road be used to create a new grid over the site.

The description of the establishment of the previous grid and suggested instructions for reestablishing a new grid indicate that Kellar had no plans to participate in the six-week 1971 field project. Kellar also suggested that the numbering system and cataloging method he employed for his 1968–1969 projects were likely not the "most appropriate" for the planned work that summer. Kellar suggested in his June 1971 response, based on the proposed plan for excavations to only explore the plow zone, that "some kind of horizontal control be built in, [as] obviously the vertical dimension and features notations would be irrelevant." Kellar also cited a recent move to the new laboratory facility at Indiana University as the reason that he could not share any notes, photographs, or slides from his then recent excavation projects due to the records being "stuffed away in some box as yet undiscovered." (It is not clear now, within the extent of this research, that all of these materials were ever unpacked or recovered.) He closed his letter with a statement that should the materials show up before he left the lab in the following week, he would send them along for the TCHA's use, but it does not appear that this ever occurred.

It therefore fell to undergraduates Larry Chowning in 1971 and Claude White in 1972 to lead excavations without firsthand knowledge or records of the previous work conducted at the site, relying on the memories of volunteers who participated in Kellar's field schools in a plowed field with no datum points. Chowning's and White's excavations were at first limited to sections of the plow zone and did not extend into undisturbed feature fill. After two years of this work under permission of the landowner, with several boxes of material recovered from the plow zone, the TCHA secured funds to purchase the few acres of land containing the established archaeological site in 1972. The TCHA then asked Chowning to return in 1973 and open an excavation block six hundred feet square in the levels below the plow zone in the southwest corner of the site. The materials that resulted from the early 1970s excavations fill two dozen archival boxes now housed at the GBL. These materials remained unwashed in their original bags until the 1990s, and they were never formally examined or analyzed (Noble 1991). The amateur excavations below the plow zone explored features suggested to be the wall trench associated with the southwest corner of the post palisade and two "aboriginal pit features" (Tordoff 1983, 146). It is unclear whether these feature interpretations are the work of the original avocational excavators or of later graduate research utilizing notes available after the project had been completed.

Records pertaining to any of these three years of excavations at the site would be useful in assembling a more detailed plan view of the site. Notes or maps pertaining to the 1973 excavations below the plow zone would likely allow for interpretation of the materials recovered in that year. While coordinates were recorded on the original artifact bags that are still curated with the archaeological materials, they do not match any of the known spatial information about the site. No copies of the original report on the 1973 materials can be located, and according to Chowning, only one copy of his report was ever made due to a lack of access to technology to make copies of documents at the time.

The original report, which Chowning typed himself in 1973, has been missing from the archives of the TCHA for an unknown length of time. However, when the report and associated notes were requested from the TCHA by a Michigan State University (MSU) graduate student in 1975, only few records could be found, indicating that it was already inaccessible. Those records relating to the 1971–1973 seasons that could be located were said to be "unusable" and created by "amateurs." When I questioned Chowning about the excavation of 1973 during my dissertation research, he expressed that the amount of time that had passed since the project took place prevented him from providing any pertinent details about his past work. After I contacted him with details about my research, he was able to locate a box of notes and artifacts from his projects at home in late 2015, which are now being curated by the TCHA. The 1973 Ouiatenon project proved to be the pinnacle project of Chowning's archaeological career. He did not pursue graduate study or professional employment in the field of anthropology or archaeology after the 1973 field season had concluded, but the notes from his work at the site are likely to contain valuable information that could inform future research focused on the southwest corner of the palisade.

INVESTIGATIONS BY MICHIGAN STATE UNIVERSITY

Rebranded as Fort Ouiatenon rather than Post Ouiatenon after its National Register designation and three years of avocational excavation, the TCHA focused its efforts on developing a more intensive, formal research program for the site. The TCHA approached the curator of the MSU Museum, Charles E. Cleland, requesting that he design a three-year exploratory research plan. Excavations were led by doctoral graduate student Judith Tordoff, who would also serve as a research assistant during the academic year.

The project was sponsored by the TCHA and the Indiana Office for Historic Preservation, and field crews of university students from MSU and other institutions as well as volunteers from the TCHA assisted in the excavations. Correspondence between Tordoff and Kellar in the GBL archives dating to September 1974 reveals that Tordoff was unsuccessful in obtaining any records or reports from Larry Chowning prior to or following the 1974 field season she led. Tordoff also asked if there was any possibility of seeing notes and slides from Kellar's work at the site. She hinted to Kellar that not having any descriptions of previous work at the site or access to existing data before beginning her dissertation fieldwork "proved unfortunate at times." Tordoff did have access to infrared photographs taken by the Purdue Laboratory for Applications of Remote Sensing in the fall of 1973; however, these are no longer accessible at Purdue and were possibly deaccessioned according to recent information provided by the laboratory's staff.

The units excavated during the 1974–1976 field seasons included nine backhoe trenches distributed across the site, placed in an attempt to delineate the palisade wall documented by Kellar. It was hoped that by locating portions of the palisade wall trenches, Tordoff and Cleland would be able to infer the remaining sections of the wall as well as the general size and shape of the post. Multiple open-block excavations were also utilized, resulting in the identification of forty features including an abandoned well and what was identified as a complete but burned twelve-by-nine-foot poteaux-en-terre storehouse (Feature 56) in the southeastern corner of the excavation area. This storehouse feature is described in great detail in Tordoff's work, and her text provides a high-resolution forensic reconstruction of the building's destruction by fire, noting probable wind direction on the day the building burned and the orientation of the wood grain in the various architectural pieces encountered in excavation (Tordoff 1983, 167–70). The storehouse was very likely a casualty of trade-based or sociopolitical warfare, but no accounts detailing its demise can be found in the remaining historical accounts of the site. Finally, the excavation strategy involved "transects," or additional slot trenches, through the estimated center of the palisaded area in an attempt to identify the locations of interior military, domestic, and trade-related structures. Fortunately, once the field season was under way, the workload created by the excavations discussed above prevented the placement of these transects. Remote sensing in the form of proton magnetometer survey was utilized in these areas during the first field season instead. Purdue University students conducted their 1974 Geoscience Research Project at the Ouiatenon site and identified anomalies using resistivity and magnetometry data to guide project directors in placing additional excavation units.

Tordoff investigated several anomalies in the center of the site identified by this remote sensing survey, which she later interpreted as a blacksmith's shop or forge area. In May 1975, archived correspondence suggests that Tordoff may have examined artifacts in the collection at the GBL, but Kellar stated he would not be there when she arrived, as he had been called away to a meeting. Later that summer during the second season of fieldwork (and after much frustration as noted in her writing), Tordoff successfully located Kellar's 1968–1969 excavation areas. It was at this time that ground-truthing revealed that Kellar's field school students' maps were made with a latitudinal error of approximately thirty-five feet and a longitudinal error of five feet or less. This presented multiple problems in interpretation of the materials and data moving forward, and from that point on the artifacts from Kellar's excavations were only examined piecemeal for studies of material types due to a lack of accurate spatial information.

Undergraduates from the Geoscience Department at MSU were granted funds by the National Science Foundation and the National Endowment for the Humanities to continue testing the applications of geophysical survey to archaeological research in 1975 over portions of Tippecanoe County. The TCHA also received a grant from the Merrill Foundation at this time to employ a research historian for one year. This three-year project alone yielded over thirty-six thousand artifacts and ninety-six thousand fragments of animal bone. In addition to the forty features identified, two separate palisade walls were interpreted by Tordoff, suggesting that the footprint of the post expanded over time or that a complete rebuilding of the palisade wall in whole was undertaken at some point rather than replacement of rotten posts or pickets as needed. A detailed description of the work that was completed in the 1974–1976 seasons is available in Tordoff's (1983) dissertation.

The first three years of MSU's exploratory research were successful enough that the TCHA sponsored an additional three years of excavation for 1977–1979, this time led by MSU graduate student Vergil Noble. For this subsequent field project Noble employed a systematic sampling methodology, applying a technique that placed test units in a checkerboard pattern over the entire northern half of the site. This fieldwork resulted in a large collection of artifacts and several ten-by-ten-foot plan maps. Noble reports that this approach was useful in "pinpointing" several structures and refuse deposits, as well as supporting Tordoff's palisade perimeter identification. In addition, the team located additional portions of wall trench, which Noble stated was of earlier construction than the wall trench identified by Kellar and Tordoff; a second well; and several burials, the latter of which were interpreted as representing the cemetery for the fort. These findings are reported in MSU interim reports on file with the MSU Museum and the TCHA as well as in Noble's (1983) dissertation.

However, the results or interpretation of the original work completed by Kellar's two field schools at the site remained unavailable to the MSU researchers, and the result was additional confusion and tenuous conclusions at the end of each project. Several of the units placed by Noble demonstrate the presence of wall trenches outside of the proposed limits of the post demonstrated on overall plan maps. While these may be associated with domestic spaces outside of the palisade walls or additions to the original footprint of the post, neither Noble nor Tordoff were able to provide additional interpretations of the features due to a lack of detail regarding the earlier work at the site (Noble, pers. comm., 2015; Tordoff, pers. comm., 2015). Tordoff began a career studying nineteenth-century Chinese mining archaeology in northern California following the completion of her PhD and has discarded all paperwork related to her work at Ouiatenon other than her final dissertation. Noble similarly has maintained an incomplete collection of notes and the results of his work, and the plan maps that once accompanied his institutionally archived annual reports on his work at the site are also missing.

In general, most work conducted at Ouiatenon since 1970 has not included or integrated any of the data or artifacts created during Kellar's time at the site. In addition, very little of the data have been published or discussed in the literature and primarily remains in dissertation form only. These dissertations also tend to discuss broader issues in historical archaeology and report the empirical evidence gathered during field research conducted for each individual project (Noble 1991, 73). Tordoff's dissertation focused on the artifact assemblage frequencies over the site to compare Ouiatenon to other eighteenth-century French colonial sites, while Noble's dissertation "assessed the usefulness of certain statistical methods and computer modeling programs in the delineation of activity areas" (Noble 1983; Noble 1991, 73; Tordoff 1983). A sample of the animal bones excavated from feature fill during both the 1974–1976 and 1977–1979 field projects was the basis of Martin's (1986) faunal analysis dissertation.

Jackson's (2005) dissertation employed the legacy collections from both the TCHA and Indiana University. She examined a subset of artifacts using folk classifications elicited from eighteenth-century French merchant and military documents from New France. A volume titled *French Colonial Archaeology* edited by John A. Walthall contained the only book chapter written on Ouiatenon for over four decades after its initial archaeological documentation; it was written by Noble and titled "Ouiatenon on the Ouabache: Archaeological Investigations at a Fur Trading Post on the Wabash River." Noble (1991, 65) notes that having been "subjected to intensive archaeological scrutiny," Ouiatenon had been the site of intensive and lengthy field research second only to those efforts expended at Fort Michilimackinac. He also notes that the findings are not widely available (i.e., trapped in gray literature or never compiled from field notes) and that early excavation data and details had not been reported at all. Due to the limitation of space allowed in the book chapter as well as the undiscovered nature of the 1969 field school students' journals, Noble was not able to provide more than very cursory details about the history of the site and research that had been completed to date.

MORE RECENT FIELDWORK AT THE SITE OF FORT OUIATENON (12T9)

In 2012, Michael Strezewski of the University of Southern Indiana and Robert McCullough of Indiana University–Purdue University Fort Wayne and later McCullough Archaeological Services, conducted a remote sensing survey under a grant from the National Park Service's American Battlefield Protection Program. During November and December 2012, the pair conducted magnetometry surveys over the site of the palisaded post and portions of the adjacent potential Native American habitation areas to the east and west, with limited nonsystematic surface collections obtained from all three sites (Strezewski 2014). The research design for this two-year survey project included searching for potential features surrounding the palisade that could identify associated Native American villages destroyed in 1791 by the Charles Scott Campaign as well as the ground-truthing of more promising anomalies to prove the existence of related subsurface deposits. As may be expected due to the quantity of metallic objects previously recovered from the 12T9 site through archaeological excavation in the 1960 and 1970s, the resulting magnetometry data was relatively noisy and suggested many potential features in both unexcavated and previously excavated areas.

These villages had been previously surveyed by James R. Jones and Neal Trubowitz between 1984 and 1990, identified during projects designed to locate and document previously unidentified historic Native American sites in Tippecanoe County (Jones 1984; Trubowitz 1992). Trubowitz's research included the Ouiatenon vicinity and the Wea village (12T6) on the south side of the Wabash. Jones also surveyed and surface-collected from the fort location, the Indigenous villages surrounding the palisade or stockade walls, and the 12T6 Wea village site.

In 2013, Strezewski led an undergraduate archaeological field school at the 12T9 site through the University of Southern Indiana, with the remaining funding provided by the American Battlefield Protection Program grant. Assisted again by Robert McCullough as well as Scott Hipskind and myself as a GBL Summer Research Fellow, this field school was designed to continue Strezewski's research on contexts surrounding the palisade or stockade walls of the post informed by analysis of the previously collected magnetometry data. Three areas identified to have high potential for containing relevant archaeological features were delineated just outside of the western edge of the palisade or stockade of the fort and were chosen as the focus of the field school excavations.

In Strezewski's (2014) report of investigations, he states that the primary goal of this project was to provide baseline information for the continued preservation of fur trade–era village sites in the Ouiatenon vicinity. Probable Native American structures and other cultural features suggested by previously collected data concentrated in the north and west outside the fort perimeter were confirmed through the 2013 field school excavations. The single structural feature that was the focus of excavation during 2013 was also confirmed to have been burned. Historic documents describe the Kickapoo-Mascouten villages on the north side of the Wabash being burned after the Scott and Wilkinson campaigns in 1791, long after the exit of the New France government from the area.

According to Strezewski's interpretation, this burning may have resulted in an alteration to the magnetic properties of the soils, as structure fires commonly reach temperatures above the ferromagnetic Curie temperature, especially fires that burn hot and to the ground (Strezewski 2014, 37). Strezewski also theorized that while most Native American dwellings were likely of lighter construction and would be difficult to detect through magnetometry survey, later structures would have possibly been of log construction and left more substantial archaeological signatures. Several weaker anomaly signatures identified by the survey were determined to be structures built using

Indigenous construction methods but could not be associated with temporal designations with any certainty. Furthermore, several of the structures were located in areas with few magnetic anomalies, and Strezewski does state that it appears that "aboriginal structures may be relatively invisible via magnetometry, unless thoroughly burned," (Strezewski 2014, 50). The most striking anomalies from the survey were not cultural in origin but rather were the result of natural sediment deposition related to flooding of the Wabash River. For a more detailed explanation of the interpretation of magnetometry data and the remote sensing surveys conducted at the 12T9 site, see Strezewski's (2014) report and chapter 3 in this volume.

This important contribution to the archaeology of the greater historical Ouiatenon occupation area is the result of Strezewski's choice to focus his research on areas outside the suggested palisade or stockade walls of the trading post, building on earlier survey work in these areas by Jones and Trubowitz. What the data suggests is that Native-built structures, even those contemporary to European and Euro-American populations, remained largely unchanged in terms of the construction methods and materials used. Essentially, homes were built using circular wall trench construction, with small post walls set into the trench and little to no ferrous metal in the furnishing of the home. This suggests continuity in the construction of domestic structures from the Late Woodland period through the mid to late eighteenth century near Ouiatenon and persistence of domestic Native American cultural tradition.

SYNTHESIZING PREVIOUS ARCHAEOLOGICAL RESEARCH

After gathering the details of all the archaeological work that has been completed at the site over the past five decades, the difficult task of integrating this information into the same data set for my dissertation analysis remained. The primary issue in terms of significance in the process of synthesizing the data was to align the 1968 and 1969 plan maps with later spatial representations to allow a comprehensive plan view of the site to be created. Geographic information systems were not employed in research on the site until the most recent fieldwork conducted by Strezewski and McCullough. All previous spatial data was recorded using traditional surveying methods and tools, and it was left to the preference of the researcher to design a grid that was measured in feet or meters and whether coordinates would increase from east to west or vice versa. In addition, small errors were reproduced over the site each year, creating a slight misalignment of the previous year's plan view with the next year's plan view. More specific definition of the spatial error recorded by Kellar's students was pursued within the scope of research for this dissertation and does allow for the salvage of Kellar's spatial data for general application to the appearance of the post. This definition and integration is discussed in depth in my dissertation (Myers 2017) and in a chapter I contributed to Allen and Ford's volume *New Life for Archaeological Collections* (Myers 2019). My dissertation research design intended to not only detail the early work by Kellar but also place the early and later work (which has been reported to varying degrees) within a singular spatial dataset that encompasses the entirety of archaeological research that has been conducted at the Ouiatenon site.

In attempting to reconstruct more than a decade of excavations at the site, it has been necessary to read through many archived sources. This has turned up several interesting anecdotes, research relationships, and personal recollections but has left many more questions than answers. The primary objectives of my archival research have been to create a complete map of the site in plan view representing all field research and spatial data collected regarding the 12T9 site and village areas included in the eighteenth-century vernacular concept of the place "Ouiatenon," verify the reported locations of each excavation area, and unify the archaeological data into a synthetic view, allowing for a "big data" approach to the work completed at Ouiatenon to date.

In digitizing and replotting the available plan maps of the excavation areas from the 1968–1979 projects (figure 2.1), it is clear that the use of the transit and surveying equipment at the time of the original excavations in 1968–1969 was subject to much human error. As discussed above, the original metal rod datum point at the north of the site that was used for the 1968 field project was removed by accident in the first few days of the 1969 field season when Kellar was working to clear the plow zone from the site using a backhoe. Again in 1971, the area was plowed and the datum markers were removed. The directions to reestablish the grid at this time were conveyed in a letter from Kellar to the director of research at the TCHA. The undergraduates who led volunteer crews in 1971–1973 likely had no experience in archaeological surveying but were required to set datum points regardless, as Kellar was unable to participate in the avocational projects.

In 1974, the grid used to map the area was again established by MSU students using a piece of rebar embedded in concrete in an attempt to prevent accidental removal in the future. This single point appears to have been used to set a grid at the beginning of each field season since, including the 2013 University of Southern Indiana field school held at the site. In effect, this suggests that no two years' maps are based on an identical grid placement. As discussed above, there is variation between each project in the recording of coordinates relating to the personal preference of the primary investigator as to whether feet or meters should be used as the unit of measurement and whether coordinates should increase in number from east to west or west to east. Therefore, it was not possible to ground-truth every excavation and link each to the others with georeferencing based on the maps that exist from each project, as each is oriented on a slightly different angle, and varying distortions have occurred longitudinally, as all work prior

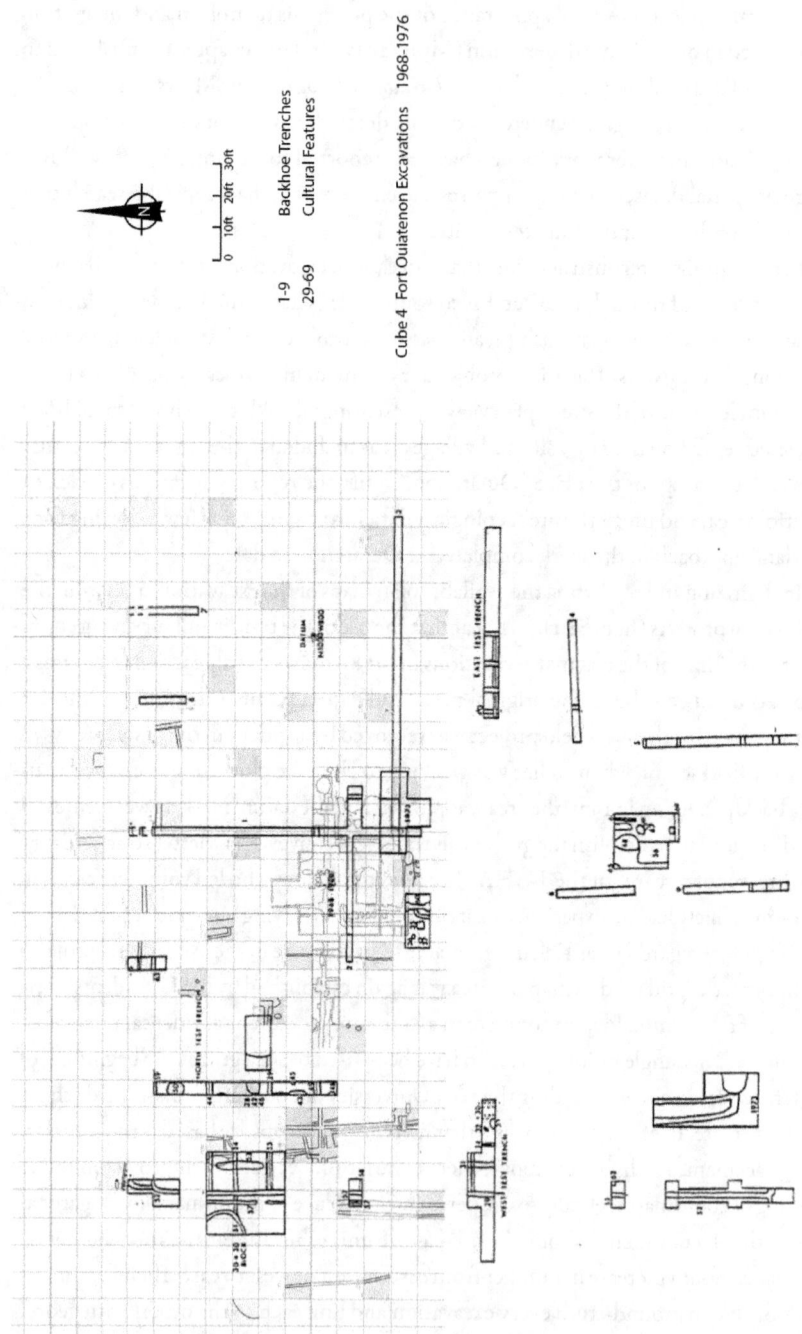

Figure 2.1. Composite map of Fort Ouiatenon Excavations based on Noble (1978), Strezewski (2014), Tordoff (1983), Myers (2017, fig. 6.4), and Myers (2019) Map 5.

to 2013 was completed without the benefit of GPS or the assembly of a geographic information system. As a control, very valuable high-resolution data produced using LiDAR and published on the Indiana Geological and Water Survey's Indiana map portal in 2015 has allowed for the visible signature of the Ouiatenon site to be aligned with the field excavations conducted to date. In addition, the recent purchase of two hundred acres surrounding the 12T9 site by the TCHA will allow access to a wide area surrounding the known site for additional remote sensing. The potential for this type of research to further rectify the confusing spatial situation of existing data is encouraging.

In 2014–2015 through funding provided by a GBL Dissertation Research Fellowship, I was able to locate, inventory, rehouse, and examine the materials resulting from the 1971–1973 excavations. The materials had previously been separated by material type to varying degrees of specificity and placed in polyethylene bags. This work was done under the supervision of various researchers including Trubowitz, who at the time was a professor at Indiana University–Purdue University Indianapolis and used the materials for teaching archaeology methods. (The loan, use, and return of these materials is briefly discussed in some of the archived correspondence discovered at the GBL.) Items more commonly of interest to avocational historians and artifact collectors, such as beads and trade silver, were identified in greater detail than other material types. Bone, ceramic, and lithic materials were lacking in identification in general. Large amounts of fire-cracked rock and botanical samples were also preserved. The boxes in which the materials had been stored had not been packed well for long-term storage, indicating that additional research may have been planned that never took place. The fire-cracked rock was placed in each box last on top of more fragile materials, resulting in fragmentation of much of the botanical and some faunal materials.

However, on conferring with Indiana University Bloomington Anthropology research associate and archaeobotany specialist Jocelyn Turner, the charcoal and other floral samples included within the materials from these excavations were collected in enough quantity and have survived storage well enough that it would be possible to gather valuable data from the macrobotanical remains in the future.

STUDENT SUMMARIES OF THE 1969 EXCAVATION

As discussed above, four field school student's journals from the 1969 field season have remained in the archives of the GBL. While no summary paper by field school student Alphonso Stadler is available, Lucianne Neff stated at the beginning of her paper that the main reason for the excavation was "establishment of the existence and location of Post Ouiatenon," which Kellar noted was only one of several reasons, all of which were equally important. Vivianne Heacox also began her journal with the objective of deciding if the site was Post Ouiatenon. Michael Whalen's (1969, 2) paper lists four objectives, the first of which aligns with the beginning of Neff's more qualitative question:

1. Are we dealing with a European (specifically French) or an Indian site?
2. Is the site chronologically eligible for the fort's location?
3. How do written descriptions of the fort compare with features revealed by excavation?
4. What evidence is there that the site under consideration actually served as a trading post?

Whalen went on to explain his interpretation (and likely that of Kellar) that the material culture of the site demonstrates a primarily European occupation, with many of the artifacts identified as French. Whalen based his interpretation on the writings of Quimby (1966) and a "virtual absence of aboriginal artifacts of any sort" (Whalen 1969, 2). However, Whalen's categorization only addresses the manufacturing origin of the artifacts rather than the specific use and ownership of the materials. In trade situations of extended culture contact, it is entirely possible for objects to pass between individuals of varying ethnicities and cultural affiliation without being modified for use in any significant way or at all. The disposal of these materials at the end of their use-life (Shott and Sillitoe 2004), however, can speak to the relationship between the object and households or neighborhoods that existed in the area. This issue of ownership and disposal and the cultural affiliation or ethnic orientation of each household was explored further in my dissertation. In addition, when reviewing the artifact lists and field specimen logs from the field school, a number of "aboriginal artifacts" as the students would have been taught to classify them, such as bone tools, stone pipes, and unglazed ceramic fragments (identified later as Woodland period ceramics), were included within the artifact assemblages. Therefore, the student's statement was likely made based on a qualitative opinion rather than quantitative analysis.

The second topic of field school student Whalen's summary paper is addressed in relation again to Quimby (1966), citing the use of early (1610–1670 CE), middle (1670–1770 CE), and late (1770–1820 CE) designations for the historic period. The student uses artifactual diagnostic criteria to determine that the site is primarily the result of an eighteenth-century settlement, largely middle historic in nature and therefore "chronologically eligible to be Fort Ouiatenon" (Whalen 1969, 5). Neff also cites artifacts as temporal indicators using several types of materials, specifically giving the averaged range of 1756–1758 CE based on the bore diameters of the kaolin tobacco pipe stems recovered. This, of course, only relates to the date of the kaolin tobacco pipes analyzed in 1969, as the post itself was known to have been occupied for nearly three-quarters of a century.

Third, the students were concerned with how well the archaeological features aligned with written descriptions of experiences at the fort. The students cited that it is commonly described, albeit quite sparsely, in contemporary eighteenth-century accounts as "a fort of upright poles," and Neff (1969, 91) quoted the description of "a double range of houses enclosed in a stockade 10' high." While wall trenches were visible in the 1969 excavations, they do not easily fit into the expected pattern of a single exterior palisade wall with two lengths of row houses within the fort. Whalen reported that "some 90 feet and a corner of a continuous trench have been revealed by two seasons' work" and describes this trench as being approximately eighteen inches wide and over four feet deep in places, with the marks of several posts visible at the bottom of the trench (specifically in N1015 W910 and N1015 W930 and perhaps at the southward turn of the trench at N1015 W860). He expressed doubt, however, that this was the true palisade line, as it was such a small amount of the total expected size for a complete stockade.

As a reminder, the discussion of Kellar's work above notes that no one involved archaeologically in the early research at the site had more than a passing familiarity with the archaeology of fortified structures and settlement of the eighteenth century. Neff (1969, 91) also wrote that the identification of this trench as the stockade trench was "not fully supported by archaeological evidence." While her objections that the trading post could not be positively identified due to incomplete excavation of the stockade and a lack of evidence that the two rows of houses cited in contemporary accounts may not conclusively negate the identification, several short runs of trench that parallel the "stockade trench" identified in multiple locations do pose interesting questions about the layout and ongoing reconstruction of the post perimeter over seven decades of occupation. According to the overall map of the site created by placing the Kellar field maps in the context of the other excavations completed in the 1970s as well as the feature descriptions of the wall trenches encountered during the field school, it is more likely that this wall trench was an exterior wall of one of the row houses. One of the many additional questions about the early archaeology is why there is no evidence of extensive burning according to the students' journals, as described in the account of Scott's American forces' attack on and sacking of the post during Pontiac's Rebellion in 1763 and as documented by the work of both Tordoff and Strezewski.

Finally, the students of the 1969 field school were concerned with the question of whether this was the site of a trading post, as evidenced by artifactual evidence. Whalen points out that although the majority of the material types recovered would be found in any French domestic habitation area, the high number of seed beads, mouth harps, and lead bale seals suggest that this was a trading area. However, the student also suggests that any French site in the area is likely to have been used for trade to some degree due to the sparse situation of sites and the important political functions of trade on the frontier. Neff did not agree that a positive identification could be made at the end of the 1969 field school based on the evidence available and suggests that both additional documentary and archaeological research were required before a decision could be made.

Both students made valid points, and I believe that the additional research Neff thought necessary has now been completed. The site is known to have been located across from the Wea village located on the south side of the river (12T6), which includes components dating back to the Archaic period, and a frontier post maintained largely as a trading site by the government of New France. Additionally, when reviewing the historical population estimates of the site based on the documentary record (discussed in chapter 3), Ouiatenon was undeniably primarily a place of Native American culture throughout its existence, and the items such as seed beads and bundles of cloth marked with lead bale seals that Whalen discusses in his field journal were very typical trade items used and owned by Native persons. Thus, if the majority of individuals at Ouiatenon were Indigenous and requested establishment of the post to facilitate trade with the French representatives for such items, why does interpretation of this site as only a French colonial trading post rather than also a Native American habitation and trading center persist? This consideration of artifact use rather than origin can help to remove the filter of mid-twentieth-century prejudices to an extent; however, in the words of Julian Thomas, "the task of circumventing our own preconceptions is unending" (2012, 220).

DEFINITION OF THE EXCAVATION GRID AND SITE PLACEMENT

The original grid for the site, laid out for the 1968 field school led by Kellar, used a permanent benchmark near a telephone pole along the dirt road leading from the property on the eastern edge of the agricultural field where the site was located (Neff 1969, 8) to establish the "zero line." A second permanent datum point was established at 35.5 feet to the south of the first datum point. The longitudinal coordinates for the 1969 field school were established based on the previous year's eastern boundary, marked with relative certainty at the southeast corner of the square known as N1000 W920.

The students, on the second day of the field school and apparently their first day of using the surveying equipment, "measured a 300' distance in line with the benchmark and the N1000 W920 stake, and sunk a marker" (Neff 1969, 8). They then measured another 300 feet of distance from the marker they had just placed, bringing them an estimated 600 feet west of the benchmark. After checking these points, the group established a permanent elevation marker off-site. The students then set about placing a stake every 10 feet over a distance of 40 feet to the east of N1000 W920, bringing them to N1000 W880. This was followed by the placement of stakes at 10 feet, 15 feet, and 25 feet to the north of N1000 W880; these increments were used to "stradle [sic] the trench" identified in the aerial photographs, which Kellar hoped would be the exterior palisade line. From the 15-foot stake, more markers were placed at 020-foot intervals to the east for 60 feet; this was repeated at the 25-foot stake.

As mentioned above, Tordoff did not find the location of Kellar's field school excavation area in the area recorded but instead located it approximately thirty-five feet to the south and slightly east. The information provided by Stadler's field journal suggests that the second datum point may have been used to label the southeast corners of each excavation unit, and by some mistake the coordinates for the two data points were conflated, or no one instructed the students to renumber the excavation units based on the new datum point or to specify that a second point was being used. Neff names Kellar as the operator of the backhoe used on-site to clear the plow zone, and it is mentioned at one point in her journal that he accidentally knocked out the datum post, suggesting that this is the point at which the data points were switched.

The squares laid out were subsequently machine-scraped to clear them of the majority of the plow zone and then tidied up by hand with shovels and trowels. Unfortunately, the daily entries of Stadler's journal are quite scanty following his description of the grid establishment. Most days are recorded with only a few sentences and lists of the artifact types found. Whalen leaves no field journal behind at all. Neff's journal is more detailed, and she includes her personal opinions and impressions alongside lists of coordinates and artifacts as well as descriptions of the areas excavated and some of the methodology used. This intermingling of excavation reporting with personal narration is likely what caused Kellar to give her work a B grade rather than an A, as he stated that her "running account was okay but might have included more about the features they were finding." However, Neff's journal provides some of the most interesting accounts and important reconstructive details that would have otherwise been left unrecorded and provides an unexpected wealth of information.

While not much of the early historical excavation records remain, these few sources do provide a variety of information about the daily experiences of the field project, an interesting and valuable social history of archaeology at the site.

REFERENCES

Allison, Harold. 1986. *The Tragic Saga of the Indiana Indians*. Paducah, KY: Graphic Design of Indiana.

Barce, Elmore, and John Wesley Whicker. 1925. "Tri-County Historical Itinerary." *Indiana Magazine of History*, March.

Brodhead, John Romeyn, Berthold Fernow, and E. B. O'Callaghan. 1853. *Documents Relative to the Colonial History of the State of New-York, Procured in Holland, England and France*. Albany, NY: Weed, Parsons and Co., Printers.

Cox, Sandford C. 1859. "Old Settlers: Recollections of the Early Settlement of the Wabash Valley." *Lafayette Daily Courier*, 1859.

Craig, Oscar John. 1893. "Ouiatanon: A Study in Indiana History." *Indiana Historical Society Publications* 22, no. 8.

Daughters of the American Revolution. 1906. *Eighth Report of the National Society of the Daughters of the American Revolution*. Washington, DC: US Government Printing Office.

Ironstrack, George. 2013. "Chapter 5: Myaamia Removal." http://teachmyaamiahistory.org/contents/section5/.

Jackson, Misty May. 2005. "Classifications by Historical Archaeologists and Eighteenth Century Montreal Merchants and Military Personnel in New France: Emic and Etic Approaches." PhD diss., Michigan State University.

Jones, James R., III. 1984. "An Archaeological Survey of an 18th Century Wea Village Near Fort Ouiatenon, in Tippecanoe County, Indiana." Department of Anthropology, Indiana University Bloomington.

Madison, James H. 2014. *Hoosiers: A New History of Indiana*. Bloomington: Indiana University Press.

Martin, Terrance J. 1986. "A Faunal Analysis of Fort Ouiatenon, an Eighteenth Century Trading Post in the Wabash Valley of Indiana." PhD diss., Michigan State University.

Miller, Robert J. 2006. *Native America, Discovered and Conquered: Thomas Jefferson, Lewis & Clark, and Manifest Destiny*. Westport, CT: Praeger.

Myers, Kelsey Noack. 2017. "Indigenous Landscapes and Legacy Archaeology at Ouiatenon, Indiana." PhD diss., University of Indiana.

———. 2019. "Reconstructing Site Provenience at Ouiatenon, Indiana." In *New Life for Archaeological Collections*, ed. R. Allen and B. Ford, 272–88. Lincoln: University of Nebraska Press.

Neff, Lucianne. 1969. "Student Journal from James Kellar's Archaeological Field School at Post Ouiatenon." West Lafayette, IN.

Noble, Vergil E. 1978. "Excavations at Fort Ouiatenon 1977 Field Season: Preliminary Report." Submitted to the Tippecanoe County Historical Association and US Department of Housing and Urban Development Community Development Program.

———. 1983. "Functional Classification and Intra-Site Analysis in Historical Archaeology: A Case Study from Fort Ouiatenon." PhD diss., Michigan State University.

———. 1991. "Ouiatenon on the Ouabache: Archaeological Investigations at a Fur Trading Post on the Wabash River." In *French Colonial Archaeology: The Illinois Country and the Western Great Lakes*, ed. John A. Walthall, 65–77. Urbana: University of Illinois Press.

Ontario. 1878. *Statutes, Documents and Papers Bearing on the Discussion Respecting the Northern and Western Boundaries of the Province of Ontario, Including the Principal Evidence Supposed to Be Either for or against the Claims of the Province*. Toronto: Hunter, Rose.

Quimby, George Irving. 1966. *Indian Culture and European Trade Goods: The Archaeology of the Historic Period in the Western Great Lakes Region*. Madison: University of Wisconsin Press.

Shott, Michael J., and Paul Sillitoe. 2004. "Modeling Use-Life Distributions in Archaeology Using New Guinea Wola Ethnographic Data." *American Antiquity* 69, no. 2: 339–55.

Smith, William Henry. 1903. *The History of the State of Indiana from the Earliest Explorations by the French to the Present Time: Containing an Account of the Principal Civil, Political and Military Events from 1763 to 1903*. Indianapolis: Western Publishing Company.

Strezewski, Michael. 2014. "Fur Trade Archeology in the Ouiatenon Vicinity: The 2012/2013 Investigations." Report submitted to the US National Park Service, American Battlefield Protection Program, Grant #GA-2255-12-025.

Thomas, Julian. 2012. "Archaeology, Anthropology, and Material Things." In *Archaeology and Anthropology: Past, Present and Future*, ed. David Shankland, 219–33. ASA Monographs 48. Abingdon, UK: Berg.

Tordoff, Judith Dunn. 1983. "An Archaeological Perspective on the Organization of the Fur Trade in Eighteenth Century New France." PhD diss., Michigan State University.

Trubowitz, Neal L. 1992. "Native Americans and French on the Wabash." In *Calumet & Fleur-de-Lys: Archaeology of Indian and French Contact in the Midcontinent*, ed. John A. Walthall and Thomas E. Emerson, 241–64. Washington, DC: Smithsonian Institution Press.

Whalen, Michael. 1969. "Student Journal from James Kellar's Archaeological Field School at Post Ouiatenon." West Lafayette, IN.

3

OUTSIDE THE FORT
Completing the Picture of the Ouiatenon Landscape

MICHAEL STREZEWSKI, UNIVERSITY
OF SOUTHERN INDIANA

BUILT IN 1717, FORT OUIATENON HAS THE DISTINCTION OF BEING THE first permanent Euro-American presence in the present state of Indiana. Throughout the remainder of the eighteenth century, the Ouiatenon area remained a hub of Native American occupation and fur trade activity, enduring through the French, British, and beginning of the American eras. After the discovery of the fort's location in the late 1960s, archaeological investigations were carried out almost every year for over a decade. Nearly all these excavations, however, were situated either within or immediately outside the fort itself, with the goal of recovering information about the activities of fur traders and military personnel who lived within its stockade walls.

For quite some time, the archaeological remains of the many Wea, Kickapoo, and Mascouten villages that were situated in the immediate area were largely overlooked, despite the wealth of documents attesting to the thousands of Native American residents who lived near the fort. It was not until the 1980s that a more systematic approach to researching these sites was undertaken. These efforts have continued sporadically over the last decades but have produced new and interesting data on the activities of the Native American peoples who lived in the area, without whom the fort would not have been built in the first place.

NATIVE AMERICAN VILLAGES IN THE OUIATENON AREA, 1690 – 1834

If the existing documents describing Fort Ouiatenon and the structures within its limits are limited, details regarding the Native American villages in the surrounding area can be considered even more sparse. In most instances, written descriptions of the Native American inhabitants in the area surrounding the fort comprise little more than an estimate of the number of warriors living the area, as this was a constant concern for the European colonial powers based on whether the Native Americans in question were considered allies or adversaries. Unfortunately, we have precious few clues as to number of villages at any point in time as well as their location and distribution and the types of structures or other facilities present.

At the beginning of sustained European contact (ca. 1665), the Wabash Valley seems to have been sparsely populated, and many tribes later found at Ouiatenon, including the Wea, Kickapoo, and Mascouten, were known to be residing in southeastern Wisconsin and northeastern Illinois, having fled west circa 1650 – 1655 to avoid Iroquois raids (Wheeler-Voegelin, Blasingham, and Libby 1974, 40). By 1691, however, with the threat from the Iroquois waning, a group of Miami had reportedly returned to the Wabash River valley (Pease and Werner 1934, 392 – 93; Jablow 1974, 128, 135; Krauskopf 1953, 24).[1] Numerous Wea (comprising at least four hundred warriors) were living on the Wabash by the first years of the eighteenth century, and by 1715 they were definitely residing at the archaeological site known today as the Wea village (12-T-6), located on the south bank of the Wabash (Beach 1877, 276). It was in this year that they requested the presence of a French official, a blacksmith, and a missionary as a means to foster trading relationships (Michigan Pioneer and Historical Society 1904, 441; Thwaites 1902, 326; Wheeler-Voegelin et al. 1974, 50, 120). In the spring of 1717, construction of the fort began on the north side of the river opposite the Wea village. A document dating to 1718 indicates that the Wea at Ouiatenon resided in five villages, "all built closely together," along with "more than two leagues of fields" (Thwaites 1902, 376).

The Ouiatenon landscape, as mapped by Ulrich et al. (1959) and Martin (1986), indicates a variety of natural vegetation zones within a few miles of the fort (figure 3.1).

Upland areas and portions of the terraces above the river bottoms were tallgrass prairie. The "Wea Plains," lying on the south side of the Wabash, were described in 1765 as a "very Fine Meadow clear for several Miles [with] fine Wild Grass and Wild Hemp 10 or 12 Feet High" (Krauskopf 1955, 224). Portions of the uplands adjacent to waterways were forested, as were the bottomlands and terraces (Martin 1986, 46–55). Areas in the immediate vicinity of the fort and villages, however, would have likely been extensively modified from this natural state, given the multidecade presence of thousands of people. Various observers noted that hundreds of acres were under cultivation in and

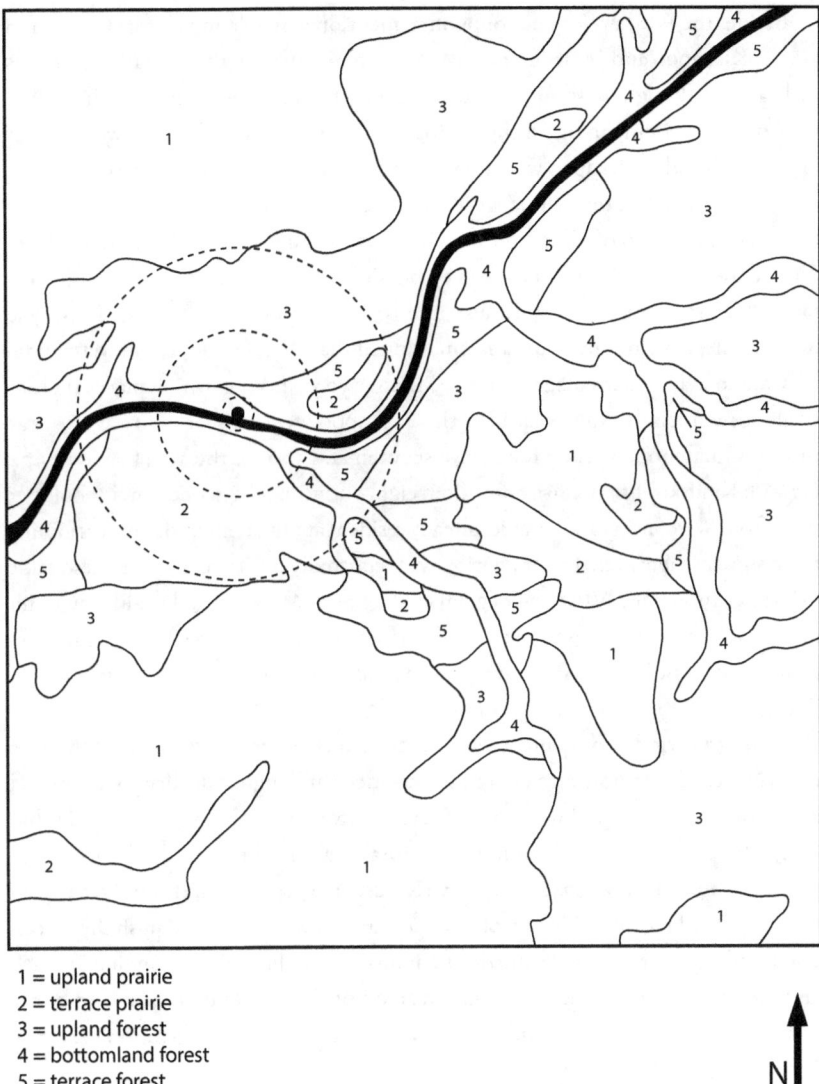

1 = upland prairie
2 = terrace prairie
3 = upland forest
4 = bottomland forest
5 = terrace forest

Figure 3.1. Vegetation zones in the Ouiatenon vicinity, based on maps by Ulrich et al. (1959, fig. 2) and Martin (1986, fig. 1). Dotted lines represent distances of 1, 5, and 10 km from the fort.

around the village areas (Imlay 1916, 14; Wheeler-Voegelin et al. 1974, 172). Certainly, the spots that were once forested were also greatly modified over the many years of habitation due to the need for lumber related to the construction of dwellings, palisade walls, and other facilities and for heating and cooking purposes.

Besides the Wea, two other groups often mentioned in relation to Fort Ouiatenon are the Kickapoo and Mascouten. A Mascouten presence on the Wabash is noted as early as 1711, though most documents place both the Kickapoos and the Mascouten west of Lake Michigan or on the St. Joseph River at this time (Jablow 1974, 141, 149–50, 177). The Kickapoo were nonetheless reportedly residents in the Ouiatenon vicinity by 1734, but they along with the Mascouten were said to be recent arrivals to the area. A group of Kickapoo were living six leagues (about fifteen miles) from Ouiatenon in the winter of 1734–1735, possibly at their winter residence (Jablow 1974, 186; Krauskopf 1953, 175; Krauskopf 1955, 147). In 1735 Jean-Baptiste Le Moyne de Bienville, governor of Louisiana, mentioned that "the Kickapoo and Mascouten . . . came to make their village with the Miami two years ago," which places their arrival more precisely.[2] One year later the Kickapoo were estimated to have 80 warriors at Ouiatenon, with 60 for the Mascouten and 300 for the Wea (Jablow 1974, 187–88; Krauskopf 1953, 186). Soon after, eight additional Mascouten households arrived from Wisconsin to join a chief already resident at Ouiatenon, with others joining them shortly thereafter. This migration was reportedly due to fear of the Mesquakie (Thwaites 1906, 336; Wheeler-Voegelin et al. 1974, 126). By 1750, the addition of numerous Kickapoo families to the area ultimately resulted in a large Native American contingent in the Wabash River area, with a total population perhaps as large as 2,400 (Barnhart and Riker 1971, 66; Jones 1989, 143).

During a period of discontent with the French circa 1751–1752, many of the Wea residents left Ouiatenon, attracted by lower-priced and higher-quality goods offered by the British at their trading town of Pickawillany in present-day west-central Ohio. Only the Kickapoo and Mascouten, who totaled about three hundred warriors, remained behind (Jablow 1974, 211, 220–21; Krauskopf 1953, 302, 311, 314, 316; Krauskopf 1955, 155). The French decided that force was the only way they could push the British traders out of territory they claimed as their own, and in June 1752 a combined French and Indian force destroyed Pickawillany, an event that resulted in the return of the Wea to Ouiatenon in August and September of that year (Pease and Jenison 1940, 731; Wheeler-Voegelin et al. 1974, 129–30).

During the post-1760 British period, Fort Ouiatenon continued to be an important regional hub for the fur trade. A 1765 report from British agent George Croghan indicates that the Kickapoo and Mascouten lived in two villages on the north side of the river (in proximity to the fort), while the Wea resided in a single village on the opposite bank (Alvord and Carter 1916, 33–34). Croghan's description of the Native American village locations is confirmed in a number of documents dating to the 1770s and 1780s (Barnhart and Riker 1971, 172; Dunn 1894, 436; Krauskopf 1955, 157; Thornbrough 1957, 80, 246). The regional primacy of Ouiatenon as a trading center likely continued through the American Revolutionary War. In 1778, Henry Hamilton stopped at

Ouiatenon en route to recapture Vincennes from the Americans. Here, he met with Wea and Kickapoo war chiefs, noting that there were likely about one thousand Native Americans living there, residing in ninety-six "cabins" of about ten inhabitants each (Barnhart 1951, 214).

Ten years later at the beginning of the American period in the Old Northwest, William Biggs, traveling in the Illinois Country, was captured by a group of Kickapoo and Wea. After traveling east for ten days, he arrived at the Wabash River and was transported through a number of Kickapoo towns and sugar camps in the area. Later, Biggs was brought to what he called the "old Kickapoo trading town" (Biggs 1977 [1825]) or the "old Weaues town" (Draper Manuscripts 1949, 5NN) about ten miles from one of the Kickapoo sugar camps. Though Biggs does not provide the Native American name of the town, its location along the Wabash River, combined with its proximity to Kickapoo towns and sugar camps (known to have been in the vicinity) suggests that the town he was speaking of was one of the Kickapoo towns adjacent to Fort Ouiatenon. Here, he made acquaintance with a number of fur traders, eventually making his way to Vincennes after buying his freedom.

In 1790, it was estimated that three hundred Wea fighting men were present at Ouiatenon, as were one hundred Kickapoo on the north side of the river, suggesting that most were determined to stay in their homeland despite increasing conflict with American settlers and threats of reprisal from the US government (Jablow 1974, 310). These difficulties, however, did create fear among some. That year, a small portion of the Wea, consisting of eighty warriors and their families, were persuaded to come under American protection. These individuals, under the leadership of Crooked Legs, established a new village farther down the Wabash between Vincennes and the mouth of the Vermillion River (Wheeler-Voegelin et al. 1974, 158–59).

Paradoxically, the most detailed written descriptions of the Native American villages at Ouiatenon were penned by those involved in their destruction. Charles Scott's narrative of his June 1791 expedition indicates that while approaching the Wea village from the south, the Kentucky militia reached the edge of an extensive tallgrass prairie (i.e., the Wea Plains) (Krauskopf 1955, 224). Proceeding to the north and approaching the Wea village on the south bank of the Wabash, Scott's forces encountered numerous small hamlets, indicating that some Native American settlements were spread out along the river rather than concentrated at Ouiatenon proper. Two villages were attacked to the west, two and four miles distant, with another larger village noted even farther to the west. A single house was also encountered, located on the high ground above the Wea village (American State Papers, Indian Affairs 1832–1834, 1, 131). In the course of destroying the town of Kethtippecanunk, located fifteen miles upriver (at the confluence of the Wabash and Tippecanoe Rivers), several additional small settlements were found and burned (Draper Manuscripts 1949, 63J, 141).

In the wake of these attacks, many of the former residents fled, at least temporarily. Some of the Kickapoo and Mascouten escaped to the Illinois River area, while others descended the Wabash to reside near Vincennes (Jablow 1974, 317, 325–26; Smith 1882, 2, 242). The destruction of their towns and villages by Scott's militia, however, did not bring about the end of Native American residence in the Ouiatenon vicinity. In August 1791 a second expedition, led by James Wilkinson, arrived at the former site of Kethtippecanunk, which he found abandoned. He did note, though, that "the enemy had returned and cultivated their corn and pulses, which I found in high perfection" (Smith 1882, 2, 237). Evidently, the former occupants were reluctant to concentrate at their previous town site for fear of attack but continued to live in the area and cultivate their crops. Wilkinson's men destroyed "about 200 acres of corn at Kathtippacanunck, Kickapoo, and the lower Weauctenau [Ouiatenon] towns" and also destroyed a Kickapoo town about ten miles west of Ouiatenon, consisting of about thirty houses (American State Papers, Indian Affairs 1832–1834, 1, 133–35; Imlay 1916, 14).

Despite a series of Native American military victories over the Americans in 1790 and 1791 (e.g., Harmar's and St. Clair's defeats), it appears that the Scott and Wilkinson expeditions had their desired effect among the people living along the central Wabash River. In March 1792, seven Wea and two Eel River Miami chiefs arrived in Vincennes and announced their intention to make peace with the United States (Heckewelder 1888, 49). Later in September 1792, the Eel River Indians and the Piankashaw, Wea, Kickapoo, Mascouten, Peoria, and Ottawa signed a treaty with the United States agreeing to cease hostilities. Though the treaty was never ratified by Congress, the Wea never again took up arms against the United States (Edmunds 1972, 248–52; Wheeler-Voegelin et al. 1974, 165).

The situation, however, was changing rapidly. In 1795, an American officer traveling down the Wabash found a group of Potawatomi now living near the former site of Kethtippecanunk, which is the first mention of their residence in this portion of the Wabash River valley (Smith 1954, 287), while another source from the same year mentions a village of Potawatomi living "a day's walk below the Wea towns on the Wabash" (Wheeler-Voegelin et al. 1974, 174–75). Thus, it would appear that a number of Potawatomi quickly filled the void created by the Scott and Wilkinson expeditions, though by their acknowledgment they were yet "dependent on their Wabash Brethren for permission," indicating that the Wabash Indians still laid claim to these lands (Jablow 1974, 333). In June 1795 Thomas Bodley, an American officer, visited the site of Ouiatenon, describing both the "old village" (the Wea village) and the "old French Village" (Fort Ouiatenon) in the past tense, suggesting that both were no longer occupied. Two hundred acres in the immediate area, however, were still reportedly in cultivation, indicating a continued Native American presence (Wheeler-Voegelin et al. 1974, 172).

Over the following years, most of the Wea moved farther south along the Wabash. In 1801 William Henry Harrison, residing in Vincennes, described the Piankashaw, Wea, and Eel River Indians as the "tribes in this immediate Neighbourhood," and by 1806, their primary village was situated near Terre Haute (Jablow 1974, 344; Temple 1975 [1958], 71; Wheeler-Voegelin et al. 1974, 177–78). The Wea eventually ceded their claims within the present state of Indiana in 1818 and 1820, and by 1832 those remaining were removed to lands west of the Mississippi River (Tanner 1987, 140).

In regard to the Kickapoo, documents dating from 1804 through 1809 mention settlements along the Vermillion River, indicating that a portion of this nation remained in the general area (Jablow 1974, 343, 346, 353). Later, large numbers of Kickapoo returned to the Wabash River (near the former site of Kethtippecanunk) after the establishment of the multitribal settlement of Prophetstown by Tecumseh and Tenskwatawa, the Shawnee Prophet, in 1808 (Callender, Pope, and Pope 1978, 662). Notably, permission for the Shawnee brothers and their followers to settle on this land was granted by the Potawatomi, who had apparently now become the de facto claimants of the area (Edmunds 1983, 68). The Kickapoo following the Shawnee Prophet's movement were primarily those who were former residents of the Wabash Valley. Following the Battle of Tippecanoe in November 1811, Prophetstown was destroyed, and the Kickapoo never again resided in the Ouiatenon vicinity. The Mascouten, who were never a numerous group, were reportedly integrated into the Kickapoo by 1813 (Goddard 1978, 670). The Kickapoo signed treaties in 1819, exchanging their lands for reservations across the Mississippi, and remaining Kickapoo on the Vermilion, lower Wabash, Embarras, and Kaskaskia Rivers were removed by 1830 in the face of increasing white encroachment on their lands (Tanner 1987, 139).

ARCHAEOLOGICAL INVESTIGATIONS OUTSIDE THE FORT

As noted in previous chapters, after much speculation and searching, the archaeological site of Fort Ouiatenon was confirmed in the late 1960s. An intensive program of investigations commenced soon after, running from 1968 through 1979 and concentrating almost exclusively on activities within the fort's limits. Despite documentary evidence for fur trade–era habitation and other activities outside the fort perimeter, it took some time before professional interest in the archaeological traces of these activities came about. Early documentation of a number of probable fur trade–era sites in the immediate area was made by Dr. Robert Mulvey, who surface-collected in the Lafayette/West Lafayette area from the 1940s through the 1970s. Systematic work in precisely locating and recording these and other sites, however, did not occur until the

1980s, when James R. Jones and Neal Trubowitz undertook a large-scale surface survey of Tippecanoe County, investigating a number of spots where historic documents suggested that fur trade–era sites were likely to be identified (Jones 1984, 1989; Jones and Trubowitz 1987; Trubowitz 1992). As part of this effort, Jones and Trubowitz surveyed a 192-hectare area around Fort Ouiatenon, including spots on both the north and south sides of the river. The areas surrounding the fort on the north side of the river have been completely surveyed from the Wabash to the base of the bluffs at the northern edge of the floodplain (Jones and Trubowitz 1987, 31). We can therefore be fairly certain that nearly all of the significant fur trade sites in the immediate vicinity have been identified. In total, twenty-five probable fur trade–era sites (represented by three or more eighteenth-century artifacts) have been found, with an additional thirteen isolated find spots identified. All but two of these sites, the Wea village (12-T-6) and site 12-T-499, are located on the north side of the Wabash River. The resulting data on Native American habitation sites paint a fairly clear picture of the archaeological remains, with sites surrounding the fort on its north, east, and west sides. In general, these sites are located on all elevated spots of any appreciable height. Even so, most areas of the floodplain (with the exception of the east-west ridge on which Fort Ouiatenon stands) are frequently inundated when the levels of the Wabash River are high, suggesting that regardless of their location, annual flooding may have been an ongoing concern in the past.[3]

Further investigation of these Native American sites has been in the form of geophysics and excavation. Work on the south side of the Wabash has been somewhat limited. In 1986, a controlled surface collection was performed over portions of the Wea village (12-T-6) opposite the fort site, which was then followed up with a small-scale magnetometry survey along a number of narrow strips largely corresponding to the areas of highest reported artifact surface density (Jones and Trubowitz 1987; Satoskar 1987). Despite the low data density of the magnetometry survey (given the relatively crude instruments available at the time), a number of anomalies were identified that may correspond to areas of intact subsurface features. Following the survey portion of the project, a total of 34 m^2 of the site was excavated. Intact features were encountered, including a midden 20–40 cm thick buried up to 80 cm below the current surface, which was identified in a number of units. A large post mold, a smudge pit, and other features were also noted (Jones and Trubowitz 1987, 62; Trubowitz 1992, 99). Despite clear indications that the Wea village site likely contains substantial information on the eighteenth-century Native American residents of the Ouiatenon area, no further work has been conducted since then.

Additional work on nonfort occupations has been conducted on the north side of the river as well. From 2009 through 2017, a large-scale magnetometry survey was performed in and around the fort area (supplemented with small areas of resistivity

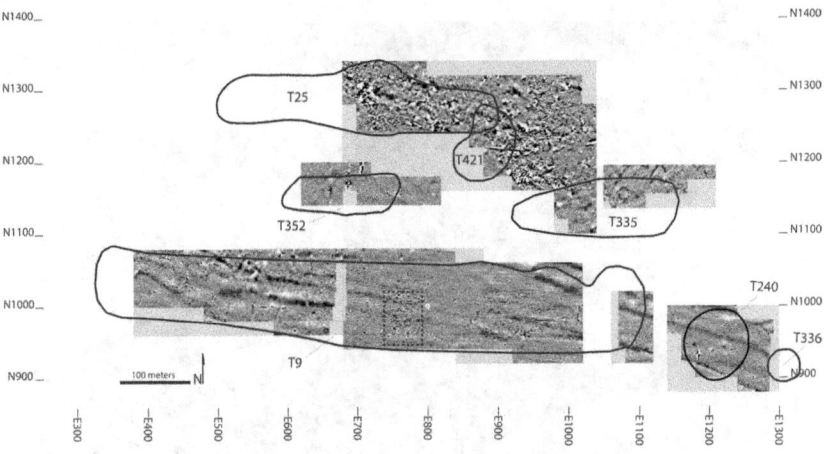

Figure 3.2. Extent of 2009–2017 magnetometry survey in and around the site of Fort Ouiatenon. The fort site itself, located within site 12-T-9, is shown with a black dotted line. Site extents are those recorded during pre-GPS research of previous decades and do not precisely correspond to the areas of highest elevation and highest apparent feature density.

survey) in an effort to better identify intact subsurface features outside the fort (figure 3.2) (Strezewski 2014; Strezewski and McCullough 2010, 2017, 2019).

These included surveys across large portions of probable village sites 12-T-25/421, 12-T-240/336, 12-T-336/507, and 12-T-352. The results of these surveys were equivocal in some instances, with indications that flood-related and agricultural erosion have likely impacted the archaeological remains. In other cases, however, there was clear evidence for intact subsurface features. This is perhaps most apparent at site 12-T-240/336, located on high ground about 400 m directly east of the fort. Here, numerous subsurface anomalies were found, likely representing trash pits and cooking features (figures 3.3 and 3.4). Although no excavations have yet been conducted to confirm these findings, the recorded presence of numerous fur trade–era artifacts on the surface suggests that a substantial eighteenth-century component is present (Jones 1984).

Magnetometry and resistivity surveys at site 12-T-9 have produced the most fruitful results. The site consists of a low rise on the floodplain running east-west and containing not only the remains of Fort Ouiatenon itself but also other fur trade–era and precontact remains, as recorded in surface collections (Jones 1984). Most notable in the magnetometry data (for the purposes of this chapter) was the identification of at least fifteen anomalies that most likely represent Native American structures (figure 3.5).

Of these, thirteen were circular to oval in shape and are thought to be Native American wigwam-type structures, based on ethnographic and ethnohistoric

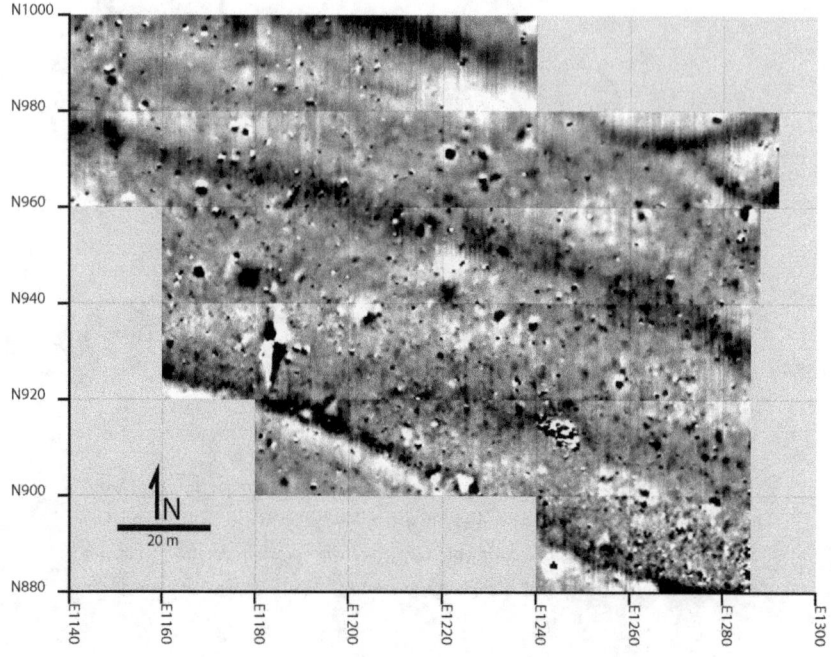

Figure 3.3. Results of the magnetometry survey of site 12-T-240/336.

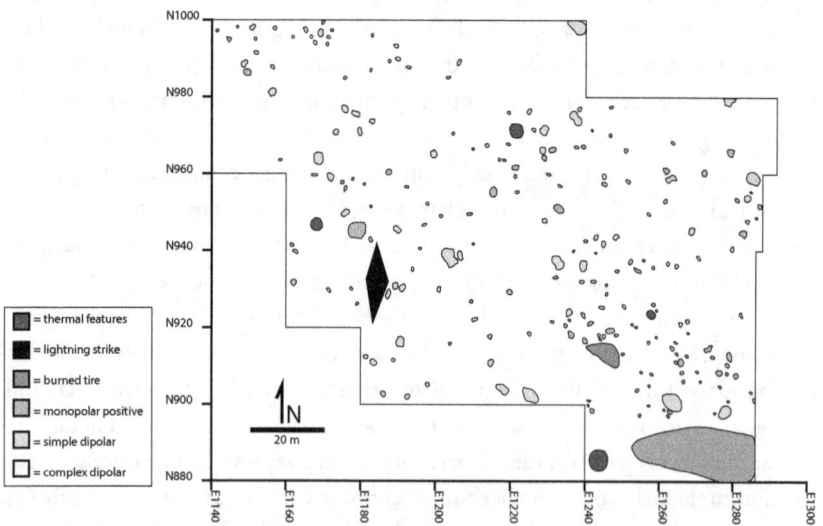

= thermal features
= lightning strike
= burned tire
= monopolar positive
= simple dipolar
= complex dipolar

Figure 3.4. Interpretation of the magnetometry survey results from site 12-T-240/336.

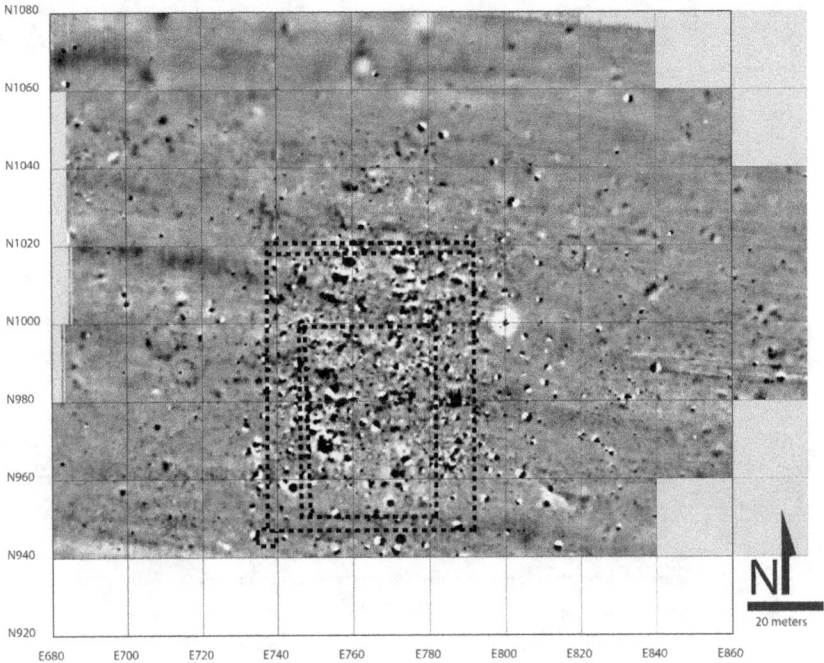

Figure 3.5. Results of the magnetometry survey in and around the site of Fort Ouiatenon.

descriptions of Kickapoo dwellings (e.g., Latorre and Latorre 1976; Ritzenthaler and Peterson 1970; Wagner 2011). The circular and oval anomalies are quite large, ranging from 5.9 to 9.0 m in diameter, with an average of 7.4 meters (figure 3.6). The remaining two anomalies were rectangular; their cultural affiliation is less certain in the absence of excavation. Most of the structures were located near the remains of the fort's northwest corner, forming a rough oval about 100 by 40 m in size with an open area in the center.

In 2013, the University of Southern Indiana opened a 30 m^2 block over the southeast portion of one of the circular magnetic anomalies (anomaly 4 in figure 3.6) as a means to test if it did indeed represent a structure. At the point of definition, the feature consisted of a very large dark-colored stain comprising jumbled charcoal fragments up to 3 cm in size and running the entire east-west length of the block. Continuing deeper, the outline of a wall trench became clear, thereby confirming our suspicions (figure 3.7).

The trench was wide and shallow, about 50 cm at the point of definition and only about 20 cm deep. Despite careful examination, only two structural posts were identified within the trench. Their general absence may be due to the small size of the posts that were used or that they were not typically driven beyond the depth of the trench.

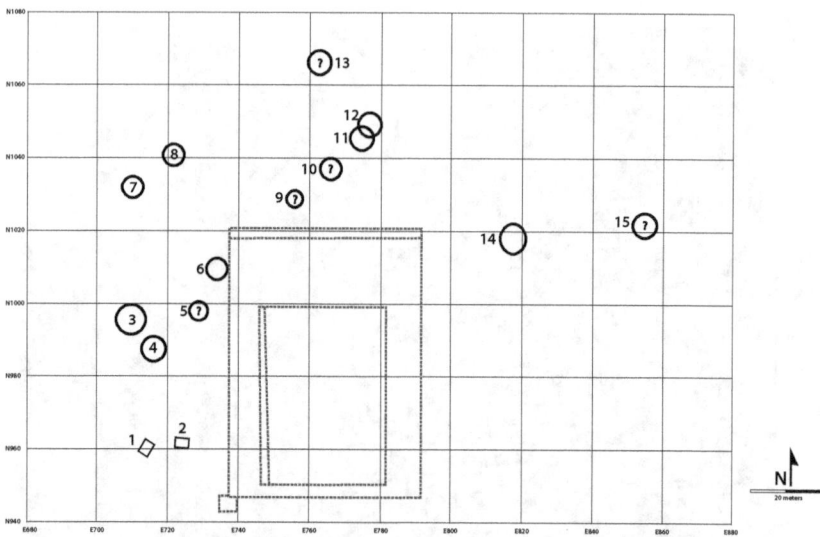

Figure 3.6. Interpretation of the magnetometry results in and around Fort Ouiatenon showing locations of possible Native American structures. Interior (earlier) and exterior (later) stockade walls are shown as dotted lines.

Figure 3.7. Block from 2013 excavation showing a circular wall trench and a linear wall trench to the left (partially excavated at previous level). View to the north.

Apart from five interior posts, no other features were identified within the structure. Most notable among these was a cluster of three small postholes, which may represent a roof support post that had been replaced at least twice. These posts were located in the center of the structure's southeast quadrant, suggesting that corresponding roof supports may have been placed in the center of the other three quadrants. Fifteen other posts, seemingly randomly arranged, were noted outside the structure. These may be nonstructural in nature and related to various domestic activities. Though centrally located internal hearths are often mentioned in ethnohistoric descriptions of Kickapoo structures (e.g., Dillingham 1963; Goggin 1951; Latorre and Latorre 1976; Wagner 2011) none was identified in the 2013 excavations. A bullseye-shaped anomaly noted in the magnetometry data and lying outside of our excavation block may represent such a hearth, however.

Apart from charcoal (g = 12,107.6) and faunal remains (g = 154.1), few other artifacts were recovered from the structure's interior. These consist of three small fragments of container glass, a portion of a brass kettle patch, worked pipestone fragments, and a single hand-wrought nail. Fire-cracked (g = 205.7) and non–fire-cracked (g = 18.0) rock were also found, albeit in small quantities.

Overall, the excavations indicate that the structure was approximately 6.2 m in maximum diameter (measured from the interior of the wall trench), encompassing approximately 30.2 m^2 of interior space. The structure was likely constructed by digging a wide and shallow trench into which small pliable saplings were placed. Woods used in its construction include both hickory and maple (Strezewski and Rubino 2017). These saplings were likely bent over and secured, creating a dome-like structure that was then covered in bark, mats, or possibly canvas. After an indeterminate period of use, the structure burned.

A portion of a linear wall trench, oriented roughly north-south, was identified along the eastern edge of the large excavation block. The feature ranged from 25 to 40 cm wide at the point of definition and extended to about 85–90 cm below the current surface. Intermittently spaced postholes were noted in some portions of the wall trench, the largest of which were 15–18 cm in diameter and extended a few centimeters beyond the depth of the trench. Notably, the linear wall trench clearly superimposed the dense charcoal zone directly outside the structure, indicating continued use and occupation of the immediate area after the structure's destruction by fire.

The function of the north-south wall trench is not clear. Unfortunately, it did not appear on the magnetometry data and so cannot be traced out beyond the limits of the 2013 excavations. It may be part of a very large *poteaux-en-terre* structure, palisade wall, or a fenced enclosure of some sort. The feature runs approximately eighteen meters west of (and nearly parallel to) the westernmost palisade wall of Fort Ouiatenon, identified during the Michigan State University (MSU) excavations and in the magnetometry data. Given this, the linear wall trench likely does not represent a previously unrecognized rebuilding of Fort Ouiatenon. Supporting this supposition is the fact that Fort Ouiatenon's outer palisade wall, excavated by MSU, extended to circa 1.4 m below the surface, about 50 cm deeper than the enigmatic linear feature in the 2013 block. Unfortunately, there were very few artifacts in this feature to suggest its function or temporal affiliation, though it almost certainly dates to the fur trade era (Strezewski 2014, 70–72).

An attempt at dating the 2013 structure via dendrochronology was made utilizing the largest available fragments of the burned structure. While both hickory and maple chronologies were developed (forty-three and thirty-five years in length, respectively), such relatively short sequences are difficult to date confidently. Coupled with the absence of reliable reference chronologies from the Ouiatenon area, the study of these remains was deemed inconclusive. It is possible, however, that a satisfactory cross date may be obtained in the future once additional historic structures are sampled (Strezewski and Rubino 2017).

Although not recognized at the time, a review of the MSU excavation records indicated that the investigations uncovered portions of a second circular Native American structure in 1975 and 1979, very similar to that found in 2013 (Noble 1983; Tordoff 1983). This structure, located just west of the northwest corner of the fort, was partially excavated and described as a "strange feature" of uncertain type, "twenty feet in diameter [and] filled up with charcoal in a matrix of brown sand" (Tordoff 1983, 147, 162). The unexcavated portion of this structure was identified during our magnetometry survey and is shown as anomaly 6 in figure 3.6. The MSU excavators noted that its wall trench was wide and shallow, comprising a structure approximately 5.2 m in diameter measured from the interior walls (approximately 1.0 m smaller than the example excavated in 2013). Like the structure found in 2013, there was a scarcity of materials found in association; these included charcoal, burned and unburned animal bone, fire-cracked rock, two pieces of glass, one piece of brass, one nail, and one fragment of shell. Notably, the feature superimposed an east-west wall trench segment, which in turn was superimposed by the fort's outer stockade wall. As the outer stockade wall is thought to postdate 1740, the excavators concluded that the structure must have been constructed after the expansion of the fort in the 1740s. Their best guess was that it may postdate the fort's occupation (Tordoff 1976, 53, 91).

Most recently, in 2022 a portion of a third structure was excavated, previously identified as anomaly 14 in the magnetometry data (see figure 3.6). The structure was chosen for excavation due to its somewhat unusual attributes. Not only did it appear to be larger than most, but it was also oval rather than circular in outline (measuring approximately 10.0 by 7.9 m in size) and isolated from the main cluster of structures situated near the northwest corner of the fort. One possibility was that it was a structure used for nonresidential purposes, perhaps a town house or other community-type structure.

A small excavation block was opened over the southern end of this anomaly, 20 m² in extent, confirming that it too was a portion of a structure. The presence of large amounts of charcoal indicated that it, like the others excavated previously, had also been destroyed by fire and was likely built by placing small posts in a shallow trench. While artifacts found within the structure were not particularly abundant, those that were recovered strongly suggest that it was utilized for habitation purposes. These materials included burned and unburned faunal material, small amounts of container glass, gun parts, gunflints, copper/brass scrap, a copper hawk bell, and a tinkling cone. Like the structure excavated in 2013, a number of pipestone fragments were also found within its limits, indicating household manufacture of these items within Native American residences. Perhaps most notable among these was a whole wedge-shaped pipe, perhaps unfinished, that was found above the western wall trench (figure 3.8).

One of the few artifact types deemed anomalous was a number of small slag fragments (n = 80) each averaging only 2.0 g in weight and representing the remains of ironworking activities. Previous excavations within the fort proper indicate that similar pieces, some quite large, were relatively common especially in an area likely devoted to blacksmithing (Tordoff 1980, 44–45). This area lay approximately 57 m southwest of the 2022 structure. Fair amounts of slag-like material were found in many other units within the fort, however, and its presence in the 2022 structure is not thought to be related to any type of metalworking within its confines.

Altogether, the three Native American structures excavated thus far at Ouiatenon correspond fairly closely to ethnographic and ethnohistoric descriptions of the types of dwellings constructed by the Kickapoo. A nineteenth-century account from Illinois indicates that

their Wigwams were nearly all made circular and were mostly made of bark. They would get the bark in the season of the year when it would peel from the tree the best.... I have seen them get off pieces perhaps 3 feet and a half wide. They would make their wigwams with a little opening at the top for the smoke of their camp-fire

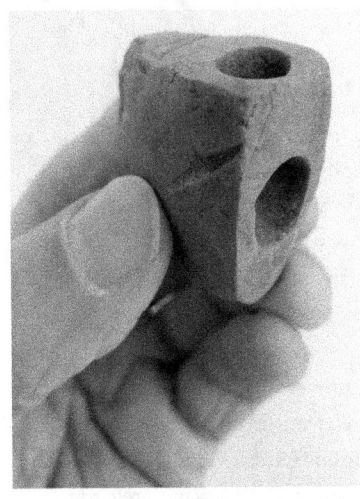

Figure 3.8. Pipe (perhaps unfinished) made of gray pipestone and found above the western wall of the 2022 structure.

to escape, as they always built their fire in the middle of their wigwams. Then they would get out their wolf and deer skins and spread them on the ground around the fire. They used the skins to sit on and lay on for their beds. (Hendrix 1889, cited in Wagner 2011, 48–49)

There are few detailed period descriptions of the methods used to construct wigwams of this type. Though describing Potawatomi structures, Harvey Lee Ross's account is one of the most detailed. His description from the Spoon River valley in Illinois dates to the 1830s:

> They had erected some twenty wigwams.... A common sized wigwam for a family of eight or ten persons would be about 12 x 16 feet in size. Small saplings would be cut and set firmly in the ground, big ends down, in rows three feet apart, all round the plat (12 x 16 feet) to be enclosed. Then the limber tops of the poles would be brought together and fastened with hickory wyths or strips of leather. Then small poles would be tied lengthwise to the saplings, making a cross-barred and solid frame. The whole would then be covered with a heavy matting that had been woven by the squaws from the coarse swamp grass yet to be found on the bottom lands. This completed the wigwam, and it had the shape of a hay stack. An opening was left as a door way and this was protected by a blanket. A pit 2 x 3 feet in size and eight or ten inches deep would be dug in the center under the wigwam for a fire-place, and there was an opening at the top for the smoke to pass through. The Indians were quite comfortable in these wigwams, with their blankets and furs, in the coldest weather. (Ross 1899, 52)

The structure described by Ross is slightly smaller than those found at 12-T-9 but appears to be otherwise similar in terms of the methods used in its construction.

Both magnetometry and excavated data indicate that the two structures west of the fort's palisade wall were part of a small village consisting of at least eleven structures running along a southwest-northeast axis and occupying an area of approximately 0.4 hectares. It is important to note, though, that most or all the structures visible via magnetometry are likely identifiable only because they were burned (thereby altering the magnetic properties of the subsurface) and that numerous other village-related features may be present but undetected. Such possible features include unburned structural remains, cemeteries, council houses, dance grounds, sweat lodges, menstrual huts, food-drying scaffolds, and agricultural fields. Another uncertainty with regard to this small village is how many of the identified structures were occupied at any given time. The fact that two of the anomalies overlap (anomalies 11 and 12 in figure 3.6) indicates that limited rebuilding at least likely took place.

In the absence of significant numbers of highly diagnostic artifacts, it is somewhat difficult to assign a date to these structures. Feature superpositioning (in the case of the MSU and 2013 structures) and information related to the artifacts found within their limits suggest that they may have been occupied after the fort had already been dismantled (i.e., after 1780 or so). Reasons for this supposition include the fact that neither the French nor the British would likely have looked favorably on having a Native American village in such close proximity to the fort, especially during the time in which it was being used as a military outpost (i.e., between 1717 and 1763). In addition, none of the post-1778 accounts of the Ouiatenon locale mention the presence of a fort, which suggests that it may have been demolished or salvaged sometime between 1778 and 1791. Though the fact that the fort was not mentioned in these accounts is not definitive proof that it did not exist at this late date, its absence in these descriptions is good indirect evidence for this conclusion.

Given the possible late eighteenth-century date for the village, the question arises as to whether any or all of the burned structures were destroyed as part of Scott's 1791 attack on Ouiatenon. While this is certainly possible, there is no conclusive evidence to link them to this event. In all three excavations relatively few artifacts were found within the structures, possibly indicating that each had been cleaned out and intentionally burned by the Native Americans themselves, perhaps after they were no longer deemed useful. Compounding our uncertainty is the fact that the artifacts found within the structures were not particularly diagnostic aside from suggesting a post-1760 date. Finally, as noted above, there is no reason to believe that all the structures in the general village area were burned or that we were able to see all of them using geophysical methods. It is unknown how many other structures may be present that had not ended their period of use in this manner.

Regardless of the numerous unanswered questions that remain, the data produced thus far are quite valuable in understanding the types of residences used by the Native American residents of Ouiatenon in the latter portion of the eighteenth century. Aside from the three excavated at Ouiatenon, there is relatively little archaeological data on probable Kickapoo structures. Although excavations have been conducted at a few Kickapoo-related sites in Illinois (e.g., Berkson 1992; Smith 1978), structures have been identified at only one, the Rhoads site (11-Lo-8), located in Logan County, that was occupied between circa 1790 and 1830 (Wagner 2011). Of the three structural outlines identified at Rhoads, one was a longhouse-like rectangular structure, at least 13.6 by 6.0 m in size, built by placing individual posts into the ground. The second was oval 5.3 by 3.5 m in size; it too was constructed by placing individual posts into the ground, with a small hearth in the interior. The final structural outline identified at the Rhoads site was difficult to discern and consisted of an area 11.0 by 11.0 m in size containing numerous postholes, likely representing one or more rebuilding episodes on the same spot. A large hearth was identified in the midst of the posts, which may have been inside one or more of the structures (Wagner 2011, 104–8).

These archaeological data from the Rhoads site indicate the use of at least two different structural forms; one is a longhouse-type structure, while the other is a wigwam-style dwelling constructed of individual posts set into the ground. Notably, none of the Rhoads sites structures was built in a manner identical to the three found at Ouiatenon, particularly in the absence of a wall trench. The notable differences in the construction techniques used at the two sites is a bit difficult to explain, though ethnohistoric sources can provide some insight. One possibility includes a change in the manner in which structures were built between the late eighteenth and early nineteenth centuries when Ouiatenon and Rhoads were occupied, respectively. Another factor may be the contemporary use of a number of different construction techniques depending on the needs of the residents, the soil or drainage conditions, and the season of occupation. The Kickapoo, like many groups of the Great Lakes area, had both summer and winter villages. Summer dwellings were typically built from a sapling framework that was covered with bark, mats, or skins, with both longhouse and smaller circular or rectangular structures mentioned (Dillingham 1963). Descriptions of winter accommodations are fewer but suggest that most were circular to oval in plan view and constructed by placing mats over a pole frame. An interior hearth was dug into the center of the floor, with a hole to allow smoke to escape (Custer 1907, 5; Dillingham 1963; Hendrix 1889; Mead 1904; Ross 1889). Unfortunately, seasonality data from the Ouiatenon Native American village is slim, making it difficult to determine what time of year this small settlement was occupied and to what degree seasonality may have played into the differences between the Rhoads and Ouiatenon structures.

CONCLUSION

Data from the 1980s through the present have conclusively demonstrated the presence of intact archaeological remains related to the various Native American groups residing in proximity to the fort. These consist of Kickapoo/Mascouten settlements on the north side of the Wabash River, surrounding the fort on three sides, and the large Wea village, situated on the south side of the river. Though no evidence of French or British occupation outside the confines of the fort has yet been confirmed archaeologically, it is certainly possible that such remains exist, possibly representing pre- or postfort occupations not recorded in the documentary sources.

Although the amount of archaeological data on the Native American habitation areas is not nearly as extensive as that collected within the fort proper, the degree to which we know about the location, size, and presence of Native American occupations is substantial when compared to many other fur trade research projects. It is hoped that future investigations will expand upon these data in order to paint a more vivid and balanced picture of the fur trade economy that fully considers the Native American contributions to this enterprise.

NOTES

1. The Wea were often considered a subgroup of the Miami and therefore grouped together with them in contemporary descriptions. It is therefore quite possible that these settlements were Wea towns.
2. Bienville is likely speaking of "the Miami" in the broad sense here, an ethnonym that often included the Wea on the Wabash.
3. The continued presence of driftwood and other debris on the Fort Ouiatenon site itself indicates that even the highest elevations on the north side of the river are sometimes inundated. Due to wetland drainage and removal of bottomland vegetation on the Wabash, flooding in the Ouiatenon area may now be more frequent or severe than in the eighteenth century. Regardless, there is evidence that seasonal flooding was a concern for the fort's residents. When British lieutenant John Butler took possession of Ouiatenon in December 1760, he noted that "last spring the water in the fort was four foot deep" (Butler 1762). Similarly, an American officer, John Bodley, noted in 1795 that "on the N.W. side [of the Wabash] was the old French Village [Fort Ouiatenon] it stood in a large Prarie part of which overflows at times" (Wheeler-Voegelin et al. 1974, 172).

REFERENCES

Alvord, Clarence W., and Clarence E. Carter, eds. 1916. *The New Régime, 1765–1767*. Collections of the Illinois State Historical Library, Vol. 11, British Series, Vol. 2. Springfield: Illinois State Historical Library.

American State Papers, Indian Affairs. 1832–1834. *American State Papers, Indian Affairs [1789–1827]*. 2 vols. Washington, DC: Gales and Seaton.

Barnhart, John D., ed. 1951. *Henry Hamilton and George Rogers Clark in the American Revolution with the Unpublished Journal of Lieut. Gov. Henry Hamilton*. Crawfordsville, IN: R. E. Banta.

Barnhart, John D., and Dorothy L. Riker. 1971. *Indiana to 1816: The Colonial Period*. Indianapolis: Indiana Historical Bureau and Indiana Historical Society.

Beach, W. W. 1877. *The Indian Miscellany: Papers on the History, Antiquities, Arts, Languages, Religions, Traditions, and Superstitions of the American Aborigines*. Albany, NY: J. Munsell.

Berkson, Alice. 1992. "Cultural Resistance of the Prairie Kickapoo at the Grand Village, McLean County, Illinois." *Illinois Archaeology* 4, no. 2: 109–205.

Biggs, William. 1977 [1825]. *Narrative of William Biggs, While He was a Prisoner with the Kickepoo Indians*. The Garland Library of Narratives of North American Indian Captivities, Vol. 37. New York: Garland Publishing.

Butler, John. 1762. "January 1st, 1762 Letter regarding the Details of Taking Possession of Forts Miamis and Ouiatenon for the British." The National Archives, War Office 34/90, Kew, United Kingdom.

Callender, Charles, Richard K. Pope, and Susan M. Pope. 1978. "Kickapoo." In *Northeast*, ed. Bruce G. Trigger, 656–67. Handbook of North American Indians, Vol. 15. Washington, DC: Smithsonian Institution Press.

Custer, Milo. 1907. Milo Custer to George J. Remsburg, January 16. George Jacob Remsburg Papers, Collection 78. Kansas State Historical Society, Topeka.

Dillingham, Betty Ann Wilder. 1963. "Oklahoma Kickapoo." PhD diss., University of Michigan.

Draper Manuscripts. 1949. *Draper Manuscript Collection* [microform]. Department of Photographic Reproduction, University of Chicago.

Dunn, Jacob Piatt. 1894. "Documents Relating to the French Settlements on the Wabash." *Indiana Historical Society Publications* 2, no. 11: 403–42.

Edmunds, R. David. 1972. "Wea Participation in the Northwest Indian Wars, 1790–1795." *Filson Club History Quarterly* 46: 241–53.

———. 1983. *The Shawnee Prophet*. Lincoln: University of Nebraska Press.

Goddard, Ives. 1978. "Mascouten." In *Northeast*, ed. Bruce G. Trigger, 668–72. Handbook of North American Indians, Vol. 15. Washington, DC: Smithsonian Institution Press.

Goggin, John M. 1951. "The Mexican Kickapoo Indians." *Southwestern Journal of Anthropology* 7, no. 3: 314–27.

Heckewelder, John. 1888. "Narrative of John Heckewelder's Journey to the Wabash in 1792 (Part II)." *Pennsylvania Magazine of History and Biography* 12: 34–54, 165–84.

Hendrix, William M. 1889. Letter of W. M. Hendrix. McLean County Historical Society Collections, Vol. I, McLean County. Historical Society, Bloomington, IL.

Imlay, George. 1916. "A Topographical Description of the Western Territory of North America, 1793." In *Indiana as Seen by Early Travelers: A Collection of Reprints from Books of Travel, Letters, and Diaries Prior to 1830*, ed. Harlow Lindley, 9–16. Indianapolis: Indiana Historical Commission.

Jablow, Joseph. 1974. *The Indians of Illinois and Indiana: Illinois, Kickapoo, and Potawatomi Indians*. New York: Garland Publishing.

Jones, James R., III. 1984. Eighteenth and Early Nineteenth Century Aboriginal and Euroamerican Occupations in the Vicinity of Lafayette, Tippecanoe County, Indiana. Glenn A. Black Laboratory of Archaeology, Indiana University, Bloomington.

———. 1989. "Degrees of Acculturation at Two 18th Century Aboriginal Villages Near Lafayette, Tippecanoe County, Indiana: Ethnohistoric and Archaeological Perspectives." PhD diss., Indiana University.

Jones, James R., III, and Neal L. Trubowitz. 1987. "1986 Archaeological Reconnaissance and Testing of Historic Occupations along the Wabash River in the Vicinity of Lafayette, Tippecanoe County, Indiana." Report submitted to the Indiana Department of Natural Resources, Division of Historic Preservation and Archaeology, Indianapolis.

Krauskopf, Frances. 1953. "The French in Indiana, 1700–1760: A Political History." PhD diss., Indiana University.

———. 1955. *Ouiatanon Documents*. Indianapolis: Indiana Historical Society.

Latorre, Felipe A., and Dolores L. Latorre. 1976. *The Mexican Kickapoo Indians*. Austin: University of Texas Press.

Martin, Terrance J. 1986. "A Faunal Analysis of Fort Ouiatenon, an Eighteenth-Century Trading Post in the Wabash Valley of Indiana." PhD diss., Michigan State University.

Mead, J. R. 1904. Mead to George J. Remsburg, February 13. George Jacob Remsburg Papers, Collection 78. Kansas State Historical Society, Topeka.

Michigan Pioneer and Historical Society. 1904. *Michigan Pioneer and Historical Society Collections*, Vol. 33. Lansing, MI: Robert Smith.

Noble, Vergil E., Jr. 1983. "Functional Classification and Intra-site Analysis in Historical Archaeology: A Case Study from Fort Ouiatenon." PhD diss., Michigan State University.

Pease, Theodore C., and Ernestine Jenison, eds. 1940. *Illinois on the Eve of the Seven Years' War*. Collections of the Illinois State Historical Library, Vol. 29, French Series, Vol. 3. Springfield: Illinois State Historical Library.

Pease, Theodore C., and Raymond C. Werner, eds. 1934. *The French Foundations, 1680–1693*. Collections of the Illinois State Historical Library, Vol. 16, French Series, Vol. 1. Springfield: Illinois State Historical Library.

Ritzenthaler, Robert E., and Frederick A. Peterson. 1970. *The Mexican Kickapoo Indians*. Milwaukee Public Museum Publications in Anthropology No. 2. Westport, CT: Greenwood.

Ross, Harvey Lee. 1899. *The Early Pioneers and Pioneer Events of the State of Illinois*. Chicago: Eastman Brothers.

Satoskar, Vijay V. 1987. "Results of a Magnetometer Survey of 12T6." In *1986 Archaeological Reconnaissance and Testing of Historic Occupations along the Wabash River in the Vicinity of Lafayette, Tippecanoe County, Indiana*, by James R. Jones III and Neal L. Trubowitz, 92–102. Report submitted to the Indiana Department of Natural Resources, Division of Historic Preservation and Archaeology, Indianapolis.

Smith, Charles R. 1978. "The Grand Village of the Kickapoo: An Historic Site." Master's thesis, Illinois State University.

Smith, Dwight. 1954. "Notes on the Wabash River in 1795." *Indiana Magazine of History* 50, no. 3: 277–90.

Smith, William Henry, ed. 1882. *The St. Clair Papers: The Life and Public Services of Arthur St. Clair, Soldier of the Revolutionary War, President of the Continental Congress, and Governor of the North-Western Territory, with His Correspondence and Other Papers*. 2 vols. Cincinnati: Robert Clarke.

Strezewski, Michael. 2014. "Fur Trade Archeology in the Ouiatenon Vicinity: The 2012/2013 Investigations." Report submitted to the US National Park Service, American Battlefield Protection Program, Grant #GA-2255-12-025.

Strezewski, Michael, and Robert G. McCullough. 2010. "Report of the 2009 Archaeological Investigations at Three Fur Trade–Era Sites in Tippecanoe County, Indiana: Kethtippecanunk (12-T-59), Fort Ouiatenon (12-T-9), and a Kickapoo-Mascouten Village (12-T-335)." Indiana University-Purdue University Fort Wayne Archaeological Survey, Reports of Investigations 903. Report submitted to the US National Park Service, American Battlefield Protection Program, Grant #GA-2255-08-016.

———. 2017. "Fur Trade Archaeology at the Ouiatenon Preserve: The 2016/2017 Geophysical Investigations." University of Southern Indiana Archaeology Laboratory, Reports of Investigations 16-03. Report submitted to the Indiana Department of Natural Resources, Division of Historic Preservation and Archaeology, Indianapolis.

———. 2019. "Fort Ouiatenon, 1717–2019: 300+ Years of Indiana History." *Indiana Archaeology* 14, no. 1: 54–88.

Strezewski, Michael, and Darrin Rubino. 2017. "Dendrochronology in the Midwest? Dating a Burned Native American Structure from Fort Ouiatenon." Paper presented at the Midwest Archaeological Conference, October 19–21, Indianapolis.

Tanner, Helen Hornbeck, ed. 1987. *Atlas of Great Lakes Indian History*. Norman: University of Oklahoma Press.

Temple, Wayne C. 1975 (1958). *Indian Villages of the Illinois Country*. Publications 2, Part 1, Supplement. Springfield: Illinois State Museum.

Thornbrough, Gayle. 1957. *Outpost on the Wabash, 1787–1791: Letters of Brigadier General Josiah Harmar and Major John Francis Hamtramck, and Other Letters and Documents Selected from the Harmar Papers in the William L. Clements Library*. Indiana Historical Society Publications, Vol. 19. Indianapolis: Indiana Historical Society.

Thwaites, Reuben Gold, ed. 1902. *Collections of the State Historical Society of Wisconsin*, Vol. 16, *The French Regime in Wisconsin I, 1634–1727*. Madison: Wisconsin State Historical Society.

———. 1906. *Collections of the State Historical Society of Wisconsin*, Vol. 17, *The French Regime in Wisconsin II, 1727–1748*. Madison: Wisconsin State Historical Society.

Tordoff, Judith D. 1976. "Report of Archaeological Excavations at Fort Ouiatenon, 1974 & 1975." Unpublished report in possession of the Tippecanoe County Historical Society, Lafayette.

———. 1980. "Excavations at Fort Ouiatenon, 1974–1976: Preliminary Report." Unpublished report in possession of the Tippecanoe County Historical Society, Lafayette.

———. 1983. "An Archaeological Perspective on the Organization of the Fur Trade in Eighteenth Century New France." PhD diss., Michigan State University.

Trubowitz, Neal L. 1992. "Thanks, but We Prefer to Smoke Our Own: Pipes in the Great Lakes–Riverine Region during the Eighteenth Century." In *Proceedings of the 1989 Smoking Pipe Conference*, ed. Charles F. Hayes, Connie C. Bodner, and Martha L. Sempowski, 97–112. Rochester, NY: Rochester Museum and Science Center.

Ulrich, H. P., T. E. Barnes, B. A. Krantz, and J. G. Wade. 1959. *Soil Survey of Tippecanoe County, Indiana*. Soil Conservation Service, Series 1940, No. 22. Washington, DC: US Department of Agriculture.

Wagner, Mark J. 2011. *The Rhoads Site: A Historic Kickapoo Village on the Illinois Prairie*. Illinois State Archaeological Survey, Studies in Archaeology No. 5. Urbana: University of Illinois.

Wheeler-Voegelin, Erminie, Emily J. Blasingham, and Dorothy R. Libby. 1974. *Miami, Wea, and Eel River Indians of Southern Indiana: An Anthropological Report on the Miami, Wea, and Eel-River Indians*. New York: Garland Publishing.

4

FRENCH COLONIAL HISTORY AND ARCHAEOLOGY AT FORT MIAMIS AND VINCENNES

MICHAEL STREZEWSKI, UNIVERSITY
OF SOUTHERN INDIANA

WHILE FORT OUIATENON HAS THE DISTINCTION OF BEING THE FIRST formal French outpost in the present state of Indiana, two other areas within the state also saw long-term French colonial occupation, a direct result of France's attempts to maintain control over the fur trade in the North American interior. The first was Fort Miamis, the archaeological remains of which are located within the present city of Fort Wayne. The fort was founded in 1722, only five years after the establishment of Fort Ouiatenon. Like Ouiatenon, Fort Miamis was situated adjacent to an established Native American settlement (in this case the Miami town of Kiihkayonki) and served primarily as a center for fur trading activities. The second concentration of French colonial activity was located on the lower Wabash River at Vincennes. Unlike Fort Miamis, the fort built at Vincennes eventually evolved into a small town of French settlers, many of whom made a portion of their living by farming, with the fur trade often occupying a lesser role in its residents' lives.

This chapter presents a summary of the history of these two French establishments with a review of the archaeological work that has been done at each. Although a great deal of knowledge has been gained through archaeological work at Ouiatenon, researchers have had much less success in locating intact eighteenth-century deposits at Fort Miamis and Vincennes. This is due to a large extent to the fact that unlike Ouiatenon, both Fort Miamis and French Vincennes were once located within urban neighborhoods. As a result, any remains that may have been present were most likely severely impacted by construction, demolition, and general landscape modification, making them much more difficult to identify and access. Regardless, work conducted at these sites has yielded some evidence of the French occupations with the hope that additional investigations may yield more substantial remains in the future.

HISTORY OF FORT MIAMIS/KIIHKAYONKI

Before the development of modern transportation routes, rivers were the main means of moving goods and people, and the most favored routes were those that required the least amount of overland travel. The Maumee-Wabash portage in northeastern Indiana was one of these links. Here, a short overland trek could be used to jump from the Maumee River drainage, which flows northeast into Lake Erie, to the Little River, which flows southwest into the Wabash, Ohio, and Mississippi River drainages (see figure I.2). The overland distance associated with the Maumee-Wabash portage was about nine miles, though the length varied depending on water levels and time of year. During periods of drought, for example, the distance could be up to twenty-five miles (Bicentennial Heritage Trail Committee 1994, 143). While a number of similar portages were used throughout the Great Lakes area, the Maumee-Wabash portage provided the shortest route from Lake Erie to the Mississippi River and was of great importance from both a military and economic standpoint, as it linked the French colonies in Canada to Louisiana and the various settlements and forts in between (Griswold 1917, 26, 35–36).

By the late seventeenth century, the Miami were residing at the eastern end of the portage trail, most at the village of Kiihkayonki (Kekionga). Though written records are scarce, a French post and a small garrison were also likely present there by 1697 or so under the command of Jean Baptiste Bissot, Sieur de Vincennes (Griswold 1917, 36–39; Bicentennial Heritage Trail Committee 1994, 109). The French, however, were not happy with the Miami's choice of settlement and tried to persuade them to move west to the Kankakee River, where they would be well removed from the British sphere of influence. The Miami, though, were adamant about staying put, and the French eventually gave in, deciding to build a proper fort at that location. In August 1721 Captain Louis-Jacques-Charles Dubuisson was sent to establish the fort, which was completed in May 1722 and officially named Fort St. Philippe des Miamis, though this was usually shortened to Fort Miamis in official correspondence (Barnhart and Riker 1971; Krauskopf 1953, 88–89, 93–100; Krauskopf 1955, 172).

FRENCH COLONIAL HISTORY AND ARCHAEOLOGY   83

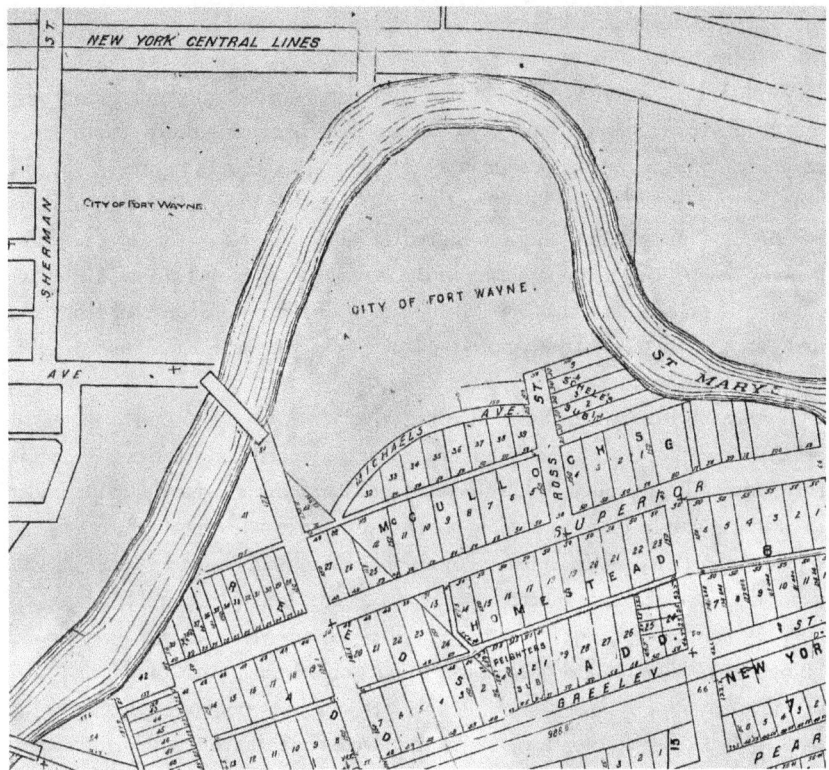

Figure 4.1. Map of Fort Wayne, 1923, showing the Guldlin Park site (south of the St. Marys River and marked "City of Fort Wayne") and neighborhood in the immediate area (Allen County Surveyor's Office 1923).

The first French fort was situated on low ground approximately half a mile downriver from the portage road. This appears to correspond more or less to the location of present-day Guldlin Park, west of downtown Fort Wayne (Ankenbruck 1972, 7; Barnhart and Riker 1971,111; Poinsatte 1976, 5; Woehrmann 1971, 2) (figure 4.1).

While there is no known map of the fort, it was reportedly of upright logs with a number of interior structures and was proclaimed in 1722 to be "one of the finest in the upper country." At the time of its completion, the garrison consisted of a commander, two cadets, a sergeant, an interpreter, and an unspecified number of soldiers. Though there is little information on the structures within the fort at any given point in time, various sources mention the presence of a barracks, a powder magazine, and a blacksmith's forge (Krauskopf 1953, 99–100, 104, 154, 194, 270; Roy 1923, 83). After its initial construction, the fort undoubtedly required repair and reconstruction on a regular basis. One such repair was made in 1732, ten years after it was built, with labor provided by *engagés* (fur company employees), who were to benefit most from its presence. The fort was also repaired in the winter of 1745 (Krauskopf 1953, 154–55, 234).

While Fort Miamis was crucial in maintaining free travel throughout trading territory claimed by France, the post played a relatively minor part in the overall fur trade economy in the Upper Country. In most years, between 250 and 300 packages of furs were shipped from the fort (Poinsatte 1976, 7). According to a 1728 document, Forts Miamis and Ouiatenon were both considered unimportant because they produced few beaver pelts, which were more desirable than other furs. Post receipts for the Upper Country in 1743 indicate that Fort Miamis' fur trade rights were leased out for 1,200 livres, about 2.5 percent of the region's total revenue for that year (Krauskopf 1953, 137; Krauskopf, 1955, 193).

In 1747, a Native American revolt against the French, brought upon by increased prices for trade goods, coupled with a feeling that the French were not treating them as partners and allies, resulted in the division of the Miamis into two factions. One, under the leadership of Le Pied Froid (Cold Foot), continued to side with the French and resided near Fort Miamis. The other, followers of La Demoiselle, favored the British, who were offering trade goods of better quality at a cheaper price (Pease and Jenison 1940, 122). In the late summer of 1747, a band of discontented Miami looted and partially burned Fort Miamis and took its eight-man garrison prisoner (Griswold 1917, 43–44; O'Callaghan 1858, 140–41, 150; White 1991, 198–99). As would be expected, the fur trade in the Upper Country was negatively impacted by the revolt, with many traders reporting heavy losses. Ensign Dubuisson, commander at the fort, spent the winter of 1747–1748 negotiating with the hostile Miami faction in order to bring them back to the French, apparently without much success. Regardless, the damaged fort was repaired, and the garrison was temporarily strengthened to thirty men (Barnhart and Riker 1971, 97; Krauskopf 1953, 255, 261, 270).

By 1749, however, the fort was reportedly again in poor condition. In September of that year Father Jean de Bonnecamps stated that when he arrived at Fort Miamis, "most of the palisades were decayed and fallen into ruin. Within there were eight houses,—or, to speak more correctly, eight miserable huts, which only the desire of making money could render endurable" (Thwaites 1896, 69, 187). At that same time, the fort was described by a captured British trader as "small, [and] stuck round with Pallisadoes," with a captain, lieutenant, and about fifty men residing within. Most of these were reportedly traders who were constantly coming and going, with only nine or ten living there on a more or less permanent basis (Barnhart and Riker 1971, 105; Griswold 1917, 52).

Charles de Raymond, who had assumed command of the fort in September 1749, reported that the majority of the Miami were ill disposed toward the French and noted that the traders were withdrawing to Detroit, as "no one is keen on staying here and having his throat cut" (Pease and Jenison 1940, 106, 119; Peyser 1997, 22). Aware of the danger, Raymond suggested that Fort Miamis be relocated about 1.3 miles to the northeast on the east bank of the St. Joseph River, which would afford a more defensible position. Arrangements for construction of a new fort began in 1750, with four *arpents* of land (about 3.4 acres) cleared to provide an open field of fire for defensive purposes (Krauskopf 1953, 326). The new fort, which was completed in 1752, was built entirely by the fur traders, with a garrison of sixteen regulars but no large guns. After its abandonment by the French, the remaining structures from the first French fort were occupied by Cold Foot and his followers, and the site became the center of a small settlement known as Cold Foot Village. Many of the villagers, however, including Cold Foot and his son, died soon after during a region-wide smallpox epidemic in 1752 (Krauskopf 1953, 321, 326, 350, 359, 372; Pease and Jenison 1940, 217; Poinsatte 1976, 9–10).

Following the September 1760 French capitulation in the French and Indian War, Fort Miamis was formally handed over to the British without incident. A report by Rangers lieutenant John Butler described the event in the following manner:

[At] ... fort Maimie I found one french officer, one serjt. And seven french Regulars and twenty-seven Canadians, the former I disarmed imidiatly, the later I administered the oath too and sent them to Detroit the next day. The fort is a good stockaded fort of 120 feet square with flankers [i.e., bastions or corner turrets] having ten houses in it all of which the french officer informd me belonged to Mr. Betales Except the Guardhouse. I found nothing there except one set of smith tools belonging to the Kings. (Butler 1762)

Formal occupation of the fort did not occur until late 1761, when an officer and fifteen men were sent to garrison each of the forts at Ouiatenon, Miamis, and St. Joseph (in southwest Michigan). Ensign Robert Holmes took command of Fort Miamis from Lieutenant Butler, and under British rule it continued to serve as a point of exchange. Fur trading resumed almost immediately. In 1761, pelts worth 140,000 livres were brought from Fort Miamis to Montreal, amounting to a little over 9 percent of the total for that year (Barnhart and Riker 1971, 133, 136, 140).

However, relations with the Miami soon went sour. This was largely due to the British air of superiority in their relations with the Native Americans and their inability to appreciate the unique commercial relationship that had been the norm during the French period. In 1763 this short-sighted policy culminated in Pontiac's Rebellion, in which a number of forts in the Great Lakes area were captured by Native Americans, including Fort Miamis. The fort was not regarrisoned after the cessation of hostilities, as the British, still seeking to reduce costs, felt that the Miami could trade instead at Detroit (Barnhart and Riker 1971, 157, 159). By 1765, Fort Miamis had fallen into disrepair and was described as a "stockade fort somewhat ruinous" containing a "runaway colony" of French who had fled Detroit during Pontiac's Rebellion. George Croghan, expressing his negative opinion of the French residents, stated that they were "a lazy, indolent people, fond of breeding mischief and spiriting up the Indians against the English, and should by no means be suffered to remain here" (Ontario 1878, 95).

The last known references to the fort include a 1769 census of the region, which lists nine individuals living within, all of whom had French surnames. A slightly later document, possibly dating to 1774, notes that the Miami live opposite the fort, which was occupied by eight or ten French families (Dunn 1894, 33, 37). The fort appears to have been abandoned shortly thereafter, as no indication of its presence is given in Normand MacLeod's and Henry Hamilton's journals of 1778 (Evans 1978, 30–67; Barnhart 1951), nor is it depicted on Major Ebenezer Denny's 1790 map of the Indian villages in the area (Denny 1860, 350). Though the fort likely ceased to exist by the late eighteenth century, numerous fur traders continued to live around and among the Miami up to and through the American period (Quaife 1921).

ARCHAEOLOGY OF THE FRENCH FORTS IN FORT WAYNE

While the "dim outlines" of the first French fort were reportedly visible as late as 1800 (Brice 1868, 13), its exact location was eventually lost to history and no contemporary maps of the fort's size, shape, or interior structures are known to exist. All these factors have made it difficult for archaeologists and historians to relocate the fort, especially within an urban setting that has seen extensive construction, demolition, and landscape modification over more than two hundred years. All sources seem to agree, however, that the first French fort was located west of downtown Fort Wayne (Brice 1868, 12–13). Some place the fort site within or immediately south of present-day Guldlin Park, on the south bank of the St. Marys River (Bicentennial Heritage Trail Committee 1994, 111; Helm 1880, 8). Others situate the fort about 950 feet farther to the southwest, within a present-day residential area (Griswold 1917, 34). Fortunately, it would appear that the area around the probable fort location has seen less development than other spots to the south and east, likely due to its low elevation and susceptibility to flooding.

The site on which Guldlin Park stands was purchased by the City of Fort Wayne in 1897, and in 1911 it became the city's first public playground (Board of Park Commissioners 1912, 61). The plan began with a public appeal for some ten thousand loads of ash and cinders to raise and level the land. Unfortunately, however, the park was in use only briefly before it was destroyed during the flood of 1913 (*Fort Wayne Journal Gazette* 1911; *Fort Wayne News* 1913, 1914). This episode, coupled with evidence from historic photographs, suggests that floodwaters have repeatedly followed the path of least resistance, flowing across the landform currently occupied by Guldlin Park. This would suggest that if the French fort was once located within the park area, any intact below-surface remains may have been washed away long ago.

It is also possible and probably more likely that the fort was originally located on somewhat higher ground south of the park. This area, located around West Superior Street, was developed in the late nineteenth and early twentieth centuries, with numerous residences eventually constructed (Andres, McCullough, and Strezewski 2008, 49) (see figure 4.1). While these homes have been demolished in recent years due to their susceptibility to flooding, ground disturbances related to their construction, use, and demolition likely adversely impacted any archaeological remains that may have been located there.

Although a number of investigations have been conducted, the archaeological remains of the first French fort have proven elusive to the present day. Shovel-testing, trenching, small excavation units, ground-penetrating radar, and resistivity surveys have been conducted within Guldlin Park proper in an attempt to locate artifacts or features related to the French fort. Unfortunately, these investigations indicate that the present surface is the result of extensive late nineteenth-century and twentieth-century infilling, shown to be greater than eight feet deep in some places. If any remains of the fort were once within the park, they are either very deeply buried or completely obliterated (Andres et al. 2008; Arnold and Graham 2013; Gaff 2007).

Testing has also been done in areas of higher elevation south and southwest of Guldlin Park. Here, it was found that most areas had experienced extensive disturbance related to later construction and demolition activities. Fortunately, some undisturbed areas were identified in the yards of former residences. While excavations recovered mostly recent materials, a small number of eighteenth-century artifacts were discovered as well, suggesting that the fort's remains may be somewhere nearby. These included a number of glass trade beads, copper/brass scrap, a lead bale seal, and a ferrous metal arrow point, typical of those fashioned by Native Americans from pieces of Euro-American metal (e.g., Strezewski et al. 2007, 159; Strezewski and McCullough 2010, 226) (figure 4.2).

Overall, the presence of fur trade–era artifacts in this area suggests that remains of the first French fort may yet be discovered one day. However, it seems that locating these remains will be difficult.

The second French fort, completed in 1752, is thought to have been located near the present-day intersection of St. Joseph Boulevard and Delaware Avenue on the eastern bank of the St. Joseph River (Griswold 1917; Krauskopf 1953, 359). No professional archaeological investigations have been conducted with the goal of ascertaining whether any remains of the fort have survived to the present day. Griswold (1917,

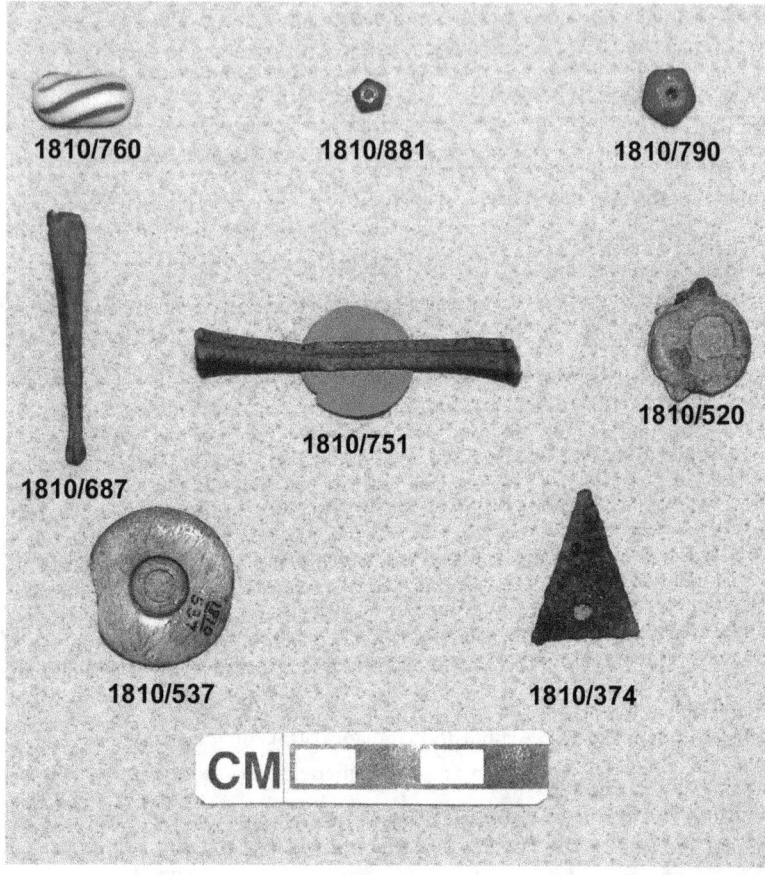

Figure 4.2. Probable eighteenth-century artifacts found during excavations near the site of Fort Miamis. Top row, glass trade beads; middle row (left to right), copper/brass aglet, copper/brass bracelet fragment, lead bale seal; bottom row (left to right), bone button and iron arrow point.

50, 52), however, reports that a number of artifacts related to its occupation were found during late nineteenth-century construction projects in the area. These items include a copper kettle, a copper box, a French medallion dated 1693, and a number of "Indian arrowheads" of unspecified type. Given the amount of later construction in this area including that of the St. Joseph River floodwall, it seems likely that most or all the archaeological deposits related to the second fort have either been destroyed or severely impacted.

HISTORY OF POST VINCENNES/ ACIIPIHKAHKIONKI

After the conclusion of Queen Anne's War in 1713, France intensified its efforts to link its two major landholdings in North America: Canada, which laid claim to the St. Lawrence River and the Great Lakes, and French Louisiana, which oversaw the greater Mississippi River drainage. The French were particularly worried about English encroachment from the east via the Ohio River valley, and the absence of a permanent French presence in this area was seen as problematic. During this time, rumors were being spread that English fur traders were circulating in the Ohio River valley and persuading Native Americans to defect (Derleth 1968, 4; Roy 1923, 88). Correspondence dated as early as 1715 indicates the desire to build a post to serve as the southwestern-most anchor for French claims in Canada (Krauskopf 1953, 62). In 1725 the Company of the Indies, which possessed a trade monopoly in Louisiana, sent a letter to the governor suggesting the construction of a post on the lower Wabash. However, a chronic lack of funds prevented this project from coming to fruition (Barnhart and Riker 1971, 78–79; Bearss 1967, 13; Derleth 1968, 4–5; Krauskopf 1953).

A few years later, however, the political will was found to begin making this new post a reality. François-Marie Bissot, Sieur de Vincennes, who had been previously posted at Forts Miamis and Ouiatenon, was sent to search for a suitable site for the new fort (Griswold 1917, 40–41; Krauskopf 1953, 63, 134). The post was to be called "Poste des Pianguichats" after the Piankashaw peoples who had been living on the lower Wabash as early as 1718 (Barnhart and Riker 1971, 67; Bearss 1967, 12; Derleth 1968, 6; Roy 1923, 95). After numerous delays, Vincennes began construction on the lower Wabash River post, which was finished by March 1733. The simple fort consisted of only two structures, Vincennes's house and a small barracks for ten soldiers surrounded by a palisade wall. Some Piankashaws were living near the fort in 1733, and they were reportedly planning to bring down the greater part of their people, who were currently residing about sixty miles upriver (Barnhart and Riker 1971, 80; Roy 1923, 92–96; Krauskopf 1953, 161–62). The village at Vincennes's post was called Aciipihkahkionki by the Piankashaw and is sometimes referred to as "Chip-kaw-kay" or "Chippecoke" in historical accounts (Ironstrack 2012; McCormick 1968).

A number of fur traders had also set up operations at the fort. Vincennes estimated that thirty thousand animal pelts could be collected here each year if the English could be prevented from interfering with the Indian trade. Vincennes's major problem, however, was a lack of trade goods (Roy 1923, 94). In the absence of goods, the Native American peoples in the vicinity would not be interested in working with him. Also lacking were funds to build other structures, including a guard house and larger barracks.

Vincennes's post was anchored by the fort, which was probably similar to those at Forts Ouiatenon and Miamis. Over the years, however, the settlement evolved into a small French village containing a number of settlers, or *habitants* (inhabitants). While deriving most of their income from the fur trade, the *habitants* also made part of their living by farming. While other similar settlements had been established in the Illinois country (e.g., Kaskaskia, Cahokia, Prairie du Rocher), this was the only such village in the Wabash River drainage. It has proven difficult to pinpoint the number of residents at any given time, as people were constantly coming and going. Population estimates vary widely, but it is likely that the growth of Vincennes was slow. In 1746 forty *habitants* and their families resided there, and by 1757 near the end of the French colonial period, the number had jumped to seventy-five, with three horse-powered mills present in the area (Thwaites 1908, 176; Wilson 1997, 12–18). In later years at least, many of the town's residents were métis, that is, children born of French fur traders and local Native American women (Peterson 1981; Wilson 1997, 43–44).

Vincennes only enjoyed a short stint as commandant of the Wabash post. In early 1736 he was ordered to assemble a force to aid in attacking the pro-British Chickasaw, who had been harassing French traders moving up and down the Mississippi River, threatening to disrupt supply lines (Bearss 1967, 17). In February 1736 Vincennes's force, consisting of 160 Piankashaw and Wea, 38 Iroquois, and the French garrison and militia from his post, arrived at Ecorce a Prudhomme near present-day Randolph, Tennessee. Learning that additional French forces were to be delayed in arriving, the decision was made to attack the Chickasaw rather than wait. This choice was to be ill-fated, as they soon encountered a much larger Chickasaw force who routed the French and their allies. Many were killed as a result, among them Sieur de Vincennes (Bearss 1967, 21–31).

After Vincennes's death, command of the post was passed to Louis Groston de Saint-Ange et de Bellerive, who was reportedly well liked by the Piankashaw. He was the son of the commandant at Fort de Chartres in Illinois and presumably had much experience with Native American relations (Barnhart and Riker 1971, 89; Krauskopf 1953, 183). St. Ange remained the post commandant for twenty-eight years, only relinquishing the office after France's defeat in the French and Indian War (Barnhart and Riker 1971, 89–90). Under St. Ange's leadership, the Piankashaw abandoned their village next to the post a number of times, further diminishing its importance as a fur trading center. This may have been a major incentive for Fort Vincennes's French residents to take up farming to supplement their income (Barnhart and Riker 1971, 109–110; Bearss 1967, 34; Krauskopf 1953, 297, 316). Supporting this view, it was often remarked in official correspondence that the post was felt to be more trouble than it was worth (in terms of fur trade revenue) but that securing the lower Wabash was deemed necessary in order to check British expansion. In 1757 only about 80 packs of furs were traded at Vincennes, compared to 250–300 at Fort Miamis and 300–400 at Fort Ouiatenon (Barnhart and Riker 1971, 94; Thwaites 1908, 176; White 1991, 229).

Though it is assumed that Fort Vincennes was repaired and modified a number of times during the decades under French administration, there are few records of these events. In 1752 during the Miami revolt against the French (described above), St. Ange enlarged the fort with small-diameter pickets to include the church, the presbytery, and shelters for the *habitants*. At the time, all the buildings within the palisade wall were described as being decayed, and the residents had difficulty securely storing provisions, as no bark could be obtained for the structures' roofs (Krauskopf 1953, 356; Pease and Jemison 1940, 485). The Piankashaw residing near the French fort had abandoned the area and had joined the pro-British Miami village at Pickawillany, Ohio (Krauskopf 1953, 339, 344, 346).

Following France's defeat in the French and Indian War, the Vincennes post became a British possession. While Forts Miamis and Ouiatenon were formally occupied by the British in December 1760, the Illinois Country (including Vincennes) was considered hostile territory due to extreme anti-British sentiment among the Native Americans. British officials planned to formally occupy Vincennes in 1763, but that same year ill will toward the British erupted into open revolt during Pontiac's Rebellion. Although many forts were seized by disaffected Native Americans during the uprising, Vincennes was spared, possibly because the English had not yet taken possession of it. British control finally came in 1765, though no garrison was assigned to the fort, as Vincennes was felt to be too distant from the region's main military establishment, Fort de Chartres, located near present-day Prairie du Rocher, Illinois (Barnhart and Riker 1971, 156; Bearss 1967, 49–51).

In 1766 Lieutenant John Rumsey of the 42nd Royal Highlanders arrived in Vincennes, made repairs to the old French fort (rechristening it Fort Sackville), and soon departed for Detroit, leaving administration of the town to its residents (Somes 1962, 56). This period of self-governance continued through the 1770s. Though documentary evidence is absent, it would appear that the rehabilitated but unoccupied French fort/Fort Sackville soon declined again into disrepair. When Captain Thomas Hutchins visited Vincennes in 1769, he did not mention the presence of a fort, a fact that Bearss (1967, 55) suggests is an indication that what remained of the French fort had fallen apart or had otherwise been salvaged.

It was not until 1777 that the documentary sources again mention the presence of a fort in Vincennes. In April of that year, British lieutenant governor Edward Abbott was sent to Vincennes. Upon his arrival and "having no fort," he erected a stockade around the two-story cabin in which he was residing, also naming it Fort Sackville. The new fort, which was constructed by the Vincennes militia, was completed in the fall. It consisted of a simple eleven-foot-high palisade wall, roughly square, with "salient angles" (i.e., projections) along the midpoint of each wall (Barnhart and Riker 1971, 180, 186; Bearss 1967, 62, 117). This fort was captured by George Rogers Clark's American forces in February 1779 and renamed Fort Patrick Henry. By 1786, however, all the fort-related structures had been demolished, and in 1803 the site of the former French fort/Fort Sackville was platted for industrial and residential use (Bearss 1967, 136; Burns 1929, 440; Jaeger Company 2008, 21).

Soon after the demolition of the former Fort Sackville, the first American fort, Fort Knox (1787), was built. This fort, however, was constructed to the northeast of the former fort sites, near the corner of present-day Buntin and First Streets (Watts 1966, 56). Fort Knox was occupied through 1803, after which it was relocated to a spot 3.5 miles northeast of the original French fort site (known today as "Fort Knox II") (Gray 1988). Later in 1813, the second Fort Knox was disassembled and floated downriver, to be reerected at or near the site of the original French fort/Fort Sackville. This last fort, now referred to as Fort Knox III, was reportedly about 82.5 by 165 feet in size, with a palisade wall 12 to 15 feet high. Fort Knox III was only occupied for a short period, and at the conclusion of the War of 1812, the fort was abandoned. With the termination of the perceived threats from Native Americans and the British, there was no further need for a military presence in Vincennes, and the town no longer held the strategic significance it once had (Bearss 1967, 268; Tomak 1972, 14; Watts 1949, 237).

ARCHAEOLOGY OF THE VINCENNES FORTS

Like Fort Miamis, the spot where Vincennes's French fort once stood eventually became part of the present-day city. A number of commercial buildings were built in the area, including a pork packing house, a cooper shop, a hotel, and various outbuildings (Sanborn-Perris Map Co. 1892, map no. 2; Sanborn Map Co. 1902) (figure 4.3).

As a result, the area undoubtedly experienced considerable construction, demolition, and earthmoving over the years, activities that almost certainly have negatively impacted the archaeological remains of the French fort and all subsequent forts built in the immediate vicinity. In 1931, the fort site was incorporated into the twenty-six-acre George Rogers Clark National Historic Park. Construction of the park and monument, which was completed in 1933, involved substantial ground disturbance. During that time existing structures were razed, low spots were filled in, and the area was covered with varying amounts of fill dirt in order to level the terrain and cover over historic features such as cisterns, streets, and structural foundations (Bearss 1970, 106; Jaeger 2008, 23–28).

While the exact location of the French fort/Fort Sackville has been the object of speculation for some time, there is no one source that precisely identifies either of the fort

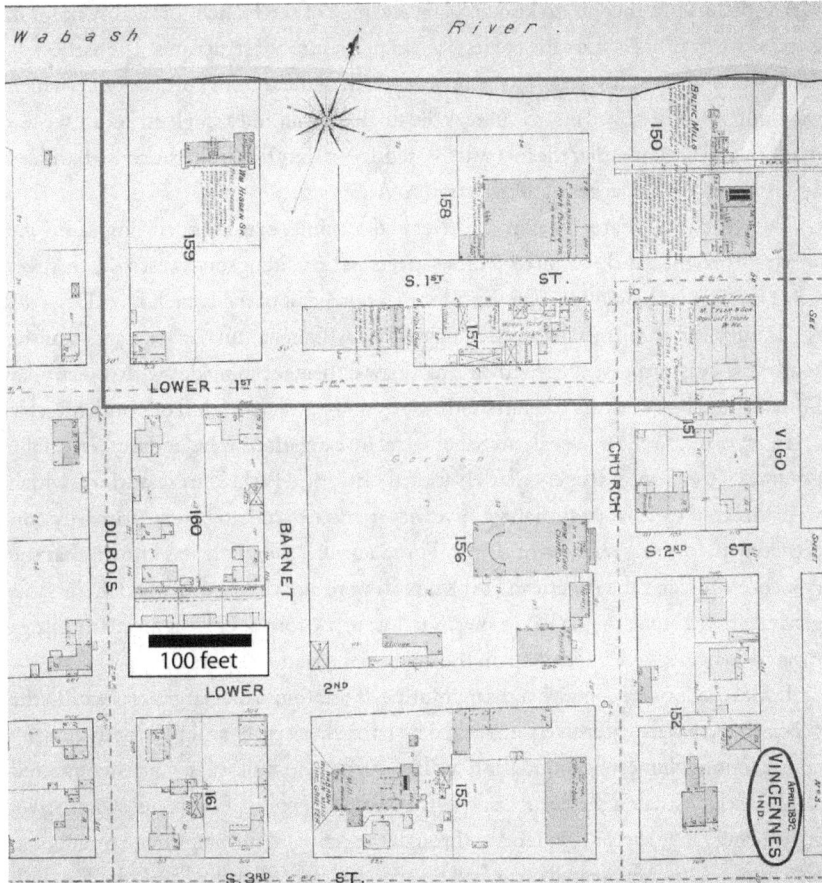

Figure 4.3. Sanborn Fire Insurance 1892 map of Vincennes, Indiana, showing buildings once located in the area where the French fort, Fort Sackville, and Fort Knox III were situated. The limits of the present-day George Rogers Clark National Historic Park are outlined.

locations relative to present-day ground features (Bearss 1967, 133; Tomak 1972, 12–13). Contemporary descriptions, however, generally agree that they were located southwest of present-day Vigo Street. In 1816 Robert Buntin, a surveyor and resident of Vincennes, produced a map that shows the location of the French fort/Fort Sackville and Fort Knox III, both of which are within the present-day grounds of the George Rogers Clark National Historical Park (Watts 1966, 56). All later researchers scouring the historic documents for evidence agree that the forts were likely located in this area, more specifically in the grassy area immediately northeast of the George Rogers Clark memorial building (e.g., Bearss 1967, 38; Cauthorn 1902, 17; Greene 1911, 72; Jaeger Company 2008).

Unfortunately, there is no known planview map of the French fort at any point in time, so we have little or no idea of its size, shape, or interior structures. The earliest depiction of one of the forts is a 1778 planview sketch of the second Fort Sackville, which was built by the British. This map shows the stockade wall and a single structure within its limits and indicates that the fort was located about sixty feet from the river (Barnhart and Riker 1971, 186; Jaeger 2008, illustration A).

The French village area lay along the river in the vicinity of the fort, encompassing the area from present-day Busseron to Willow Streets and extending southwest to Sixth Street, while the Piankashaw village was likely located northeast of the French fort (Day 1988, 15). Though not confirmed by archaeological means, Greene (1911, 27) suggests that the southwest and northeast edges of the Piankashaw settlement coincided with present-day Busseron and Perry Streets and ran southeast from the river to Eighth or Ninth Streets.

In 1970 and 1971, large-scale archaeological investigations were undertaken on the grounds of the George Rogers Clark National Historical Park. The excavations, which were directed by various Indiana University graduate students, were primarily concerned with locating remains of British Fort Sackville, though it was known that the French-era fort and the American Fort Knox III were most likely also found in the same general area (Tomak 1972, 1). As a means to locate the fort, a series of mechanically excavated trenches were opened up on the memorial grounds (figure 4.4).

Initial results were somewhat disappointing. It was found that large areas within the park property were extensively disturbed by later nineteenth- and twentieth-century construction. Numerous foundation walls, cisterns, and walkways were encountered, all of which postdated the occupation of the forts. A portion of the former First Street right-of-way that had once extended through the center of the memorial grounds was also found. Other excavated areas had been completely disturbed and filled in with sand, gravel, or both to various depths (Tomak 1972, 17).

Fortunately, portions of the park grounds were found to have intact archaeological remains related to the period of interest. The most notable of these were two long palisade wall segments, designated Wall A and Wall B. Both ran in a northwest-southeast direction perpendicular to the Wabash River shoreline and parallel to one another. Wall A was traced for a total of 162 feet. It was disturbed, however, in a number of spots by more recent construction, and the excavators could not be certain that all of the Wall A sections were in fact parts of a single wall. Wall A consisted of a trench that had once contained wooden posts. The trench was about 2.0–2.5 feet wide on the northern end, narrowing to about 1.0 foot on the south end. Each of the posts within the trench was between 5 and 9.5 inches in diameter and extended about 2.0 feet below the level of the trench. The trench was not completely straight; rather, it jogged to the west about midway through. This may be part of a corner bastion or one of the "salient angles" mentioned in the 1778 descriptions of Fort Sackville.

FRENCH COLONIAL HISTORY AND ARCHAEOLOGY

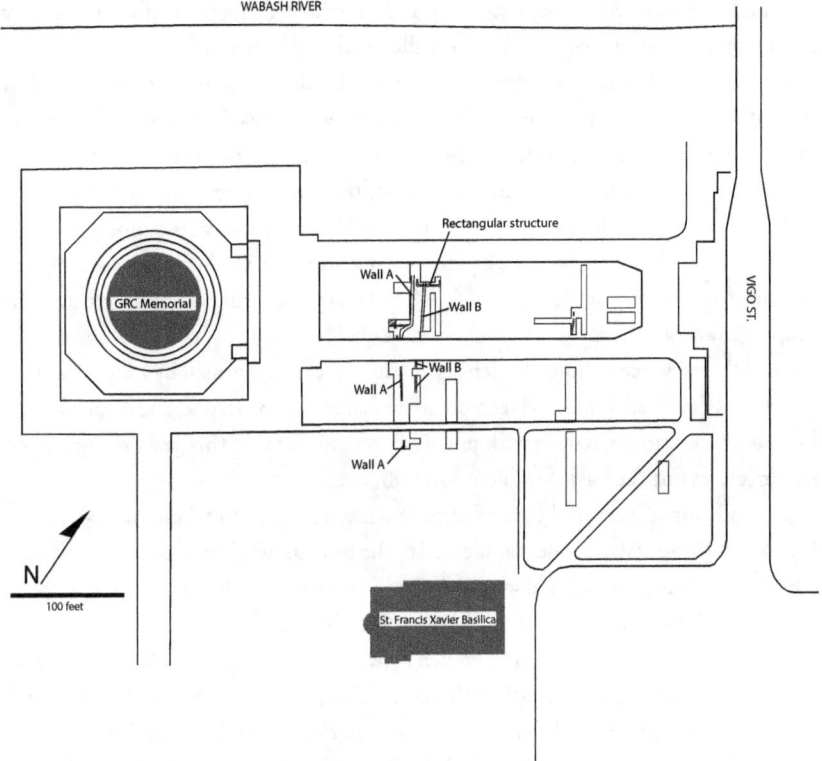

Figure 4.4. Map of fort-related features identified during Tomak's (1972) excavations within the limits of the George Rogers Clark National Historic Park.

Unfortunately, relatively few artifacts were found in association with Wall A that could be used to date its construction. One of these was a piece of pearlware likely dating to the late eighteenth or early nineteenth century. Other artifacts include a plain creamware sherd, likely dating to the 1760–1810 period; a creamware sherd with a "tortoiseshell" design dating to 1750–1775; and a number of small "seed beads" (i.e., tiny glass trade beads) dating to ca. 1760–1820 (Quimby 1966, 87–88). Though evidence is slim, the presence of these artifacts suggests that Wall A may be a portion of Fort Sackville or possibly the American Fort Knox III, which was built in 1813 and abandoned in 1816 (Tomak 1972).

The second of the two wall segments, Wall B, was located to the east of Wall A. Wall B was also disturbed in spots by later construction. The trench making up the wall was traced for a total of 102 feet and was from 1.0 to 2.0 feet wide, extending from 1.0 to 3.0 feet below the original ground surface. Like Wall A, Wall B also contained posts; in this case, the posts were mostly between 6 and 7 inches in diameter. Unfortunately, few cultural materials were recovered from Wall B, making it rather difficult to date its construction. The only artifacts of note were two seed beads, which, as noted above, date to the post-1760 period. Given this, we can tentatively state that Wall B is likely not part of the original French fort, but little else can be said regarding its age (Tomak 1972, 37).

Nickel (2002, 9) has suggested that some of these wall segments may be related to picket fences surrounding late eighteenth- or early nineteenth-century homes once located in this area rather than one or more of the known forts. Such fences were common in ethnic-French settlements such as Ste. Genevieve, Missouri, and were used for keeping grazing animals out of the house lot (Eckberg 1996, 284–85; Peterson 2001, 10–11). The presence of house lot fences in Vincennes is confirmed by a 1796 observer who stated that "each house, as is customary in Canada, stands alone, and is surrounded by a court and garden, fenced with poles" (Bearss 1967, 229). This practice continued in Vincennes until at least 1817 (Peterson 1981, 174).

An additional excavated feature of note was a portion of a rectangular structure found just east of Wall A and parallel to it. The only intact part of the structure consisted of the southeast wall and small portions of two other walls; unfortunately, the remainder of the structure was completely disturbed by later construction. Evidence indicates that it was constructed in the French *poteaux-en-terre* style. The intact wall from the structure was 23 feet in length with a total of 48 postmolds identified, each placed between 1.0 and 1.5 feet in the ground. Unfortunately, few artifacts were found in association with the structure. These included a few pieces of glass, two handwrought nails, and half a dozen glass seed beads. Though information is sparse, our best guess is that the structure may date to the later eighteenth or early nineteenth century. Just south of the structure, a small pit feature was identified containing charred corncobs, brass fragments, and three .55-caliber musket balls (Tomak 1972, 29). Other features of note include a few short segments of overlapping wall trenches, most of which were found in the western edge of the excavated area. Again, artifacts were few, though these features may to be related to the fort-era occupation of the vicinity (Tomak 1972, 39–40, 43).

The only area of the excavation that produced a fair quantity of eighteenth-century artifacts was identified during "general digging" in the easternmost trench, close to present-day Vigo Street. Materials found here included glass trade beads, bone and shell buttons, French tin-glazed *faience*, redware ceramics, and British and French gunflints (Tomak 1972, 52–61). In general, these artifacts are consistent with a date between circa 1775 and 1800. This suspicion is confirmed by measurement of the bore diameters of the white clay pipe stems found in the deposit, suggesting an assemblage dating between 1720 and 1800 in keeping with the French/British/American forts (Deetz 1996, 28).

Overall, the 1970s excavations on the park grounds suggest the presence of intact archaeological remains related to the eighteenth-century occupation of the general area. Unfortunately, it would appear that a great deal of these remains were disturbed by later construction during the nineteenth and early twentieth centuries. This disturbance continued through the period of the memorial's construction in the 1930s, which involved substantial earthmoving (e.g., Nickel 2002, fig. 3). Ironically, this activity may have destroyed the archaeological remains of the fort that the memorial was (in part) built to memorialize. Unfortunately, the George Rogers Clark memorial was built during a time when the archaeological remains of historic sites were not considered of great importance. While the excavations indicate that it is quite likely that intact remains related to the fort era are still to be found within the limits of memorial grounds, the presence of substantial amounts of fill dirt covering the archaeological remains and the extensive disturbance of the fort sites will make it difficult to locate additional deposits of interest. Since the 1970–1971 excavations, a number of other archaeological investigations have been conducted in and around the immediate area, most of which were related to minor construction-related projects on the memorial grounds (e.g., Bringelson 2010; Kaufmann et al. 2012; Kellar 1975; Nickel 2002, 7–9; Ruby 1997). No archaeological investigations, however, have yet identified any additional fort-related remains.

Though a fair amount of effort has been expended in attempting to locate the archaeological remains of Fort Miamis and French Vincennes, we have been largely unsuccessful in identifying intact features related to these two important sites. In each case as noted above, this is mostly due to the fact that the former fort sites are within and surrounded by modern development. The French recognized these well-situated landforms when choosing a place to build their forts, and, unfortunately so did others who came after them. Consequently, the fact that Fort Ouiatenon has escaped this fate makes it all that more important in telling the story of the fur trade period in the Great Lakes area.

Most authors (e.g., Bearss 1967) place the origin of the name "Fort Sackville" with Abbott's 1777 construction of a palisade wall around his residence, a fortification that was later modified and strengthened by Governor Henry Hamilton. Others (e.g., Greene 1911, 10; Somes 1962, 56) mention that the name originated in 1766 when Lieutenant Rumsey (also cited as Ramsey) of the 42nd Royal Highlanders repaired the French fort and rechristened it Fort Sackville. Unfortunately, neither of the above sources provides a citation for the original document from which this information was gathered, making it difficult to verify. However, Harold Allison, local historian and columnist for the *Washington Times Herald*, saw the original document on Rumsey's 1766 fort reconstruction in a private collection in the 1970s and made notes as to its contents (Harold Allison, pers. comm., August 2016). Unfortunately, the document has never been published, and its current whereabouts are unknown. Allison published a newspaper column on Rumsey's visit to Vincennes (Allison 2016). The reported presence of the 42nd Royal Highlanders in Vincennes in 1766 matches well with the documented deployments of this unit, which is known to have been present in the Ohio River vicinity and at Fort de Chartres during the 1765–1766 period before being ordered back to Great Britain in 1767 (Wauchope 1908, 14–15).

REFERENCES

Allen County Surveyor's Office. 1923. Map of the City of Fort Wayne Indiana. https://archive.org/details/mapofcityoffort00alle.

Allison, Harold. 2016. "Clark's Capture of Fort Sackville Has Significance." *Washington Times Herald*, April 28.

Andres, Christopher R., Dorothea McCullough, and Michael Strezewski. 2008. "Intensive Survey of the Forts of Fort Wayne, Allen County, Indiana." Reports of Investigations 801. Fort Wayne: Indiana University–Purdue University Fort Wayne Archaeological Survey.

Ankenbruck, John. 1972. *Five Forts*. Fort Wayne, IN: Lion's Head.

Arnold, Craig R., and Colin Graham. 2013. "Intensive Investigations at Three Contact Era Locales in Northeast Indiana." Reports of Investigations 1302. Fort Wayne: Indiana University–Purdue University Fort Wayne Archaeological Survey.

Barnhart, John D., ed. 1951. *Henry Hamilton and George Rogers Clark in the American Revolution with the Unpublished Journal of Lieut. Gov. Henry Hamilton*. Crawfordsville, IN: R. E. Banta.

Barnhart, John D., and Dorothy L. Riker. 1971. *Indiana to 1816: The Colonial Period*. Indianapolis: Indiana Historical Bureau and Indiana Historical Society.

Bearss, Edwin C. 1967. *George Rogers Clark and the Winning of the Old Northwest*. Washington, DC: National Park Service, US Department of the Interior.

———. 1970. *George Rogers Clark Memorial Historic Structures Report Historical Data*. Washington, DC: National Park Service, Division of History, US Department of the Interior.

Bicentennial Trail Heritage Committee. 1994. "On the Heritage Trail, Fort Wayne, Indiana: A Walking Guide to the Fort Wayne Heritage Trail." Fort Wayne: ARCH and the Essex Group.

Board of Park Commissioners. 1912. "8th Annual Report." Fort Wayne, IN.

Brice, Wallace A. 1868. *History of Fort Wayne, from the Earliest Known Accounts of This Point, to the Present Period*. Fort Wayne: D. W. Jones and Son.

Bringelson, Dawn. 2010. *Archaeological Monitoring for Proposed Utility Upgrades, George Rogers Clark National Historical Park, Knox County, Indiana*. Lincoln: National Park Service, Midwest Archaeological Center.

Burns, Lee. 1929. "Life in Old Vincennes." *Indiana Historical Society Publications* 8, no. 9: 437–60.

Butler, John. 1762. "January 1st, 1762 Letter Regarding the Details of Taking Possession of Forts Miamis and Ouiatenon for the British." The National Archives, War Office 34/90, Kew, United Kingdom.

Cauthorn, Henry S. 1902. *A History of the City of Vincennes, Indiana from 1702 to 1901*. Terre Haute, IN: Moore and Langen.
Day, Richard. 1988. *Vincennes, a Pictorial History*. St. Louis: G. Bradley Publishing.
Deetz, James. 1996. *In Small Things Forgotten: An Archaeology of Early American Life*. 2nd ed. New York: Anchor Books.
Denny, Ebenezer. 1860. "Military Journal of Major Ebenezer Denny." *Memoirs of the Historical Society of Pennsylvania* 7: 205–498.
Derleth, August. 1968. *Vincennes: Portal to the West*. Englewood Cliffs, NJ: Prentice-Hall.
Dunn, Jacob Piatt. 1894. "Documents Relating to the French Settlements on the Wabash." *Indiana Historical Society Publications* 2(11).
Eckberg, Carl J. 1996. *Colonial Ste. Genevieve*. 2nd ed. Tucson: Patrice.
Evans, William A., ed. 1978. *Detroit to Fort Sackville, 1778–1779: The Journal of Normand MacLeod*. Detroit: Wayne State University Press.
Fort Wayne Journal Gazette. 1911. "Wanted—Ten Thousand Loads of Ashes for Playground." February 26.
Fort Wayne News. 1913. "Getting Playgrounds Ready." May 1.
———. 1914. "What Is the Matter with Guldlin Playground?" June 24.
Gaff, Donald. 2007. "Archaeological Testing at Guldlin Park, City of Fort Wayne, Allen County, Indiana." Report on file, Indiana Department of Natural Resources, Division of Historic Preservation and Archaeology.
Gray, Marlesa A. 1988. "The Archaeological Investigations of Fort Knox II." Research Reports No. 9. Glenn A. Black Laboratory of Archaeology, Indiana University, Bloomington.
Greene, George E. 1911. *History of Old Vincennes and Knox County, Indiana*. Chicago: S. J. Clarke.
Griswold, B. J. 1917. *The Pictorial History of Fort Wayne, Indiana*. 2 vols. Chicago: Robert O. Law.
Ironstrack, George. 2012. "The Crooked Trail to Pickawillany (1747–1752)." https://aacimot aatiiyankwi.org/2012/04/19/the-crooked-trail-to-pickawillany-1747-1752/.
Jaeger Company. 2008. "George Rogers Clark National Historical Park, Vincennes, Indiana." Cultural Landscape Report/Environmental Assessment, submitted to the US National Park Service, Washington, DC.
Kaufmann, Kira E., Timothy Schilling, Michael J. Hambacher, and Katherine A. Guidi. 2012. "George Rogers Clark Park Phase I and II Archaeological Investigations Knox County, Indiana (GERO 157423)." Report submitted to the US National Park Service, Denver, Colorado.
Kellar, James H. 1975. "George Rogers Clark National Monument Interpretive Center Construction: Archaeological Report." Glenn A. Black Laboratory of Archaeology. Lincoln: National Park Service, Midwest Archaeological Center, Lincoln.
Krauskopf, Frances. 1953. "The French in Indiana, 1700–1760: A Political History." PhD diss., Indiana University.
———. 1955. *Ouiatanon Documents*. Indianapolis: Indiana Historical Society.

McCormick, Mary Anne. 1968. *Ouiatanon: A Detailed Description and History, Trade and Ordinance Lists*. Manuscript on file, Glenn A. Black Laboratory of Archaeology, Indiana University, Bloomington.

Nickel, Robert K. 2022. *An Archaeological Overview and Assessment of George Rogers Clark National Historical Park*. Technical Report No. 83. Lincoln: Midwest Archaeological Center.

O'Callaghan, E. B., ed. 1858. *Documents Relative to the Colonial History of the State of New York; Procured in Holland, England, and France*. Vol. 10. Albany, NY: Weed, Parsons.

Ontario, Province of. 1878. *Statutes, Documents and Papers Bearing on the Discussion Respecting the Northern and Western Boundaries of the Province of Ontario*. Toronto: Hunter, Rose.

Pease, Theodore C., and Ernestine Jenison, eds. 1940. *Illinois on the Eve of the Seven Years' War, 1747–1755*. Collections of the Illinois State Historical Library, Vol. 29. Springfield: Illinois State Historical Library.

Peterson, Charles E. 2001. *Colonial St. Louis: Building a Creole Capital*. Tucson: Patrice.

Peterson, Jacqueline L. 1981. "The People in Between: Indian-White Marriage and the Genesis of a Métis Society and Culture in the Great Lakes Region, 1680–1830." PhD diss., University of Illinois.

Peyser, Joseph L. 1997. *On the Eve of the Conquest: The Chevalier de Raymond's Critique of New France in 1754*. East Lansing: Michigan State University Press.

Poinsatte, Charles. 1976. *Outpost in the Wilderness: Fort Wayne, 1706–1828*. Fort Wayne: Allen County Fort Wayne Historical Society.

Quaife, Milo M. 1921. "Fort Wayne in 1790." *Indiana Historical Society Publications* 7, no. 7: 295–361.

Quimby, George I. 1966. *Indian Culture and European Trade Goods*. Madison: University of Wisconsin Press.

Roy, Pierre-Georges. 1923. "Sieur de Vincennes Identified." *Indiana Historical Society Publications* 7, no. 1: 81–105.

Ruby, Bret J. 1997. *Plan for an Archaeological Reconnaissance of Properties within the Boundaries of George Rogers Clark National Historical Park, Vincennes, Knox County, Indiana*. Plan and field notes on file, National Park Service, George Rogers Clark National Historical Park, Vincennes, Indiana.

Sanborn Map Co. 1902. *Insurance Maps of Vincennes, Knox County, Indiana*. New York: Sanborn Map.

Sanborn-Perris Map Co. 1892. *Vincennes, Indiana, Knox Co*. New York: Sanborn-Perris Map.

Somes, Joseph H. V. 1962. *Old Vincennes: The History of a Famous Old Town and Its Glorious Past*. New York: Graphic Books.

Strezewski, Michael, and Robert G. McCullough. 2010. "Report of the 2009 Archaeological Investigations at Three Fur Trade–Era Sites in Tippecanoe County, Indiana: Kethtippecanunk (12-T-59), Fort Ouiatenon (12-T-9), and a Kickapoo-Mascouten Village (12-T-335)." Reports of Investigations 903. Fort Wayne: Indiana University–Purdue University Fort Wayne Archaeological Survey.

Strezewski, Michael, Robert G. McCullough, Dorothea McCullough, Craig Arnold, and Joshua J. Wells. 2007. "Report of the 2006 Archaeological Investigations at Kethtippecanunk (12-T-59), Tippecanoe County, Indiana. Reports of Investigations 703." Fort Wayne: Indiana University–Purdue University Fort Wayne Archaeological Survey.

Thwaites, Reuben Gold, ed. 1896. *The Jesuit Relations and Allied Documents*, Vol. 69. Cleveland, OH: Burrows Brothers.

———. 1908. *Collections of the State Historical Society of Wisconsin*, Vol. 18. Madison: State Historical Society of Wisconsin.

Tomak, Curtis H. 1972. *Archaeological Investigations at the George Rogers Clark National Historical Park, Vincennes, Indiana*. Report on file at the Indiana Department of Natural Resources, Division of Historic Preservation and Archaeology, Indianapolis.

Watts, Florence G. 1949. "The Death of a Legend." *Indiana Magazine of History* 45, no. 3: 233–48.

———. 1966. "Fort Knox: Frontier Outpost on the Wabash." *Indiana Magazine of History* 62, no. 1: 51–78.

Wauchope, Arthur G. 1908. *A Short History of the Black Watch (Royal Highlanders), 1725–1907*. Edinburgh, UK: William Blackwood and Sons.

White, Richard. 1991. *The Middle Ground: Indians, Empires, and Republics in the Great Lakes Region, 1650–1815*. Cambridge: Cambridge University Press.

Wilson, Denise M. 1997. "Vincennes: From French Colonial Village to American Frontier Town, 1730–1820." PhD diss., West Virginia University.

Woehrmann, Paul. 1971. *At the Headwaters of the Maumee: A History of Fort Wayne, Indiana*. Indianapolis: Indiana Historical Society.

PART II

ARTIFACT STUDIES

5

USE OF ANIMALS AT FORT OUIATENON

TERRANCE J. MARTIN, CURATOR EMERITUS OF
ANTHROPOLOGY, ILLINOIS STATE MUSEUM

THIS CHAPTER IS A SUMMARY OF A MUCH LARGER WORK IN WHICH ANImal exploitation on the eighteenth-century French frontier in North America was investigated by means of predictions of available animal resources, site catchment analysis, and identification and analysis of animal remains that were recovered during six years of excavations at the site of Fort Ouiatenon by the Michigan State University (MSU) Museum. These efforts culminated in a characterization of French colonial frontier subsistence strategies involving local animal resources in the central Wabash River valley (Martin 1986). Comparison of the pattern discerned for Fort Ouiatenon to zooarchaeological assemblages at other well-studied contemporaneous French regime sites permits examination of factors that may account for similarities and differences, such as environmental setting, site function, class and ethnic composition, and intensity of culture contact with local Native American groups. Forts Ouiatenon and St. Joseph (in southwestern Michigan) were similar in that both sites actively participated in the fur trade and experienced close interaction with their respective local Native American allies. Both sites functioned as "local distribution centers" (Tordoff 1983). In contrast, post-1730 Fort Michilimackinac and Fort de Chartres functioned as "regional distribution centers" in that both served as administrative centers, had more formal military installations, and maintained fewer intimate contacts with local Native American populations (Martin 1991a; Tordoff 1983).

Reviews of the historical background of Fort Ouiatenon and summaries of previous archaeological investigations of the site have been presented elsewhere (Moussette and Waselkov 2013, 341–43; Noble 1991; Strezewski and McCullough 2019; chapter 2, this volume). Excavations in 1968 and 1969 by James Kellar (1970) confirmed the location of Fort Ouiatenon. Three seasons of excavations by the MSU Museum were directed by Judith Tordoff (1980, 1983) between 1974 and 1976, and this work delineated parts of the stockade wall, exposed numerous other features, and eventually relocated Kellar's block excavation. This was immediately followed by three additional seasons of excavations by the MSU Museum that were directed by Vergil Noble (1983) between 1977 and 1979 in the northern half of the site. These later investigations revealed another stockade wall along with additional features and discrete activity areas.

Although the Euro-American presence has been the primary focus for studies of Fort Ouiatenon, there were as many as five large and separate Native villages that together made up the greater Ouiatenon community (Sleeper-Smith 2018, 58; chapter 3, this volume). Whereas the Wea was the dominant Native group, others periodically included the Mascouten, Kickapoo, and Piankeshaw (Jones 1988; Sleeper-Smith 2018, 58; Strezewski and McCullough 2019, 55; Trubowitz 1992). The culmination of the French and Indian War in 1760 resulted in the end of the French regime in the Wabash River valley. Pontiac's Rebellion terminated a brief British occupation in 1763 (Strezewski and McCullough 2019, 56). Sleeper-Smith (2018, 137) reported that Native Americans at Ouiatenon allowed the fort to disintegrate, with most of the Euro-American fur traders moving upriver to the ethnically mixed trading village of Kethtippecanuck. In light of these historical events, the question of temporal changes in local subsistence and animal procurement is of interest. Does Fort Ouiatenon's archaeological record reflect political and demographic changes at Ouiatenon? Are there any indications of depleting animal resources?

ENVIRONMENTAL SETTING AND RESOURCE POTENTIAL

Tippecanoe County, Indiana, has a humid, continental, and temperate climate (Ulrich et al. 1959, 3–4) and is located within a physiographic zone referred to as the Tipton Till Plain (Schneider 1966, 42). The terrain consists of gently rolling uplands, steep hillsides, rich alluvial river bottoms, and level till plains (Gorby 1886, 61). The most pronounced topographic relief is north of West Lafayette, where steep, highly dissected slopes mark the transition between the till plain and the Wabash River bottom (Ulrich et al. 1959, 3). The valley transforms from being narrow with precipitous bluffs to being over ten km wide, with well-rounded, gently sloping bluffs (McBeth 1902, 237; Neill and Tharp 1907, 785). Coincidently, the location of Ouiatenon historically marked the transition to deepwater navigation downstream on the Wabash River (Lindley 1916, 7;

Sleeper-Smith 2018, 137). The Wea Plain is a prominent landform on the south side of the Wabash River, a second terrace that rises twelve to twenty-four meters above the low alluvial first terrace bottomlands and extends five to thirteen km back from the river (Gorby 1886, 67; Neill and Tharp 1907, 786). There are at least ten tributary streams to the Wabash in the area, including the Tippecanoe River and Wild Cat Creek.

The most detailed accounts of local plant communities for the various vegetation zones in the vicinity of Fort Ouiatenon are by Ulrich et al. (1959) and Petty and Jackson (1966). The differences in their respective scenarios seem to reflect descriptions of different forest succession stages in the central Wabash River valley. Although the site is located within the Beech-Maple Forest Region (Braun 1950), the Prairie Peninsula section of the Northern Oak-Hickory Forest Region is just to the north (Transeau 1935). Early descriptions indicate that except for the tallgrass prairie in northwestern Indiana, the Tipton Till Plain was heavily forested, and the Neo-Boreal climatic episode (1300–1800 CE) was responsible for cooler and moister conditions (Petty and Jackson 1966, 268). Lindsey, Crankshaw, and Qadir (1965, 162) suspected that early floodplain forests resembled the mesic beech-maple association much more than the oak-hickory forest that is indicated on early maps. The transitional vegetation between the beech-maple association and prairie consisted of oak-hickory forests and oak openings, but fire may have been important in determining the vegetation in many areas (Anderson and Brown 1983; Potzger, Potzger, and McCormick 1956).

For the purpose of constructing a model of faunal resource use for the central Wabash River valley near Fort Ouiatenon, a circular site territory of 38.8 km^2 (15 mi^2) was employed. This does not imply that inhabitants of Fort Ouiatenon restricted acquisition of animals to this territory but does provide a way to determine how selective hunters and trappers were in procuring various animals in their local environmental setting (B. Smith 1979). Fort Ouiatenon was located relatively close to many resource zones, especially the vast Wea Plain terrace, which makes up 37 percent of the defined site territory. Bottomland forest composes 29 percent. Other resource zones consisted of well-drained upland forest (12.5 %), forested terrace (9%), slopes (7%), poorly drained upland forest (2%), the Wabash River (2%), and wet upland prairie (1%). A brief summary of the environmental setting presented by Trubowitz (1992, 245–47) included Frances King's assessment that the many miniature prairie-forest ecotones on the floodplain made the area near Ouiatenon one of the richest areas for obtaining wild food resources.

Several early travelers, including Jacques-Charles de Sabrevois in 1718, Thomas Hutchins in 1762, and George Croghan in 1765, commented on the early French settlements on the Wabash. The "extensive natural meadow" that we know as the Wea Plain was across the river where one of five local Native villages was located. The extensive upland prairie was visited by herds of bison during the early summer, and these provided local Native populations with robes for the fur trade and meat for their large villages. Based on various early eighteenth-century accounts, Belue (1996, 160) opined that "certainly there were once thousands [of bison] there" in Indiana prior to the early 1800s. White-tailed deer, black bear, and other wild game were also said to be abundant in adjacent upland and bottomland forests (Krauskoft 1955, 161–62; McCord 1970, 11–12, 20–21; Sleeper-Smith 2018, 59, 137). According to naturalist David Thomas, bison were no longer present by the early nineteenth century, but wapiti could still be found in some places. He also noted that wild turkeys, geese, and ducks were abundant; greater prairie chickens inhabited the prairie during the winter; and pelicans, swans, and sandhill cranes were common migrants. Thomas observed that fish in the Wabash River were plentiful and of diverse species and that freshwater mussels were so abundant that they were gathered and the shells burned for lime (Lindley 1916, 118). The occasional entries of beef, bacon, and venison in the payment vouchers sent by the various fort commandants to Montreal prior to 1761 are the only mentions of subsistence practices for Fort Ouiatenon. Cattle, swine, and horses were undoubtedly present at the fort, but historical documents do not imply that livestock was the staple source of meat.

Several studies have demonstrated the utility of applying research by wildlife ecologists to provide information on animal populations that is pertinent for precontact situations (Keene 1981; Munson, Parmalee, and Yarnell 1971; Reidhead 1981; Smith 1975; Styles 1981). Following these approaches, estimates of animal densities, potential annual yields, and annual effective biomass were calculated for twenty-four species or groups of animals formerly present near Fort Ouiatenon (Martin 1986, 75). Some estimates in the model are more speculative than others, especially for migratory waterfowl and passenger pigeons, and bison and wapiti are problematic because these large mammals were extirpated from the region at an early date, and their respective behaviors and ecological patterns in the rich deciduous forest biome east of the Mississippi River is poorly understood. Factors affecting hunting and trapping of animal populations by human groups include biological potential and reproductive rate of a species, size of the prey species in terms of edible meat per individual, the relative ease of capture, and seasonal peaks in density levels (Smith 1975, 137–38).

Aquatic habitats offer the highest total animal biomass for the Fort Ouiatenon resource model. Fish and waterfowl are obvious first-line animal resources because they can be harvested annually in virtually unlimited numbers, and fish can be efficiently captured. Although beavers, river otters, and other mustelid species were important for the fur trade, these aquatic mammals would be quickly depleted in an area if heavily hunted and trapped. Whereas riverine turtles were abundant, they require considerable labor to capture and process. Forests were the primary habitats for many animals, but only white-tailed deer qualify as a first-line prey species due to their abundance, relatively large size, and predictably high seasonal densities over relatively small geographical areas. Black bears are perceived as a secondary prey species due to their low reproductive rate, lower abundance, high mobility, less sociable manner, and hostile temperament (Styles 1981, 86). Wapiti would have been an important supplemental species, but their availability is unknown. Raccoons and wild turkeys are the only medium-sized animals having attributes as first-line prey species. Small animals native to forest habitats that were likely exploited as supplementary resources include passenger pigeons, eastern box turtles, eastern cottontails, gray and fox squirrels, and ruffed grouses. For prairie habitats, documents attest to the presence of both bison and wapiti when Fort Ouiatenon was inhabited, and these offer the two largest "meat packages" available. However, despite having high reproductive rates, both bison and wapiti wandered over wide expanses of territory, and neither may have been predictable concerning when and where respective aggregations would occur. The only medium-sized mammal on the prairies was the badger, which was solitary and widely dispersed across northern Indiana. Small animals available on the prairies included two species of ground squirrel, bobwhites, and ornate box turtles. Thus, greater prairie chicken is the only species that would have been a regular and abundant source of meat on the upland prairie. Consideration of factors such as these provides for an objective appraisal of faunal resources that were available to the human population at Fort Ouiatenon and provides a way to view zooarchaeological collections from the site in order to evaluate how efficient or selective eighteenth-century animal procurement was. A report in preparation will consider the faunal collections that were encountered by Kellar's initial work at the site in 1968 and 1969 (see chapter 2, this volume).

ZOOARCHAEOLOGY METHODS

Because of the abundance of animal remains that were encountered during the six years of excavations at the Fort Ouiatenon site by the MSU Museum excavations, an emphasis of the faunal analysis was placed on feature contexts. However, attention was also given to sheet midden contexts in order to determine if the site's faunal assemblage from features is representative of the site at large. A grand total of 100,654 animal remains were analyzed, 66,637 (66.2%) being associated with 59 features. Midden samples were obtained from forty-seven test units, most of which were excavated during the 1974–1976 field seasons, but some samples from units and features from the 1977–1979 excavations were also included. The faunal collection from the 1974–1979 excavations are curated by the Tippecanoe County Historical Association in Lafayette, Indiana.

Identifications of animal remains from the Fort Ouiatenon site were accomplished by comparing archaeologically derived osteological specimens to skeletal specimens from known reference skeletons in the osteology collections at the MSU Museum (East Lansing) and the Illinois State Museum (Springfield). Published manuals were also consulted; especially important was the volume by Balkwill and Cumbaa (1992) for distinguishing postcranial bones of cattle from bison. Scientific and common names for animals follow the Integrated Taxonomic Information System website (Integrated Taxonomic Information System 2020). Data recorded included provenience, class of animal, taxon (order, family, subfamily, genus, or species), anatomical skeletal element, side, skeletal portion, status of epiphyseal closure, body size or 8-cm-size class for fish, burning, natural modifications (e.g., carnivore- or rodent-gnawing), human modifications (e.g., cut marks), weight of specimen in grams, number of specimens, and comments. These topics are discussed in depth by Reitz and Wing (1999). All data were entered into a microcomputer for sorting and quantification, which included number of specimens, number of identified specimens (NISP), total weight of specimens for each taxon, and minimum number of individuals (MNI) for each taxon. MNI estimates were based on the most frequently encountered specimen having the same anatomical portion and included consideration of the biological age of the animal, size, and symmetry of left and right anatomical specimens. The criterion of size was especially significant for estimating MNI for fish (see Parmalee, Paloumpis, and Wilson 1972, 11; Styles 1981, 118, 146–53). In the case of white-tailed deer, attention was also given to assessing size compatibility of various anatomical specimens in addition to the most abundant elements. Specimen weights also permitted the application of an allometric scaling technique in order to derive biomass estimates (Reitz and Cordier 1984; Reitz et al 1987). As described by Reitz and Scarry (1985, 18), "the weight of the archaeological bone is used in an allometric formula [see Reitz and Scarry 1985, 67] to predict the quantity of biomass for the skeletal mass recovered rather than the total original weight of the individual animal represented by the recovered bone." This approach avoided the problem of basing meat estimates on MNI and determining whether the meat from entire animals was consumed at the site from which the archaeological sample was acquired. Despite the problems inherent in the various techniques used to estimate biomass and usable or edible meat (see Jackson 1989; for discussion and critiques, see Lyman 2008, 84–108), the interpretive value of such measures is the relative importance of the various taxa rather than the absolute quantities. For the Fort Ouiatenon faunal collection, biomass was calculated for each taxon separately by feature or area and then summed to obtain totals for the samples from Fort Ouiatenon that were analyzed.

OVERVIEW OF FORT OUIATENON ZOOARCHAEOLOGY

The analyzed faunal assemblage exceeds one hundred thousand specimens, of which 11.6 percent by count and 54.2 percent by weight were identified more specifically than the taxonomic level of class (table 5.1). Mammals were clearly the dominant class, followed in decreasing order by birds and fish. Although significant, reptiles and freshwater mussels are represented by small quantities in proportion to the entire Fort Ouiatenon assemblage. Recovery techniques may have resulted in a bias against small specimens from fish, small birds, and small mammals, since standard procedures involved screening all matrix below the plow zone through .64-cm mesh hardware cloth. Flotation and dry-screening through 0.16-cm mesh was applied on a limited basis.

TABLE 5.1. SPECIES COMPOSITION OF ANIMAL REMAINS FROM THE FORT OUIATENON SITE, 1974–1979

Animal Taxa	NISP[1]	MNI	NISP Weight (g)	Biomass (Kg)
MAMMALS	**86,480**	**263**	**138,079.8**	**1,502.138**
Opossum, *Didelphis virginiana*	8	3	8.3	.177
Short-tailed shrew, *Blarina brevicauda*	8	3	1.2	.031
Eastern mole, *Scalopus aquaticus*	48	12	16.7	.331
Eastern cottontail, *Sylvilagus floridanus*	13	1	6.3	.138
Eastern chipmunk, *Tamias striatus*	17	3	2.9	.069
Woodchuck, *Marmota monax*	3	1	1.4	.036
Thirteen-lined ground squirrel, *Ictidomys tridecemlineatus*	1	1	.1	
Gray squirrel, *Sciurus carolinensis*	64	7	22.0	.425
Tree squirrel sp., *Sciurus* sp.	19	—	3.0	.071
Beaver, *Castor canadensis*	138	6	587.8	8.172
Deer/white-footed mouse, *Peromyscus* sp.	5	1	.3	.009
Meadow vole, *Microtus pennsylvanicus*	2	1	.5	.014
Vole sp., *Microtus* sp.	3	2	.3	.009
Muskrat, *Ondatra zibethicus*	10	1	4.1	.094
Unidentified rodent	17	—	1.8	.045
Dog/coyote, *Canis* sp.	67	3	103.1	1.706
Fox sp., *Vulpes/Urocyon*	1	1	10.3	.215
Black bear, *Ursus americanus*	153	6	2,853.8	33.875

Animal Taxa	NISP[1]	MNI	NISP Weight (g)	Biomass (Kg)
Raccoon, *Procyon lotor*	964	39	1,249.7	16.111
Fisher, *Martes pennanti*	8	2	18.3	.360
Mink, *Mustela vison*	1	1	.6	.017
Badger, *Taxidea taxus*	2	1	1.1	.029
River otter, *Lontra canadensis*	16	3	29.6	.555
Domestic cat, *Felis catus*	6	3	5.8	.132
Bobcat, *Lynx rufus*	1	1	—	—
Horse/ass, *Equus* sp.	59	2	1,629.5	20.457
Pig, *Sus scrofa*	313	12	2,677.9	31.990
Wapiti, *Cervus elaphus canadensis*	8	2	287.3	4.290
White-tailed deer, *Odocoileus virginianus*	5,072	139	57,627.6	506.487
Wapiti/deer, Family Cervidae	12	—	118.7	1.936
Bison, *Bison bison*	1	1	294.4	4.386
Domesticated cattle, *Bos taurus*	15	2	1,736.7	21.665
Cattle/bison, *Bos/Bison*	88	3	2,933.5	275.834
Unidentified mammal	79,337	—	65,845.2	572.469
BIRDS	**10,143**	**204**	**4,919.5**	**53.222**
Common loon, *Gavia immer*	1	1	2.3	.044
Grebe spp., *Podilymbus/Podiceps*	3	1	.9	.019
Swan sp., *Cygnus* spp.	16	3	65.9	.923
Canada goose, *Branta canadensis*	275	12	487.7	5.705
cf. Canada goose, small race	2	1	2.0	.038
Goose sp., Tribe Anserini	1	—	.5	.011
Wood duck, *Aix sponsa*	7	2	4.2	.075
Mallard, *Anas platyrhynchos*	81	12	74.5	1.032
cf. Pintail, *Anas* cf. *acuta*	2	1	.6	.013
cf. Gadwall, *Anas* cf. *strepera*	1	1	.4	.009
Blue-winged/green-winged teal, *Anas discors/creca*	37	7	15.0	.240
Surface-feeding ducks, *Anas* spp.	33	5	22.9	.353
cf. Canvasback, *Aythya* cf. *valisineria*	3	2	3.2	.059
cf. Redhead, *Aythya* cf. *americana*	1	1	.8	.017
Canvasback/redhead, *Aythya valisineria/americana*	1	—	.2	.005
cf. Ring-necked duck, *Aythya* cf. *collaris*	2	1	1.4	.028

Animal Taxa	NISP[1]	MNI	NISP Weight (g)	Biomass (Kg)
cf. Lesser scaup, *Aythya* cf. *affinis*	1	1	.3	.007
Bay ducks, *Aythya* spp.	5	3	2.5	.047
Common goldeneye, *Bucephala clangula*	3	1	1.3	.026
Bufflehead, *Bucephala albeola*	6	2	3.7	.041
Hooded merganser, *Lophodytes cucullatus*	1	1	1.0	.020
Common merganser, *Mergus merganser*	9	4	8.7	.146
Red-breasted merganser, *Mergus serrator*	1	1	.1	.003
Merganser sp., *Mergus* sp.	3	—	2.3	.044
Duck spp., Subfamily Anatinae	642	23	234.8	2.933
Cooper's hawk, *Accipiter cooperii*	1	1	.5	.011
Red-tailed hawk, *Buteo jamaicensis*	5	1	2.6	.049
cf. Red-shouldered hawk, *Buteo* cf. *lineatus*	2	1	.4	.009
Soaring hawk spp., *Buteo* sp.	1	—	1.1	.017
Hawk sp, Family Accipitridae	4	—	1.1	.022
Bald eagle, *Haliaeetus leucocephalus*	2	1	3.4	.062
Red junglefowl (domestic chicken), *Gallus gallus*	306	17	222.4	2.791
Ruffed grouse, *Bonasa umbellus*	17	3	4.1	.074
Prairie chicken/sharp-tailed grouse, *Tympanuchus* sp.	127	9	73.9	1.024
Wild turkey, *Meleagris gallopavo*	1,434	30	3,338.0	32.838
Northern bobwhite, *Colinus virginianus*	12	2	2.4	.045
Fowls/gallinaceous birds, Family Phasianidae	36	—	17.6	.278
Black-bellied/lesser golden-plover, *Pluvialis* sp.	2	1	.6	.013
Plover sp., *Charadrius* sp.	1	1	.1	.003
Greater yellowlegs, *Tringa melanoleuca*	9	2	2.6	.049
cf. Lesser yellowlegs, *Tringa* cf. *flavipes*	1	1	.1	.003
cf. Solitary sandpiper, *Tringa* cf. *solitaria*	2	1	.3	.007
cf. Pectoral sandpiper, *Calidris* cf. *melanotos*	1	1	.1	.003
Shorebird spp., Order Charadriiformes	9	3	1.3	.026
Mourning dove, *Zenaida macroura*	1	1	.1	.003
Passenger pigeon, *Ectopistes migratorius*	451	26	96.0	1.300
Cuckoo sp., *Coccyzus* sp.	1	1	.1	.003

Animal Taxa	NISP[1]	MNI	NISP Weight (g)	Biomass (Kg)
Common nighthawk, *Chordeiles minor*	1	1	.4	.009
Woodpecker sp., Family Picidae	2	2	.5	.011
American crow, *Corvus brachyrhynchos*	1	1	.4	.009
Songbird spp., Order Passeriformes	67	11	9.6	.160
Unidentified bird	6,510	—	202.6	2.565
REPTILES	**206**	**17**	**215.0**	**2.485**
Common snapping turtle, *Chelydra serpentina*	1	1	11.1	.150
Common musk turtle, *Sternotherus odoratus*	8	1	5.5	.099
Spiny softshell turtle, *Apalone spinifera*	4	1	2.4	.057
Softshell turtle sp., *Apalone* sp.	33	—	40.5	.378
Eastern box turtle, *Terrapene carolina*	15	3	31.2	.317
Ornate box turtle, *Terrapene ornata*	6	2	4.1	.081
Box turtle spp., *Terrapene* spp.	4	—	2.5	.058
Northern map turtle, *Graptemys geographica*	4	1	11.8	.165
False map turtle, *Graptemys pseudogeographica*	1	1	1.0	.032
Map turtle spp., *Graptemys* spp.	5	—	5.5	.099
Painted turtle, *Chrysemys picta*	7	2	10.6	.154
Slider, *Trachemys scripta*	1	1	.4	.017
Painted turtle/slider, *Chrysemys/Trachemys*	11	—	7.8	.125
Blanding's turtle, *Emydoidea blandingii*	19	3	31.8	.321
Pond turtle spp., Family Emydidae	82	—	48.3	.425
Fox/rat snake spp., *Pantherophis* spp.	5	1	.5	.007
AMPHIBIANS	**46**	**?**	**5.7**	**—**
Toad sp., *Bufo* sp.	11	?	1.2	—
Frog sp., *Lithobates* sp.	4	?	.7	—
Frog/toad, *Bufo/Lithobates*	31	?	3.8	—
FISHES	**924**	**58–69**	**428.2**	**10.892**
Shovelnose sturgeon, *Scaphirhynchus platorynchus*	167	3(+)	39.4	.579
Longnose gar, *Lepisosteus osseus*	2	1	.7	.093
Gar sp., *Lepisosteus* sp.	3	—	.3	.045

Animal Taxa	NISP[1]	MNI	NISP Weight (g)	Biomass (Kg)
Bowfin, *Amia calva*	3	1	1.1	.137
Northern pike, *Esox lucius*	4	1	4.1	.424
Smallmouth/black buffalo, *Ictiobus bubalus/niger*	7	3	6.1	.596
Bigmouth buffalo, *Ictiobus cyprinellus*	1	1	.9	.115
Buffalo spp., *Ictiobus* spp.	26	2–5	17.4	1.468
Carpsucker sp., *Carpoides* sp.	1	1	.2	.032
Silver redhorse, *Moxostoma anisurum*	2	1	.2	.032
Black redhorse, *Moxostoma duquesnei*	4	3	1.2	.147
cf. Black redhorse, *Moxostoma* cf. *duquesnei*	1	—	.3	.045
Golden redhorse, *Moxostoma erythrurum*	4	3	.8	.104
Shorthead redhorse, *Moxostoma macrolepidotum*	4	2	2.1	.238
Redhorse spp., *Moxostoma* spp.	48	2–7	21.2	1.740
Northern hog sucker, *Hypentelium nigricans*	1	1	.1	.017
Sucker spp., Family Catostomidae	2	—	.2	.032
Brown bullhead, *Ameiurus nebulosus*	1	1	.2	.004
Channel catfish, *Ictalurus punctatus*	89	11	132.3	2.068
Bullhead/catfish spp., *Ameiurus/Ictalurus*	5	—	3.2	.060
Flathead catfish, *Pylodictis olivaris*	1	1	1.3	.026
Catfish sp., *Ictalurus/Pylodictis*	1	—	.2	.004
White bass, *Morone chrysops*	1	1	.2	.032
Smallmouth bass, *Micropterus dolomieui*	8	4	2.8	.068
Largemouth bass, *Micropterus salmoides*	1	1	.3	.045
Black bass spp., *Micropterus* spp.	21	1–4	8.1	.161
Sunfish sp., Family Centrarchidae	1	1	.1	.017
Walleye/sauger, *Sander* sp.	25	5	20.5	.338
Freshwater drum, *Aplodinotus grunniens*	29	7	47.3	.843
Unidentified fish	461	—	115.4	1.382
UNIDENTIFIED VERTEBRATA	1,813	—	421.0	—
GASTROPOD	1	1	3.7	—
Jay's river snail, *Lithasia jayana*	1	1	3.7	—
BIVALVES	1,041	193	3,834.6	—
Pistolgrip, *Tritogonia verrucosa*	1	1	21.2	—

Animal Taxa	NISP[1]	MNI	NISP Weight (g)	Biomass (Kg)
Rabbitsfoot, *Theliderma cylindrica*	4	4	60.0	—
Monkeyface, *Theliderma metanevra*	2	2	65.1	—
Threeridge, *Amblema plicata*	10	9	197.7	—
Wabash pigtoe *Fusconaia flava*	1	1	8.8	—
Sheepnose, *Plethobasus cyphyus*	1	1	44.1	—
Ohio pigtoe, *Pleurbema cordatum*	9	9	208.3	—
Clubshell, *Pleurobema clava*	39	38	353.5	—
Elephant-ear, *Elliptio crassidens*	42	38	765.8	—
Spike, *Elliptio dilatata*	9	8	184.5	—
Mucket, *Ortmanniana ligamentina*	9	8	161.8	—
Hickorynut, *Obovaria olivaria*	2	2	41.5	—
Round hickorynut, *Obovaria subrotunda*	14	13	80.5	—
Ring pink, *Obovaria retusa*	1	1	12.1	—
Black sandshell, *Ligumia recta*	2	2	44.5	—
Pocketbook, *Lampsilis ovata*	61	49	418.8	—
Tubercled blossum, *Epioblasma torulosa*	7	7	51.3	—
Unidentified freshwater mussel	827	—	1,115.1	—
Totals	100,654	736–747	147,907.5	1,568.737
Totals identified	11,706	736–747	80,208.2	992.321
% identified	11.6		54.2	63.3

[1]Abbreviations: NISP, number of identified specimens; MNI, minimum number of individuals.

Mammals

Mammal specimens make up nearly 86 percent of all animal remains and 61 percent of those identified below class. In terms of specimen weight and biomass, mammals contribute over 90 percent for each measure, regardless of whether total assemblage or only identified specimens are considered.

White-tailed deer dominates all measures of quantification and was obviously the staple animal in the Fort Ouiatenon economy. Articulated deer bones were rarely observed during excavations, and except for carpals, tarsals, and phalanges, whole specimens are extremely rare. Observations of age and sexual composition of the Fort Ouiatenon deer can be the basis to hypothesize whether hunting was selective (by stalking) or nonselective (by drives or surrounds) or if there was selective harvesting of animals from a mass kill (Cleland 1966, 219–20; Emerson 1980; Waselkov 1978).

Criteria for assessing tooth eruption, replacement, and wear in mandibles (Severinghaus 1949) and knowledge of the timing and order of postcranial epiphyseal closure (Purdue 1983a) provides ways to assess biological ages of deer in an archaeological collection. For Fort Ouiatenon, only fifteen mandibles were recovered, and five (33.3%) were from individuals less than two years of age (including three fawns). However, distal tibiae are the single most abundant anatomical deer element in the Fort Ouiatenon collection, and only 36 of 158 distal tibiae (22.8%) were from individuals less than two years of age based on epiphyseal closure. This suggests that hunting was selective for older individuals and that hunters may have been concentrating on obtaining deer hides from larger deer for the fur trade. Due to the low recovery of deer pelvises and cranial frontal bones, the sex ratio of the Fort Ouiatenon deer was made through metrical analyses of selective postcranial bones and discriminant function analysis using control samples of modern deer of known sex (Purdue 1983b). Forty-one percent (54 of 136 specimens) of distal tibiae from adult individuals (i.e., bones with fused epiphyses) were classified as males, whereas 45.5 percent (15 of 33 specimens) of astragali were classified as male. The average November live weight for the 15 astragali that were classified as males was 85.1 kg, in comparison to an average of 56.6 kg for the 18 astragali that were classified as females (Purdue 1986; see Purdue 1983b for discussion of sex determination).

The composition of deer skeletal portions is presented in table 5.2 along with a similar breakdown for the deer remains from the Fort St. Joseph site (Martin, Hearns, and Becker 2019, 54–55). Although all parts of the body are represented, the proportions reveal that the two sites are remarkably similar except for a higher proportion of ribs and vertebrae fragments at Fort St. Joseph and a greater proportion of bones from the upper hind legs at Fort Ouiatenon. The apparent underrepresentation of bones from the lower legs and feet at both sites, less than 10 percent, is striking. Investigations of several Native American habitation sites of the late precontact and early contact periods show a different pattern in that lower leg and foot bones constitute from 26 to 44 percent (Garland et al. 2001; Martin 2015; Martin and Kuehn 2017, 445; Martin and Richmond 1996, 168; Martin, Richmond, and Brand 2003). Ethnographic and ethnoarchaeological accounts indicate that Native hunters and craftspeople preferred marrow from metacarpals and metatarsals over that from other long bones for food and technological uses (Binford 1978; Logan 1998, 359; Nassaney and Martin 2017). Hypothetically, the lower legs of deer were systematically culled at the two French fur trade posts so that they could be processed for marrow elsewhere.

Cut marks resulting from skinning, dismemberment, filleting, and marrow extraction were recorded for deer bones from Fort Ouiatenon feature contexts. Excluding antlers, cut marks were observed on ninety-nine specimens (approximately 6%). The highest proportion of cut marks occurs on distal humeri, proximal radii, distal femurs, and astragali, anatomical locations that were apparently points of dismemberment. Filleting cuts are

TABLE 5.2. WHITE-TAILED DEER SKELETAL PORTIONS AT FORT OUIATENON AND FORT ST. JOSEPH SITES

Skeletal Portion	Fort Ouiatenon NISP[1]	%	Fort St. Joseph NISP	%
Cranium	**741**	**14.6**	**577**	**15.0**
Cranial bones	146	2.9	188	4.9
Mandible	56	1.1	48	1.2
Isolated teeth	389	7.7	328	8.5
Antler fragments	150	3.0	6	.2
Hyoid	0	—	7	.2
Axial Bones	**1,015**	**20.0**	**1,211**	**31.5**
Vertebrae	209	4.1	460	12.0
Rib	740	14.6	740	19.2
Rib/vertebral spine fragments	54	1.1	0	—
Costal cartilage	0	—	4	.1
Sternum	12	2.4	7	.2
Proximal forequarter	**1,110**	**21.9**	**844**	**21.9**
Scapula	356	7.0	154	4.0
Humerus	345	6.8	297	7.7
Radius	251	4.9	251	6.5
Ulna	158	3.1	142	3.7
Proximal hindquarter	**1,770**	**34.9**	**978**	**25.4**
Pelvis	94	1.9	148	3.8
Femur	762	15.0	359	9.3
Patella	82	1.6	49	1.3
Tibia	832	16.4	422	11.0
Distal legs and feet	**436**	**8.6**	**237**	**6.2**
Carpal bones	74	1.5	45	1.2
Metacarpal	17	.3	14	.4
Astragalus	82	1.6	22	.6
Calcaneus	65	1.3	36	.9
Miscellaneous tarsal bones	58	1.1	41	1.1
Metatarsal	32	.6	27	.7
Carpal/tarsal fragments	15	.3	0	—
Metapodial fragments	19	.4	16	.4
Sesamoid	4	.1	1	<.1
Phalanges	70	1.4	35	.9
Grand totals	5,072	100.0	3,847	100.0

[1]NISP, number of identified specimens.

much less frequent but were noted as longitudinal cuts on scapula blade fragments, on upper long bones (especially humeri), and on vertebral dorsal spines and ribs. Antlers were subjected to additional modification. Whereas seventeen cut and carved pieces of antlers were included in previous artifact inventories (Noble 1983; Tordoff 1983), faunal collections from the well, the forging area, and five other features included approximately eighty antler fragments that had been drilled, cut, or sawed into crude disks or were selected to eventually be made into tool handles or projectile points (figure 5.1).

A conservative approach to recording damage by scavenging animals resulted in the finding that 11 percent of the deer bones from features were gnawed by rodents or chewed by carnivores, such as dogs and coyotes. Similar to the pattern recorded by Binford (1981, 44–49), bones most affected by carnivores were proximal humeri, proximal femurs, distal femurs, pelvises, patellae, phalanges, calcanei, proximal tibiae, proximal ulnae, and vertebrae. Deer bones exhibiting rodent-gnawing were rare, but traces were noted on many small unidentified mammal bone fragments. The finding

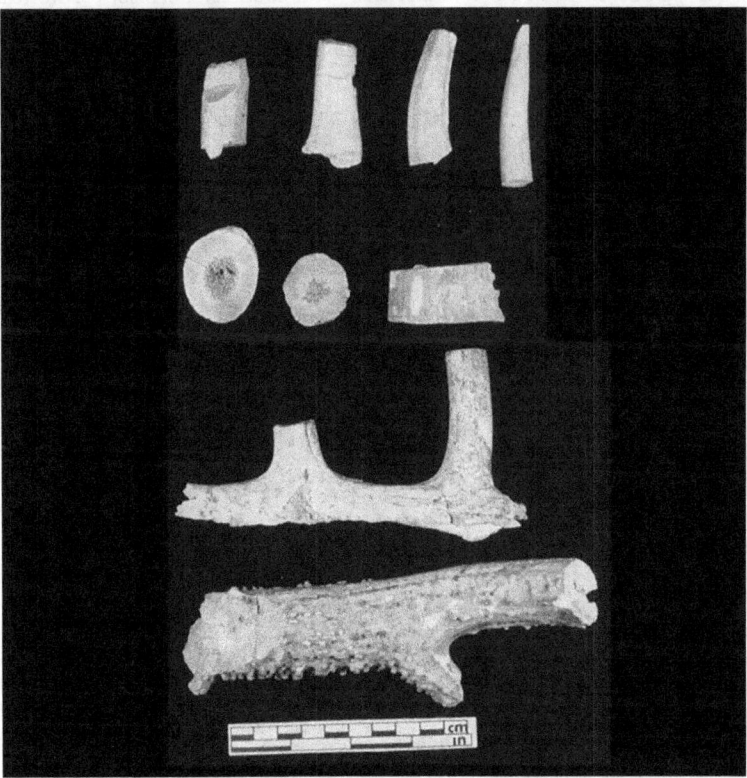

Figure 5.1. Examples of cut deer antlers; seven at top are from the forging area, two on bottom are from Well No. 1. Photographs by Philip J. Franz.

that nearly every refuse deposit displays carnivore damage is an indication that faunal remains in most features were the result of secondary refuse disposal.

Trauma was encountered on three deer bones (figure 5.2). An ulna and a radius from Well No. 1 were conjoined by callus formation resulting from a fracture at the midshafts. A distal humerus from the forging area also displayed remodeling after a fracture. A proximal humerus from the west stockade wall trench exhibits inflammation below the proximal epiphysis. Deer bones from at least two other early contact sites exhibit similar healed traumatic injuries, all involving humeri and radius-ulnae (Martin et al. 2019, 52–53; Parmalee and Klippel 1983, 282). These examples, all from the front legs, attest to how individual deer in the wild are capable of surviving injuries that might initially be considered to be fatal (Martin and Lawler 2014).

The second most significant group of mammals is comprised of large bovids, that is, cattle and bison. Together large bovids account for less than 2 percent of the identified mammal specimens but 32.5 percent in terms of biomass from identified mammals. Despite documentary accounts attesting to the abundance of bison on the nearby

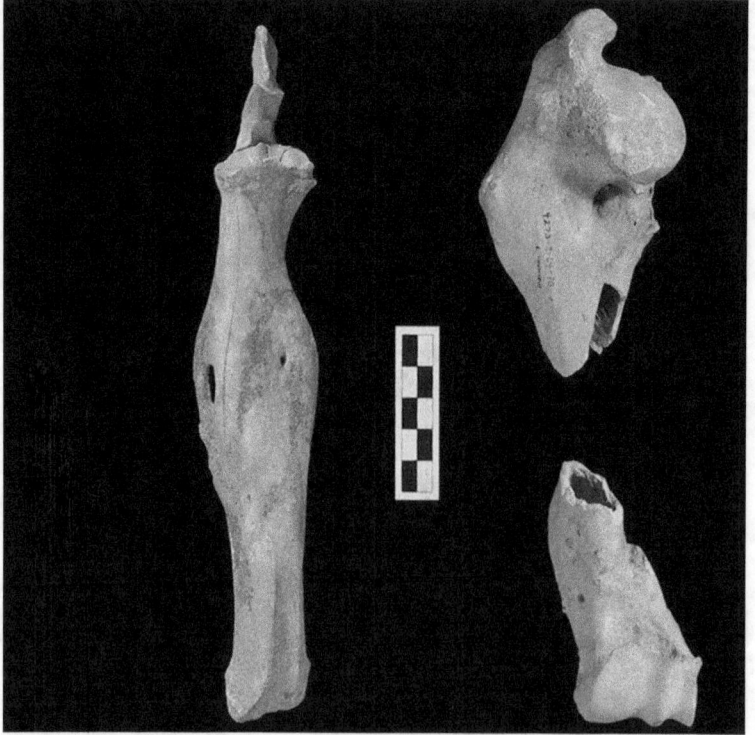

Figure 5.2. White-tailed deer remodeled traumatic bone injuries: radius-ulna on left; proximal humerus on upper right; distal humerus on lower right. Photographs by Doug Carr.

upland prairie, only one distal tibia was identified as bison, in contrast to fifteen from cattle. Although eighty-eight specimens could not be confidently distinguished between cattle and bison, cattle are better represented. Reminiscent of Hennepin's description of how the Miami hunted and processed bison in the 1670s (Thwaites 1972, 147), bison killed on the prairie near Fort Ouiatenon were likely processed where they were killed, with only the meat and hides brought to the fort. In contrast, cattle were present at the French outpost, as indicated by statements of supplies periodically sent to Montreal by the various commandants (e.g., Archives Nationales, Colonies, Series C11A, Vol. 118). An example for July 8, 1747, reads "1 beef for the savages....130# [livres]" and implies that cattle were being presented to Native Americans as gifts for their trade. Except for a nearly complete cattle scapula recovered from the well, the indistinguishable cattle/bison specimens consist of highly fragmented bones. A noteworthy find in the north-central part of the site was a portion of a cattle cranium from which both horns had been removed, presumably to be made into artifacts.

Horse bones and teeth were found widely scattered about the site, including a nearly complete cranium with teeth that were found in the well. No mandibles or vertebrae were present, and no cut marks or other modifications were observed. The combined weight of the cranium, a distal humerus, and a distal femur accounts for the high biomass estimate for horse in the Fort Ouiatenon faunal assemblage.

Wapiti was slightly better represented than bison, with ten identified specimens. An MNI estimate of two is based on the presence of two right astragali. Similar to bison, the large sizes of wapiti were probably an incentive for hunters to process carcasses at kill sites and transport few bones to the fort.

Bones and teeth from black bear were surprisingly common, more numerous in fact than bones and teeth from beavers. The large omnivore was actively sought, since the estimated potential annual yield of black bear in the 39-km^2 (15-square-mile) Fort Ouiatenon site area is only two or three individuals. In addition to meat and fat, the pelt was sold on the open fur market during the early eighteenth century (Eccles 1969, 135). More than 47 percent of the bear specimens at Fort Ouiatenon are from the feet. This pattern is generally consistent with other French forts sites in the Midwest in that foot bones make up the greatest proportion of bones from all other skeletal portions (Martin 2020, 115). Fort Ouiatenon's faunal collection includes two bones that had been modified into artifacts. An awl that was made from a fibula was found in the western area within the fort's interior. Especially significant is a mandible that was recovered from just outside the east stockade wall in a midden that was not associated with any special activity area. The mandible has an oval perforation, 25 mm in diameter, in the ascending ramus (the coronoid process was broken off) with use-polish present on the anterior surface of the perforation (figure 5.3). This is similar to bear mandible babiche tools that were found at several Native habitation sites in the northern Great Lakes

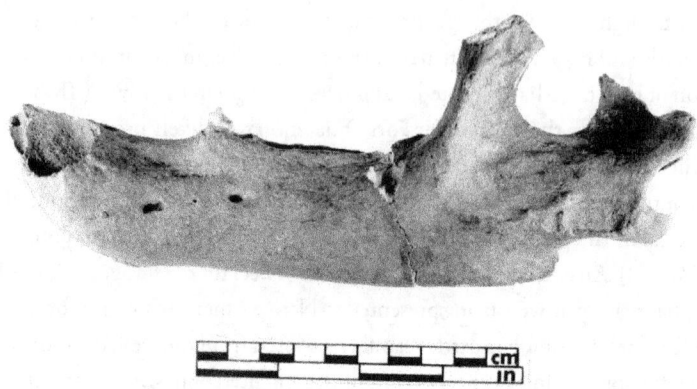

Figure 5.3. Modified black bear mandible with perforation in the ascending ramus. Photograph by Philip J. Franz.

region ranging in age from the early seventeenth century to the early nineteenth century (Martin 2020). This and several other modified animal specimens may be possible indicators of the close interaction between the French and Native peoples who resided in the Ouiatenon community (Martin 1991b).

Pigs rank third among mammals in terms of NISP and MNI and fourth in terms of biomass. Nearly half of all identified pig specimens consist of isolated teeth followed by fragments of crania and mandibles. An MNI of seven mature individuals was derived from seven right ulnae, whereas a minimum of five immature individuals are represented by right mandibles. This estimate of a minimum of twelve individuals is undoubtedly conservative for the faunal collection. Bacon was frequently listed in the statement of supplies sent by the fort commandant to the governor-general of Canada. Because few written accounts pertaining to Fort Ouiatenon mention livestock, the practice followed in the Illinois Country may have applied to the Wabash Valley as well. Concerning numbers of pigs, "how many there really were no one probably ever knew, for they ran loose in the woods, and though they were branded with their owners' marks, they had to be hunted almost as wild beasts" (Belting 2003 [1948], 57). When left to forage for themselves, pigs thrived on mast including hickory nuts, walnuts, acorns, and beech mast (Towne and Wentworth 1950, 109).

Raccoons were the most plentiful medium-sized mammal, but due to smaller body size, they rank seventh among all mammals in terms of biomass. Although their pelts were of low value in comparison to beaver, river otter, and other river mammals, their natural abundance resulted in a steady trade of raccoon furs coming from Indiana. In the case of Fort Ouiatenon, not only would the natural habitat be favorable for raccoons, but the gardens and refuse deposits in and around the settlement would quickly become part of a raccoon's foraging rounds.

Although beaver remains are present, their numbers are far less than expected for a settlement where the fur trade was the major activity of its inhabitants. This scarcity is consistent with information available from later trading posts in Indiana. Mumford and Whitaker (1982, 298) cite fur traders' records for northern Indiana as evidence that beaver populations were depleted by the early nineteenth century, and apparently Europeans and their Native trading partners had already exerted considerable pressure on Wabash Valley beavers by the early eighteenth century. Although trappers may have turned to muskrats as an alternative, traders' records from the early 1800s fail to reveal that (Mumford and Whitaker 1982, 372). Despite our model's prediction that muskrats would have reached four hundred to five hundred individuals in the vicinity of Fort Ouiatenon, the aquatic rodent is relatively rare in the faunal assemblage. Perhaps some aspect of the local aquatic habitats, such as more rapid current or widely dispersed stands of emergent vegetation, was unconducive. Perhaps the value of deer hides and the greater local availability of deer made muskrat trapping less appealing. Opossums were also apparently underexploited. Because extremely cold winters occasionally decimated opossum populations in Indiana (Mumford and Whitaker 1982, 88), the marsupial may not have been well established in the central Wabash River valley when Fort Ouiatenon was inhabited.

Species of the mustelid family identified at Fort Ouiatenon include fisher, mink, badger, and river otter. Consistent with the biomass model for the area, these animals did not constitute more than incidental prey in the faunal assemblage. Although highly valued as fur bearers, local mustelid populations could not have withstood sustained trapping. The hardiest were river otters, and fur trade records document their presence during the early 1800s (Mumford and Whitaker 1982, 101). Similarly, otters were apparently regularly procured by Fort Ouiatenon trappers but not in large numbers. The presence of fisher in the faunal assemblage is noteworthy in that this species was never abundant in Indiana (Mumford and Whitaker 1982, 95). Forested floodplains would have provided the only suitable habitat, and its presence reflects its value in the fur trade. Minks, in contrast, were more numerous and occurred near water in both forested and unforested areas (Mumford and Whitaker 1982, 459). However, a mandible is the only mink specimen encountered in the faunal collection. Similarly, two isolated teeth found in a stockade trench constitute the only badger specimens. Badgers are restricted to open habitats and have low population densities due to the nonoverlapping home ranges of males.

A total of sixty-seven canid remains were identified, and all are probably from domesticated dogs. A well yielded a concentration of bones from an immature, probably articulated individual. At least two mature individuals were identified from the site at large, but no formal burials were encountered. The only other canid at the site is a fox, but no determination could be made as to whether the tibia from the forging area is from red fox or gray fox.

The family Felidae is represented at Fort Ouiatenon by two species. Domesticated cat specimens were found widely dispersed at the site and represent at least three individuals. A fragment of a bobcat mandible was noted from one of the random test units in the north-central area. The wild and secretive bobcat would have inhabited the wooded bottomlands and slopes near the site (Mumford and Whitaker 1982, 477).

Several small mammal species were also identified. Eastern cottontail remains were widely scattered across the site, the largest concentration consisting of three bones that were associated with the forging area. Most numerous among rodents of the squirrel family are gray squirrels. Although metrical criteria cannot always separate gray and fox squirrels (Purdue 1980), the absence of specimens in the modern size range of fox squirrels seems significant and is consistent with the assessment for northern Indiana offered by Mumford and Whitaker (1982, 261, 271). Eastern chipmunks are also surprisingly well represented at Fort Ouiatenon, whereas only one specimen from a thirteen-lined ground squirrel was identified. Woodchucks were also available, but only three bones from the large ground-dwelling member of the squirrel family were encountered. Other small mammals were incidental to the human occupation of the site. Eastern moles and short-tailed shrews are fairly numerous, but their occurrence is probably fortuitous due to their fossorial habits. Intrusive voles and field mice were also commonly found.

Birds

A total of 10,143 specimens, representing 10.1 percent of the total faunal assemblage by count and 3.3 percent by specimen weight, are from birds. Estimates of biomass indicate that all birds contributed less than 4 percent.

Wild turkey was the most significant avian species. The MNI estimate is a distant second to all waterfowl, but their importance is compensated by the large size of the individuals. Not only were the forested floodplains of the central Wabash River valley an optimal habitat, but the year-round availability also made wild turkeys a first-line food resource. The Fort Ouiatenon sample of twenty-seven tarsometatarsus shaft fragments suggest a fairly balanced composition of fifteen males (indicated by the presence of spurs) and twelve hens and juveniles. While this ratio may suggest a deliberate hunter selection for males, sex and age ratios change with the season, and local population characteristics may vary considerably (Mosby 1967, 119, 123). A small tarsometatarsus shaft fragment is unique in exhibiting a remnant of a spur after the pointed end had been deliberately cut off (figure 5.4). Associated with the well (Feature 50), perhaps this is from a wild turkey raised at the settlement, and the detached spur made the bird easier to handle and less dangerous to other captive birds. Although Bruce Smith (1975, 80) observed that most early historic accounts suggest that fall and winter were the favored time for hunting wild turkeys, the presence of turkey bones at Fort

Figure 5.4. Midshaft of a wild turkey tarsometatarsus with a cut spur shown next to an unmodified wild turkey tarsometatarsus with intact spur. Photograph by Philip J. Franz.

Ouiatenon having medullary bone deposits (Rick 1975) indicates that the large birds were also hunted in the spring.

Considered as a single grouping, waterfowl were also very important. Several species of ducks along with Canada geese and swans account for approximately one-third of the NISP and MNI for birds and nearly one-fourth of the biomass. Despite several diagnostic morphological features (Oates, Boyd, and Raemaekers 2003; Woolfenden 1961), fewer than 25 percent of the archaeological duck specimens could be identified more precisely than to the level of subfamily. Each of the three major groups of ducks (dabbling ducks, diving ducks, and fish-eating ducks) are represented in the Fort Ouiatenon faunal assemblage. Canada geese are not as numerous as the various ducks, but their biomass contribution is second only to wild turkey. A smaller subspecies of Canada goose was noted for two specimens. The abundance of Canada geese is not surprising, given that the Wabash River is within the migration corridor taken by Canada geese between the northern Great Lakes and the Ohio Valley (Bellrose 1968, 15). Somewhat surprising is the absence of bones from lesser snow geese (*Chen caerulescens*) even though they pass through northwestern Indiana during their fall migrations (Bellrose 1968, 17). Swan bones were found, but the fragmentary specimens could not be confidently identified to species. Trumpeter swan (*Cygnus buccinator*) is most likely, since these swans formerly bred in Indiana (Bellrose 1976, 89; Bent 1925). Tundra (or whistling) swans (*Cygnus columbianus*) rarely occur as migrants in the area and were probably never very common south of their west-to-east migration corridor, which passes through Wisconsin and Michigan and on to Chesapeake Bay (Bellrose 1976, 96–97).

Because all of Indiana was within the principal nesting area (Schorger 1955, 257), high seasonal population densities of passenger pigeons probably occurred in the vicinity of Fort Ouiatenon during years in which mast was plentiful. The abundance of passenger pigeon bones at the site supports this expectation. The smaller body size of the passenger pigeon relegates the estimated biomass for the species as less than that for wild turkey, waterfowl, and domestic chicken but greater than all other birds in the Fort Ouiatenon assemblage.

More than three hundred bones from domestic chickens (formally known as red junglefowl) were recovered at Fort Ouiatenon. These were likely left to fend for themselves around the settlement but would nearly always be available as a supplemental food, and chicken eggs may have been an important by-product. Chicken bones from French contexts at Fort Michilimackinac and Fort St. Joseph are present, but they are not numerous (Martin et al. 2019, 60; Scott 1985). There are no mentions of chickens for the French settlement at Kaskaskia in the Illinois Country (Belting 2003 [1948]), but chicken bones were identified at the Laurens site, one of the previous locations of Fort de Chartres prior to the stone fort in the Illinois Country (Jelks, Ekberg, and Martin 1989, 82).

Bones that were identified as either greater prairie chicken or sharp-tailed grouse rank sixth among all bird taxa in both NISP and MNI and are unique in being the only avian taxa that occurs almost exclusively on the prairies.Bones of these two prairie species are indistinguishable in most cases. During the late spring, greater prairie chickens congregate at "booming grounds" that extend over several acres, and these areas of courtship are used repeatedly over a number of years. With large flocks forming in the autumn, greater prairie chickens were a highly predictable avian resource that was vulnerable to human hunters (Trippensee 1948, 241).

Shorebirds and passerine songbirds are surprisingly well represented in the faunal assemblage. The first group seems to reflect more than an incidental occurrence, and perhaps early French inhabitants killed them for sport as a frontier form of "bay-bird shooting" (Bent 1927, 330). Songbirds were probably killed for sport or for the purpose of acquiring colorful feathers for use as decoration or as body adornment.

Fifteen specimens were identified as birds of prey and minimally include bald eagle, Cooper's hawk, red-tailed hawk, and a possible red-shouldered hawk. These were associated with a variety of contexts at the site. Often bones from raptorial birds at native habitation sites are limited to wings and legs, suggesting use of plumage and special anatomical parts for decorative or ceremonial functions (Parmalee and Klippel 1983, 268–69). At Fort Ouiatenon, the recovery of cranial parts, pelvises, and synsacrum fragments in addition to wing bones suggests more generalized use.

Overall, the diverse avian taxa indicate a rather balanced pattern of procuring birds from the Wabash River, its tributaries, and its floodplains; the forested slopes and the uplands; and the upland prairie. This fondness for many varieties of wild birds is echoed by eighteenth-century accounts from Lower Louisiana (Dawdy 2010, 398–99).

Reptiles and Amphibians

Reptile and amphibian bones make up a relatively small part of the faunal assemblage, with most of the herptile taxa consisting of a diverse array of both terrestrial and aquatic turtles. Nonetheless, turtles are significant in that they contribute a unique perspective on how some animals were used for both food and artifacts. The fragmentary and disarticulated condition of most of the turtle remains made identifications challenging and likely resulted in MNI estimates that are highly conservative. Whereas our resource model suggests that both species of box turtle were underexploited, the same is true for common snapping turtles. Softshell turtles, in contrast, may have been captured in numbers greater than predicted based on the number of specimens that were recovered. Among the various pond turtle species, Blanding's turtles were surprisingly abundant. The natural distribution for this semiaquatic turtle includes the northern lake plains section of Indiana and the northern half of Illinois that was originally prairie (Minton 1972, 160; Smith 1961, 132).

Thirteen carapace specimens show some form of human modification. Vertebrae and costal ribs were removed from neural and pleural bones, and smoothed margins on peripheral bones were made by cutting and grinding. These modifications suggest the production of bowls, containers, or both on eight Blanding's turtle specimens, one eastern box turtle, two painted turtles, one common map turtle, and one unidentified pond turtle. Two nearly whole modified carapaces are represented by an eastern box turtle (from midden context) and a Blanding's turtle (from near the storehouse) (figure 5.5). Similar modifications on Blanding's turtle carapaces were found at the Bell site, a Meskwaki habitation site in east-central Wisconsin (Parmalee 1963, 63). The Fort Ouiatenon examples also reflect Native American influences.

The other herpetofaunal remains consist of isolated vertebrae from nonvenomous snakes and isolated bones from frogs and toads. In northwestern Indiana, the genus *Pantheerophis* includes the western fox snake (*P. ramspotti*) that occurs in prairie areas and the black rat snake (*P. obsoletus*) that prefers wooded bluffs (Minton 1972, 271, 274). The snake, frog, and toad bones from these excavations may be the remains of intrusive animals.

Fishes

A total of 463 identified fish specimens from nearly two dozen taxa compose just under 4 percent of the number of specimens for the Fort Ouiatenon faunal assemblage.

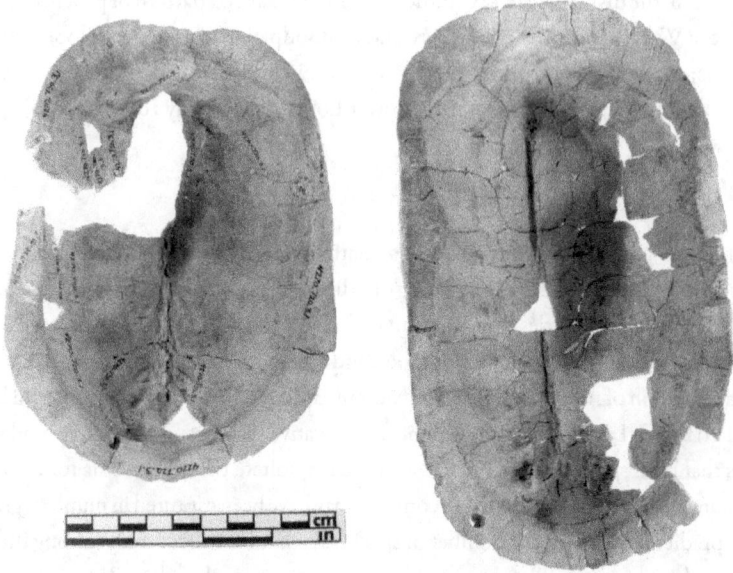

Figure 5.5. Modified turtle carapaces: eastern box turtle on left; Blanding's turtle on right. Photographs by Philip J. Franz.

This diverse collection represents only about 1 percent of the biomass from the NISP but is important for providing information about aquatic habitats when the site was occupied as well as fish procurement techniques. A total of eighteen iron fish hooks were found during the 1974–1979 excavations (Noble 1983, 180–81). Fisheries statistics compiled for the Wabash River for 1894 (Smith 1898, 513–17) and 1899 (Townsend 1902, 674–76) help provide ways to evaluate the archaeological assemblage. This must be done with caution, however, since conditions and status of the fishery in the late nineteenth century constitute an imperfect analogue for the eighteenth-century setting. Siltation, desiccation during droughts, invasive species interactions (i.e., introduction of the common carp, *Cyprinus carpio*, during the 1880s), and agricultural and industrial pollution are some of the factors responsible for changes in midwestern riverine fauna (Smith 1971). Locally, construction of the Wabash and Erie Canal near Lafayette in 1843 and soil erosion caused by forest clearing and modern agriculture have had adverse impacts on fish populations (Gammon 1977).

Catostomidae (suckers) and Ictaluridae (catfishes) were two fish families that were prevalent at Fort Ouiatenon. River catfish (i.e., channel and flathead catfish) may have been the most significant single group of fish at Fort Ouiatenon, especially when considering the larger size of most individual catfish (ten of the twelve individuals were greater than 50 cm in standard length). Catfish constitute just over 20 percent of the fish NISP, about 20 percent of the fish MNI, and 22 percent of fish biomass. Channel catfish were prevalent, but both channel catfish and flathead catfish occur in medium-sized and large rivers, especially those having clear water, a fast current, and sand or gravel substrates (P. Smith 1979, 183).

Redhorse suckers were also important, especially in terms of biomass (nearly 25% of all identified fish) and total number of individuals. This genus formerly included as many as six species in midwestern rivers and are distinctive in generally having a low tolerance for turbid water, silty substrates, and pollution (Pflieger 1975, 194–98; P. Smith 1979, 159–64). Curry and Spacie (1978, 187) observed redhorse suckers to be "extremely abundant" in Wildcat Creek during spring spawning. Another group of suckers is buffalofish, which are second only to redhorse in terms of estimated biomass. Three species of buffalo are extant in the Midwest, and all are generally distributed in medium-sized and large rivers as well as in the mouths of tributaries and occasionally in backwater lakes (P. Smith 1979, 151–52).

A fish species that is difficult to evaluate for the archaeological assemblage is the shovelnose sturgeon. Although most numerous at the site in terms of NISP, obtaining estimates of MNI and biomass are highly speculative. Sturgeons have cartilaginous skeletons, and only their bony cranial dermal plates from the dorsal skull, ventral bones of the neurocranium, and postcranial dermal scutes will be found at archaeological sites. At Fort Ouiatenon, dermal bones and scutes were most often recovered as isolated and fragmented specimens that could not be identified to specific element (Findeis 1993, 1997). Individuals of the species are much smaller than lake sturgeons (*Acipenser fulvescens*) that occur in the Great Lakes and their large tributary rivers. In the Ohio River, for example, female shovelnose sturgeons have average lengths of 64.5 cm and weights of 1.5 kg, in comparison to males that average 55.1 cm and 0.9 kg (Bailey and Cross 1954, 198–99). A common commercial species for many years, shovelnose sturgeons have been more abundant in the Wabash River because flood-control dams and other modifications have not been as restrictive as elsewhere (P. Smith 1979, 14). These fish feed off river bottoms, their diet consisting of small prey that is mostly insect larvae (Findeis 1993, 54–55). Although shovelnose sturgeons prefer the strong currents of large river channels along with sand or gravel substrates, reduced current in some areas due to river impoundments has probably been more detrimental than increased turbidity (Bailey and Cross 1954, 197–98).

Several other fishes that were identified in the Fort Ouiatenon collection were probably significant as supplemental taxa. Freshwater drums thrive in turbid water over a mixed sand and silt substrate and usually prefer the main channels of large rivers (P. Smith 1979, 299). Black bass are important game fish and consist of largemouth bass (*Micropterus salmoides*), smallmouth bass (*M. dolomieui*), and spotted bass

(*M. punctatus*), all of which are difficult to distinguish from fragmentary bones. Whereas smallmouth and spotted bass are usually found in cool, clear streams with moderate currents and gravelly bottoms, largemouth bass are more tolerant of conditions and occur in large rivers as well as in weedy backwaters, swamps, and creeks (P. Smith 1979, 230–33). The large percid bones at the site are probably from walleye (*Sander vitreum*) rather than sauger (*S. canadensis*), since the estimated standard lengths were greater than 32 cm, the maximum size for normal sauger (P. Smith 1979, 257). Walleyes occur in large rivers and adjacent backwaters, where they prefer aquatic vegetation while avoiding warm, turbid water and silty bottoms (P. Smith 1979, 258).

Several other fish taxa represent incidental catches. Gars, bowfins, bullheads, and small sunfish are poorly represented in the Fort Ouiatenon faunal collection. This may indicate that backwater lakes were not present near the outpost or, if present, were underexploited. The taxa and sizes observed seem indicative of an emphasis on larger fish, but the lack of systematic flotation recovery may have introduced a bias against the recovery of small fish remains. Nonetheless, the fishing techniques employed and the spring seasons of exploitation when large fish enter areas of shallow water for spawning may account for the profile of the Fort Ouiatenon fish assemblage.

Mollusks

A gastropod shell that is unique in light of its known distribution is Jay's river snail. The single specimen was found in midden debris near a building trench at N1010W964. There is a perforation in the aperture of the shell and the outer lip has been worn away, but it is uncertain if this is the result of intentional human modification (figure 5.6). Records for the species exist for the Cumberland, Tennessee, and Duck Rivers in Kentucky and Tennessee (Bogan and Parmalee 1983, 92; Burch and Tottenham 1980, 162–63), but Goodrich and van der Schalie (1944, 303) report that it was also known from the lower Ohio River and the Wabash River from its mouth to Mt. Carmel, Illinois.

A total of seventeen species of freshwater mussels are represented among 214 identified bivalve shells. The occurrence of so many mussel shells at a site inhabited by Europeans is rather surprising, although Native residents or visitors may have also been responsible. One shell that was recovered from near a forging area had been modified by having a hole cut or drilled through the valve (Tordoff 1980, 22; Tordoff 1983, 430). Three species—pocketbook, elephant-ear, and clubshell—comprise two-thirds of the identified shells. Pocketbook, elephant-ear, Ohio pigtoe, and sheepnose are species typical of deep water in large rivers and together make up just over 50 percent of the total MNI. Mussels that mainly inhabit small streams, such as Wea Creek, are represented by 25 percent of the MNI and consist of Wabash pigtoe, clubshell, and threeridge. Threeridge shells from the site (none greater than seven cm in length) are the small river

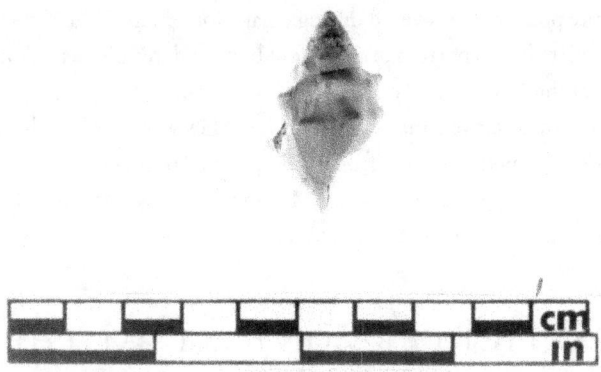

Figure 5.6. Jay's river snail. Photograph by Philip J. Franz.

form, as denoted by the compressed shell and slightly elevated beak (Parmalee 1967, 26). As an assemblage, the species composition is indicative of a mixture of sand and gravel substrates, moderate to strong current, and depths of 1.8 m or less, although a deeper channel may also have been present (Parmalee 1967; Warren 1991). Twentieth-century studies of mussels in the Wabash River indicate that Tippecanoe County is the transition from the river's headwater zone to the large river zone, and the 48 species documented at Lafayette is only surpassed downstream at New Harmony, where 50 species were recorded (Goodrich and van der Schalie 1944; Krumholz, Bingham, and Meyer 1970). Noteworthy is the complete absence of the elephant-ear from the Lafayette locality in both of these inventories.

Miscellaneous Modified Animal Specimens

At least eighty-two specimens made from bone, ivory, or antler were modified for use as artifacts, and these were included in artifact inventories presented in appendices by Tordoff (1983) and Noble (1983). Specific items include fifteen carved bone beads, six fine-toothed comb fragments, at least twenty-one scales for utensil handles (including incised and polished specimens), and fragments of awls, needles, tubes, discs, pegs, antler tips, gaming pieces, and fragments of unknown function that were drilled, engraved, carved, scored, and polished. Modified specimens from black bear and various turtles were previously discussed. There are also two projectile points that were made from bone or antler. One of these is diamond-shaped in cross section with a socketed base that was found in unit N875W875 (figure 5.7, right). Parmalee and Klippel (1983, 274, 297) described and illustrated a point from the Rhoads site, a late eighteenth-century Kickapoo camp in central Illinois that is similar in shape and size.

A less elaborate point was recovered during excavation of unit N861W865 (figure 5.7, left). A triangular-shaped portion of cancellous bone with red pigment along one edge was found near the forging area (figure 5.8). Similar examples of these tools have been reported from other Native American sites, where they were attributed to patellae or proximal ends of humeri or femurs from bison that had been modified to function as pigment applicators for decorating hides (Martin 2015, 81, 83; Martin and Parker 2017, 323; Mazrim 2015, 17, 18; Morrissey 2015, 25, 27).

PARTICULAR CONTEXTS AT THE FORT OUIATENON SITE

Following the exploratory excavations by James Kellar, Judith Tordoff's excavations resulted in the discovery of 40 features in addition to over 36,000 artifacts and 96,000 animal remains (Tordoff 1983, 149). During 1974 and 1975, Ralph van Frese (Purdue University) conducted proton magnetometer and soil resistivity surveys and detected anomalies that Tordoff's crews discerned to be the remains of a small semisubterranean storehouse (Feature 56) and a forging area (Features 35, 36, 37, and 60) (von Frese and Noble 1984). Tordoff also investigated a deep well (Feature 50). Faunal samples for each of these contexts were large, and the species compositions were diverse. Feature 56 yielded 294 identified specimens (37 taxa; MNI = 48). The forging area included 2,293 identified specimens (56 taxa; MNI = 158). Feature 50 contained 825 identified specimens (39 taxa; MNI = 97). Areas outside of features also had abundant animal remains in sheet middens.

Features versus Sheet Midden Contexts

A topic of interest was if there is a contextual bias being introduced by emphasizing animal remains from discrete features over areas of undifferentiated sheet midden. Because of the disparity in how MNI can be calculated for the Fort Ouiatenon collection, rarefaction curves (Styles 1981, 42–43) were constructed by plotting the number of taxa against NISP. The total NISP for sheet midden was 3,288 and 70 taxa, compared to features that had a total NISP of 8,348 and 78 taxa. The curves were comparable in terms of taxonomic richness; hence, both sheet midden and refuse deposits seem to share the same underlying structure of taxonomic diversity. Following the preferences of Grayson (1979, 154–58) and Tipper (1979), two-sided Smirnov tests (Conover 1971, 309–14) were used to compare the species-abundance distributions between sheet midden and features for mammals, birds, and fish. Even at a significance level of 0.20, no significant differences were found.

Figure 5.7. Bone or antler projectile points. Photographs by Philip J. Franz.

Figure 5.8. Cancellous bone paint applicator. Photograph by Leslie Martin Conwell.

A difference of proportions test (Blalock 1972, 228–30) was used to determine if twenty-one taxa are represented in the same proportions in both midden and feature contexts. There is a slightly higher proportion of deer remains associated with midden samples, and this is probably why the same tendency holds for all identified mammals. In contrast, the proportion of all identified bird bones is slightly higher in the feature collections, even though there are no significant differences for any individual avian species. Attention to ordinal rankings of all taxa shows that shovelnose sturgeon ranks fifth in NISP for midden contexts but eighteenth for features.

These subtle differences may be due to taphonomic factors such as trampling and sweeping in areas of sheet midden. Carnivore-gnawed bones occur in feature deposits as well as in middens, which suggests that wall trenches and refuse pits received secondary refuse. Unlike larger osteological specimens, small and fragile dermal cranial bones and postcranial scutes from shovelnose sturgeon were more abundant in sheet midden faunal refuse. Identifiable bird bones apparently survived better in refuse pits.

Temporal Perspective: Changes over Time?

Charles Cleland compared the French and British subsistence patterns using faunal samples from nine refuse pits at Fort Michilimackinac in northern Michigan (Cleland 1970). He surmised that (1) the French exploited a greater variety of animal species, especially among mammals; (2) the French hunted moose (*Alces alces*) and black bears to a greater extent than did the British, who instead relied more on domesticated animals; and (3) the French obtained a greater proportion of their diet from wild fowl and deepwater fish species than did the British. Later studies of faunal samples from other contexts at that site showed additional complexity and heterogeneity in diets, possibly resulting from ethnic, religious, and occupational backgrounds as well as interactions with Native Americans including marriage (Carlson 2012; Scott 1985, 1996, 2001; Shapiro 1979).

Similarly, conditions at Fort Ouiatenon were not static over the seventy-five years of Euro-American occupation. Whereas Fort Michilimackinac was transformed from a French palisaded trading town into a major British military post after 1761 (Heldman and Grange 1981), Fort Ouiatenon had a different history. It was garrisoned by a small British detachment for less than two years before Pontiac's Rebellion terminated the British military presence in the Wabash River valley. The outpost then reverted to essentially the same fur trade families of French descent who lived there prior to the French and Indian War but without the support of New France. Although a British store operated at Ouiatenon in 1782 (Barnhart and Riker 1971, 230) and British agents sporadically visited the Wabash Valley posts, there is little indication that British influence brought about major changes in daily life and subsistence activities. Perhaps the large

Native populations in the vicinity depleted local animal populations, and this would have forced hunters and trappers to shift their reliance to alternative wild and domesticated animals.

Thirty features have the potential to reveal temporal animal exploitation patterns at Fort Ouiatenon. Based on artifact associations, nineteen features were attributed to an early period of occupation (i.e., 1717–1761), and these consist of fifteen wall trenches, two refuse pits, and two wells (i.e., the lower fill of Feature 50 and the total fill from Feature 102). Eleven features were assigned to the later occupation (i.e., post-1761), and these include six wall trenches, three refuse pits, one hearth, and one well (i.e., the upper fill of Feature 50). The cumulative faunal assemblage for the early period totals 12,261 specimens, compared to 11,785 specimens that were associated with late period features. The early period sample of 1,921 NISP with sixty-five taxa is only slightly more diverse in species composition than the late period sample of 1,943 NISP with fifty-nine taxa. The data for animal remains from all features assigned to a period were treated as one large faunal assemblage, and a conservative minimum distinction approach (Grayson 1973) was used to calculate MNI values.

When the thirty collections are considered as two groups, the difference of proportions test was used to assess whether observed differences in the relative proportions for a taxon is statistically significant. For NISP values, three differences were noteworthy. White-tailed deer specimens occur in the late assemblage in a higher proportion (50.5%) than in the early assemblage (43.4%). This influences NISP proportions for all identified mammals: 68.8 percent for the late sample versus 59.6 percent for the early sample, a difference that was highly significant (probability does not exceed 0.01). Although bird bones are more numerous in the early refuse and the taxa are slightly more diverse, none of the bone counts for any of the individual taxa exhibited significant differences. However, when NISP for all birds are compared, the difference between early and late samples was highly significant (probability does not exceed 0.01). The tests failed to reveal any significant differences when MNI and biomass were the values being considered. Thus, white-tailed deer appears to have been more important for the Fort Ouiatenon inhabitants following the onset of the British administration in 1761. Perhaps the increased importance of deer hides during the later years of occupation could reflect depletion of beavers and other fur-bearing mammals (Nassaney 2015, 86). Meanwhile, both pig and cattle appear to have been consumed at roughly equivalent rates during both early and late occupations. These tendencies were examined in more detail by applying the comparison of means test (Steel and Torrie 1980, 106–7) to individual feature collections that made up the two aggregate temporal samples. Individual features having fewer than thirty identified species were excluded, resulting in only thirteen of the original nineteen early features and nine of eleven late features. The tests demonstrated that there is more variation for individual refuse deposits within both the early and late collections than there is between the two periods when the combined assemblages are considered.

Unlike Fort Michilimackinac and the French settlement at Detroit, both of which functioned as regional distribution centers, Forts Ouiatenon, St. Joseph, and Miamis are examples of local distribution centers that had more intimate connections, interactions, and commerce with neighboring Native population centers. The local centers were more remote in terms of distance and infrequent communications and had smaller numbers of French civilians and military personnel. Concerning animal procurement, the local centers were more dependent on wild species, with domesticated livestock providing supplementary sources of meat. Aside from the French commandant and his small garrison, the families residing at Fort Ouiatenon were essentially the same after 1761 when the British took possession of the Wabash Valley posts. This political transition apparently had little influence on daily economic pursuits and activities at Fort Ouiatenon. Although wild animal resources may have become even more important, there is also no archaeological evidence for a perceptible depletion in wild animal resources in the later part of the eighteenth century.

INTERSITE COMPARISONS

The significance of Fort Ouiatenon's faunal assemblage is best understood by using a comparative approach and examining other contemporaneous French colonial fort and outpost sites in the Midwest to find if patterns exist that inform us if these sites share similarities in economic orientations. Despite analyses of several Fort Michilimackinac faunal collections, consideration of the French regime at the Straits of Mackinac is exceptional due to the stark contrast in the environmental setting of the northern Michigan site compared to the French sites to the south. The mixed hardwood forest of coniferous and deciduous trees in the northern location was unfavorable to large game animals (Cleland 1966, 764–65), which is reflected by the emphasis that was placed on deepwater fish at the Straits of Mackinac. Elizabeth Scott's biomass calculations indicate that fish, mainly lake trout (*Salvelinus namaycush*) and lake whitefish (*Coregonus clupeaformis*), contributed as much as 86 percent of the meat in several of the midden deposits that she analyzed (Scott 1985, 154–55). This presents a major contrast to Fort Ouiatenon.

Sites of French forts and outposts located in environmental settings more similar to Fort Ouiatenon are available for consideration. These include Fort St. Joseph (20BE23) in southwestern Michigan (Martin et al. 2019); Fort de Chartres No. 3 at the Laurens site (11R125) in the Mississippi River valley in Randolph County, Illinois (Jelks et al. 1989; Martin 2014; Mazrim 2011, 195–207); and Fort de Chartres No. 4

(11R127), located about 1 km to the west (Keene 1991; Martin and Masulis 1988). All four sites have abundant well-preserved faunal samples. Whereas Forts Ouiatenon and St. Joseph functioned as "local distribution centers," Fort de Chartres was a "regional distribution center" (Tordoff 1983). An alternative model proposed by Keene (1991, 40) views the French colonial forts as a "series of entrepots," with Forts Ouiatenon and St. Joseph engaged in the "extraction, processing, and shipping of natural resources, e.g., furs," in contrast to Fort de Chartres, which was involved with the "production, processing, and shipping of surplus agricultural goods." Each of these economic pursuits was characterized by its own basic settlement and land-use pattern and population structure. A key aspect of animal exploitation for both models concerns the relative importance of domesticated and wild species. The local distribution center and extractive resource sites are expected to exhibit a greater reliance on wild animals, especially those species that were valued for the fur trade. In contrast, the regional distribution center and agricultural sites would reflect places where habitants were primarily concerned with growing crops and raising domesticated animals for local consumption as well as possible export to other local centers and fur trade outposts.

In order to make broad comparisons, importance values were combined for deer, wapiti, bison, and black bear to make a category of large wild mammals. Similarly, the large domesticated mammals consist of horse, pig, cattle, sheep (*Ovis aries*), and goat (*Capra hircus*). Because diagnostic cattle were much more common than bison at each site, indeterminate large bovid specimens were grouped with cattle. Biomass is used to illustrate intersite patterns. Whereas the biomass from all large mammals (wild and domesticated) constitutes 87 percent for all identified animals at Fort St. Joseph, these account for approximately 91 percent of the biomass at Fort Ouiatenon as well as at the two Illinois Country sites. Figure 5.9 presents comparisons using percentages of biomass. The hypothesized dichotomy between wild and domesticated mammals appears to be valid, but there is a significant difference between the two trading post sites. Whereas Fort Ouiatenon shows a greater proportion of biomass for large wild mammals, cattle apparently contributed an important periodical source of supplemental meat. Sleeper-Smith (2018, 59, 133) emphasized the importance of native women's extensive river bottom cornfields near the Ouiatenon villages for sustaining a large local population, and payment vouchers sent by French commandants attest to the presence of some cattle at Fort Ouiatenon. Inclusion of horse bones probably also inflates the importance of domesticated animals at Fort Ouiatenon. Although mid-eighteenth-century documents suggest that livestock were also being raised at Fort St. Joseph (Brandão and Nassaney 2019, 32), the quantity of domesticated large mammal remains among the archaeological collections is relatively minuscule. In contrast, domesticated mammals make up more than 70 percent of the biomass from large

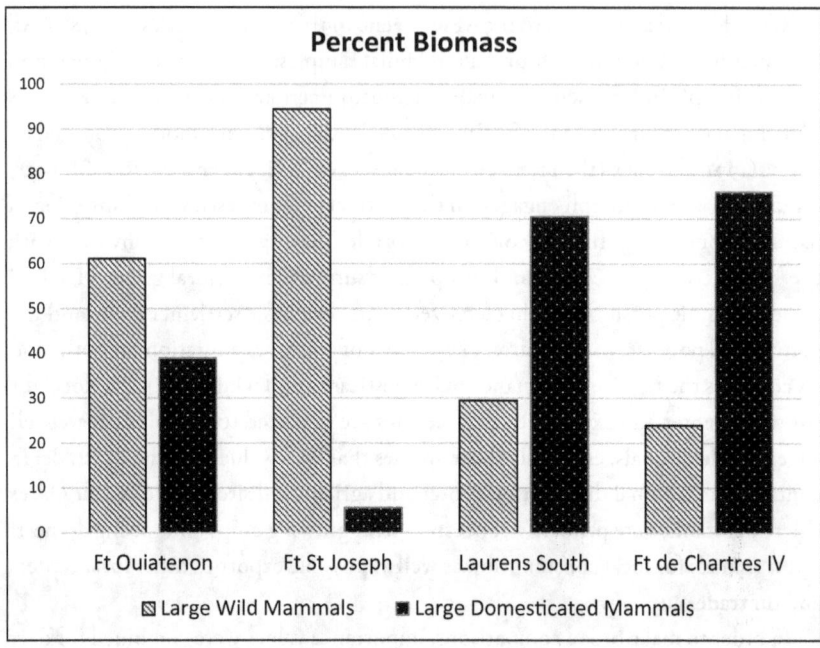

Figure 5.9. Percentage biomass from large wild mammals and large domesticated mammals at four French colonial fort sites. Laurens South is the archaeological site of Fort de Chartres No. 3.

mammals at both Illinois Country sites. Fort de Chartres No. 4 is unique in being the only site that had sheep or goat remains. Although additional excavations took place in the northern part of the Laurens site in 2011 and 2012, the identified animal remains occurred in proportions that are consistent with those from the previous excavations in the southern area (Martin 2014).

Figure 5.10 shows biomass contributions for all other animals except large mammals at the four sites with miscellaneous mammals consisting only of medium-sized and small species. There is much more variability among the sites, but Fort Ouiatenon and Laurens South are similar in having large proportions of avian remains. Waterfowl (ducks, geese, and swans) and wild turkey are the dominant taxa at all sites, but domestic chickens and passenger pigeons are also present at each. Consistent with its function as a fur trade post, Fort St. Joseph is unique in having abundant remains of raccoon, beaver, and porcupine (*Erethizon dorsatum*), along with lesser numbers of various rodents, mustelids, canids, and bobcats. Fort de Chartres No. 4 is unusual in having greater biomass contributions from large aquatic turtles and large river fish resulting in a more balanced profile, but this may be sample bias and a smaller overall faunal sample.

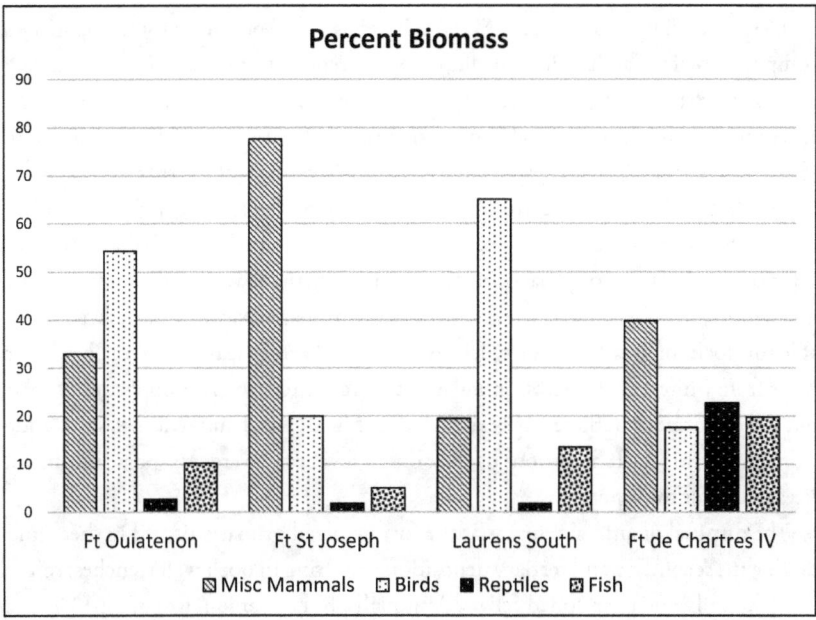

Figure 5.10. Percentage biomass from miscellaneous vertebrate animals at four French colonial fort sites, exclusive of large wild mammals and large domesticated mammals shown in figure 5.9. Laurens South is the archaeological site of Fort de Chartres No. 3.

CONCLUSION

An upper Wabash Valley animal exploitation pattern may be discerned when the Fort Ouiatenon faunal assemblage is compared to other French colonial forts and trading posts in the Midwest. The large well-preserved faunal assemblage provides insights on animal exploitation at a Wabash River valley French fur trade site that prevailed over time as an isolated trading post and enclave for the French-descended traders and their families, even after the fall of the French regime.

Wild animals were prevalent in the subsistence economy. Although many kinds of animals were sought for both food and furs, white-tailed deer was by far the most significant single species. Individual mature deer were selectively hunted or utilized, and this attests to the importance of deer as a principal source of hides and meat. Waterfowl, wild turkey, and raccoon were important secondary food animals. Although cattle, pig, and horse make up less than 10 percent of the NISP and MNI, these species contributed just less than 40 percent of the biomass from all animals in the analyzed Fort Ouiatenon sample and comprised a notable supplement.

Despite the importance of the Wabash River as a transportation route, the species composition of the archaeological sample mostly reflects terrestrial habitats occurring within approximately 40 km² of Fort Ouiatenon. Local aquatic habitats contained and supported bountiful animal populations, but according to our Fort Ouiatenon resource model, these resources were underutilized. Riverine animals that were targeted include large fish, especially catfishes, redhorses, and buffalos, along with turtles, freshwater mussels, and waterfowl. In addition to the main channel of the Wabash River, local tributary streams would have drawn attention where spawning fish and freshwater mussels may have been more accessible on a seasonal basis. Nearby prairies were favorable for flocks of greater prairie chickens, and these were at least occasionally sought. Aside from white-tailed deer, bison and wapiti were hunted when the opportunity arose, but the importance of these large extirpated mammals is difficult to assess, since aside from hides and selected portions of meat only a few bones were transported from kill sites to the fur trade post.

The disposal of animal remains at the fort involved primary discard in sheet middens, with secondary and tertiary deposition occurring in open wall trenches, refuse pits, old wells, and abandoned cellars. Although a horse cranium was dumped in one of the wells and many pieces of cut deer antlers were discarded in small concentrations near particular features, the only other noticeable pattern was the greater occurrence of small dermal bones from shovelnose sturgeons in sheet midden deposits instead of in trenches or pits.

The end of the French regime at Fort Ouiatenon and the political transition to British control seems to have had little influence on daily economic pursuits. Any depletion of wild animal resources near the Ouiatenon community during the second half of the eighteenth century is also imperceptible. The underrepresentation of beaver and mustelid species in the fort's archaeological faunal assemblage, even during its early occupation, may indicate that the harvest of local populations of these fur trade species could not be sustained during the span of the site's occupation.

Insights into the people who resided at Fort Ouiatenon and what life was like for them may also be gleaned from some of the bone, antler, and shell artifacts that were encountered during the excavations. Distinct from Fort Ouiatenon, excavations at the Laurens site (Fort de Chartres No. 3) yielded European-made bone artifacts such as cutlery handle scales, buttons, combs, and a die. In contrast, many of the modified animal remains at Fort Ouiatenon consist of local Native-made objects including turtle carapace bowls or rattles, projectile points, bird bone tubes, bone awls, a cancellous bone paint applicator, a perforated bear mandible, and a mussel shell digging tool. These artifacts reflect interactions with local Miami and Wea populations, the presence of Native partners and wives, and the likely assimilation of some of the French traders and their métis descendants into local Native societies.

ACKNOWLEDGMENTS

Thanks to Kory Cooper, Misty Jackson, and David Hovde for their work in organizing this volume. The work reported on in this chapter was made possible by the collaboration of the Tippecanoe County Historical Association and the MSU Museum at Michigan State University, Charles E. Cleland, principal investigator. Work space, laboratory facilities, and equipment at the MSU Museum were provided by former museum directors Rollin H. Baker and C. Kurt Dewhurst and at the Illinois State Museum by former museum director R. Bruce McMillan and former assistant director for science James E. King. Enthusiastic support was also given by Bonnie W. Styles and James R. Purdue. I thank Philip J. Franz, Doug Carr, and Leslie Conwell for photographs of various specimens. Assistance with specimen identifications was given by the late J. Alan Holman (snake vertebrae), Leslie Fay (small rodents), Mona Colburn (fish), Robert Warren (mussels), and John B. Burch (*Lithasia* shell). Rick Purdue furnished his expertise on all matters pertaining to white-tailed deer. Judy Tordoff and Vergil Noble provided detailed insights on the MSU excavations, and I received advice and support from my dissertation committee members Charles Cleland (chair), the late Moreau Maxwell, William Lovis, and Lawrence Robbins. I am indebted to many colleagues then at the MSU Museum, the MSU Department of Anthropology, and the Illinois State Museum for their interest and encouragement over the years. Most of all, thanks to Claire Fuller Martin and to Tim Martin.

REFERENCES

Anderson, R. S., and L. E. Brown. 1983. "Comparative Effects of Fire on Trees in a Midwestern Savannah and an Adjacent Forest." *Torrey Botany Club Bulletin* 110: 87–90.

Bailey, Reeve M., and Frank B. Cross. 1954. "River Sturgeons of the American Genus *Scaphirhynchus*: Characters, Distribution, and Synonomy." *Papers of the Michigan Academy of Science, Arts, and Letters* 39: 169–208.

Balkwill, Darlene McCuaig, and Stephen L. Cumbaa. 1992. *A Guide to the Identification of Postcranial Bones of* Bos taurus *and* Bison bison. Syllogeus No. 71. Ottawa: Canadian Museum of Nature.

Barnhart, John D., and Dorothy L. Riker. 1971. *Indiana to 1816: The Colonial Period*. Indianapolis: Historical Bureau and Indiana Historical Society.

Bellrose, Frank C. 1968. *Waterfowl Migration Corridors East of the Rocky Mountains in the United States*. Biological Notes No. 61. Urbana: Illinois Natural History Survey.

———. 1976. *Ducks, Geese and Swans of North America*. Harrisburg, PA: Stackpole Books.

Belting, Natalia Maree. 2003 (1948). *Kaskaskia under the French Regime*. Carbondale: Southern Illinois University Press.

Belue, Ted Franklin. 1996. *The Long Hunt: Death of the Buffalo East of the Mississippi*. Mechanicsburg, PA: Stackpole Books.

Bent, Arthur Cleveland. 1925. *Life Histories of North American Wildfowl: Order; Anseres (Part II)*. Bulletin 130. Washington, DC: United States National Museum.

———. 1927. *Life History of North American Shore Birds*. Bulletin 142. Washington, DC: United States National Museum.

Binford, Lewis R. 1978. *Nunamiut Ethnoarchaeology*. New York: Academic Press.

———. 1981. *Bones: Ancient Men and Modern Myths*. New York: Academic Press.

Blalock, Hubert M., Jr. 1972. *Social Statistics*. 2nd ed. New York: McGraw-Hill.

Bogan, Arthur E., and Paul W. Parmalee. 1983. *Tennessee's Rare Wildlife*, Vol. 2, *The Mollusks*. Nashville: Tennessee Department of Conservation.

Brandão, José António, and Michael S. Nassaney. 2017. "The Historical and Cultural Context of Fort St. Joseph." In *Fort St. Joseph Revealed: The Historical Archaeology of a Fur Trading Post*, ed. Michael S. Nassaney, 15–39. Gainesville: University Press of Florida.

Braun, Emma Lucy. 1950. *Deciduous Forests of Eastern North America*. Philadelphia: Blakiston.

Burch, J. B., and John L. Tottenham. 1980. *North American Freshwater Snails; Species List, Ranges and Illustrations*. Transactions of the POETS Society, No. 3. Society for Experimental and Descriptive Malacology. Ann Arbor: University of Michigan.

Carlson, Jenna K. 2012. *Culinary Creolization: Subsistence and Cultural Interaction at Fort Michilimackinac, 1730–1761*. Archaeological Completion Report Series No. 18. Mackinac Island, MI: Mackinac State Historic Parks.

Cleland, Charles E. 1966. *The Prehistoric Animal Ecology and Ethnozoology of the Upper Great Lakes Region*. Anthropological Papers No. 29. Ann Arbor: University of Michigan.

———. 1970. "Comparison of the Faunal Remains from French and British Refuse Pits at Fort Michilimackinac: A Study in Changing Subsistence Patterns." *Canadian Historic Sites: Occasional Papers in Archaeology and History* 3:7–23.

Conover, W. J. 1971. *Practical Nonparametric Statistics*. New York: Wiley.

Curry, Kevin D., and Anne Spacie. 1978. "Distribution of Stream Fishes in Tippecanoe County, Indiana." *Proceedings of the Indiana Academy of Science* 87:182–88.

Dawdy, Shannon Lee. 2010. "'A Wild Taste': Food and Colonialism in Eighteenth-Century Louisiana." *Ethnohistory* 57: 389–414.

Eccles, William J. 1969. *The Canadian Frontier, 1534–1760*. New York: Holt, Rinehart and Winston.

Emerson, Thomas E. 1980. "A Stable White-tailed Deer Population Model and Its Implications for Interpreting Prehistoric Hunting Patterns." *Midcontinental Journal of Archaeology* 5: 117–32.

Findeis, Eric K. 1993. "Skeletal Anatomy of the North American Shovelnose Sturgeon *Scaphirhynchus platorynchus* (Rafinesque 1820) with Comparisons to Other Acipenseriformes." PhD diss., University of Massachusetts.

———. 1997. "Osteology and Phylogenetic Interrelationships of Sturgeon (Acipenseridae)." *Environmental Biology of Fishes* 48: 73–126.

Gammon, J. R. 1977. "The Status of Indiana Streams and Fish from 1800 to 1900." *Proceedings of the Indiana Academy of Science* 86: 209–16.

Garland, Elizabeth B., Kathryn E. Parker, Terrance J. Martin, and Arthur L. DesJardins. 2001. The Wymer West Knoll Site (20BE132): An Upper Mississippian Habitation in a Multicomponent Site on the Lower St. Joseph River in Berrien County, Michigan. Completion Report prepared for the Michigan Department of Transportation. Department of Anthropology, Western Michigan University, Kalamazoo.

Goodrich, Calvin, and Henry van der Schalie. 1944. "A Revision of the Mollusca of Indiana." *American Midland Naturalist* 32: 257–326.

Gorby, S. S. 1886. "Geology of Tippecanoe County." In *Indiana Department of Geology and Natural History Fifteenth Annual Report*, ed. Maurice Thompson, 61–96. Indianapolis: William B. Burford.

Grayson, Donald K. 1973. "On the Methodology of Faunal Analysis." *American Antiquity* 39: 432–39.

———. 1979. "On the Quantification of Vertebrate Archaeofaunas." In *Advances in Archaeological Method and Theory*, Vol. 2, ed. Michael B. Schiffer, 199–237. New York: Academic Press.

Heldman, Donald P., and Roger T. Grange Jr. 1981. *Excavations at Fort Michilimackinac: 1978–1979; The Rue de la Babillarde*. Archaeological Completion Report Series No. 3. Mackinac Island, MI: Mackinac Island State Park Commission.

Integrated Taxonomic Information System. 2020. Information retrieved October 3, 2020, from the Integrated Taxonomic Information System online database. http://www.itis.gov.

Jackson, H. E. 1989. "The Trouble with Transformations: Effects of Sample Size and Sample Composition on Meat Weight Estimates Based on Skeletal Mass Allometry." *Journal of Archaeological Science* 16: 601–10.

Jelks, Edward B., Carl J. Ekberg, and Terrance J. Martin. 1989. *Excavations at the Laurens Site: Probable Location of Fort de Chartres I*. Studies in Illinois Archaeology No. 5. Springfield: Illinois Historic Preservation Agency.

Jones, James R., III. 1988. "Degrees of Acculturation at Two Eighteenth Century Aboriginal Villages Near Lafayette, Tippecanoe County, Indiana." PhD diss., Indiana University.

Keene, Arthur S. 1981. *Prehistoric Foraging in a Temperate Forest: A Linear Programming Model*. New York: Academic Press.

Keene, David. 1991. "Fort de Chartres: Archaeology in the Illinois Country." In *French Colonial Archaeology: The Illinois Country and the Western Great Lakes*, ed. John A. Walthall, 29–41. Urbana: University of Illinois Press.

Kellar, James H. 1970. "The Search for Ouiatenon." *Indiana History Bulletin* 47, no. 11: 123–33.

Krauskopf, Frances, ed. 1955. "Ouiatenon Documents." *Indiana Historical Society Publications* 18, no. 2: 132–234.

Krumholz, Luis A., Roy L. Bingham, and Edward R. Meyer. 1970. "A Survey of the Commercially Valuable Mussels of the Wabash and White Rivers of Indiana." *Proceedings of the Indiana Academy of Science* 79: 205–26.

Lindley, Harlow, ed. 1916. *Indiana as Seen by Early Travelers*. Indianapolis: Indiana Historical Society.

Lindsey, Alton A., William R. Crankshaw, and Syed A. Qadir. 1965. "Soil Relations and Distribution Map of the Vegetation of Presettlement Indiana." *Botanical Gazette* 126, no. 3: 155–63.

Logan, Brad. 1998. "Fat of the Land: White Rock Phase Bison Hunting and Grease Production." *Plains Anthropologist* 43: 349–66.

Lyman, R. Lee. 2008. *Quantitative Paleozoology*. Cambridge Manuals in Archaeology. Cambridge: Cambridge University Press.

Martin, Terrance J. 1986. "A Faunal Analysis of Fort Ouiatenon, an Eighteenth Century Trading Post in the Wabash Valley of Indiana." PhD diss., Michigan State University.

———. 1991a. "An Archaeological Perspective on Animal Exploitation Patterns at French Colonial Sites in the Illinois Country." In *French Colonial Archaeology: The Illinois Country and the Western Great Lakes*, ed. John A. Walthall, 189–200. Urbana: University of Illinois Press.

———. 1991b. "Modified Animal Remains, Subsistence, and Cultural Interaction at French Colonial Sites in the Midwestern United States." In *Beamers, Bobwhites, and Blue-Points: Tributes to the Career of Paul W. Parmalee*, ed. James R. Purdue, Walter E. Klippel, and Bonnie W. Styles, 409–19. Scientific Papers Vol. 23. Springfield: Illinois State Museum.

———. 2014. "Use of Animals at the Laurens North Site, the Location of Fort de Chartres III in the Illinois Country." Paper presented at the 47th Annual Conference on Historical and Underwater Archaeology, Quebec City.

———. 2015. "Foodways and the Illinois: Archaeozoological Samples from Grid A." In *Protohistory at the Grand Village of the Kaskaskia: The Illinois Country on the Eve of Colony*, ed. Robert F. Mazrim, 65–88. Studies in Archaeology No. 10. Illinois State Archaeological Survey, Prairie Research Institute. Urbana: University of Illinois.

———. 2020. "Use of Black Bears in the Western Great Lakes Region and the Riddle of the Perforated Bear Mandibles." In *Bears: Archaeological and Ethnohistorical Perspectives in Native Eastern North America*, ed. Heather A. Lapham and Gregory A. Waselkov, 108–37. Gainesville, University of Florida Press.

Martin, Terrance J., Joseph Hearns, and Rory J. Becker. 2019. "The Use of Animals for Fur, Food, and Raw Material at Fort St. Joseph." In *Fort St Joseph Revealed: The Historical Archaeology of a Fur Trading Post*, ed. Michael C. Nassaney, 40–78. Gainesville: University Press of Florida.

Martin, Terrance J., and Steven R. Kuehn. 2017. "Faunal Analysis." In *The Hoxie Farm Site Main Occupation Area: Late Fisher and Huber Phase Components in South Chicago*, ed. Douglas

K. Jackson, 415–93. Research Report No. 40, Illinois State Archaeological Survey, Prairie Research Institute. Urbana: University of Illinois.

Martin, Terrance J., and Dennis F. Lawler. 2014. "Animal Pathologies at French Colonial Sites in the Midwest: Case Studies of White-tailed Deer at Forts St. Joseph and Ouiatenon." Paper presented at the 79th Annual Meeting of the Society for American Archaeology, Austin.

Martin, Terrance J., and Mary Carol Masulis. 1988. "Appendix D: Preliminary Report on Animal Remains from Fort de Chartres (11R127)." In *Archaeological Excavations at Fort de Chartres:1985–87*, ed. David Keene. Springfield: Illinois Historic Preservation Agency.

Martin, Terrance J., and Kathryn E. Parker. 2017. "Ritual Feasting at Cahokia?: Animal and Plant Remains from an Early Eighteenth-Century Illinois Occupation on the First Terrace of Monks Mound." *Illinois Archaeology* 29: 301–54.

Martin, Terrance J., and J. C. Richmond. 1996. "Animal Remains from 12-Hu-1022." In *Archaeological Excavations at the Ehler Site (12-Hu-1022): An Early 19th Century Miami Indian Habitation Site Near the Forks of the Wabash, Huntington County, Indiana*, ed. Rob Mann, 158–76. Report of Investigation 95IN0062-P3r01, Landmark Archaeological and Environmental Services, Sheridan, Indiana. Submitted to Indiana Department of Transportation, Indianapolis.

Martin, Terrance J., J. Chris Richmond, and Erin Brand. 2003. *An Archaeozoological Analysis of 23CK116, the Illini Village of the Marquette and Jolliet Voyage of 1673*. Technical Report 2003-1478-8, Landscape History Program, Illinois State Museum, Springfield. Submitted to the Missouri Department of Natural Resources, Jefferson City.

Mazrim, Robert F. 2011. *At Home in the Illinois Country: French Colonial Domestic Sites Archaeology in the Midwest, 1730–1800*. Studies in Archaeology No. 9, Illinois State Archaeological Survey, Prairie Research Institute. Urbana: University of Illinois.

———. 2015. "The Seventeenth Century Samples and Affiliations at Grid A." In *Protohistory at the Grand Village of the Kaskaskia: The Illinois Country on the Eve of Colony*, ed. Robert F. Mazrim, 13–27. Studies in Archaeology No. 10. Illinois State Archaeological Survey, Prairie Research Institute. Urbana: University of Illinois.

McBeth, William A. 1902. "Wabash River Terraces in Tippecanoe County, Indiana." *Proceedings of the Indiana Academy of Sciences* 11: 237–43.

McCord, Shirley S., ed. 1970. *Travel Accounts of Indiana, 1679–1961*. Indiana Historical Collections Vol. 47. Indianapolis: Indiana Historical Bureau.

Minton, Sherman A., Jr. 1972. *Amphibians and Reptiles of Indiana*. Indianapolis: Indiana Academy of Science Monograph.

Morrissey, Robert Michael. 2015. *Empire by Collaboration: Indians, Colonists, and Governments in Colonial Illinois Country*. Philadelphia: University of Pennsylvania Press.

Mosby, Henry S. 1967. "Population Dynamics." In *The Wild Turkey and Its Management*, ed. Oliver H. Hewitt, 113–36. Washington DC: Wildlife Society.

Moussette, Marcel, and Gregory A. Waselkov. 2013. *Archéologie de l'Amérique colonial française*. Montreal: Lévesque éditeur.

Mumford, Russel E., and John O. Whitaker, Jr. 1982. *Mammals of Indiana*. Bloomington: Indiana University Press.

Munson, Patrick J., Paul W. Parmalee, and Richard A. Yarnell. 1971. "Subsistence Ecology of Scovill, a Terminal Middle Woodland Village." *American Antiquity* 36: 410–31.

Nassaney, Michael S. 2015. *The Archaeology of the North American Fur Trade*. Gainesville: University Press of Florida.

Nassaney, Michael S., and Terrance J. Martin. 2017. "Food and Furs at French Fort St. Joseph." In *Archaeological Perspectives on the French in the New World*, ed. Elizabeth M. Scott, 83–111. Gainesville: University Press of Florida.

Neill, N. P., and W. E. Tharp. 1907. "Soil Survey of Tippecanoe County, Indiana." In *Field Operations of the Bureau of Soils, 1905*, ed. Milton Whitney, 781–813. Washington, DC: US Department of Agriculture.

Noble, Vergil E., Jr. 1983. "Functional Classification and Intra-site Analysis in Historical Archaeology: A Case Study from Fort Ouiatenon." PhD diss., Michigan State University.

———. 1991. "Ouiatenon on the Ouabache: Archaeological Investigations at a Fur Trading Post on the Wabash River." In *French Colonial Archaeology: The Illinois Country and the Western Great Lakes*, ed. John A. Walthall, 65–77. Urbana: University of Illinois Press.

Oates, David W., Ed D. Boyd, and Jennifer S. Raemaekers. 2003. *Identification of Waterfowl Breastbones and Avian Osteology (Sterna) of North American Anseriformes*. Special Publication No. 10. Martinsville: Virginia Museum of Natural History.

Parmalee, Paul W. 1963. "Vertebrate Remains from the Bell Site, Winnebago County, Wisconsin." *Wisconsin Archeologist* 44: 58–69.

———. 1967. *The Fresh-Water Mussels of Illinois*. Popular Science Series Vol. 8. Springfield: Illinois State Museum.

Parmalee, Paul W., and Walter E. Klippel. 1983. "The Role of Native Animals in the Food Economy of the Historic Kickapoo in Central Illinois." In *Lulu Linear Punctated: Essays in Honor of George Irving Quimby*, ed. Robert C. Dunnell and Donald K. Grayson, 253–321. Anthropological Papers No. 72, Museum of Anthropology. Ann Arbor: University of Michigan.

Parmalee, Paul W., Andreas A. Paloumpis, and Nancy Wilson. 1972. *Animals Utilized by Woodland Peoples Occupying the Apple Creek Site, Illinois*. Reports of Investigations No. 23. Springfield: Illinois State Museum.

Petty, R. O., and M. T. Jackson. 1966. "Plant Communities." In *Natural Features of Indiana*, ed. Alton A. Lindsey, 264–96. Indianapolis: Indiana Academy of Science.

Pflieger, William L. 1975. *The Fishes of Missouri*. Jefferson City: Missouri Department of Conservation.

Potzger, John E., Margaret E. Potzger, and Jack McCormick. 1956. "The Forest Primeval of Indiana as Recorded in the Original US Land Surveys and an Evaluation of Previous Interpretations of Indiana Vegetation." *Butler University Botanical Studies* 13: 95–111.

Purdue, James R. 1980. "Clinal Variation of Some Mammals during the Holocene in Missouri." *Quaternary Research* 13: 242–58.

———. 1983a. "Epiphyseal Closure in White-tailed Deer." *Journal of Wildlife Management* 47: 1207–13.

———. 1983b. "Methods of Determining Sex and Body Size in Prehistoric Samples of White-tailed Deer (*Odocoileus virginianus*)." *Transactions of the Illinois State Academy of Science* 76: 351–57.

———. 1986. "The Size of White-tailed Deer (*Odocoileus virginianus*) during the Archaic Period in Central Illinois." In *Foraging, Collecting, and Harvesting: Archaic Period Subsistence and Settlement in the Eastern Woodlands*, ed. Sarah W. Neusius, 65–69. Occasional Paper No. 6, Center for Archaeological Investigations. Carbondale: Southern Illinois University.

Reidhead, Van A. 1981. *A Linear Programming Model of Prehistoric Subsistence Optimization: A Southeastern Indiana Example*. Prehistoric Research Series 6(1). Indianapolis: Indiana Historical Society.

Reitz, Elizabeth J., and Dan Cordier. 1984. "Use of Allometry in Zooarchaeological Analysis." In *Animals and Archaeology 2: Shell Middens, Fishes, and Birds*, ed. C. Grigson and J. Clutton-Brock, 237–52. BAR International Series 183. London: British Archaeological Reports Oxford Ltd.

Reitz, Elizabeth J., Irvy R. Quitmyer, H. Stephen Hale, Sylvia J. Scudder, and Elizabeth S. Wing. 1987. "Application of Allometry to Zooarchaeology." *American Antiquity* 52: 304–17.

Reitz, Elizabeth J., and C. Margaret Scarry. 1985. *Reconstructing Historic Subsistence with an Example from Sixteenth-Century Spanish Florida*. Special Publication Series No. 3. Glassboro, NJ: Society for Historical Archaeology.

Reitz, Elizabeth J., and Elizabeth S. Wing. 1999. *Zooarchaeology*. Cambridge Manuals in Archaeology. Cambridge: Cambridge University Press.

Rick, Anne. 1975. "Bird Medullary Bone: A Seasonal Dating Technique for Faunal Analysts." *Canadian Archaeological Association Bulletin* 7: 183–90.

Schneider, Allen F. 1966. "Physiography." In *Natural Features of Indiana*, ed. Alton A. Lindsey, 40–56. Indianapolis: Indiana Academy of Science.

Schorger, Arlie W. 1955. *The Passenger Pigeon; Its Natural History and Extinction*. Madison: University of Wisconsin Press.

Scott, Elizabeth M. 1985. *French Subsistence at Fort Michilimackinac, 1715–1781: The Clergy and the Traders*. Archaeological Completion Report Series No. 9. Mackinac Island, MI: Mackinac Island State Park Commission.

———. 1996. "Who Ate What? Archaeological Food Remains and Cultural Diversity." In *Case Studies in Environmental Archaeology*, ed. Elizabeth J. Reitz, Lee A. Newsom, and Sylvia Scudder, 339–56. New York: Plenum.

———. 2001. "Faunal Remains from House D of the Southeast Rowhouse, British Period (1760–1781), Fort Michilimackinac." In *House D of the Southeast Row House: Excavations at Fort Michilimackinac, 1989–1997*, ed. Lynn L. M. Evans, 60–66. Archaeological Completion Report Series No. 17. Mackinac City, MI: Mackinac Island State Park Commission.

Severinghaus, C. W. 1949. "Tooth Development and Wear as Criteria of Age in White-tailed Deer." *Journal of Wildlife Management* 13: 195–216.

Shapiro, Gary. 1979. "Early British Subsistence Strategy at Michilimackinac: A Case Study in Historical Particularism." *Conference on Historic Sites Archaeology Papers 1978* 13: 315–56.

Sleeper-Smith, Susan. 2018. *Indigenous Prosperity and American Conquest: Indian Women of the Ohio River Valley, 1690–1792*. Chapel Hill: Omohundro Institute of Early American History and Culture, Williamsburg, Virginia, and University of North Carolina Press.

Smith, Bruce D. 1975. *Middle Mississippi Exploitation of Animal Populations*. Anthropological Papers No. 57, Museum of Anthropology. Ann Arbor: University of Michigan.

———. 1979. "Measuring the Selective Utilization of Animal Species by Prehistoric Human Populations." *American Antiquity* 44: 155–60.

Smith, Hugh M. 1898. "Statistics of the Fisheries of the Interior Waters of the United States." In *Report of the Commissioner for the Year Ending June 30, 1896*, 489–574. Washington, DC: US Commission of Fish and Fisheries.

Smith, Philip W. 1961. *The Amphibians and Reptiles of Illinois*. Bulletin Vol. 28, Article 1. Urbana: Illinois Natural History Survey.

———. 1971. *Illinois Streams: A Classification Based on Their Fishes and an Analysis of Factors Responsible for Disappearance of Native Species*. Biological Notes No. 76. Urbana: Illinois Natural History Survey.

———. 1979. *The Fishes of Illinois*. Urbana: University of Illinois Press.

Steel, Robert G. D., and James H. Torre. 1980. *Principles and Procedures of Statistics*. 2nd ed. New York: McGraw Hill.

Strezewski, Michael, and Robert G. McCullough. 2019. "Fort Ouiatenon, 1717–2019: 300+ Years of Indiana History." *Indiana Archaeology* 14, no. 1: 54–88.

Styles, Bonnie Whatley. 1981. *Faunal Exploitation and Resource Selection: Early Late Woodland Subsistence in the Lower Illinois Valley*. Archeological Program Scientific Papers No. 3. Evanston, IL: Northwestern University.

Thwaites, Reuben Gold, ed. 1972. *A New Discovery of a Vast Country in America*, by Father Louis Hennepin, Vols. 1 and 2. Reprint ed. New York: Krause Reprint. Originally published 1903, A. C. McClung, Chicago.

Tipper, John C. 1979. "Rarefaction and Rarefiction: The Use and Abuse of a Method in Paleoecology." *Paleobiology* 5: 423–34.

Tordoff, Judith D. 1980. *Excavations at Fort Ouiatenon, 1974–1976 Seasons: Preliminary Report*. Submitted to the Tippecanoe County Historical Association, Lafayette, Indiana. East Lansing: Michigan State University.

———. 1983. "An Archaeological Perspective on the Organization of the Fur Trade in Eighteenth Century New France." PhD diss., Michigan State University.

Towne, Charles W., and Edward N. Wentworth. 1950. *Pigs: From Cave to Corn Belt*. Norman: University of Oklahoma Press.

Townsend, C. H. 1902. "Statistics of the Fisheries of the Mississippi River and Tributaries." In *Report of the United States Commissioner of Fish and Fisheries for the Fiscal Year Ending June 30, 1901*, 659–740. Washington, DC: US Commission of Fish and Fisheries.

Transeau, E. N. 1935. "The Prairie Peninsula." *Ecology* 16: 423–37.

Trippensee, Reuben Edwin. 1948. *Wildlife Management: Upland Game and General Principles*, Vol. 1. New York: McGraw Hill.

Trubowitz, Neal L. 1992. "Native Americans and French on the Central Wabash." In *Calumet and Fleur-de-Lys: Archaeology of Indian and French Contact in the Midcontinent*, ed. John A. Walthall and Thomas E. Emerson, 241–64. Washington DC: Smithsonian Institution Press.

Ulrich, H. P., T. E. Barnes, B. A. Krantz, and J. G. Wade. 1959. *Soil Survey of Tippecanoe County, Indiana*. US Series 1940, No. 22. Washington, DC: US Department of Agriculture.

von Frese, Ralph R., and Vergil E. Noble. 1984. "Magnetometry for Archaeological Exploration of Historical Sites." *Historical Archaeology* 18: 38–53.

Warren, Robert E. 1991. "Freshwater Mussels as Paleoenvironmental Indicators: A Quantitative Approach to Assemblage Analysis." In *Beamers, Bobwhites, and Blue-Points: Tributes to the Career of Paul W. Parmalee*, ed. James R. Purdue, Walter E. Klippel, and Bonnie W. Styles, 23–66. Scientific Papers Vol. 23. Springfield: Illinois State Museum.

Waselkov, Gregory A. 1978. "Evolution of Deer Hunting in the Eastern Woodlands." *Midcontinental Journal of Archaeology* 3: 15–34.

Woolfenden, Glen E. 1961. *Postcranial Osteology of the Waterfowl*. Bulletin of the Florida State Museum Vol. 6, No. 1. Gainesville: Florida State Museum.

6

SYMBOLISM, NATIONALITY, IDENTITY, AND GENDER AS INTERPRETED FROM AN EIGHTEENTH-CENTURY RING FROM FORT OUIATENON

MISTY M. JACKSON, ARBRE CROCHE CULTURAL RESOURCES LLC, AND H. KORY COOPER, ASSOCIATE PROFESSOR, DEPARTMENT OF ANTHROPOLOGY

IN 1973 LARRY CHOWNING CONDUCTED EXCAVATIONS FOR THE TIPPECANOE County Historical Association at the site of Fort Ouiatenon. Chowning reported that while working at the southwest corner of the fort's original stockade he recovered a possible signet ring in the plow zone (Chowning, pers. comm., July 6, 2011; Tordoff 1983, 146–47). The unusual symbolism exhibited on the ring, that of a man astride a fish or dolphin, invites a close study to determine its meaning. Research suggests that it represented the Dauphin of France, Louis XV, and by extension it may have belonged to a high-ranking male of the post.

Excavations began at the fort site in 1968 and 1969 by Indiana University. In addition, Chowning worked at the site from 1971 to 1973, and Michigan State University followed with excavations from 1974 to 1979 (Noble 1983, 17; Tordoff 1983, 145–49). These excavations resulted in a large legacy collection that has been subjected to only a few studies to date and has the potential to yield much more information about life at the fort (see chapter 2 in this volume for a summary of the excavations).

DESCRIPTION OF THE RING

The possible signet ring consists of a translucent, nearly colorless, oval-shaped stone with brilliant cut on the beveled edges that is held in a copper alloy setting by seventeen points (figure 6.1). At the time of its recovery a gold-colored gilding, probably either of tombac or similor (see chapter 7 in this volume for a discussion of these materials), was evident (Chowning, pers. comm., July 6, 2011). The crown of the bezel displays an incised intaglio design of a male figure astride a fish or dolphin. The male figure holds a harp or lyre and wears a garment around the waist, which also trails behind the neck and shoulders in scarf-like fashion. The fish or dolphin floats above arcs representing waves. The ring band, which collapsed sometime after recovery, wraps around the back of the stone (figure 6.2). It consisted of scroll or filigree-work in the figure of a bird. Though the bird's head was missing at the time of recovery, when worn it would have appeared inverted to the wearer. If used as a seal, the intaglios's design would stand out in relief when pressed into wax.

IDENTIFYING THE RING'S COMPOSITION

The ring resides in the collections of the Tippecanoe County Historical Association in Lafayette, Indiana. On June 28, 2010, Jeff Kessler, master graduate gemologist of Stall and Kessler Jewelers of Lafayette, examined the ring in order to identify the stone's composition. The original assumption given its color was that it consisted of glass or quartz. Kessler visually inspected the material. The abrasions, nicks, and chips required that it be studied further under magnification, which revealed what appeared to be a very clear gemstone. However, it did not exhibit identifying characteristics typical of most gemstones such as garnet. Kessler conducted another test utilizing a refractometer, which gives the refractive index of a gemstone. Because the stone's surface showed much wear, registering an accurate reading proved difficult. This test produced a refractive index reading of approximately 1.77. According to Kessler, most glass objects test between 1.50–1.70. He indicated that gemstones registering in the 1.77 vicinity are garnet and corundum, also known as ruby and sapphire, but that the refractive index test is by no means conclusive. A determination could be achieved through other tests, such as specific gravity testing and magnification of the stone's back. However, these would require removing the stone from its setting, and that option was not pursued.

Figure 6.1. Possible signet ring from Fort Ouiatenon in the Tippecanoe County Historical Association collection. Photograph by Misty M. Jackson.

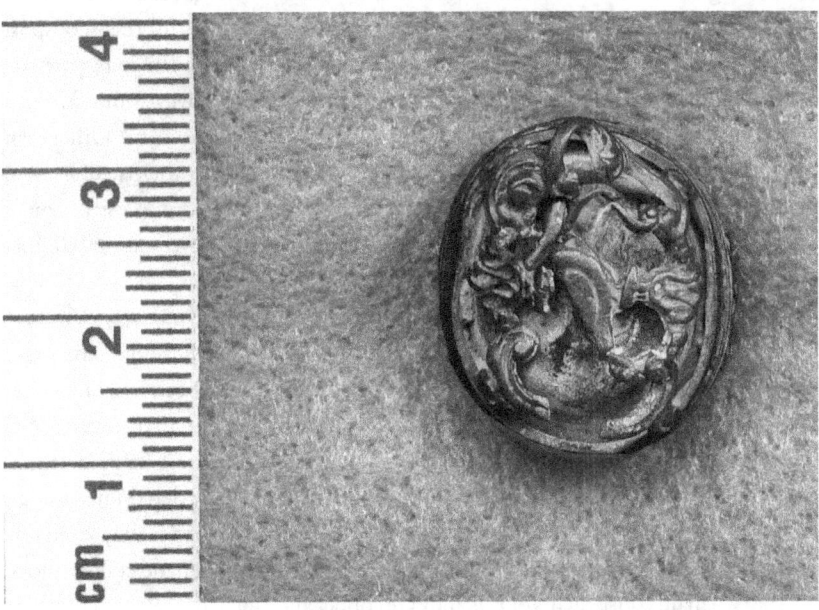

Figure 6.2. Back of the possible signet ring from Fort Ouiatenon in the Tippecanoe County Historical Association collection. Photograph by Brooke Sauter.

Kessler stated, "In summary, I am almost 100 percent certain it is not glass, and my best guess is garnet" (pers. email comm., July 14, 2010).

Garnets come in all colors but blue. According to Kessler, the refractive index of 1.77 is a high number for a garnet but is an almost perfect number for corundum (ruby and sapphire). The mineral corundum consists of aluminum oxide and can exhibit in any color. Varieties of red corundum are rubies, and all other varieties of corundum are sapphires. Given that corundum is second in hardness only to the diamond and that the ring's stone exhibits some chips and nicks, it appeared that the stone was garnet rather than corundum (Kessler, pers. telephone comm., October 8, 2010; Bonewitz 2005, 148–51, 300–303).

Garnets were a popular semiprecious gemstone throughout the eighteenth century, and the results of the analysis seemed plausible. White (2005, 98–99) refers to an advertisement in the June 1, 1758, *Pennsylvania Journal* listing precious and semiprecious stones including garnets for rings and earrings and cornelians for rings and seals. Jewelers commonly used the technique of backing garnets with foil to achieve a crimson appearance, but the ring from Fort Ouiatenon does not appear to have had such a backing.

To test the results of the stone's refractive index reading and also analyze the composition of the ring's band, the authors investigated the stone's and band's compositions using a Bruker Trace-III SD portable X-ray fluorescence (PXRF) instrument. Investigations employing PXRF instruments to analyze artifacts for their compositions have increased probably due to the relatively low cost, the ability to test artifact types composed of metal and other materials, and the nondestructive nature of the process to the artifact (Abel and Burke 2014; Shugar 2013; Barone et al. 2017). Other techniques including atomic absorption spectrometry, electron probe microanalysis, and scanning electron microscopy–energy dispersive spectrometry require destruction of a small portion of the artifact and therefore tend to be less attractive options (Cooper and Al-Saad 2015, 87; Dussubieux et al. 2008).

The metal portion of the ring was analyzed for one hundred seconds at 40 kV, 10.90 mA, using an Al Ti filter. The stone portion of the signet and of additional garnet samples were analyzed for one hundred seconds at 40kV, 10.90 mA, both without a filter and using a variety of filters. The results using the Al Ti filter and no filter produced nearly identical spectra. The metal portion of the signet ring is brass (copper-zinc alloy). The quantitative results for the metal (shown in table 6.1) were determined using a custom-made calibration file composed of sixty-two copper and copper alloy standards. This calibration file was designed to identify historic period copper and copper alloys.

The two main constituents of this alloy are copper and zinc. The weight percentage column does not add up to 100 percent. This is most likely due to the complicated geometry of the object being analyzed. The spectrum for the metals analysis (figure 6.3)

TABLE 6.1. PXRF RESULTS OF METAL IN WEIGHT PERCENTAGE

Element	Weight %
MnKa1	0.460108292
FeKa1	1.436339919
NiKa1	1.835758059
CuKa1	77.84146748
ZnKb1	5.482979179
AsKb1	0.789794427
PbLb1	1.384977254
BiLb1	0.331341655
AgKa1	0.637277909
CdKa1	0.307196596
SnKa1	0.415200359
SbKa1	0.369988181

shows very few other components. The real percentage of copper and zinc are both probably higher, but the object would still be identified as brass with no other intentional alloying additions such as tin. The lead detected could be an intentional addition or accidental component of the brass alloy or could originate from the stone portion of the signet. Additionally, along with nickel and iron, both of which may be present in the amounts indicated but probably not as intentional alloying constituents, the lead may be present on the object due to it not having been cleaned of all of the original soil matrix.

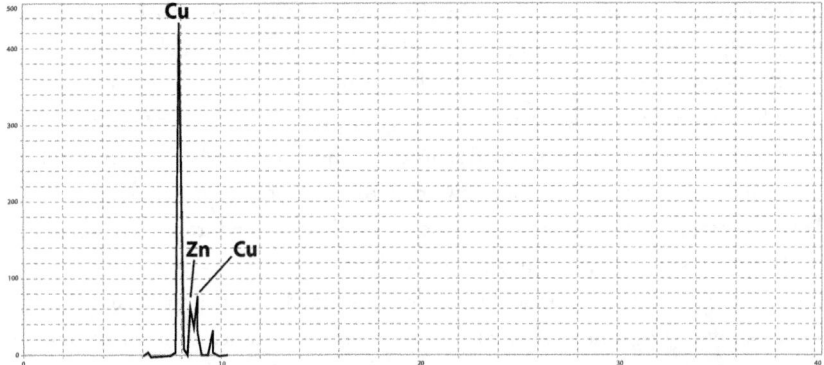

Figure 6.3. Spectra of metal portion of signet ring showing primarily copper and zinc.

Figure 6.4 shows the result of the analysis of the ring's stone in comparison with the analysis of a 100 percent Pb powder standard. The L-shell peaks are shown and match very closely, showing that the stone is not garnet but rather a paste like that associated with costume jewelry developed in eighteenth-century France. The L-shell analysis is shown because for both samples there is so much lead, in the case of the powder standard 100 percent, that the analyzer is essentially overloaded with the Pb energy signal. The difference in peak height is probably related to the Pb in both objects being in different forms, which affects X-ray geometry.

As part of the process of confirming the composition of the ring's stone, samples of garnet were also analyzed following the procedures. A small red garnet donated by Stall and Kessler Jewelers was analyzed; the results are shown in figure 6.5. The spectrum is dominated by iron. Additionally, a yellowish stone identified as garnet and purchased by one of the authors at the Eddy Discovery Center, Waterloo Recreation Area, Chelsea, Michigan, was tested for comparison; results of the analysis are shown in figure 6.6. The signal is largely dominated by calcium. A comparison of these four spectra, the ring, Pb powder standard, and two garnet samples demonstrates without a doubt that the ring's stone is not garnet but rather a paste, that is, an artificially created stone substitute of glass composed largely of lead.

HISTORY OF PASTE STONES

Paste refers to a "heavy, very transparent flint glass that simulates the fire and brilliance of gemstones because it has relatively high indices of refraction and strong dispersion (separation of white light into its component colours).... Before 1940 most imitation gems were made from glass with a high lead content. Such glasses were called paste because the components of the mixture were mixed wet to ensure a thorough and even distribution.... Cut paste stones may be distinguished from real ones in several ways... [including] hardness (paste is softer than real stones and will not scratch ordinary glass), [and] index of refraction (1.50–1.80, less than diamond at 2.42)" (Britannica, n.d.c).

While paste, or strass jewelry, as it also became known in the eighteenth century, does not have the same value as actual gemstones, this innovation became very popular. The numerous examples of costume jewelry in the form of rings and buckles from the Fort Ouiatenon excavations are likely also composed of paste and attest to its popularity.

The process of adding lead to glass began thousands of years ago in Mesopotamia, but its reintroduction in the modern era is first attributed to British glassmaker George Ravenscroft of England in 1675. He rediscovered the practice in an effort to combat the loss of transparency that occurred in glass several months after manufacture. Though his work centered on blown glass for tableware, others began to use blown

SYMBOLISM, NATIONALITY, IDENTITY, AND GENDER 157

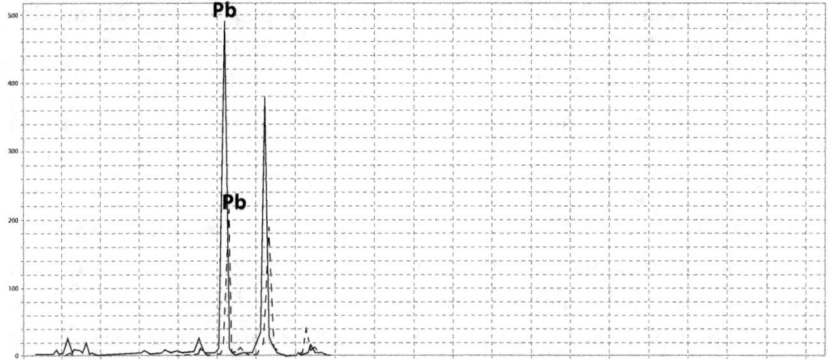

Figure 6.4. The red spectra is the stone in the ring. The blue line is from the analysis of a 100 percent Pb powder.

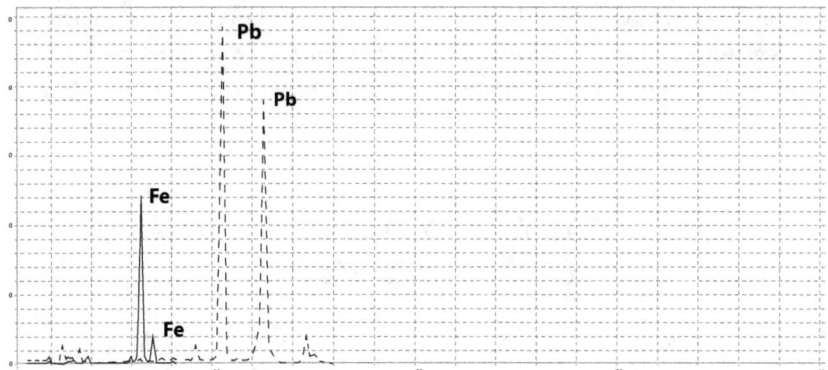

Figure 6.5. Ring's stone spectrum shown in red, Stall & Kessler garnet in green.

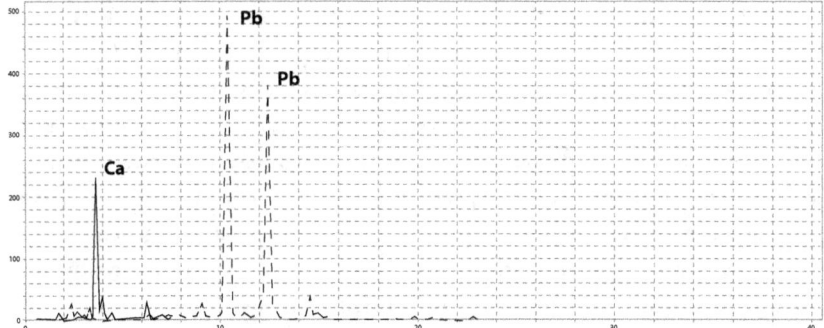

Figure 6.6. Ring's stone spectrum shown in red, EDC garnet in green.

glass extensively in Britain and elsewhere for jewelry. Its popularity grew in the eighteenth century stemming from three of its qualities: brilliance when cut with facets by new techniques thereby simulating gemstones, affordability for the middle class, and feasibility as a substitute when highwaymen made carrying gemstones during travel a risk. Paste was used in all types of jewelry, especially finger rings, and settings included silver and pewter (Britannica, n.d.b; Newman 1981, 182–83, 228).

Georges-Frédéric Strass invented a particularly successful formulation of brilliant paste composed of borosilicate of potassium and lead with small amounts of alumina and arsenic. Designed to imitate transparent gemstones including diamonds, the result came to be named for him. Born near Strasbourg, he learned to make jewelry and artificial gems before moving to Paris in 1724 around age twenty-three. From 1730 to 1734 he invented the technique for making imitation stone, though imitation diamonds were known in Paris in the seventeenth century. His "strass" gained adherents among the court of Louis XV and won Strass the appointment as jeweler to the king in 1734. Strass continued his work until 1752, when he ceded the commerce of strass glass to the fiancé of his niece, and it continued to be produced through the eighteenth century (Newman 1981, 292–93; Challamel, Lillie, and Hoey 1882, 148; Haug 1961, 179–82).

HISTORY AND DESCRIPTION OF SIGNET RINGS

The history of signet or seal rings extends back at least 3,500 years among Mediterranean cultures including the Mycenaeans, Egyptians, Greeks, and Romans. They utilized cut, also referred to as intaglio, gemstones or engraved gold bands to impart a raised impression on soft materials such as wax and clay. In medieval Europe the engraved designs included animals, heraldic and emblematic devices, initials, and names (Scarisbrick 1994, 60), and rings were worn on the first finger or thumb (Murdoch 1991, 132). Newman (1981, 280) states, "They were often used by a messenger as a credential," with crown servants among those given official signets apparently for use in their office, and "by the eighteenth century the need for seals was less, but signet rings continued in use at least as ornamental pieces, especially those with an engraved gemstone." Merchants and tradesmen used them with their personal devices or initials (Scarisbrick 1994, 150). Neoclassical designs for both men and women gained popularity in general and for seals in particular beginning in the 1770s through the early nineteenth century, following styles in painting and architecture. In Britain particularly during the early nineteenth century, royal portraits on cameos and intaglios depicted contemporary monarchs and their Hanoverian ancestors (Scarisbrick 1994, 226, 334). The simple gold band with an engraved or raised monogram on the flat bezel also gained popularity in the nineteenth century (Newman 1981, 280).

In addition to gemstones, jewelers employed glass and coral. Seals mounted on shanks of various metals including steel as well as porcelain, usually three to five centimeters in height, were worn in the sixteenth century on neck chains and chatelaines and from the seventeenth century by men on a watch chain (Newman 1981, 274). Excavations at Fort Michilimackinac produced two glass seals that are either of the latter type or of the small desk variety (Evans 2003, 24). Whether or not the need for seals had declined by the eighteenth century, the signet ring was out of fashion for most of that century and replaced by the fob or shank seal (Scarisbrick 1994, 221, 296).

SEAL RINGS IN INVOICES AND INVENTORIES

The eighteenth-century trade invoices for goods shipped to French fur trade posts in Canada and referred to as the Montreal Merchant Records and a number of inventories prepared by personnel of various French military posts in the same region together list seventeen finger ring entries described as "seal" rings (see chapter 7 in this volume for more on the Montreal Merchant Records and post inventories).

The military listed the term "seal ring" for nine entries and also used the variables "small" in one entry and "trade" in two entries. Five of its twelve entries occur under the section "Munitions (Stores) and merchandise for the trade" in the documents. All of these were described as seal or small seal rings. Under variations of the section heading "Munitions and Merchandise making part of the stock/property of the Estate of the King," two entries specify trade rings, and three entries list simply seal rings. Seal rings were included under two sections in a single inventory, "Munitions and Merchandise coming from those sent from the port of Rochefort" and "Munitions and Merchandise ... from Quebec." These appeared in "Extract/Abstract of Munitions, Merchandise and Food that have been delivered ... to Indians domiciled [or settled] there and others who have come there for the service of his Majesty." From this it is clear that seal rings were also "trade" rings in at least seven of the military entries given their location within the inventories (Jackson 2005, 404).

Finger rings never sold in quantities of less than a dozen. The largest quantity recorded appears in Fort Niagara's 1737 inventory: thirty-six gross and seventy-nine seal rings. Similar to the military inventories, two of the entries in the Montreal Merchant Records specifying seal rings came from documents titled "Extract/Abstract of Munitions, Merchandise and Food that have been delivered ... to Indians domiciled [settled] there and others who have come there for the service of his Majesty" for

1731–1732 and 1735–1736. During 1731–1732 the French distributed five gross of seal rings, and during 1735–1736 they distributed four dozen of them. The merchants did not use the variable "trade" to describe any seal rings, and they listed only "large" seal rings, with none listing the variable "small."

Seal rings comprised more than half of the rings in the military inventories. Perhaps not surprisingly given the quantities in which they were sold, they were also the cheapest variety of ring in the lists with the exception of "gold colored rings," which may have comprised simple bands with no ornamentation. Seal rings' lowest price registered at one livre fifteen sols per gross for the years 1736 and 1737 (Jackson 2005, 405).

As demonstrated by Carol Mason (2003, 1–25) and by the finds from LaSalle's shipwreck *La Belle*, what archaeologists commonly referred to as "Jesuit rings" were among those carried by the military. It is plausible that seal rings served as the merchants' and military personnel's category for so-called Jesuit rings, given their cheapness and plenitude in the invoices and inventories and the engraving on the bezels that suggest a seal. There is direct evidence that at least one missionary, Jacques Gravier, used the term "seal ring" himself in a letter to France requesting supplies. The document appears in *The Jesuit Relations* (Thwaites 1896–1901, 66:25–31) and is discussed by both Walthal (1993, 498) and Mason (2003, 10). In the original French, Gravier asks for, among other things, *bagues au cachet* (rings with seal). The Montreal Merchant Records and the post storehouse inventories used the same terminology. It is unlikely that the missionaries referred to something different from the merchants' and military's terminology, given the evidence discussed by Mason. Among the French, seal ring may have simply been understood to mean a ring typically bearing engraving including religious and other iconography, though it may have had other meanings in other contexts. Mason and Ehrhardt (2009, 6) discuss many possible alternate meanings including luck and romantic associations. The Catholic worldview pervaded eighteenth-century French society, accompanied by the ubiquitous presence of religious iconography in the form of medals, necklaces, finger rings, and crucifixes. It is plausible that the merchants and the military shared the terminology of religious leaders and listed them simply as seal rings without specific reference to the pictorial ornamentation, use, or meanings associated with them (Jackson 2005, 407–8).

OTHER RINGS IN THE INVOICES AND INVENTORIES

The seal rings noted in the merchant invoices and military documents appear to not be of the same type as that represented by the signet ring with the intaglio of the man on the dolphin. The documents list other rings as well, and rings with colored "stones" were more expensive than the seal rings in the records. While large seal rings cost three livres ten sols per gross in 1746, a gross of finger rings "with stones" cost a little over two livres more at five livres twelve sols in 1772. Ring band material, specifically similor, may have increased the cost as well. An alloy of copper and zinc, similor was invented in Lille, France, in 1729 to resemble gold in color and to imitate pinchbeck, an English equivalent (see chapter 7 in this volume). The name refers to the Latin *similis* (similar) and the French *or* (gold) (Newman 1981, 281). The single entry for a gross of similor rings "with colored stones" in 1748 sold for fourteen livres eight sols. Unfortunately, the fourteen silver rings "with diamond" had no prices associated with them in the invoices, but the single listing for a dozen rings "with diamond" registered the highest price of all the rings at five livres ten sols per dozen, or ninety livres per gross, in 1737. Clearly, these rings were not truly expensive at less than a livre each (12.5 sols each), but they carried a much higher price of any of the other rings in the documents examined. They made up part of a trading outfit for the Winnebago and no specific post is mentioned, so it cannot necessarily be assumed that these were meant solely for French consumption. Whether "diamond" refers to the gemstone or to the fine paste stone is not clear.

ARION AND THE DOLPHIN

Investigation conducted to identify the figures depicted on the paste "stone" of the signet ring indicates that they represent the Greek legend of Arion. Herodotus relates the story of how the historical master musician and poet was returning home by sea after touring Sicily and Magna Graecia. The Corinthian sailors he hired demanded his prize money from the competition he had just won and that he throw himself overboard or kill himself while on the ship. Arion requested their permission to dress in the full costume of his profession and sing one final song accompanied by his lyre, which they permitted. Upon hearing the song, a dolphin rescued him when he flung himself into the sea and carried him on its back to Taenarum. From there he walked to Corinth. Arion reported to his friend Periander, the tyrant of the city, who at first did not believe the story. Periander confronted the sailors who admitted their guilt when they saw Arion. After that he was honored in the shrine at Taenarum by a small figure in bronze representing him on a dolphin. He and the dolphin also became the constellations Lyra and Delphinus (Britannica n.d.a; Herodotus 1997, 14–16).

Understanding the meaning and place of the story of Arion in French culture during the eighteenth century provides clues that aid in answering the question regarding to whom the ring belonged or who may have used it. Though the British and Americans both also held or occupied Fort Ouiatenon, the French officially and unofficially occupied it the longest. In addition, the fame of Francois Boucher's *Arion on the Dolphin* (1748) suggests a French origin for the ring. The painting and a play based on it are directly associated with the Dauphin of France, Louis XV (figure 6.7).

Betsy Rosasco, research curator of European painting and sculpture at the Princeton University Art Museum, has detailed the history of Boucher's painting, its relationship to Louis XV, and the play representing him as Arion. As she explains,

> The subjects were chosen for personal, self-referential reasons. In the act representing Water, Arion plays the lyre and is called a "worthy son of Apollo." He symbolizes Louis XV, successor to the Sun King. Arion was saved by a dolphin, according to Herodotus's Histories, when, returning to Greece from a singing tour to Italy, he was robbed by the ship's crew and threw himself overboard to avoid being murdered. The dolphin must refer to the title of the heir to the throne, dauphin (from the French province of Dauphiné); a dolphin, its homonym, was shown in the dauphin's coat of arms. In 1721, Arion's survival probably referred to Louis XV's survival of the epidemic that killed his father and brother, and his assumption of the title of dauphin. In 1748, it could also have alluded to his survival of a near-fatal illness in 1744, the nation's prayers for his survival, and the joy with which he was named "le Bien-Aimé" (the well-loved), when he recovered (Rosasco 2010, 5).

Figure 6.7 Francois Boucher's *Arion on the Dolphin* (1748). Princeton University Art Museum/Art Resources NY.

Louis XV's mistress Madame de Pompadour hung the painting and its companion over the doors of his Chateau de la Muette, where they remained until 1750. At that time their coded meanings no longer were useful to her, as she had lost the status of king's mistress but gained even more influence as his friend. "At an unknown date, the paintings appear to have been returned to Boucher. After Mme de Pompadour's death in 1764, they were reproduced in prints by Augustin Saint-Aubin and Jacques Jean Pasquier, dated 1765–66. For reasons not yet understood, one figure of a triton in Arion's entourage was omitted in the print.... A scarf trailing behind the musician has been painted over, and he now wears a cape that billows behind him" (Rosasco 2010, 7).

Evidence for the association between the Dauphin and the story of Arion dates to at least the beginning of the seventeenth century. Jean de Beaugrand published *Panchrestographie* in Paris in 1604 in which appears his lineographic representation of the arms of the Dauphin of France (figure 6.8). Lineography involved the creation of drawings with a single line produced by not lifting the drawing implement during execution of the work. The technique originated in France in the seventeenth century. De Beaugrand included in this representation male figures astride fish or dolphins flanking the coat of arms as well as birds above the figures. The bird motif on the band of the ring from Fort Ouiatenon appears to be significant for further linking the ring's symbolism to the Dauphin, given de Beaugrand's depiction of birds. It should be noted that the royal signet ring of Charles I, produced between 1623 and 1655, bears a lion and a unicorn on the shoulders of the ring band, suggesting that such treatment of bands with animal motifs may not have been uncommon (Newman 1981, 263). In a coat of arms as on Charles I's ring and in de Beaugrand's drawing, such flanking motifs are referred to as "supporters."

WHAT DOES THIS MEAN FOR THE OCCUPANTS OF FORT OUIATENON?

While rings were and are items of personal adornment, it is possible that an officer would be provided a signet or letter seal that represented his position rather than his personal mark. It is not clear how frequently officers among the French, British, and Americans used signets or seals for documents, but the presence of the two seals at Fort Michilimackinac suggests that they saw some use. Two letters by George Rogers Clark dated 1778 bear his seal of a rampant lion and a star and crescent (Thwaites 1888, 114, 178).

Given the associations with the Dauphin, the owner of the ring depicting Arion may have been a male of high rank. This is not to say that all commandants at Fort Ouiatenon, however, held high rank. Of the thirteen French commandants recorded

Figure 6.8. From Jean de Beaugrand's 1604 *Panchrestographie*.
Courtesy of the Newberry Library, Chicago.

in the documents translated by Krauskopf (1955), at least one, the trader Simon Reaume, may have been of low rank. The first person sent to the post, an ensign by the name of Bellestre, may have been of relatively high social though not high military rank. The knights of five baronies including the barony of Bellestre were part of the Chevaliers de la Sainte-Ampoule. This order was purported to have been created by Clovis I on the occasion of his baptism, during which a miraculous dove from Heaven brought a flask containing the oil to anoint him, referred to as la Sainte-Ampoule. Documents indicate that the knights participated in the coronations of Louis XIII, Louis XIV, Louis XV, and Louis XVI. Four knights of the baronies held the four posts of the "dais," or canopy (baldachin) over the flask containing the holy ointment for the sacrament of the kings (Velde 2010). Pierre-Alexandre d'Auger, baron de Bellestre, served at the coronation of Louis XVI. The relationship between him and the Bellestre of Ouiatenon and his son Marie-François Picoté de Bellestre, commandant of Detroit at the time of capitulation, is not currently known. As a symbol of the Dauphin it would not be necessary for the ring to have belonged to a Bellestre or any other official, but the connection is at least coincidental and suggestive.

Table 6.2 provides an overview of known commandants at Fort Ouiatenon along with their titles and ranks. It is of interest that the documents indicate the necessity of sending officers to manage the post in order to provide prominence. Native Americans made it clear that they respected French officers more than subordinates (Krauskopf 1955, 142, 159).

Another explanation for the presence of the ring lies in the possibility of an officer at the post who had previously served in the Dauphin's royal dragoon or cavalry regiments in France. The king, queen, prince or Dauphin, and noblemen, specifically Orleans, all commanded royal regiments, and the uniforms marked each accordingly. Evidence as to whether officers wore an item such as an identifying ring has yet to be found (Pengal and Hurt 2002, 2, 4, 26, 40, 42, 43, 66, 78).

Even if the ring never functioned in the sealing of documents, its size is such that it would have been conspicuous, even ostentatious. Given its associations with the Dauphin, educated elites would no doubt have readily recognized it and possibly all French citizens. During the eighteenth century the nobility studied classical literature and art, and it is likely they were familiar with the story of Arion. Merchants, on the other hand, as members of the nouveau riche emphasized "practical studies" in the education of their children. In relation to this it is important to note that Joseph Peyser's research based on Chevalier de Raymond's critique of New France in 1754 indicates that the officers suffered the serious problem of inadequate and fixed pay. Some were reduced to begging, while others asked leave to return to France in order to find work and place their children with those who would feed them. They also borrowed from merchants and apparently not uncommonly died without settlement of their debts (Peyser 1997, 77–78, 132). Raymond wished to disabuse his readers of the notion that officers lived in comfort or were held in esteem by their fellow Canadians. Merchants in large measure had the financial means for a middle-class or higher lifestyle during this time of contested social boundaries when rank and nobility competed with the shifts in power structure developing from the mercantile capitalist system. In relation to this it should be noted that during the eighteenth century both male and female ruling elites in the American colonies as well as after independence from Britain availed themselves of fashionable paste jewelry and buckles (Cadou 2002, 16, 19; Murdoch 1991, 56).

To complicate further the situation of determining who may have owned the ring, signet rings and letter seals have been recognized as indication of literacy, yet it has been pointed out that "all classes of society, men and women, made use of seals when involved in any formal or legal transaction" (Murdoch 1991, 128, 132).

The ring depicting Arion remains an ambiguous artifact in terms of who possessed it, and as such we must "honor ambiguity and problematize certitude" with "underdetermined conclusions" rather than force an interpretation (Gero 2007, 315). The ring may symbolize high rank, power, and an official relationship to the king of France. The fashionable and desirable nature of paste in the eighteenth century provides a strong possibility that a person of higher status owned the ring. The gold-colored substance

TABLE 6.2. KNOWN COMMANDANTS AT FORT OUIATENON, 1717–1763

Date	Commandant	Comments	References
Spring 1717	Ensign François Picoté de Bellestre	Sent with four soldiers and three other Frenchmen to establish the post.	Krauskopf 1953, 70–71; Krauskopf 1955, 159–60.
August 1720	Ensign Réformé Dumont and Simon Réaume	Sent to command in country of Ouiatenon and Miamis (resident at Ouiatenon?).	Barnhart and Riker 1971, 74; Krauskopf 1953, 88; Krauskopf 1955, 165–68
1721	Charles Renaud Dubuisson	Governor and Lieutenant General Vaudreuil requested that he receive a Cross of St. Louis, used to reward distinguished army and naval officers.	Krauskopf 1955, 159
1721–1730	Cadet François-Marie Bissot de Vincennes	Post supervisor, serving under Captain Dubuisson at Fort Miamis. Promoted to second ensign and (later) half-pay lieutenant.	Barnhart and Riker 1971, 75; Krauskopf 1953, 95
1732	Simon Réaume	Réaume (former voyageur) was acting commandant until his death in late 1733 or early 1734.	Barnhart and Riker 1971, 83; Krauskopf 1953, 88; Krauskopf 1955, 146
1734	Cadet François de l'Espervanche de Villemure		Barnhart and Riker 1971, 85; Krauskopf 1953, 168
1735	Louis Godefroy, Sieur de Normanville		Barnhart and Riker 1971, 86; Krauskopf 1953, 179; Krauskopf 1955, 184

TABLE 6.2. CONTINUED

1736 or 1737	René Godefroy, Sieur de Linctot		Barnhart and Riker 1971, 90; Krauskopf 1953, 190
Fall 1739	unnamed commandant	Died soon after arriving at Ouiatenon, possibly shot by a voyageur.	Barnhart and Riker 1971, 90; Krauskopf 1953, 201a
Summer 1740	Henri Albert de St. Vincent fils		Barnhart and Riker 1971, 91; Krauskopf 1953, 209
1743	Ensign de la Perrière		Krauskopf 1953, 225
1745	Ensign Chevalier de la Pèrade fils		Krauskopf 1953, 235, 264
May 1748	Claude Drouet de Richardville, Sieur de Carqueville		Barnhart and Riker 1971, 98; Krauskopf 1953, 264; Krauskopf 1955, 209
June 1751	François-Marie le Marchand de Ligneris (Lignery)		Barnhart and Riker 1971, 106; Krauskopf 1953, 368
1754	Mézière		Krauskopf 1953, 369
1757	Ensign Camet Bayeul		Barnhart and Riker 1971, 122; Thwaites 1904, 175–76
Late 1761– June 1763	Lieutenant Edward Jenkins	British took possession of Ouiatenon, likely early 1761. Jenkins and British garrison arrived later. Taken prisoner in Pontiac's Rebellion, June 1763. Fort not regarrisoned.	Barnhart and Riker 1971, 140, 143

In Strezewski (2014, 13), with minor additions; used with permission.

present on the ring band at the time of its recovery may have consisted of similor or tombac, giving the base metal of copper alloy the appearance of gold.

The ring may instead signal the identity someone wished to craft by exhibiting the fashion of the day and by wearing what may have served as a commemorative piece symbolizing France and the ascent of the Dauphin to the throne in 1715. The ring was neither the cheapest nor the most expensive that one could buy, and the middle class had access to desirable brilliant paste. It cannot be ruled out that a merchant or a woman may have worn it.

One other possibility remains for interpreting the ring, though the supporting bird motif on the band makes the option less likely. A man riding a dolphin also served as the family crest of the Irish name O'Coffey (Coat of Arms and Family Crests Store). Given the British and American presence at Fort Ouiatenon, brief though it was, in order to present all evidence this heraldry must be noted.

What upon first examination appears to be a signet ring worthy of an officer of high rank and associated in some manner with the Dauphin of France in the final analysis may have been the possession of a merchant with the means of signaling his or her desired status. As Chevalier de Raymond pointed out, the merchants had great financial means more often than was the case for military officers. While it seems likely that the ring belonged to a French inhabitant of the fort, one cannot rule out that a Native American or métis person might have owned it at some point in its history. Ambiguity is eschewed, while certitude is honored. For now, ambiguity must be preserved.

ACKNOWLEDGMENTS

Jackson would like to thank Rick Conwell of the Tippecanoe County Historical Association, Lafayette, Indiana, for initial conversations in which he speculated on the possible link between the symbolism of the ring and the Dauphin of France. She also thanks him for sharing his knowledge of the original condition of the ring prior to the collapse of the band. Larry Chowning, who excavated the ring, also kindly answered questions and provided his knowledge concerning its recovery. Jackson would like to extend her deepest thanks to Research Curator of European Painting and Sculpture Betsy J. Rosasco, Princeton University Art Museum, who shared with her knowledge of representations of Arion at Versailles in addition to that at the Château de la Muette. To her brother-in-law Philip W. Johnston she is indebted for sharing his vast knowledge and resources on seventeenth- and eighteenth-century French uniforms and military organization.

REFERENCES

Abel, Timothy J., and Adrian L. Burke. 2014. "The Protohistoric Time Period in Northwest Ohio: Perspectives from the XRF Analysis of Metallic Trade Materials." *Midcontinental Journal of Archaeology* 39, no. 2 (May): 179–99.

Barnhart, John D., and Dorothy L. Riker. 1971. *Indiana to 1816: The Colonial Period*. Indianapolis: Indiana Historical Bureau and Indiana Historical Society.

Barone, Germana, Danilo Bersani, Paolo Mazzoleni, and Simona Raneri. 2017. "Portable XRF: A Tool for the Study of Corundum Gems." *Open Archaeology* 3: 194–201.

Bonewitz, Ronald Louis. 2005. *Rock and Gem*. New York: DK Publishing.

Boucher, Francois. 1748. *Arion on the Dolphin*. Oil on canvas. 33 7/8 x 53 3/8 in. Princeton University Art Museum/Art Resource, New York.

Britannica. n.d.a. "Arion." Encyclopedia Britannica Online. https://www.britannica.com/biography/Arion-Greek-poet-and-musician.

Britannica. n.d.b. "George Ravenscroft." Encyclopedia Britannica Online. https://www.britannica.com/biography/George-Ravenscroft.

Britannica. n.d.c. "Paste." Encyclopedia Britannica Online. https://www.britannica.com/technology/paste-glass-product.

Cadou, Carol Borchert. 2002. "The Best of Every Article: The Style of Martha Washington." In *The Annual Report of the Mount Vernon Ladies' Association of the Union*. Mount Vernon, VA: Mount Vernon Ladies Association.

Challamel, Augustin, John Lillie, and Frances Cashel Hoey. 1882. *The History of Fashion in France, or, The Dress of Women from the Gallo-Roman Period to the Present Time*. New York: Scribner and Welford.

Coat of Arms and Family Crests Store. 2013. "O'Coffey." https://coatofarmsgifts.com/search?q=O%27Coffey.

Cooper, H. Kory, and Ziad Al-Saad. 2015. "Metal Jewelry from Burials and Socioeconomic Status in Rural Jordan in Late Antiquity." *Mediterranean Archaeology and Archaeometry* 15, no. 2: 81–99.

De Beaugrand, Jean. 1604. *Panchrestographie: Toutes les figures cy bessus sont formées d'un seul traict*. Par I. de Beaugrand, escrivain du roy et de ses bibliotheques et secretaire ordinaire de la chambre de sa Majesté. Paris: P. Firens sculpsit.

Dussubieux, Laure, Aurelie Deraisme, Gérard Frot, Christopher Stevenson, Amy Creech, and Yves Bienvenu. 2008. "LA-ICP-MS, SEM-EDS and EPMA Analysis of Eastern North American Copper-based Artefacts: Impact of Corrosion and Heterogeneity on the Reliability of the LA-ICP-MS Composition Results." *Archaeometry* 50, no. 4: 643–57.

Evans, Lynn L. M. 2003. *Keys to the Past: Archaeological Treasures of Mackinac*. Mackinac Island, MI: Mackinac State Historic Parks.

Gero, Joan M. 2007. "Honoring Ambiguity/Problematizing Certitude." *Journal of Archaeological Method and Theory* 14, no. 1 (March): 311–27.

Haug, Hans. 1961. "Les Pierres de Strass et Leur Inventeur." *Cahiers de la Céramique, du Verre et des Arts du Feu* 23: 175–83.

Herodotus. 1997. *The Histories*. Translated by George Rawlinson. New York: Everyman's Library Alfred A. Knopf.

Jackson, Misty. 2005. "Classifications by Historical Archaeologists and Eighteenth Century Montreal Merchants and Military Personnel in New France: Emic and Etic Approaches." PhD diss., Michigan State University.

Krauskopf, Frances. 1953. "The French in Indiana, 1700–1760: A Political History." PhD diss., Indiana University, Bloomington.

———, trans. and ed. 1955. *Ouiatanon Documents*. Indianapolis: Indiana Historical Society. Reprint, West Lafayette, IN: Chien Noir Trading Company, 2000.

Mason, Carol. 2003. "Jesuit Rings, Jesuits and Chronology." *Midcontinental Journal of Archaeology* 28, no. 2 (Fall): 1–25.

Mason, Carol I., and Kathleen L. Ehrhardt. 2009. "Iconographic (Jesuit) Rings in European/Native Exchange." *French Colonial History* 10: 55–74.

Murdoch, Tessa. 1991. *Treasures and Trinkets: Jewellery in London from Pre-Roman Times to the 1930s*. London: Museum of London.

Newman, Harold. 1981. *An Illustrated Dictionary of Jewelry*. London: Thames and Hudson.

Noble, Vergil E, Jr. 1983. "Functional Classification and Intra-site Analysis in Historical Archaeology: A Case Study from Fort Ouiatenon." PhD diss., Michigan State University.

Pengel, R. D., and G. R. Hurt. 2002. *French Cavalry & Dragoons: Uniforms and Flags of the Seven Years War, 1740–1762*. Facsimile ed. Hopewell, NJ: On Military Matters.

Peyser, Joseph L., trans. and ed. 1997. *On the Eve of the Conquest: The Chevalier de Raymond's Critique of New France in 1754*. East Lansing: Michigan State University Press.

Rosasco, Betsy. 2010. *A Royal Commission: Francois Boucher's Water and Earth Reunited*. Princeton, NJ: Princeton University Art Museum. Published in conjunction with an exhibition of the same title organized by and presented at the Princeton University Art Museum, March 13–May 13, 2010.

Scarisbrick, Diana. 1994. *Jewellery in Britain 1066–1837: A Documentary, Social, Literary and Artistic Survey*. Wilby, Norwich: Michael Russell Publishing.

Shugar, Aaron N. 2013. "Portable X-ray Fluorescence and Archaeology: Limitations of the Instrument and Suggested Methods to Achieve Desired Results." *Archaeological Chemistry VIII* 1147: 173–93.

Strezewski, Michael. 2014. *Fur Trade Archaeology in the Fort Ouiatenon Vicinity: The 2012/2013 Investigations*. University of Southern Indiana Archaeological Laboratory Reports of Investigations 13-03.

Thwaites, Reuben G., ed. 1888. "Papers from the Canadian Archives—1778–1783." In *Collections of the State Historical Society of Wisconsin*, Vol. 11, ed. Reuben G. Thwaites, 97–212. Madison, WI: Democrat Printing.

———. 1896–1901. *The Jesuit Relations and Allied Documents: Travels and Explorations of the Jesuit Missionaries in New France, 1610–1791; the Original French, Latin, and Italian Texts, with English Translations and Notes*. 73 vols. Cleveland, OH: Burrows Brothers.

———. 1904. *Early Western Travels, 1748–1846*, Vol. 1. Cleveland, OH: Arthur H. Clark.

Tordoff, Judith Dunn. 1983. "An Archaeological Perspective on the Organization of the Fur Trade in Eighteenth Century New France." PhD diss., Michigan State University.

Velde, François. 2010. "Orders of Chivalry in France." Mythical Orders: Chevaliers de la Sainte-Ampoule. https://www.heraldica.org/topics/france/frorders.htm.

Walthal, John. 1993. "Stylistic and Temporal Analysis of Jesuit Rings in the Illinois Country." *Illinois Archaeology* 5, nos. 1–2: 489–507.

White, Carolyn. 2005. *American Artifacts of Personal Adornment, 1680–1820: A Guide to Identification and Interpretation*. Lanham, MD: Rowman & Littlefield.

7

BUCKLES FROM FORT OUIATENON

Searching for Interpretive Clues in the Documents and Testing for Their Composition

MISTY M. JACKSON, ARBRE CROCHE CULTURAL RESOURCES LLC, LINA C. PATINO, NATIONAL SCIENCE FOUNDATION, AND DAVID W. SZYMANSKI, DEPARTMENT OF NATURAL AND APPLIED SCIENCES, BENTLEY UNIVERSITY

EIGHTEENTH-CENTURY FRENCH MERCHANT TRADE INVOICES AND MILItary storehouse inventories of New France offer a rich glimpse into the way a variety of trade and other items were viewed and classified by these segments of French colonial society. These classifications differ from those of archaeologists for some artifacts types. Historic documents and laser ablation inductively coupled plasma mass spectrometry (LA-ICP-MS) were used to identify one particular material variable, that of tombac, and related variable similor , which eighteenth-century French employed for describing buckles but archaeologists have not. We examined a sample of buckles from the site of Fort Ouiatenon for evidence of tombac. The implications for identifying and using this variable for classifying artifacts is explored, specifically tombac's role in establishing, maintaining, or contesting French social boundaries.

A total of ninety-six buckles and buckle fragments have been excavated or collected from the site of Fort Ouiatenon. Seventy-two of these are in the Tippecanoe

County Historical Association (TCHA) collection in Lafayette, Indiana. Michigan State University excavations in the 1970s led by Tordoff (1983, 187, 190–93) and Noble (1983, 114–19) recovered fifty-five of the seventy-two buckles. An additional twenty-four buckles and buckle fragments are part of the Fort Ouiatenon collection at Indiana University's Glenn Black Laboratory of Archaeology. They include those made of copper alloy, iron, pewter, and possibly steel. A sample of twelve copper alloy buckles from the TCHA collection was selected based on their color as determined by visual inspection for testing by LA-ICP-MS in order to determine their relative (ratio) material compositions (figure 7.1). The results are compared to their appearances to explore whether visual inspection can be used as a way to identify buckles and other jewelry using the same descriptions as the French and other contemporary merchants, manufacturers, and consumers would have. This can lead to a clearer understanding of what the buckles and jewelry meant to Europeans of the eighteenth century.

In regard to artifact classifications, it is a long-standing observation that "we need more rather than fewer classifications" (Brew 1946). However, researchers may come to the conclusion when reading the archaeological literature that standard universal classifications based on artifact form are the most common. Archaeologists have commonly used standardized formal classification systems such as that of Lyle Stone's to classify artifacts from eighteenth-century sites in the Great Lakes region, which place the variables used to describe an artifact's physical characteristics in a hierarchical framework (Stone 1974). In historical archaeology, folk classifications—that is, the terms used by the producers, distributors, or consumers of an object—are also useful for understanding artifacts as they would have been understood by those same producers, distributors, or consumers and allow for movement beyond formal description and toward interpretation (Jackson 2005).

For items traded in New France during the eighteenth century, the "Business and Fur Trade Records of Montreal Merchants, 1712–1806," also known as the Montreal Merchant Records (MMR), and a number of fort and military storehouse inventories housed at the Library and Archives of Canada in Ottawa, Ontario, offer a rich glimpse into the way the recorders of the documents viewed and classified a variety of material culture. These classifications differ from those of archaeologists for a variety of artifact types. While some familiar trade goods, particularly knives, kettles, and axes, rank among those artifacts that archaeologists classify differently from eighteenth-century merchants and military personnel of New France, the buckle has received less attention. The Montreal Merchant Records and fort and military storehouse inventories use variables to describe buckles that allow for a more nuanced interpretation of this artifact type (Jackson 2005, 34).

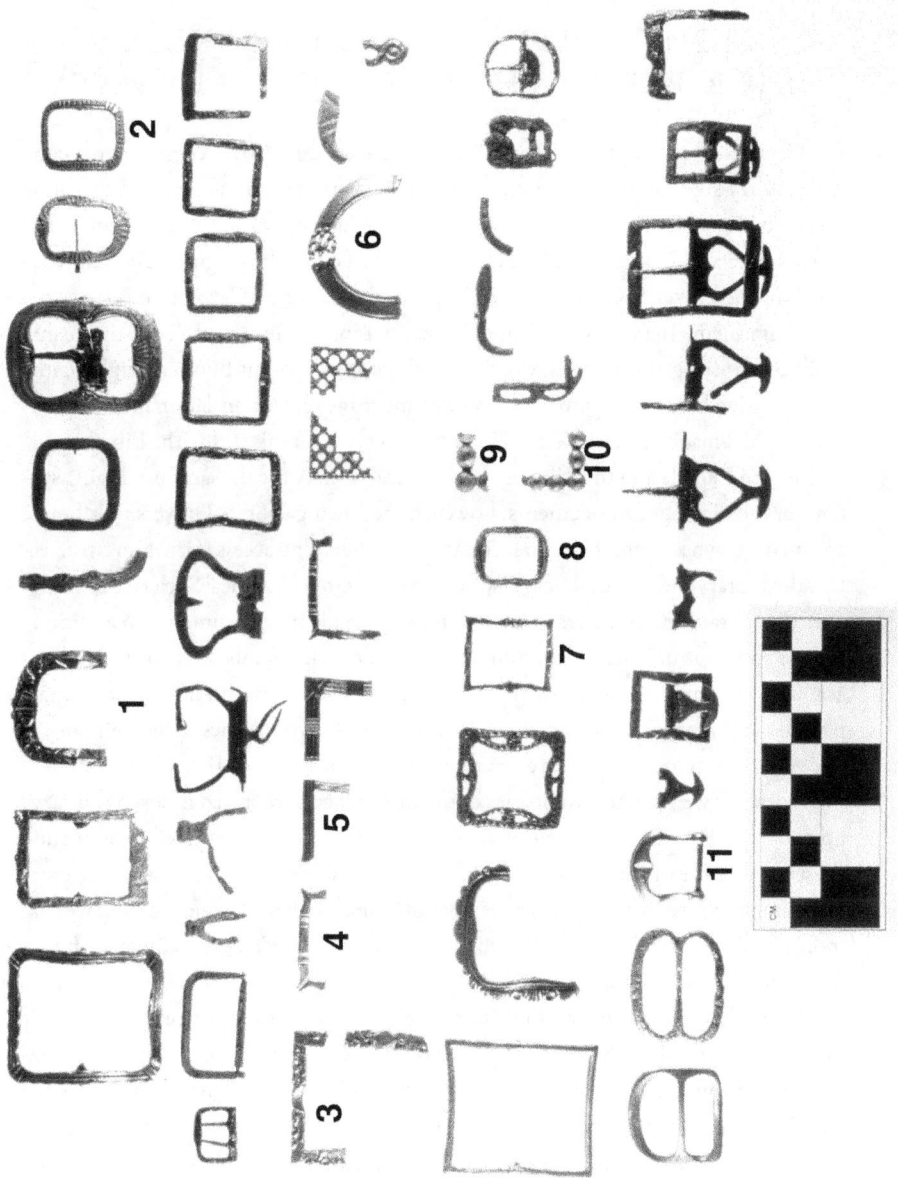

Figure 7.1. Buckles from the TCHA Fort Ouiatenon collection tested by LA-ICP-MS. Numbers refer to the following accession numbers 1: 4270.5G; 2: 4270.57.7; 3: 4270.978.5; 4: 4270.956.1; 5: 4270.958.1; 6: 4270.T23.1; 7: 4270.285.3; 8: 4270.T17.2; 9: 4270.57.2; 10: 4270.38.4; 11: 4270.T17.P. Buckles #9 and #10 have clear paste stones, which are uncommon in the collection. Photograph by Misty M. Jackson.

EIGHTEENTH-CENTURY BUCKLES DESCRIBED IN THE DOCUMENTARY DATA

The historical documents used for this study include the MMR. These records consist of thirty-six volumes of account books and ledgers concerning personal and business activities of ten French merchants and are invaluable as primary documents. The Antiquarian and Numismatic Society of Montreal owns the originals and allowed the Public Archives of Canada (now Library and Archives of Canada) in Ottawa to microfilm them. The Michigan State University Library purchased a copy of the microfilm consisting of nine reels, which it cataloged as "Account Books of Eighteenth Century Merchants of Montreal" (catalog number 19014). A translation into English of the MMR made by Marie Gerin-Lajoie was accessed for this study. The Library and Archives of Canada and the Minnesota Historical Society use the same cataloging system for referencing the documents; however, the Michigan State University Library assigned its own reel numbers. To facilitate researchers who access microfilms from either the Library and Archives of Canada or the Minnesota Historical Society, this study cites the Library and Archives of Canada number to identify documents. In addition, the account book or journal title, volume number, and page numbers when given in the account books are also included. Volume numbers reflect the account book or journal position within the microfilm reels. Reels cover at least two volumes or account books (see Anderson 1992 and Jackson 2005 for more details on the MMR).

A total of twenty-four inventories of the material culture stored at seven military posts in New France spanning the years 1694 to 1744 were also examined to better understand folk classifications. A comparison of the military inventories with the merchant invoices reveals both similarities and differences in their classifications, of which more detail is provided below. The Library and Archives of Canada retain microfilms of the storehouse inventories.

The MMR and the fort and military storehouse inventories record forty-three buckle entries, the majority (N = 35, or 81.4%) of which appear in the merchant records, with the remainder authored by military personnel. The merchant Alexis Moniere Sr., whose invoices make up the majority of those in the MMR, recorded fifteen, with five other merchants' invoices also contributing data. The documents span the period from 1699 to 1770.

Buckles were described using sixteen variables in various combinations. They include belt, waist belt/sword belt, garter, shoe, steel, similor, tombac, yellow, with colored stones, one tongue, two tongue, polished, pair, small, large, men's, and women's. Since Marie Gerin-Lajoie's translation into English was used, the original French for these variables is not included here. They can be grouped under typical archaeological classification categories of function, material, construction, treatment, quantity, size, and gender. The military used five of the variables, three of which reflected material or color (yellow, steel, and tombac) and two of which reflected function (waist belt/sword belt and shoe). The merchants recorded greater detail and precise description by employing all but two of the variables, yellow and waist belt/sword belt. Two of the variables of interest due to their lesser use by archaeologists are tombac and the related term "similor."

Similor appears five times in the merchants' invoices. Brouillard, the younger Moniere, designated men's (one entry) and women's (two entries) buckles as being composed of similor in 1758. In addition, the merchant Pascaud made an entry for one dozen similor buckles for men. An additional entry by Pascaud lists a dozen similor buckles with colored stones at six livres, considerably less than the eighteen livres for a dozen similor buckles for men in the first entry. Pascaud listed both of these similor entries in a 1748 ship's insurance claim he made at Quebec included in the MMR (Library and Archives of Canada, 1712–1806, MG 1 Vol. 1376, reel F-1697). Unfortunately, the younger Moniere did not list prices; hence, we only have Pascaud's invoices for an indication of the value of similor buckles. The "stones of color" were probably glass rather than stone. Given the differences in the way Pascaud listed the two entries as well as the prices, the buckles of similor and stones may be for women or may be knee or stock buckles.

Similor, like brass, was "an alloy of copper and zinc, resembling gold in colour. It was invented in France by Renty, of Lille, c. 1729, and later improved by Leblanc, of Paris. It was an imitation of pinchbeck, and was sometimes called 'goldshine.' The name is derived from Latin, *similus* (similar), and French, *or* (gold)" (Newman 1981, 281). Pinchbeck, similor, and tombac were developed to mimic gold cheaply. Around 1720 the London watchmaker Christopher Pinchbeck created the copper and zinc alloy that bears his name. Pinchbeck kept his alloy's composition secret, but the most reliable sources place it at 83 percent copper with 17 percent zinc (Newman 1981, 240). According to Paul Craddock of the British Museum Research Laboratory, it can range from 80 to 85 percent copper, with 15–20 percent zinc and possible iron contents of 0.3–1 percent (Craddock, pers. email comm., November 12, 2001). A second range of composition places the copper at 85–88 percent, with 12–15 percent zinc (James 1998, 48). Pinchbeck, similor, and tombac could pass for gold but were much lighter in weight. Jewelers, watchmakers, and toy makers used it to manufacture buttons, buckles, jewelry, and snuff boxes. Manufacturers might thinly gild pinchbeck, but the difference between the gold and the imitation was barely detectable if the wash wore off. Silver might also be used for gilding (Earle 1903, 381).

Similor, pinchbeck, and tombac as well as colored stones of paste, while inexpensive, were not just for the poor or middle classes. It has been noted that "much imitation jewellery was worn by all people even of great wealth. Perhaps imitation is an incorrect word. The old paste jewels made no assertion of being diamonds" (Earle 1903, 381). By the 1730s paste stones had become popular (Lewis 1970, 36). "Costume" jewelry was its own desirable and highly valued item. Examples from the American colonies and the new American republic demonstrate their adoption by elites there. Jonathan Belcher, governor of Massachusetts from 1730 to 1741 and a man of economic means, ordered fine clothing in 1739 made up with matching accessories including silver and pinchbeck buckles (Earle 1903, 404). The "macaronis" of the 1770s wore their large shoe buckles made of gold, silver, pinchbeck, or steel (Laver 1995, 139). Martha Washington owned many pieces of jewelry, including shoe buckles, with paste stones, deemed appropriate for a woman of her position (Cadou 2002, 16). "Semi-precious stones, paste jewellery, ... pinchbeck and cut steel (much used for male accessories, such as buckles, watch and seal chains), all contributed to ingenious but relatively inexpensive jewellery throughout the [eighteenth] century" (Murdoch 1991, 56; see chapter 6 in this volume for further discussion of paste jewelry).

Tombac appears once in each of three different merchants' invoices and twice in the 1741 Quebec General Inventory. Moniere sent ten pairs of women's tombac buckles to the Sioux post in 1736, and Pascaud in 1748 recorded in Quebec four dozen tombac buckles for women. Pierre Guy in 1737 listed for Detroit one pair of tombac buckles, with no other descriptive variable.

In the military inventory for Quebec, two pairs of tombac buckles and four pairs of tombac shoe buckles appear in two different sections of the document. The first occurs in an untitled section, and the shoe buckles are categorized under "Merchandise." This particular inventory does not conform to the general outline of the other inventories in terms of the overall heading, section titles, and prices, which were omitted for the buckles.

Comparison of the prices of steel, tombac, and similor buckles reveals that steel buckles cost less than similor. Men's polished steel buckles cost six livres ten sols per dozen in 1741 and one livre for one pair in 1747. A dozen men's similor buckles in 1748 cost eighteen livres. Unfortunately, the merchant did not list or the translator Marie Gerin-Lajoie did not include the price of women's similor buckles for comparison to men's and to tombac buckles. Likewise, the military personnel did not record prices for their steel and tombac buckles.

Tombac was an alloy of copper and zinc with approximately the same percentages of these metals as in similor and pinchbeck (Newman 1981, 307). Like those alloys, tombac was also used to make and gild inexpensive jewelry and buckles that resisted tarnish and could be mistaken for gold. The ambassadors from Siam introduced it to France when they brought it to the court of Louis the XIV. The French claimed that the Siamese esteemed it more than gold, and initially the French thought that it was not an alloy but instead came from mines (Savary 1723–1741, 3:305). Eventually French chemists disabused themselves of this notion, though supposedly they still did not know the percentages of composition by 1762 (Savary 1762, 3:930, 1008, 1047). This lack of compositional knowledge at such a late date is interesting, and the entry in the 1762 edition of Savary's *Dictionaire Universel* might be an unrevised one from an earlier edition. Savary also mentions tombac in his 1741 edition under the entry *Me'tail De Prince*, defined as an extremely refined copper and a type of French tombac (Savary 1723–1741, 3:381). He spelled it variously as "tambac" and "tambaque."

It is interesting to note how the merchants used the variables of similor and tombac. Pascaud used both within the same document, the 1748 ship's insurance claim made at Quebec, suggesting a difference between similor and tombac. Similor was considerably more expensive at eighteen livres for a dozen men's buckles and six livres for a dozen with colored stones. By way of comparison, the women's tombac buckles cost one livre sixteen sols per dozen. The women's may simply have been smaller and unadorned. Moniere used the variable tombac, while his son used similor. Whether the terms similor and tombac were interchangeable or whether there was a perceived if not real difference between the two is not clear.

TABLE 7.1. TOMBAC, STEEL, AND SIMILOR BUCKLES BY QUANTITY, PRICE, AND YEAR

Variable 1	Variable 2	Variable 3	Quantity	Price	Year
tombac	women's		10 pairs	7 s each	1736
tombac			1 pair	No price	1737
tombac	for women		4 dozen	36s/dozen: 7#4s	1748
steel	polished	for men	1 pair	1#	1747
steel			4 pairs	7s6d/pair: 1#10s	1743
steel			3 pairs	15s/pair: 2#5s	1744
steel	polished	for men	6 pairs	6#10s/dozen: 3#5s	1741
similor	for men		1 dozen	18#	1748
similor	with colored stones		1 dozen	6#	1748

The terms "tombac," "pinchbeck," and "similor" are not ones used by archaeologists to describe buckle material. How does one identify tombac or related material today? Were all copper and zinc alloy buckles and jewelry composed of tombac, similor, or pinchbeck as opposed to the golden-colored copper alloy referred to generally as brass?

Published examples of purported pinchbeck buckles and, by extension, most likely tombac and similor appear in *Buckles 1250–1800* (Whitehead 1996, 112) and in the *Catalogue of Shoe and Other Buckles in Northampton Museum* (Northampton Borough Council 1981). Pinchbeck purportedly imitated gold rather well, resisting tarnish for use in the manufacture of jewelry, buttons, buckles, clocks, and other "toys." Burgess (1937, 306) tells us that "Such jewellery has been preserved, and in many instances when carefully cleaned still presents an attractive appearance—like modern 'substitutes,' for gold 'pinchbeck' could be worn without fear of detection when exposed in candlelight or seen at a little distance."

Compositional analysis allows for testing of the hypothesis that all golden-colored buckles are composed of pinchbeck, tombac, similor, or a gilding of these materials, thereby helping us to know whether it is possible to visually identify these variables. This in turn could save time and costs in the analysis of buckles, buttons, and jewelry of the eighteenth century.

SEMIQUANTITATIVE COMPOSITIONAL ANALYSIS OF BUCKLES BY LA-ICP-MS

LA-ICP-MS is an excellent technique for comparing the elemental composition of buckles, and researchers have utilized it to analyze other copper-based artifacts (Dussubieux et al. 2008; Hawkins et al. 2016; Bassett, Stevenson, and Dussubieux 2019). With this technique, a sample is placed inside a chamber filled with an inert carrier gas that sweeps across the sample. A laser beam ablates a very small area of the sample (micron scale). The ablated sample is carried into argon plasma, where it is atomized, ionized, and then analyzed by a mass spectrometer. Since this technique requires no sample preparation and removes only a very small volume of material, it is virtually nondestructive. Craters in inconspicuous areas of the samples are less than one hundred microns in diameter. In addition, the laser technique can accommodate the size and irregular surface morphology of the buckle fragments.

Quantitative elemental analysis of samples via LA-ICP-MS requires an external standard of known and relatively similar composition as well as an internal standard (i.e., element of known concentration) for the sample itself. The nature of laser pulsing results in variable sample yields over the course of the analysis and requires standardization to known values of at least one element in the sample to determine the concentration of other elements. Although there are external standards for tombac, the samples used for this study had no internal standard values, and element concentrations could not be determined.

However, since the samples are assumed to be relatively homogenous, it is possible to compare the elemental compositions by the relative proportions of zinc, copper, and iron in the samples. The ratio of counts for each element in each sample can be used to compare the relative composition of samples within a run. Although this technique does not yield absolute (e.g., weight %) proportions of those elements, it does allow for comparisons among groups of samples.

As previously stated, tombac's known composition included 83 percent copper with 17 percent zinc (Newman 1981, 240) or ranged from 80 to 85 percent copper with 15–20 percent zinc and possible unintentional iron contents of 0.3–1 percent (Craddock, pers. comm., 2001). Zinc could also run as low as 12–15 percent (James 1998, 48). A study by Craddock (1978, 12) of Roman copper alloy objects determined that "an alloy containing about 13% of zinc was preferred. This is the approximate zinc content of modern pinchbeck or gilding metal, widely used now, as in Roman times, for decorative metal."

In order to analyze the buckles using LA-ICP-MS, it is useful to understand how eighteenth-century craftspeople produced copper alloys. The zinc mixed with copper that resulted in tombac consisted of pure metallic zinc mostly from China and India, though furnaces with specially adapted flues at Rammelsberg, Germany, near Goslar also produced pure zinc. Cheaper calamine zinc ores were more readily available in Europe. Manufacture of most brass for utilitarian wares utilized a cementation process in which finely divided copper, charcoal, and calcined zinc ores were heated together (Craddock, pers. comm., 2001). Copper alloys produced by the cementation process should contain between 22 and 28 percent zinc or even more (Craddock 1978, 10). In addition, the iron in the zinc ores generally gives the alloys produced by the cementation process an iron content of typically 0.3–1 percent and not uncommonly as high as 3 percent. This stands in contrast to the lower 0.01–0.3 percent iron content also present in the copper and therefore present in copper alloys incorporating pure zinc. Having stated these generalities, it is also possible for the copper to have higher iron content and for the cementation process to result in lower iron (Craddock, pers. comm., 2001).

To determine the manner in which copper and zinc alloys were produced, the most important metal to measure is iron. Items with appreciably more iron likely result from the cementation process, reflecting common utilitarian items. Tombac or pinchbeck should have about the same iron content as the copper, given that their zinc additive would have been incorporated not through the cementation process but instead as a pure additive to the copper. Analysis should begin with contemporary copper items to give an idea of the background iron in them and then analyze the copper alloys in question, in this case buckles (Craddock, pers. comm., 2001).

Investigation of a sample of twelve buckles from the collection at the TCHA used laser ablation with an inductively coupled plasma mass spectrometer Cetac LSX200+ instrument located in the Geological Sciences Department and ICP-MS Laboratory at Michigan State University. Investigators took five measurements per artifact for both zinc to copper and iron to copper ratios. For both of the ratios the highest and lowest values of the five analyses were eliminated, keeping three analyses. The peaks were then integrated, and analysis used the heights of the peak for each element in the data analyses.

The buckles were selected for testing based on their visual appearance that the researchers assumed to represent the spectrum of copper alloy material composition of the buckles in the collection held at the TCHA. They ranged from one buckle that exhibits the appearance of red-colored copper (4270.57.7) to those with the general appearance of yellow or golden-colored brass. Two buckles based on visual inspection appear to have a golden-colored gilding over copper or copper alloy (4270.28.4 and 4270.958.1); the gilding was interpreted as possibly representing tombac. One buckle has the appearance of gold (no accession number and referred to here as 5G), and two others also have a golden brass appearance (4270.956.1 and 4270.T17.P). These last three buckles might represent tombac, pinchbeck, or similor, which most closely resemble the appearance of gold. In summary, the buckle sample was selected based on visual inspection of the range of colors present in the assemblage from red copper color to yellow brass color, which are assumed to represent a range of compositions of brass with higher zinc and iron (utilitarian wares) to lower zinc and iron content (probably tombac, similor, or pinchbeck). The results suggest whether it is possible to identify through visual inspection a buckle's composition as tombac, similor, or pinchbeck.

Since the goal was to test whether it is possible to perform visual inspection for tombac and, by extension, pinchbeck and similor (Newman 1981, 307), selection of buckles for analysis did not include those with the appearance of copper or steel with the exception of one buckle of red-colored copper/copper alloy (4270.57.7) and those that exhibited the tarnish. Few buckles distinguished themselves as having a golden appearance, thereby limiting the sample. Other buckles might exhibit a gold appearance if cleaned properly, particularly those from the collections at the Glenn Black Laboratory of Archaeology. The sample is not statistically valid, and results must be considered preliminary. The few buckles in the collection, at least among those held at the TCHA, with a golden appearance seem to resist tarnish, which might be argument enough for assuming that their composition or gilding is composed of tombac, pinchbeck, or similor. However, LA-ICP-MS testing for composition may allow researchers a basis for making visual determinations and move toward ascertaining composition as opposed to assuming it.

To aid in determining the potential amount of background iron as well as the ratios of zinc that can be present in copper alloys, five copper alloy kettle scraps exhibiting a red copper appearance from the collection held by the TCHA and three raw copper ore fragments from England, Hungary, and Germany were tested. The kettle scraps were selected from different excavation units and levels throughout the Fort Ouiatenon site in an effort to obtain scraps that might have originated from different kettles. In regard to the raw copper for comparison of background iron, the three countries selected are known to have produced copper for export historically. Savary (1723–1741, 1:992; 1762, 1:1229-30) lists the countries of Europe with copper mines. Sweden was the premiere provider, but Norway, Hungary, and Germany also ranked in the top four producing the best and most abundant sources. Efforts to procure a sample from the Falun Mine in Sweden, the main and most probable seventeenth-century source, proved unsuccessful due to its closure around 1992 after nine hundred years of production (Lars Laris, senior state geologist of Sweden, pers. email comm., February 7, 2002). Peter Molnar, a dealer in rocks and minerals operating out of Budapest, Hungary, provided a small sample of raw ore copper collected in 2000 from the Andrássy I Mine in Rudabánga, Hungary. The Mineralogical Research Company in San Jose, California, provided a sample containing copper, cuprite, and malachite from the Hot Lode United Downs Mine in Cornwall, England. This company also provided a sample of copper from the Kauser Steimel Mine near Daaden, Westerwald, Germany.

The results of testing that yielded ratio readings of zinc to copper and of iron to copper were visually compared to their buckles. The research design set the expectation that a lower zinc content and lower iron content reflects the composition of tombac as opposed to brass produced by the cementation process. The copper alloy kettle fragments provide a general background for measuring both iron and zinc as it would appear in copper alloys with a reddish appearance.

The bar graphs show the ratio data for iron/copper (Fe/Cu) (figure 7.2) and zinc/copper (Zn/Cu) (figure 7.3) resulting from the LA-ICP-MS investigation. The five bars on the left side of the charts give the ratios for the five kettle scraps. The three bars on the right side of the charts show ratios for the three samples of raw copper ore. The twelve bars between the scrap and raw copper ore data record the ratio data for the buckles. Figure 7.2 shows a range of iron content in the kettle scraps, and the raw copper samples also vary from a very high to a very low iron content. The iron content in the buckles lies within the range of and generally less than that in the five scrap samples, as is expected for brass produced with pure zinc rather than by the cementation process. All buckles except 4270.57.2 contain a lower iron to copper ratio than four of the five kettle scraps, again as expected for items produced with pure zinc (decorative metals) and zinc ores in the cementation process (utilitarian wares). One kettle scrap, 4270.2.39.3b, contains a low iron/copper ratio similar to three of the buckles (4270.956.1, 4270.L1, and 4270.2.85.3). The German and English raw copper samples display the highest ratios of iron to copper. The low iron content of the Hungary sample is similar to that of the buckle 4270.958.1.

The results of measurement for zinc to copper ratios as seen in the bar graph in figure 7.3 generally conforms to expectations considering that lower zinc content in copper alloys allows for retention of a reddish appearance, as in the case of the kettle scraps of copper or copper alloy. While the raw copper ore samples contain very low or no zinc as expected, nine of the twelve buckles exhibit higher zinc/copper ratios than the brass kettle scraps. The three buckles with low zinc to copper ratios (4270.57.2, 4270.57.7, and 4270.958.1) not surprisingly have a copper-like appearance, with buckle 4270.958.1

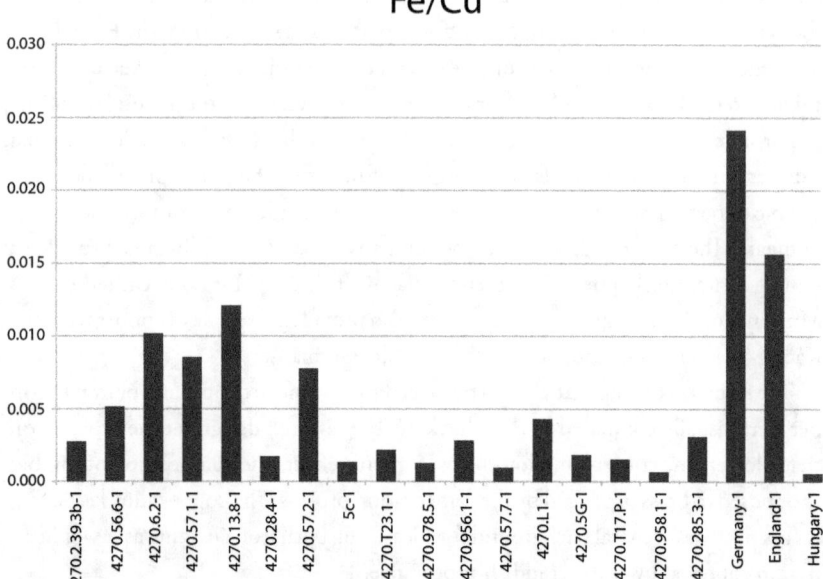

Figure 7.2. Bar graph showing ratio data for iron to copper content in five kettle or other utensil scraps (far left), three fragments of copper ore (far right), and twelve buckles in the center of the bar graph. The copper ore samples from the sources in Germany and England contain the highest ratios of iron to copper. Buckle 4270.958.1 and the copper ore from Hungary have the smallest ratios of iron to copper. The iron in the zinc ores used in the cementation process to produce copper alloys generally results in a higher iron content than tends to be present in copper or copper alloys incorporating pure zinc. The buckles in general differ from the copper alloy scraps in that they contain less iron and therefore likely represent copper alloys such as tombac produced with pure zinc. Measured by LA-ICP-MS.

possibly exhibiting brass or tombac gilding. Conversely, buckle 4270.5G shows the highest zinc/copper ratio, but it is also copper-like in appearance. However, buckle 4270.5G also appears to have a gold-colored gilding, and the underlying copper or copper alloy may have received the ablation during testing.

To summarize the LA-ICP-MS test results, while quantification of absolute metal abundance in the samples is not possible without an internal standard value, elemental ratios provide a useful tool for sample comparison. Repeat measurements on the same sample provide evidence of relative sample homogeneity and precision of the method. Ratios of metals (i.e., Zn/Cu and Fe/Cu) provide a high-level comparison of relative composition of alloys with a quasi-nondestructive analytical method. If one considers only the iron/copper (Fe/Cu) ratio data, then many of the buckles appear to result from the low iron, pure zinc manufacturing process characteristic of tombac and pinchbeck

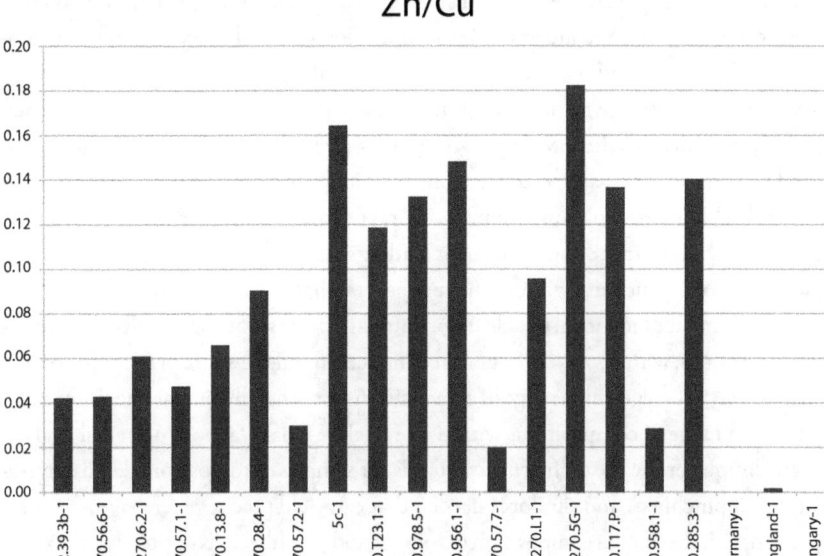

Figure 7.3. Bar graph showing ratio data for zinc to copper content in five kettle or other utensil scraps (far left), three pieces of raw copper (far right), and twelve buckles in the center of the bar graph. Nine of the twelve buckles have higher ratios of zinc to copper than the five copper alloy scraps. The three buckles with low Zn/Cu ratios have a copper-like appearance. As expected, the copper ores contain no or only a trace amount of zinc. Measured by LA-ICP-MS.

and probably also similor. However, this includes those that have a copper appearance, such as 4270.57.7 and 4270.958.1, the latter exhibiting possible gilding by tombac or brass produced by the cementation process. The data and the appearance of the cleaned copper or copper alloy scraps suggest that the kettles or other utensils from which they came comprise low zinc/copper (Zn/Cu) alloys produced by a cementation process, as expected. Buckle 4270.57.7 presents another unexpected result in that it exhibited a low Fe/Cu ratio while also exhibiting a low Zn/Cu ratio. Given its red copper appearance, low zinc is expected, but low iron is not necessarily expected.

DISCUSSION

The results of the current analysis suggest five possible conclusions. First, based on the lower iron to copper ratio, all but one buckle, 4270.57.2, consists of tombac or the related pinchbeck or similor, resulting from a noncementation process. Buckle

4270.57.2 has the appearance of a reddish copper alloy, which is expected based on the iron-to-copper ratio. Second, visual inspection allows us to identify what is likely tombac, pinchbeck, or similor at least sometimes but would not necessarily allow such identification in all cases, given that one of the buckles, 4270.5G, exhibits a reddish copper alloy appearance despite having a higher zinc content compared to the kettle scraps but low iron content, as expected for tombac, pinchbeck, and similor. Third, gilding, which might in some unknown number of cases no longer remain on the buckle, can influence both appearance and instrument readings, which probably is the case with the aforementioned buckle 4270.5G, which appears to have residual gilding. Fourth, the two very similar or identical buckle fragments with paste stones have different composition readings, with 4270.38.4 containing higher zinc and lower iron ratios to copper than 4270.57.2, suggesting a range of compositions for generally similar buckles or even possibly a range of compositions within one buckle. Finally, a more powerful analytical technique or the use of internal standards for samples of tombac or related compositions of pinchbeck and similor is needed that can yield precise percentages for comparison with the known composition of tombac and pinchbeck, as opposed to the ratio approach necessitated by the buckles in the Fort Ouiatenon collection.

The results obtained by Moreau and Hancock (1998, 335–40) using another technique, instrumental neutron activation analysis, for testing copper alloy utilitarian items including kettles, tinkling cones, and other metal artifacts for zinc and other elements indicate the range of percentages of composition of these artifacts. Percentages allow one to see the progression over time from low or no zinc kettles in the sixteenth and seventeenth centuries to increasingly more zinc in the eighteenth century in the range suggested by Craddock for cementation process brass. The technique demonstrates a range of composition for the tested kettles and might serve as an appropriate technique for further testing of copper alloy composition for artifacts suspected of having compositions consistent with tombac, pinchbeck, and similor.

IDENTITY: ETHNICITY AND STATUS

Buckles are European manufactures worn by Europeans. However, Native Americans used them too, making it impossible to draw a straightforward relationship between buckles and ethnicity at archaeological sites such as Fort Ouiatenon. Buckles do not tend to be obvious in drawings and paintings of Native Americans even into the nineteenth century in the area occupied by France, and they do not appear in burials such as those at the Lasanen and Fletcher cemeteries in Michigan (Cleland 1971; Mainfort 1979). However, a cursory look at artifact data from two Native American sites in Illinois dating to the seventeenth and eighteenth centuries, the Zimmerman site/Grand Village of the Illinois (11Ls13) and the Guebert site, indicate that 11Ls13 produced one buckle, while the Guebert site produced three buckles (Brown 1975; Rohrbaugh et al. 1999, 151, 177, 259; Good 1972, 131, 135). Wittry (1963) recorded no buckles at the eighteenth-century Bell site in Wisconsin. The Tomotley site, an east Tennessee Cherokee village occupied circa 1760–1776, produced three buckles and a buckle tang (Baden 1983), and the Trudeau site, a cemetery of the Tunica Indians in Louisiana, contained one pewter buckle (Brain 1979, 162).

It should be noted that two hundred pairs of "yellow" buckles are recorded in a document included among the MMR translated by Gerin-Lajoie, dated 1731 and titled "Statement/Invoice of the merchandise which are necessary at La Mobile (Fort Condé) for the presents for the Indians during the year 1732" (Library and Archives of Canada, 1712–1806, MG 1/C 13 B, Corr. Gén., Louisiane, Microfilm F-581, 26 bis, folio 6f). The document indicates provisioning to Native Americans with what were probably shoe or knee buckles, given their occurrence as pairs. Regardless, they may not have used them for their originally intended purpose. Only waist belt or sword belt buckles were listed specifically for French consumption in the Quebec inventory of 1741 (Library and Archives of Canada, 1697–1763, MG1 Vol. 112, reel F-112, 29–37). Likewise, in an MMR invoice for Fort Ouiatenon in 1736, waist belt or sword belt buckles as well as six pairs of women's buckles were the only ones listed, indicating that the recipients were settlers/engagés (Library and Archives of Canada, 1712–1806, Monière, Vol. 4, Journal 3, 797–801).

While buckles were not used solely by the French, they can be linked to shared European meanings for the French, particularly that of status. Documents record fine shoe buckles for men made of steel as well as gold, silver, and pinchbeck (Laver 1995, 139). Indeed, buckles served as important indicators of status. According to one source, "In the eighteenth century a whole protocol of shoe buckles was codified and a man's social position as well as his taste could be guessed from them. The rich farmer or the small squire had silver for week-days and decent gilt for Sundays; the country dandy cut steel and paste; the courtier diamonds" (Evans 1953, 179). Also, "*The Gentleman's Magazine* of June 1777 observed: 'All our young fops of quality, and even the lowest of our people in London, wear coach-harness [shoe] buckles, the latter in brass, white metal and pinchbeck'" (Pratt and Woolley 1999, 52). "White metal" referred to tin or pewter. Pewter buckles were surpassed in lowliness only by those of iron (Hume 1991, 86).

The military also made distinctions reflected in buckles. Soldiers wore the lowliest and cheapest iron shoe buckles. Officials of the colony displayed gold, possibly gilded, shoe buckles with iron chapes and stock buckles of silver. In 1740 an engineer's inventory included a tombac belt buckle (Proulx 1971, 39, 55, 57).

Tombac represents a material worn by Europeans of high status and over time by those of low status, with the potential of blurring social boundaries and providing a means for the low to mimic the well off, at least in this area of dress as it became more available to the lower classes. The association of related pinchbeck later in the eighteenth century with lower status indicates its shift in fashion and falling out of favor with elites. Its presence at a site provides ambiguous data as to the social standing of the wearer unless the context from which artifacts derive can be tightly dated, but it indicates a desire to appear fashionable and well off.

BUCKLES AND THE PEOPLE AT FORT OUIATENON

Eighteenth-century merchants and military personnel of New France used the related material terms tombac and similor, both of which bear similarity to pinchbeck, to describe buckles and buttons as well as finger rings. The items had the ability to reflect status as a ranking of materials obtained, among which tombac took its place. The order from most expensive to least not surprisingly assigned diamonds to the nobility or those of great economic means as well as gold for this group and military officials. After that followed paste "stone" insets (see chapter 6 in this volume for further discussion of paste), steel cut, silver, and gilded buckles on the same general ranking for the rich farmer, small squire, and "country dandy." The rich merchant and military officials also would have fallen into this category of consumer, though some also fell within the wealthiest category. Lower ranks of society displayed brass, pewter, and pinchbeck or tombac and probably, by extension, similor. The lowest ranking, such as the common soldier, wore iron buckles. It should be noted that this ranking of tombac and related alloys among the lowest of materials comes in 1777, decades after its introduction. Initially those of means wore it as a gold substitute suitable for traveling jewelry when highway robbery that might relieve travelers of their gold and gems made such a substitute useful and acceptable.

Results of the analysis of the elemental composition of the sample buckles utilizing LA-ICP-MS have not indicated conclusively which of the sample buckles consist of tombac or tombac gilding or the related variables of similor or pinchbeck. Though definitive visual identification of these materials remains only suggestive, buckles within the collection exhibit golden-colored copper alloy that appears to be consistent with descriptions of the copper alloy materials.

Among the invoices of the MMR, only eight listed goods headed for Fort Ouiatenon, and of these only one dated 1736 listed buckles (Library and Archives of Canada, 1712–1806, Monière, Vol. 4, Journal 3, pp. 797–801). These included two belt buckles ("2 *boucles de centrue a fl a 14s*") at fifteen sols each and six pairs of women's buckles ("6 *pairs de boucle a feme*") at eight sols per pair. One French pound (*livre*) equaled twenty sols. The invoice specifies both types as items for settlers or engagés and indicates the presence of women at Fort Ouiatenon. What is not clear is whether they were French, métis, or Native American.

The French wearers of tombac and similar alloys whether in buckles or jewelry at Fort Ouiatenon would have seen them as reflecting greater status and value earlier in the eighteenth century and representing lesser status as the century progressed. Where possible, tight dating of deposits at eighteenth-century sites will allow for a more accurate interpretation of how the French there viewed the value and significance of tombac or similor and its potential for reflecting the class and status of the wearers. The presence of buckles of golden-colored copper alloy, some of them ornately designed and including paste stones, indicates that some segment of the French population at Fort Ouiatenon valued the fashions of the period, signaled their status, and maintained this aspect of French identity. Soldiers at the site would have worn the iron buckles in the collection, which signaled their lower status. How Native Americans viewed these alloys and how they used buckles remain questions to explore.

REFERENCES

Anderson, Dean Lloyd. 1992. "Documentary and Archaeological Perspectives on European Trade Goods in the Western Great Lakes Region." PhD diss., Michigan State University.

Baden, William. 1983. *Tomotley: An Eighteenth Century Cherokee Village*. Tennessee Valley Authority Publications in Anthropology 35. University of Tennessee, Department of Anthropology, Report of Investigations 36.

Bassett, Madeleine Gunter, Christopher M. Stevenson, and Laure Dussubieux. 2019. "Re-examining Trade Networks in Late Woodland Virginia (900–1600 CE): An LA-ICP-MS Analysis of Copper Artifacts." *Journal of Archaeological Science: Reports* 27: 1–13.

Brain, Jeffrey P. 1979. *Tunica Treasure*. Cambridge, MA: Peabody Museum of Archaeology and Ethnology, Harvard University and Peabody Museum of Salem.

Brew, J. O. 1946. *The Archaeology of Alkali Ridge, Southwestern Utah*. Papers of the Peabody Museum of Archaeology and Ethnology 24. Cambridge, MA: Harvard University.

Brown, Margaret Kimball. 1975. *The Zimmerman Site: Further Excavations at the Grand Village of Kaskaskia*. Reports of Investigations 32. Springfield: Illinois State Museum.

Burgess, Fred W. 1937. *Antique Jewelry and Trinkets*. New York: Tudor Publishing.

Cadou, Carol Borchert. 2002. "The Best of Every Article: The Style of Martha Washington." In *The Annual Report of the Mount Vernon Ladies' Association of the Union*, 13–19. Mount Vernon Ladies Association.

Cleland, Charles E., ed. 1971. *The Lasanen Site: An Historic Burial Locality in Mackinac County, Michigan*. Publications of the Museum, Anthropological Series 1 (1), 1–147. East Lansing: Michigan State University.

Craddock, Paul. 1978. "The Composition of the Copper Alloys Used by the Greek, Etruscan and Roman Civilizations, 3: The Origins and Early Use of Brass." *Journal of Archaeological Science* 5: 1–16.

Dussubieux, Laure, Aurelie Deraisme, Gérard Frot, Christopher Stevenson, Amy Creech, and Yves Bienvenu. 2008. "LA-ICP-MS, SEM-EDS and EPMA Analysis of Eastern North American Copper-based Artefacts: Impact of Corrosion and Heterogeneity on the Reliability of the LA-ICP-MS Composition Results." *Archaeometry* 50, no 4: 643–65.

Earle, Alice Morse. 1903. *Two Centuries of Costume in America*, Vols. 1 and 2. New York: Macmillan.

Evans, Joan. 1953. *A History of Jewellery, 1100–1870*. New York: Pitman Publishing.

Good, Mary Elizabeth. 1972. *Guebert Site: An 18th Century, Historic Kaskaskia Indian Village in Randolph County, Illinois*. Central States Archaeological Societies Memoir Series 2.

Hawkins, Alicia L., Joseph A. Petrus, Lisa Marie Anselmi, and Gary Crawford. 2016. "Laser Ablation-Inductively Coupled Plasma-Mass Spectrometry Analysis of Copper-Based Artifacts from South Ontario and the Chronology of the Indirect Contact Period." *Journal of Archaeological Science: Reports* 6: 332–41.

Hume, Ivor Noël. 1991. *A Guide to Artifacts of Colonial America*. New York: Vintage Books.

Jackson, Misty May. 2005. "Classifications by Historical Archaeologists and Eighteenth Century Montreal Merchants and Military Personnel in New France: Emic and Etic Approaches." PhD diss., Michigan State University.

James, Duncan. 1998. *Antique Jewellery: Its Manufacture, Materials, and Design*. Princes Risborough, UK: Shire Publications.

Laver, James. 1995. *Costume and Fashion a Concise History*. New York: Thames and Hudson.

Lewis, M. D. S. 1970. *Antique Paste Jewellery*. Boston: Boston Book and Art.

Library and Archives of Canada. 1697–1763. Fonds des Colonies (MG1) Series C11A: Correspondance Général, Canada. Ottawa, Ontario.

———. 1712–1806. Antiquarian and Numismatic Society of Montreal Collection: Account Books and Records of the Fur Merchants at Montreal. Ottawa, Ontario.

Mainfort, Robert C., Jr. 1979. *Indian Social Dynamics in the Period of European Contact: Fletcher Site Cemetery, Bay County, Michigan*. Publications of the Museum, Anthropological Series 1(4), 269–418. East Lansing: Michigan State University.

Moreau, J. F., and R. G. V. Hancock. 1998. "Faces of European Copper Alloy Cauldrons from Québec and Ontario 'contact' sites." In *Metals in Antiquity*, ed. S. M. M. Young, 326–41. BAR International Series 792. Oxford, UK: British Archaeological Reports.

Murdoch, Tessa. 1991. *Treasures and Trinkets: Jewellery in London from Pre-Roman Times to the 1930's*. London: Museum of London.

Newman, Harold. 1981. *An Illustrated Dictionary of Jewelry*. New York: Thames and Hudson.

Noble, Vergil. 1983. "Functional Classification and Intra-Site Analysis in Historical Archaeology: A Case Study from Fort Ouiatanon." PhD diss., Michigan State University.

Northampton Borough Council. 1981. *Catalogue of Shoe and Other Buckles in Northampton Museum.* Northampton, UK: Northampton Borough Council Museums and Art Gallery.

Pratt, Lucy, and Linda Woolley. 1999. *Shoes.* London: V & A Publications.

Proulx, Gilles. 1971. *Le Costume Militaire à Louisbourg 1713–1758.* Service des Lieux Historiques, Travail Inédit Numéro 45. Ministère des Affaires Indiennes et du Nord Canadien.

Rohrbaugh, Charles L., Lenville J. Stelle, Thomas E. Emerson, Gregory R. Walz, and John T. Penman. 1999. *The Archaeology of the Grand Village of the Illinois: Report of the Grand Village Research Project, 1991–1996; Grand Village of the Illinois State Historic Site (11LS13), LaSalle County, Illinois.* 2nd ed., revised. Illinois Transportation Archaeological Research Program Research Reports 60. Second Edition, Revised.

Savary des Brûlons, Jacques. 1723–1741. *Dictionnaire Universel de Commerce: Contenant Tout ce qui Concerne le Commerce qui se Fait dans les Quatre Parties du Monde....* 3 vols. Paris: Chez la Veuve Estienne.

Savary des Bruslons, Jacques, and Philémon Louis Savary. 1762. *Dictionnaire universel de commerce: Contenant tout ce qui concerne le commerce qui se fait dans les quatre parties du monde, par terre, par mer, de proche en proche, & par des voyages de long cours tant en gros qu'en détail ; explication de tous les termes qui ont rapport au negoce ... les edits, declarations, ordonnances, arrets, et reglemens donnés en matiére [sic] de commerce.* Nouvelle edition, exactement repvüe, corrigée, & enrichie de beaucoup d'additions dans laquelle le supplément est rangé en sa place. Geneva: Chez les Héritiers Cramer & freres Philibert.

Stone, Lyle M. 1974. *Fort Michilimackinac 1715–1781: An Archaeological Perspective on the Revolutionary Frontier.* Anthropological Series. East Lansing: MSU Museum in cooperation with Mackinac Island State Park Commission.

Tordoff, Judith Dunn. 1983. "An Archaeological Perspective on the Organization of the Fur Trade in Eighteenth Century New France." PhD diss., Michigan State University.

Whitehead, Ross. 1996. *Buckles, 1250–1800.* Hatfield Peverel Chelmsford, Essex, UK: Greenlight Publishing.

Wittry, Warren L. 1963. "The Bell Site, Wn9, an Early Historic Fox Village." *Wisconsin Archeologist* 44, no. 1–2 (March): 1–57.

8

FLINTLOCKS ON THE FRONTIER

A Case Study of Fort St. Joseph (20BE23), Niles, Michigan

KEVIN P. JONES

THROUGHOUT THE LATE SEVENTEENTH AND EIGHTEENTH CENTURIES, flintlocks were the modern military weapons for the armies of France, England, and other European powers (Brown 1980, 77; Neumann 1998, 10). Not only did flintlocks form the foundation of European armies of the time, but trappers, traders, and woodsmen also relied heavily on them (Brown 1980, 77). Flintlocks were so widely sought after by Native Americans that their preferences helped shape the forms of many trade guns (Brown 1980, 153; Gale 2010, 9; Russell 1957, 11), and thousands of weapons were made in the workshops of Europe, intended for the hands of Native Americans (Russell 1957, 15–16).

In light of these facts as well as their persistent and widespread usage during the fur trade era, flintlock weapons represent valuable artifacts of archaeological interest for those studying this time period. This is doubly so in the context of fur trade forts and outposts. These sites provided the primary locations at which owners of flintlock weapons could have their weapons serviced, a task often requiring a skilled tradesman (Bodoh 2003; Hamilton 1980, 116).

This chapter provides a case study of flintlock materials at one such fort, Fort St. Joseph (20BE23) in Niles, Michigan. Excavations of Fort St. Joseph have been carried out regularly since 2002 by Western Michigan University archaeologists (Nassaney

2015, 164). Among the artifacts recovered during these excavations are numerous flintlock components. Additionally, available historical documents demonstrate the use and maintenance of flintlocks at Fort St. Joseph. This combination of historical documentation and archaeological material provideS ample opportunity for comparative analyses.

HISTORICAL REVIEW

Fort St. Joseph was occupied from 1691 to 1781. Established initially as a mission, it was well situated near the portage between the St. Joseph and Kankakee Rivers (Nassaney, Cremin, and Lynch 2002; Brandão 2006). During the course of occupation at Fort St. Joseph, the fort saw use by French, English, and Native Americans, particularly the Potawatomi and Miami. The French occupied the fort for the majority of its use (1691–1761), and it was during this time that a gunsmith named Antoine Dehaître lived and worked at the fort. Documentation shows that from at least 1739 to 1752, Dehaître repaired flintlocks, provided supplies, and conducted various other services at the behest of both Native American and French individuals (Giordano 2005, 37; Hulse 1977, 214; Nassaney 2015, 182; Peyser 1978, 99, 121, 123, 141). Translations of French manuscripts by Joseph Peyser (1978) provide a look into some of these activities. Within these translations are a number of vouchers that record services provided by Antoine Dehaître and a gunsmith named Durivage (Peyser 1978, 99). These records indicate that nearly every part of a flintlock musket could frequently be repaired or replaced by gunsmiths. Figure 8.1 illustrates the frequency of specified gunsmithing activities (in black) and the types of gun parts worked on by these smiths (in gray) as recorded in these vouchers (data from Peyser 1978, 99, 992, 121, 123, 141). Figure 8.2 shows some of the standard parts of a flintlock musket.

ARCHAEOLOGICAL DATA

Among the artifacts recovered at Fort St. Joseph is a collection of over 250 flintlock components. Over 125 of these artifacts were recovered from one context, Feature 4, interpreted as a French gunsmith's cache (Nassaney 2015, 181). Despite this initial review of artifact inventories, the final sample consisted of 176 artifacts. Some flintlock artifacts found at Fort St. Joseph were not included in the study because they could not be located in museum collections or were not actually flintlock components. However, the predominant reason for excluding artifacts from the study was degradation beyond identification. The conditions of the Fort St. Joseph site have contributed significantly

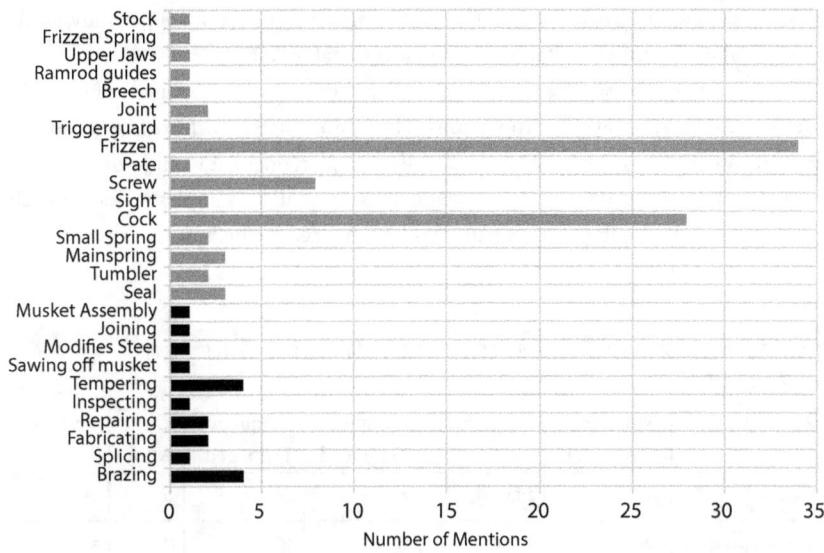

Figure 8.1. Frequency of gunsmithing repairs mentioned in translated vouchers (Peyser 1978).

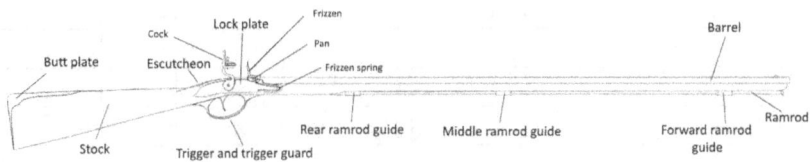

Figure 8.2. The components of a flintlock musket. Drawing by Kevin P. Jones.

to the deterioration of ferrous artifacts. The soil of the site is typically saturated if not entirely flooded, leading many of the artifacts recovered to be little more than unidentifiable fragments or rust concretions. Approximately 15 percent of the artifacts that could be located fell into this category. Such artifacts were excluded from the study. As can be seen from table 8.1, the most numerous types of artifacts were cocks (19.9%), breech plugs (18.2%), and frizzens (17.6%). These three artifact types made up over half (55.7%) of the artifacts studied. The remaining artifact types appeared at rates of 6.8 percent or less each, with the least common types—barrels and escutcheons—both having only one example each (0.6%). Among other variables, artifacts were assessed by raw material. All of the 176 artifacts fell into two material groups: ferrous and copper alloy metals. Copper alloy artifacts were limited to flintlock furniture such as butt plates, escutcheons, finials, ramrod guides, sideplates, and trigger guards. These artifact types are notably decorative in nature. No artifact types were found in both ferrous and copper alloy forms. Twenty-five (14.2%) of the studied artifacts consist of copper alloy, while 151 (85.8%) of all studied artifacts were ferrous (see table 8.1).

Nearly 60 percent of the artifacts included in the study were damaged or broken in some way. Table 8.1 shows the proportions of broken artifacts in each artifact group. For the purposes of this study, a "damaged" artifact implies one that would not be usable for its intended purpose with or without extensive repairs. Examples include breech plugs that lack their plug or tang, pans that have burned through, and cocks with broken jaws or necks.

TABLE 8.1. SUMMARY OF ARTIFACTS BY TYPE, DAMAGE, AND RAW MATERIAL

Artifact Type	Number of Artifacts	Frequency	Number Damaged	Frequency Damaged	Cu Alloy	Ferrous
Cocks	35	19.9%	21	60.0%	0	35
Breech plugs	32	18.2%	18	56.3%	0	32
Frizzens	31	17.6%	17	54.8%	0	31
Mainsprings	12	6.8%	11	91.7%	0	12
Pans	11	6.3%	4	36.4%	0	11
Butt plates	7	4.0%	5	71.4%	7	0
Trigger guards	7	4.0%	7	100.0%	7	0
Side plates	5	2.8%	5	100.0%	5	0
Vice screws	5	2.8%	1	20.0%	0	5
Bridles	3	1.7%	2	66.7%	0	3
Frizzen springs	3	1.7%	2	66.7%	0	3
Gun worms	3	1.7%	3	100.0%	0	3
Lock plates	3	1.7%	0	0.0%	0	3
Ramrod guides	3	1.7%	1	33.3%	3	0
Sears	3	1.7%	1	33.3%	0	3
Tumblers	3	1.7%	0	0.0%	0	3
Finials	2	1.1%	2	100.0%	2	0
Screws	2	1.1%	1	50.0%	0	2
Triggers	2	1.1%	0	0.0%	0	2
Upper jaws	2	1.1%	0	0.0%	0	2
Barrel	1	0.6%	1	100.0%	0	1
Escutcheon	1	0.6%	1	100.0%	1	0
Totals	176	100.0%	103	58.5%	25	151

The three most common artifact types—breech plugs, cocks, and frizzens—were all damaged at similar rates of just over half (56.3%, 60.0%, and 54.8%, respectively). Similar rates are common to bridles (66.7%) and frizzen springs (66.7%). Greater percentages of butt plates (71.4%) and mainsprings (91.7%) were damaged, while all barrels, escutcheons, finials, gun worms, sideplates, and trigger guards were damaged. Only half of screws were damaged (50.0%), while less than half of the pans (36.4%), ramrod guides (33.3%), sears (33.3%), and vice screws (20.0%) exhibited damage. None of the lock plates, triggers, tumblers, and upper cock jaws were damaged beyond usability. At least one artifact, a butt plate (04-1-115.01), is known to have been damaged during excavation, with the finial being snapped off. It was, however, complete at deposition and is not counted among the damaged artifacts. Regardless of the source of this damage (pre- or postdeposition), determining the country of origin and age of such artifacts becomes more difficult, since attributes and details on artifacts are absent or obscured. For instance, one lock plate (10-2-148.01) appears to have etchings beneath the pan. However, heavy surface pitting obscures these details. As another example, several cocks retained only the body or the neck/jaw/comb section. Recovering only half of a cock eliminates the ability to compare the relative sizes of cocks' bodies, necks, and jaws to one another, which serves as an important distinguishing characteristic. Other artifacts are remarkably well preserved, however, particularly those made of copper alloy. In fact, several copper alloy butt plates retain essentially all the detail of their etchings.

ARTIFACT DETAILS

Determinations of age were made for twenty-seven artifacts, representing 15.3 percent of the overall sample (table 8.2). These determinations ranged from circa 1680 to circa 1770, coinciding nicely with the occupation range of the fort itself. Many of these ages clustered around the 1710s and the 1740s. The second of these clusters, the 1740s, coincides with the approximate age of Feature 4. These findings fit with the expectation that the ages of artifacts would be roughly contemporaneous with Fort St. Joseph's occupation. Sixteen of these artifacts (59.3%) consisted of copper alloy, and eleven artifacts (40.7%) were ferrous. Five of these artifacts (18.5%) were determined to be English in origin, seventeen (63.0%) were determined to be of French origin, and five (18.5%) were of undetermined origin.

Of the total 176 sampled artifacts, I was able to establish a country of origin for 17.6 percent (n = 31) of the sample. Twenty of the identified artifacts (64.5%) were determined to be of a probable French origin, while 11 artifacts (35.5%) were determined to be of probable English origin. Of the artifacts for which origin could be determined, copper alloy artifacts stand out as overrepresented, with 74.2 percent (n = 23) of copper alloy and 25.8 percent (n = 8) of ferrous, compared to only 14.2 percent (n = 25) of the overall 176 sampled artifacts consisting of copper alloy. Of the 31 artifacts for which country of origin could be determined, 67.8 percent (n = 21) exhibited damage beyond usability.

TABLE 8.2. ARTIFACTS BY DETERMINED AGE

Artifact Number	Artifact Type	Country of Origin	Date Range
08-1-107.01	Butt plate	French	1680–1690
02-1-182.07d	Cock	English	1690–1715
02-1-182.06	Lock plate	English	1690–1720
98-3-0.36a	Trigger guard	French	1700–1715
98-3-0.36b	Trigger guard	French	1700–1715
02-1-115.17	Trigger guard	French	1700–1725
02-1-128.17	Sideplate	French	1700–1725
02-1-202.07f	Cock	English	1700–1725
02-1-203.08	Lock plate	French	1700–1725
04-1-074.18	Sideplate	French	1700–1725
08-2-63.11	Escutcheon	French	1705–1720
15-2-015	Sideplate	French	1710–1730
10-2-148.01	Lock plate	French	1715–1740
10-2-109.01	Cock	French	1720–1740
98-3-0.31	Cock	Unknown	1725–1750
02-1-115.09m	Cock	Unknown	1725–1750
02-203.05	Cock	Unknown	1725–1750
10-2-113.01	Cock	Unknown	1725–1750
13-2-123.01	Cock	Unknown	1725–1750
98-3-0.38	Sideplate	French	1730–1750
98-3-0.35b	Butt plate	English	1740–1760
98-3-0.42	Butt plate	French	1740–1760
06-2-93w.22	Finial	French	1740–1760
08-2-45w.15	Finial	French	1740–1760
04-1-54.18	Sideplate	French	1745–1760
98-3-178.15	Trigger guard	French	1750–1760
04-1-115.01	Butt plate	English	1750–1770

Twenty artifacts were determined to be of French origin (table 8.3). Artifact types included butt plates, cocks, escutcheons, finials, lock plates, sideplates, and trigger guards. Of these artifacts, 85.0 percent (n = 17) consisted of copper alloy, and 15.0 percent (n = 3) consisted of ferrous metal. Of all twenty French artifacts, a total of 85.0 percent (n = 17) had sustained damage beyond usability. Eleven artifacts are of English origin (table 8.4). Artifact types included butt plates, cocks, frizzen springs, lock plates, and ramrod guides. Six (54.5%) of these artifacts consisted of copper alloy, while five (45.5%) consisted of ferrous metal. Only four (36.4%) of the English artifacts exhibited damage beyond usability.

TABLE 8.3 ARTIFACTS IDENTIFIED AS FRENCH IN ORIGIN

Artifact Number	Artifact Type	Damaged	Cu Alloy	Ferrous
98-3-0.36a	Trigger guard	✓	✓	
98-3-0.36b	Trigger guard	✓	✓	
98-3-0.38	Sideplate	✓	✓	
98-3-0.41a	Trigger guard	✓	✓	
98-3-0.41b	Trigger guard	✓	✓	
98-3-0.42	Butt plate	✓	✓	
98-3-178.15	Trigger guard	✓	✓	
02-1-61.22	Trigger guard	✓	✓	
02-1-115.17	Trigger guard	✓	✓	
02-1-128.17	Sideplate	✓	✓	
02-1-203.08	Lock plate			✓
04-1-54.18	Sideplate	✓	✓	
04-1-074.18	Sideplate	✓	✓	
06-2-93w.22	Finial	✓	✓	
08-2-45w.15	Finial	✓	✓	
08-2-63.11	Escutcheon	✓	✓	
08-1-107.01	Butt plate	✓	✓	
10-2-109.01	Cock			✓
10-2-148.01	Lock plate			✓
15-2-015	Sideplate	✓	✓	
Total		17	17	3

TABLE 8.4 ARTIFACTS IDENTIFIED AS ENGLISH IN ORIGIN

Artifact Number	Artifact Type	Damaged	Cu Alloy	Ferrous
98-3-0.35a	Butt plate		✓	
98-3-0.35b	Butt plate	✓	✓	
98-3-0.40	Ramrod guide		✓	
98-3-0.57	Butt plate	✓	✓	
02-1-182.06	Lock plate			✓
02-1-182.07d	Cock			✓
02-1-202.07f	Cock			✓
02-1-202.09b	Frizzen spring			✓
04-1-115.01	Butt plate		✓	
06-2-087.14	Frizzen spring	✓		✓
10-2-146.01	Butt plate	✓	✓	
Total		4	6	5

SUMMARY OF ARTIFACT AGES AND ORIGINS

Artifacts that could be assigned to dates or origins showed a bias toward copper alloy flintlock furniture. This is in part due to the better preservation of copper alloy compared to ferrous artifacts, allowing for observation of more details. However, copper alloy flintlock furniture encompasses the most visibly distinct and information-rich components of a flintlock musket and thus provide ample details with which to make the determinations. Due to these factors, the artifacts that can be assigned dates or origins are also biased toward flintlock furniture over internal components. The number of artifacts assignable to age or origin is also small compared to the size of the overall sample (15.3%). This low number of determinations limits the strength of inferences possible based on the data. As with the bias toward copper alloy artifacts, some types (e.g., breech plugs) had no examples assignable to age or origin. One interesting observation is the presence of three early English artifacts. Two cocks (02-1-182.07d and 02-1-202.07f) and a lock plate (02-1-182.06) date between approximately 1690 and 1725. Given that the French occupied the fort at that time and for several decades after, these artifacts are surprising. One possible explanation is that these artifacts came to the fort by way of a civilian, such as a trader, trapper, or Native American individual. These individuals might not have limited themselves to the arms of any particular country. Alternatively, these components could have been deposited later in the history of the fort from older weapons still in use at that time. This is unlikely, as all three of these artifacts originate from Feature 4, the gunsmith's cache, which probably originated during the French occupation of the fort. Finally, these artifacts could be misidentified either by age or origin.

TYPES OF WEAPONS

The sample of artifacts included examples of both military and civilian or trade flintlock components. Of the thirty-six artifacts for which age or origin were determined, 58.3 percent (n = 21) came from trade or civilian muskets, 11.1 percent (n = 4) originated from military weapons, and 30.6 percent (n = 11) were undetermined. Table 8.5 shows a detailed breakdown of artifacts of identified age or origin and the type of weapon from which they originated. Of the twenty-one trade musket artifacts, 95.2 percent (n = 20) were composed of copper alloy and 4.8 percent (n = 1) of ferrous metal. Eighteen trade musket artifacts (85.7%) exhibited evidence of French origin, and three (14.3%) artifacts were of English origin. Of the French trade musket artifacts, 44.4 percent (n = 8) dated to 1725 or earlier, 16.7 percent (n = 3) dated to 1725–1750, and 22.2 percent (n = 4) dated to 1750 or later. Of the English trade musket artifacts, 33.3 percent (n = 1) dated to 1750 or later. Of the military musket artifacts, 75.0 percent (n = 3) consisted of copper alloy, while 25.0 percent (n = 1) were of ferrous metal. All four military musket artifacts were of English origin, three of which (75.0%) evidence Land Pattern musket attributes. Most likely, these three artifacts date to around the same period, approximately 1740 to 1760. All eleven artifacts of undetermined weapon type consisted of ferrous metal. Four of these artifacts (36.4%) exhibited traits of English origin, two (18.2%) exhibited traits of French origin, and five (45.5%) were of undetermined origin. These findings correlate well to the known occupation history of the fort, with French artifacts dominating the early period of occupation and English artifacts dating to the last periods of occupation. Additionally, the types of weapons display a further pattern, with French artifacts consisting overwhelmingly of trade musket components, while English artifacts include predominantly military musket components, which show up late in the fort's archaeological record.

FEATURE 4

Feature 4 has been interpreted as a blacksmith's cache based on the quantity of gun parts in a concentrated area (Nassaney 2015, 181). Of the 176 artifacts analyzed, 54.5 percent (n = 96) came from Feature 4. Figure 8.3 shows the number of each artifact type that came from inside or outside of Feature 4, while figure 8.4 illustrates the proportions of each.

TABLE 8.5. TYPES OF WEAPONS

Artifact Number	Artifact Type	Cu Alloy	Ferrous	Weapon Type
98-3-0.35a	Butt plate	✓		Military
98-3-0.35b	Butt plate	✓		Military
98-3-0.40	Ramrod guide	✓		Military
98-3-0.57	Butt plate	✓		Trade
02-1-182.06	Lock plate		✓	Unknown
02-1-182.07d	Cock		✓	Military
02-1-202.07f	Cock		✓	Unknown
02-1-202.09b	Frizzen spring		✓	Unknown
04-1-115.01	Butt plate	✓		Trade
06-2-087.14	Frizzen spring		✓	Unknown
10-2-146.01	Butt plate	✓		Trade
English Total		6	5	
98-3-0.36a	Trigger guard	✓		Trade
98-3-0.36b	Trigger guard	✓		Trade
98-3-0.38	Sideplate	✓		Trade
98-3-0.41a	Trigger guard	✓		Trade
98-3-0.41b	Trigger guard	✓		Trade
98-3-0.42	Butt plate	✓		Trade
98-3-178.15	Trigger guard	✓		Trade
02-1-61.22	Trigger guard	✓		Trade
02-1-115.17	Trigger guard	✓		Trade
02-1-128.17	Sideplate	✓		Trade
02-1-203.08	Lock plate		✓	Unknown
04-1-54.18	Sideplate	✓		Trade
04-1-074.18	Sideplate	✓		Trade
06-2-93w.22	Finial	✓		Trade
08-2-45w.15	Finial	✓		Trade
08-2-63.11	Escutcheon	✓		Trade
08-1-107.01	Butt plate	✓		Trade
10-2-109.01	Cock		✓	Unknown
10-2-148.01	Lock plate		✓	Trade
15-2-015	Sideplate	✓		Trade
French Total		17	3	

TABLE 8.5. CONTINUED

98-3-0.31	Cock		✓	Unknown
02-1-115.09m	Cock		✓	Unknown
02-203.05	Cock		✓	Unknown
10-2-113.01	Cock		✓	Unknown
13-2-123.01	Cock		✓	Unknown
Unidentified Total		0		5

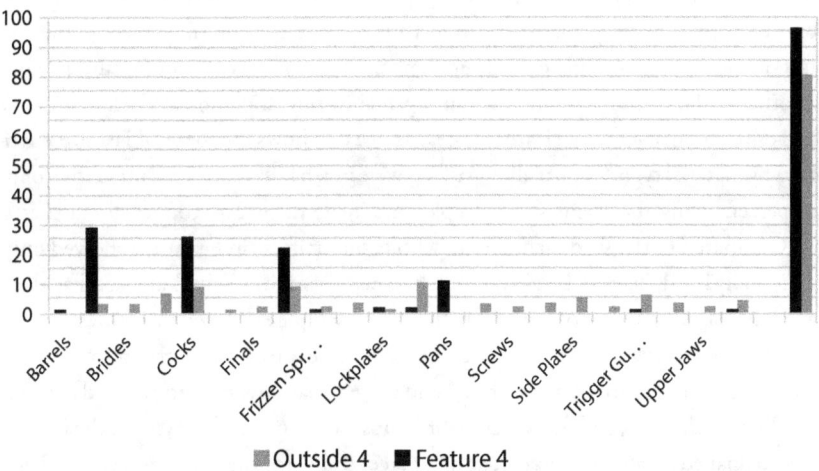

Figure 8.3. Number of artifacts by artifact type within and outside of Feature 4

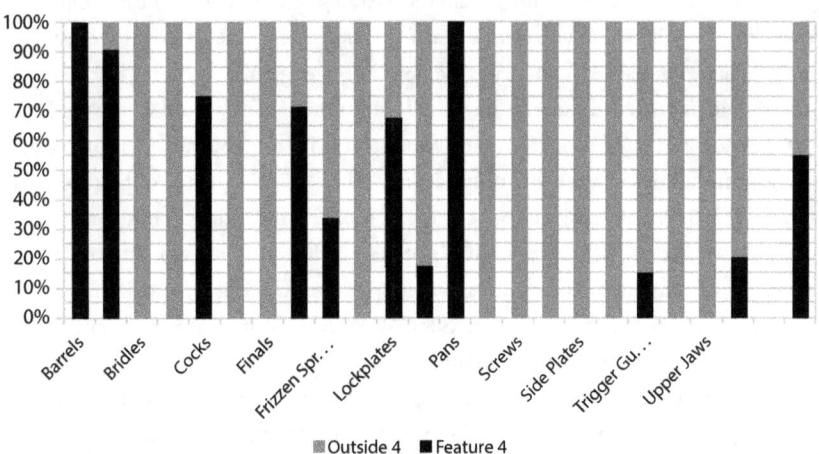

Figure 8.4. Proportions of artifacts by artifact type within and outside of Feature 4

As with the overall study sample, the most numerous flintlock artifact types found in Feature 4 consisted of breech plugs, cocks, and frizzens. All three of these artifact types made up a larger percentage of the artifacts in Feature 4 than they did in the overall sample. The majority of these artifact types (greater than 70.0% of each) came from Feature 4. Feature 4 contained 90.6 percent of all breech plugs as well as 74.3 percent of cocks and 71.0 percent of frizzens. Breech plugs, cocks, and frizzens made up 30.2 percent, 27.1 percent, and 22.9 percent of Feature 4, respectively, representing 80.2 percent of flintlock artifacts in this study taken from Feature 4. In the overall study sample, however, these three artifact types were only 55.7 percent of the total. All pans (n = 11) and the only barrel in this study originated from Feature 4 and made up 11.5 percent of the artifacts in the feature. Lock plates made up 2.1 percent of artifacts from the Feature 4, while all other artifact types (barrel, frizzen spring, mainspring, trigger guard, and vice screw) had only one artifact in the feature (1.0%). Table 8.6 shows the totals of Feature 4 artifacts by material type. Copper alloy artifacts were much less common, representing only 1.0 percent, while the overall study sample contained 14.2 percent copper alloy artifacts.

Compared to the study sample as a whole, the artifacts in Feature 4 showed only marginally less damage or breakage. Only 51.0 percent of the feature's artifacts had damage, whereas 58.5 percent of artifacts in the overall sample exhibited this trait. Table 8.6 shows the proportions of broken artifacts in Feature 4 by artifact group and in overall total. All of the barrels, mainsprings, and trigger guards from Feature 4 had damage. Cocks, breech plugs, and frizzens, the three most common artifact types in the feature, were damaged at rates of 61.5 percent, 55.2 percent, and 40.9 percent, respectively. Pans from the feature showed damage at a rate of 36.4 percent. However, all of the frizzen springs, lock plates, and vice screws recovered from the feature appeared whole. Rates of damage were lower in Feature 4 than the overall study sample for breech plugs, frizzens, frizzen springs, and vice screws. Rates of damage registered higher for cocks and mainsprings. For barrels, lock plates, pans, and trigger guards from this feature, their rates of damage equaled those in the overall study sample. This would seem to indicate that Feature 4 differed little from the overall sample in terms of damaged gun parts.

Determinations of age could only be made for 7.3 percent (n = 7) of Feature 4 artifacts (Table 8.7). They ranged from circa 1690–1745, coinciding with the early to middle occupation range of the fort itself. Six of these artifacts (85.7%) consisted of ferrous artifacts, and only one artifact (14.2%) was copper alloy. Three of these artifacts (42.9%) were identified as English, two artifacts (28.6%) were identified as French, and two artifacts (28.6%) are of undetermined origins.

Of the ninety-six artifacts in Feature 4, I determined the country of origin for 6.3 percent (n = 6) of them. Four (66.7%) were determined to be English, and two artifacts (33.3%) were determined to be French. Of the artifacts from Feature 4 for which origin could be assigned, ferrous artifacts predominated, making up 83.3 percent (n = 5) of the

TABLE 8.6. FEATURE 4, SUMMARY OF ARTIFACTS BY TYPE AND DAMAGE

Artifact Type	Artifact (Count)	Frequency within Feature 4	Percent of Study Sample	Damaged (Count)	Damaged within Feature 4	Damaged within Total Study Sample	Cu Alloy	Ferrous
Barrel	1	1.0%	100.0%	1	2.0%	100.0%	0	1
Breech plugs	29	30.2%	90.6%	16	32.7%	56.3%	0	29
Cocks	26	27.1%	74.3%	16	32.7%	60.0%	0	26
Frizzens	22	22.9%	71.0%	9	18.4%	54.8%	0	22
Frizzen Springs	1	1.0%	33.3%	0	0.0%	66.7%	0	1
Lock plates	2	2.1%	66.7%	0	0.0%	0.0%	0	2
Mainsprings	2	2.1%	16.7%	2	4.1%	91.7%	0	2
Pans	11	11.5%	100.0%	4	8.2%	36.4%	0	11
Trigger guards	1	1.0%	14.3%	1	2.0%	100.0%	1	0
Vice screws	1	1.0%	20.0%	0	0.0%	20.0%	0	1
Totals	96	100.0%	54.5%	49	100.0%	58.5%	1	95

sample, with copper alloy artifacts making up only 16.7 percent (n = 1). This compares to ferrous metal artifacts making up 85.8 percent of the overall artifact total, with copper alloy artifacts comprising the remaining 14.2 percent. Of the Feature 4 artifacts for which origin was determined, only one (16.7%) had sustained damage beyond usability. Table 8.8 presents the details of Feature 4's artifacts identifiable by country of origin and date. They include a trigger guard composed of copper alloy and a lock plate composed of ferrous metal. The trigger guard exhibited damage beyond use; however, the lock plate appears to have been usable.

TABLE 8.7. FEATURE 4 ARTIFACTS OF DETERMINED AGES

Artifact Number	Artifact Type	Country of Origin	Date Range
02-1-182.07d	Cock	English	1690–1715
02-1-182.06	Lock plate	English	1690–1720
02-1-115.17	Trigger Guard	French	1700–1725
02-1-202.07f	Cock	English	1700–1725
02-1-203.08	Lock plate	French	1700–1725
02-1-115.09m	Cock	Unknown	1725–1750
02-203.05	Cock	Unknown	1725–1750

TABLE 8.8. FEATURE 4 ARTIFACTS IDENTIFIED AS FRENCH IN ORIGIN

Artifact Number	Artifact Type	Damaged	Cu Alloy	Ferrous
02-1-115.17	Trigger guard	✓	✓	
02-1-203.08	Lock plate			✓
Total		1	1	1

Four artifacts in Feature 4 were determined to be English in origin. Table 8.9 shows the details of these artifacts. Artifact types included a lock plate, two cocks, and a frizzen spring. Ferrous metal comprised all of these artifacts, and none had damage beyond usability.

TABLE 8.9. FEATURE 4 ARTIFACTS IDENTIFIED AS ENGLISH IN ORIGIN

Artifact Number	Artifact Type	Damaged	Cu Alloy	Ferrous
02-1-182.06	Lock plate			✓
02-1-182.07d	Cock			✓
02-1-202.07f	Cock			✓
02-1-202.09b	Frizzen spring			✓
Total		0	0	4

Feature 4 yielded examples of both military and civilian or trade flintlock components. Of the eight artifacts for which age or origin were determined, 12.5 percent (n = 1) originated from a trade weapon, 12.5 percent (n = 1) from a military weapon, and the remaining 75.0 percent (n = 6) from undetermined types of firearms. Table 8.10 shows a detailed overview of artifacts of identified age or origin and the type of weapon from which they originated.

TABLE 8.10. FEATURE 4 TYPES OF WEAPONS

Artifact Number	Artifact Type	Cu Alloy	Ferrous	Weapon Type
02-1-182.06	Lock plate		✓	Unknown
02-1-182.07d	Cock		✓	Military
02-1-202.07f	Cock		✓	Unknown
02-1-202.09b	Frizzen spring		✓	Unknown
English Total		0	4	
02-1-115.17	Trigger guard	✓		Trade
02-1-203.08	Lock plate		✓	Unknown
French Total		1	1	
02-1-115.09m	Cock		✓	Unknown
02-203.05	Cock		✓	Unknown
Unidentified Total		0	2	

Along with the flintlock components recovered from Feature 4, two other artifacts (02-1-202.10a and 02-1-202.10b) likely represent makeshift screwdrivers, or "turnscrews" (figure 8.5). They take the form of shafts terminating in rounded loops or eyelets. The other end of the shafts have flattened heads. Initially, it was thought that these two objects may be vice screws in a style similar to Spanish miquelet locks. However, there is no evidence on the shaft of the objects for any threading, and the overall size of the artifacts appears too large for vice screws. The shafts also appear to have pronounced flattening along their length and in general are too large to have likely been vice screws.

However, when compared to published examples of turnscrews, these objects share a number of striking similarities. The shape and design of these artifacts share traits with examples depicted by Hamilton (1980, 123) and Mullins (2008, 48). Further, the lack of threads, the overall size, the length, and the flattened form of the artifacts lend more support to their being turnscrews rather than vice screws. As noted, these two artifacts were recovered from Feature 4, which was interpreted as a gunsmith's cache.

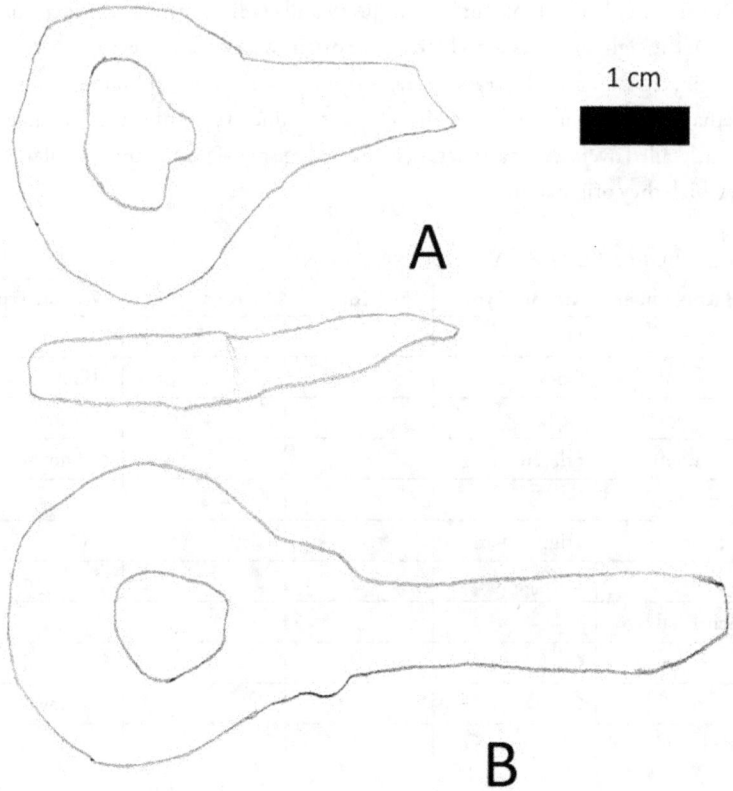

Figure 8.5. Feature 4 turnscrews. Drawing by Kevin P. Jones.

DISCUSSION

It is possible that the earlier English artifacts were outliers traded or brought by civilians (i.e., traders, trappers, and Native Americans) that were then deposited during the French occupation of the fort. Such an explanation leaves several questions. First, while it may be easier to dismiss a few outlying English artifacts, it is harder to account for nearly half of the artifacts of identifiable origin being English. Second, the presence of English military flintlock parts is more difficult to explain than civilian and trade parts.

While it is possible that this represents a mistake on my part in the process of identifying artifacts, this is an unsatisfying answer, particularly as several artifacts are most certainly English. First, it is important to note that smiths could have procured these components in locations other than Fort St. Joseph, including from civilians and Native

Americans far removed from the fort and less inclined to discriminate in their weapon choices. With this caveat in mind, I believe the answer for this is related to the designs of these weapons. Of the four military weapon components recovered, all were English in origin. No French military artifacts were identified. As noted previously, English military weapons were outfitted with copper alloy furniture, whereas French military weapons were outfitted with iron furniture. Due to this, English military components preserved much better than their French military counterparts. Thus, material choice in design of these weapons presents a bias that may account for the higher than expected frequency of English artifacts at Fort St. Joseph. It is also possible that English components are more common due to English occupation being more recent than French occupation both at the fort itself and around the region as a whole. Undoubtedly, many more flintlock artifacts existed that have not been recovered from Fort St. Joseph, and future excavations may provide data that serve to explain the ratio of English and French artifacts.

A LOOK AT FORT OUIATENON

While the previously discussed research was performed on artifacts sourced from Fort St. Joseph, the methods of this study can be applied to many other forts of a similar age and geographic location. One prime example is Fort Ouiatenon, for which the collection containing large amounts of flintlock materials from past excavations is readily available. I have taken a cursory look at this collection in order to provide a brief overview of its contents in light of my work with the Fort St. Joseph collection.

At a glance, the collection of flintlock components from Fort Ouiatenon is more substantial than that at Fort St. Joseph. In particular, Fort Ouiatenon includes many more components, which are highly informative in determining age, origin, and type of weapon. For example, the number of lock plates, sideplates, butt plates, and trigger guards is larger than at Fort St. Joseph. The Ouiatenon collection also contains a greater number of artifacts of smaller, delicate, or easily corroded types, such as gun worms or bridles. This could indicate that a larger number of weapons existed at Fort Ouiatenon, or it might reflect the poorer quality of preservation at Fort St. Joseph. Regardless, these components provide a prime opportunity to develop an understanding of what kinds of flintlock weapons were present at Fort Ouiatenon and the ways in which they were used, maintained, and modified.

Another observation of note regarding the flintlock materials at Fort Ouiatenon is that the vast majority appear to be French in origin. While there are English components within the collection, notably a portion of an English lockplate marked "Farmer 1747," many more components clearly reflect a French origin. Many of the French components have styles that indicate dates of manufacture in the range of 1730–1760, with very clear Rococo design elements. Several components exhibit earlier styles in a range closer to 1700–1720 but are far fewer in number. Figures 8.6 and 8.7 show examples of Fort St. Joseph and Fort Ouiatenon buttplates, respectively, while figures 8.8 and 8.9 show the same comparison for sideplates. The similarities in the styles of the artifacts are apparent. Several butt plates have bow and quiver motifs, and both sites have sideplates with hunting dog, serpent, and Rococo scrolling line designs.

Finally, among the flintlock artifacts exist a number of components that appear to have undergone modification from their original form. Several of these artifacts are copper alloy butt plates, some of which appear to have been cut, and one appears to be a handmade replacement. Additionally, the collection includes many sections of gun barrel, and some of these also appear to have been cut, as opposed to having been corroded or burst. Either of these observed modifications could represent evidence of gunsmiths modifying, repairing, or otherwise making use of old flintlock materials. As such, there appears to be a greater amount of artifacts in the Fort Ouiatenon collection that could provide information on maintenance and repair of the flintlock supply chain during the

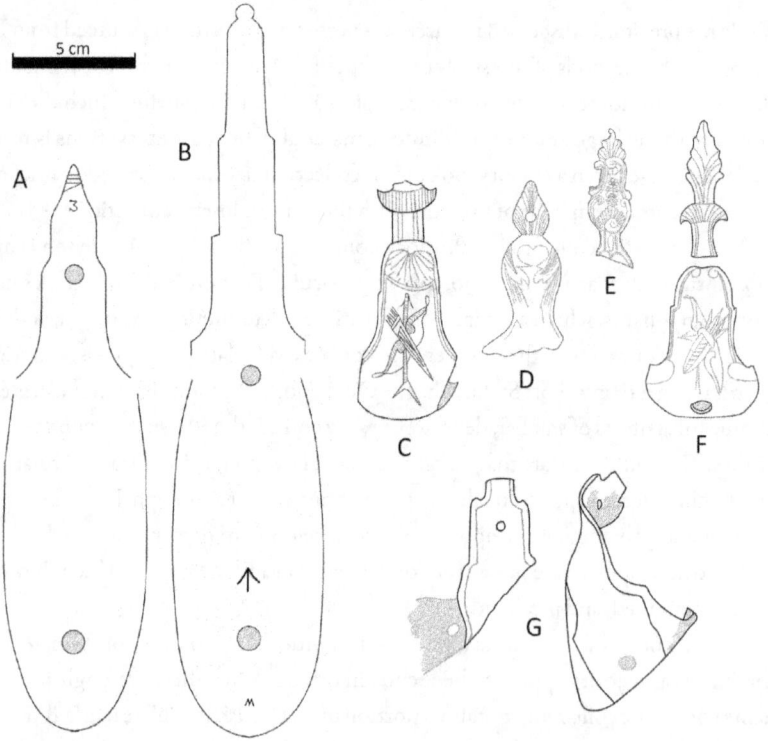

Figure 8.6. Fort St. Joseph butt plates in the Niles History Center collection. Drawing by Kevin P. Jones.

Figure 8.7. Fort Ouiatenon butt plates in the Tippecanoe County Historical Association collection. Photograph by Misty M. Jackson.

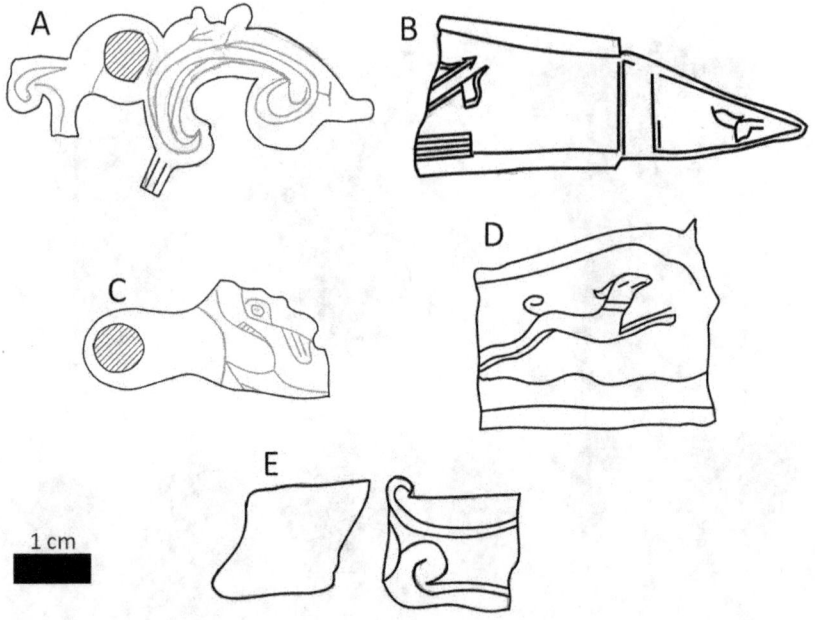

Figure 8.8. Fort St. Joseph sideplates in the Niles History Center. Drawing by Kevin P. Jones.

Figure 8.9. Fort Ouiatenon sideplates in the Tippecanoe County Historical Association collection. Photograph by Misty M. Jackson.

fur trade. Due to this as well as the previously mentioned observations about the flintlock artifacts in the collection, it is clear that Fort Ouiatenon represents a great opportunity for furthering knowledge of fur trade flintlocks and their use and their maintenance as well as the overall supply chain within which they existed.

REFERENCES

Bodoh, Bradley W. 2003. "Meskwaki Flintlocks: Cultural Accommodation and Adaptation during the Early Fur Trade in the Western Great Lakes." Master's thesis, Northern Illinois University.

Brandão, Josè A., and Michael S. Nassaney. 2006. "A Capsule Social and Material History of Fort St. Joseph and Its Inhabitants (1691–1763)." *French Colonial History* 7: 61–76.

Brown, M. L. 1980. *Firearms in Colonial America: The Impact on History and Technology, 1492–1792*. Washington, DC: Smithsonian Institution Press.

Gale, Ryan R. 2010. *For Trade and Treaty: Firearms of the American Indians, 1600–1920*. Elk River, MN: Track of the Wolf.

Giordano, Brock. 2005. "Crafting Culture at Fort St. Joseph: An Archaeological Investigation of Labor Organization on the Colonial Frontier." Master's thesis, Western Michigan University.

Hamilton, T. M. 1976. *Firearms on the Frontier: Guns at Fort Michilimackinac, 1715–1781*. Midland, MI: Pendell Printing.

———. 1980. *Colonial Frontier Guns*. Union City, TN: Pioneer.

Hulse, Charles A. 1977. "An Archaeological Evaluation of Fort St. Joseph: An Eighteenth-Century Military Post and Settlement in Berrien County, Michigan." Master's thesis, Michigan State University.

Mullins, Jim. 2008. *Of Sorts for Provincials: American Weapons of the French and Indian War*. Elk River, MN: Track of the Wolf.

Nassaney, Michael S. 2015. *The Archaeology of the North American Fur Trade*. Gainesville: University Press of Florida.

Nassaney, Michael S., William M. Cremin, and Daniel P. Lynch. 2002. "The Identification of Colonial Fort St. Joseph, Michigan." *Journal of Field Archaeology* 29, no. 3–4: 309–21.

Neumann, George C. 1998. *Battle Weapons of the American Revolution*. Texarkana, TX: Scurlock Publishing.

Peyser, Joseph L. 1978. *Fort St. Joseph Manuscripts: Chronological Inventory and Translations*. Niles, MI: Self-published.

Roache-Fedchenko, Amy S. 2013. "Technological Adaptation on the Frontier: An Examination of Blacksmithing at Fort Michilimackinac, 1715–1781." PhD diss., Syracuse University.

Russell, Carl P. 1957. *Guns on the Early Frontiers: From Colonial Times to the Years of the Western Fur Trade*. Berkeley: University of California Press.

PART III

COMMUNITY, STAKEHOLDERS, AND PRESERVATION

9

MYAAMIAKI (MIAMI PEOPLE)

A Living People with a Past

DIANE HUNTER, TRIBAL HISTORIC PRESERVATION
OFFICER (RET.), MIAMI TRIBE OF OKLAHOMA

SINCE TIME IMMEMORIAL, THE WEA PEOPLE LIVED IN A VILLAGE CALLED Waayaahtanonki, near present-day Lafayette, Indiana, at the confluence of what are now known as the Wabash River and Wea Creek, and Myaamiaki (Miami) people, including the Wea, have lived in what is now Indiana since time immemorial.

In the only extant account of the origins of Myaamiaki, Waapanaakikaapwa (Gabriel Godfroy) recounted that "mihtami myaamiaki nipinkonci saakaciweeciki" (at first the Myaamia came out of the water) (figure 9.1).

According to this story, the first Mihtohseeniaki, as Myaamiaki called themselves at that time, emerged near the confluence of Kihcikami (Lake Michigan) and the Saakiiweesiipiiwi (St. Joseph River in southwestern Michigan), so they called the place Saakiweeyonki (the place of the confluence). When the first people emerged from the water, they told each other to take hold of the tree limbs and pulled themselves out of the water. They formed a town at Saakiiweeyonki, located on the Saakiiweesiipiiwi between Kihcikami and current-day South Bend (Costa 2010, 52–53). Myaamiaki currently do not have information about the period before the time of their origin story, but from that time to today they have been a distinct people who came to call themselves Myaamiaki. The Miami Tribe of Oklahoma exists because of the decisions made since time immemorial by their ancestors and their leaders. Throughout their history, from their emergence in what is now Indiana and the surrounding areas to the present

Figure 9.1. The Miami Nation Council House mural illustrates the story of Myaamia emergence. Photograph by Karen L. Baldwin. Courtesy of Miami Tribe of Oklahoma Archive.

day, Myaamiaki have created a line of continuity as a unique and distinct people who repeatedly return to that land of their emergence.

According to nineteenth-century Myaamia leaders Pinšiwa (J. B. Richardville) and Meehcikilita, as told to C. C. Trowbridge, one of the communities of Mihtohseeniaki who lived near a whirlpool on the Saakiiweesiipiiwi chose to leave Saakiiweeyonki.

They traveled south to the confluence of the Waapaahšiki Siipiiwi (Wabash River) and Wea Creek. At the time, the akima (male civil leader) of this community was named Waayaahtanwa. So, their village was called Waayaahtanonki, and the community was the Waayaahtanooki (Wea) (figure 9.2). After some time, likely in response to either a dramatic population increase, which decreased the availability of food sources, or to political differences, a segment of Waayaahtanooki separated themselves from their community and migrated farther down the Waapaahšiki Siipiiwi to its confluence with the Oonsaalamooni Siipiiwi (Vermilion River). It was here that they became known as Peeyankihšia (Piankeshaw), which translates as "split-ear people." While living on the Oonsaalamooni Siipiiwi, the Peeyankihšiaki came in contact with another Indigenous community called the Kaahkaahkia (Kaskaskia), whom the Peeyankihšia incorporated and assimilated into their community. After some time, a group of intermarried Peeyankihšiaki and Kaahkaahkiaki migrated farther down the Waapaahšiki Siipiiwi to its confluence with the Embarras River at a place called Aciipihkahkionki

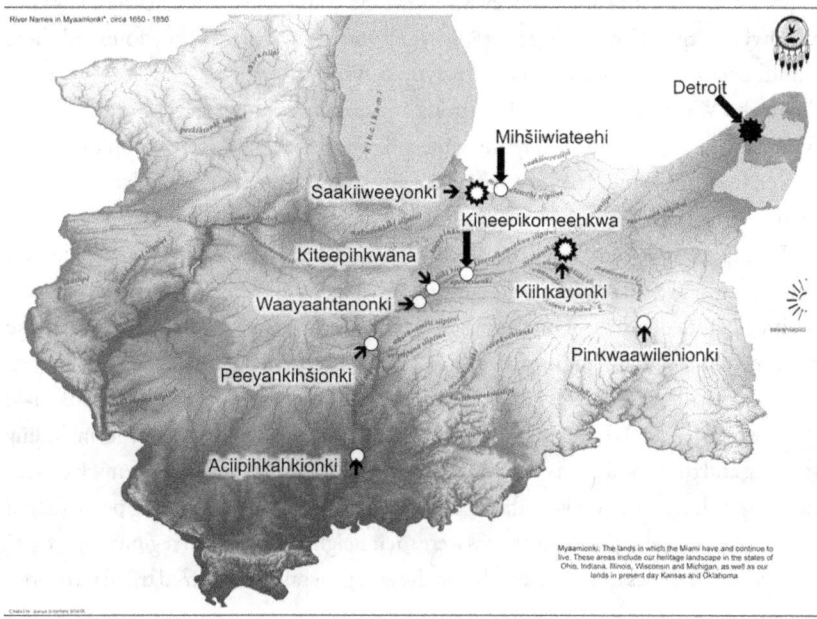

Figure 9.2. Myaamia villages. Map by Brett Governanti, Joshua Sutterfield, and George Ironstrack. Courtesy of the Miami Tribe of Oklahoma Archive.

(Vincennes), after which they simply referred to themselves as Kaahkaahkiaki. This community at Aciipihkahkionki eventually migrated westward as they splintered into other groups, including the Peewaaliaki (Peoria). These western communities of Mihtohseeniaki came to refer to themselves as Inohka and were eventually called Illinois (Trowbridge 1938, 9–12). Today the Wea and Piankeshaw peoples are citizens of the Peoria Tribe of Oklahoma.

Following the Waayaahtanooki's departure from Saakiiweeyonki, three more migrations occurred to the Aankwaahsakwa Siipiiwi (White River), the Ahseni Siipiiwi (Great Miami River), and the Taawaawa Siipiiwi (Maumee River) near Roche de Bout. After four separate migrations, the remaining Mihtohseeniaki at Saakiiweeyonki left the village and traveled down the Saakiiweesiipiiwi until they made camp at the confluence with a river soon to be known as the Mihšiiwiateehi Siipiiwi (Elkhart River). During their stay, an "elk was killed there and a woman who got possession of the heart hung it upon a tree." (Trowbridge 1938, 9–12) While it was hanging, "another woman stole it, and when the other came to seek her property she lamented the loss so much that the river thence took its name of Elk's Heart." Eventually, the community from Saakiiweeyonki arrived at the confluence of the Kociihsasiipi (St. Joseph River, in northwest Indiana) and Nameewa Siipiiwi (St. Marys River), where the Taawaawa Siipiiwi emerged (Trowbridge 1938, 9–12). One of the villages they founded there would eventually be known as Kiihkayonki. From there, they traveled westward down the Waapaahšiki Siipiiwi, forming communities along the tributaries of the Waapaahšiki Siipiiwi, including the Kineepikomeekwaki (Eel River people), among others. Eventually, these Mihtohseeniaki would refer to themselves as Myaamiaki and then were called Miami.

Though geographically separated, Myaamiaki continued as a distinct people, connected through a shared language, culture, and ancestry. Their villages, however, were politically independent of one another, and they each retained their ability to make their own independent political decisions. Within each village, men and women each organized their own councils headed by akimaki (male civil leaders) and akimaahkwiaki (female civil leaders). Female leaders coordinated activity within the village, including farming and the production of material goods. Male leaders concerned themselves with hunting, fishing, and foreign affairs, including going to war and leading peace delegations (Trowbridge 1938). Other tribes were their neighbors in shared regions (figure 9.3). No fixed boundaries existed, but tribes in the area generally recognized tribal territories.

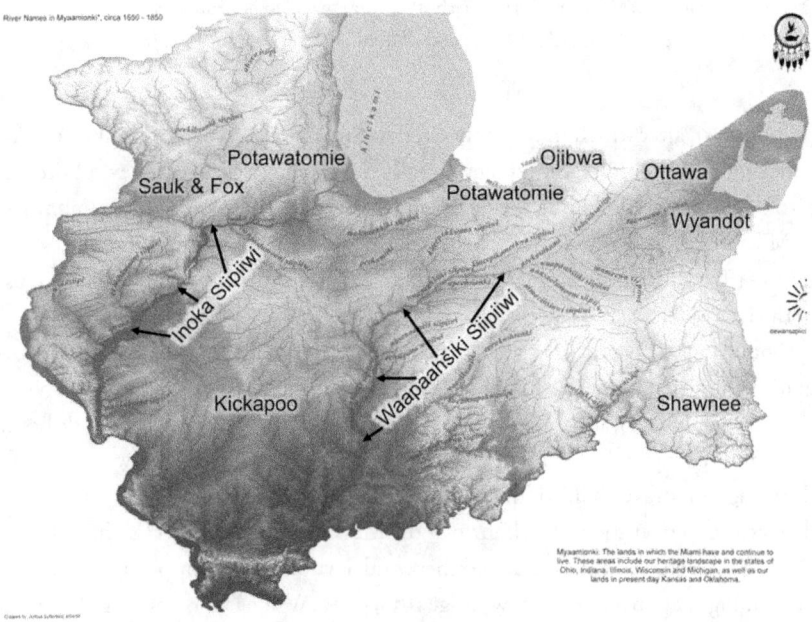

Figure 9.3. Myaamia shared territories. Map by Brett Governanti, Joshua Sutterfield, and George Ironstrack. Courtesy of Miami Tribe of Oklahoma Archive.

Their first contact with Europeans came through disease and trade goods, which they received through other tribes. By at least the mid-1600s, European diseases and aggression by the Iroquois Confederacy known as the Beaver Wars, forced the Myaamiaki to remove west and north into what is now Illinois and Wisconsin. Their first contact with French people came during this time at Kihcikami Kaakaamionki Alikonci (Lake Huron) and in the Green Bay area, and the *Jesuit Relations* described them as a "newly discovered nation" (Thwaites 1896, 44:246). Though spread throughout areas far from the place of their emergence, the Myaamiaki continued to establish villages near each other, as exemplified in the seventeenth century near present-day Chicago. Various bands of Myaamiaki, including Waayaahtanooki, lived in villages in the area where French Jesuits built the Mission of the Guardian Angel and began working on a dictionary of the Myaamia language. When their homelands were safe once again in the first decade of the eighteenth century, the Myaamiaki returned to their former villages in present-day Indiana, including Waayaahtanonki. They continued their relationship with the French, who came into Myaamionki (the land of the Miami) seeking to build trading relationships. In response, the French established a fort near Waayaahtanonki and named it Ouiatenon after the people living there. By the mid-eighteenth century, the Myaamiaki established economic relationships with the British and reaffirmed relationships with the Shawnee, Delaware, and Seneca peoples through a new village at Pinkwaawilenionki (Pickawillany).

The Myaamiaki allowed the French to establish forts that often served as trading posts in Myaamionki but never ceded their land to them. From a Myaamia perspective, in the 1763 Treaty of Paris following the French and Indian War, the French ceded their diplomatic relationship and trading rights to the British, not the land itself. After the 1783 Treaty of Paris ending the American Revolutionary War, the fledgling United States believed that the British had given them the land that they soon called the Northwest Territory. Myaamia perspectives were not considered in the treaty, and they had not agreed to cede their land. Nevertheless, following the revolution, Americans came in large numbers onto Myaamionki, illegally settling on lands shared by Myaamiaki, Shawnees, Wyandots, Delawares, and others.

Initially, the American government argued that the Treaty of Paris had given the United States complete control over all lands claimed by the British Empire south of the Great Lakes, leading to numerous attacks on and by the squatters. Through the conflict, the Myaamiaki and their allies from neighboring tribes succeeded in a number of battles, most notably St. Clair's Defeat (Battle of the Wabash) in 1791, which is often regarded as the largest defeat in the history of the United States. Even with their victories, the Myaamiaki sustained significant losses, as American soldiers destroyed their villages and vast cornfields. After a loss at the Battle of Fallen Timbers, the Myaamiaki realized that no matter how great their victories might be, the Americans could continue to supply more men to fight them. The Myaamiaki also saw that if they continued to fight the United States, even with victories they would lose so many people that they would no longer exist. As a result, Myaamia leaders signed the Treaty of Greenville in 1795, in which they gave up most of what is now the state of Ohio and small parcels of current-day Indiana. From their perspective, this treaty was intended to bring peace and enable them to be good neighbors with the Americans, each with their own land. Nevertheless, Americans kept coming farther into Myaamionki.

During this time, the Weas allied politically with other Myaamia bands under the newly formed Miami National Council. Following the War of 1812, however, Waayaahtanwa leadership was pressured by the United States to migrate from Myaamionki to the Mihsi-Siipiiwi (Mississippi River), near Shawnee, Delaware, Peewaalia, and Kaahkaahkia communities. Agreeing to a treaty at St. Marys in 1818, several Waayaahtanwa leaders, including Šako, Ahsenahamanka (Stone Eater), Meehkwaakonanka (Negro Legs), and Šiikwia (Little Eyes), ceded their claims within Myaamionki with the exception of a small reservation in western Indiana (Kappler 1904, 169–70). Two years later, Meehkwaakonanka, Šiikwia, and their followers signed a subsequent treaty ceding that reservation and requested that their resulting annuity payments be paid to them at Kaskaskia, Illinois, where they planned to move (Kappler 1904, 190; Parke 1820). They rejoined their relatives, the Peeyankihšiaki, who migrated to the area in the 1810s, forming settlements on either side of the Mihsi-Siipiiwi near Kaskaskia and along the St. Francis River in the Missouri Territory (United States Congress 1832–1861, 2:76; Carter 1934, 253–56).

Nevertheless, their removal treaty was a controversial decision, as evidenced by the absence at the negotiations of the Waayaahtanwa community from Kaawinšaahkionki (Terre Haute, Indiana) at the mouth of Ahsenaamiši Siipiiwi (Sugar Creek) on the Waapaahšiki Siipiiwi. The akimaki Šako, Kekequah, and Newapamida and the neenawihtoowaki (war leaders) Waapankia and Kiišiwaawa, who represented roughly 170 Waayaahtanooki, were "determined to abandon their annuity rather than go receive it at Kaskaskia" (Hays 1822; *Western Sun* 1824; "Statement of Jocco, Kekekqua, and Newapamida," United States Office of Indian Affairs 1964, roll 359). After several years without any financial support from the federal government, however, they agreed to remove themselves from Indiana at their own expense, and in the early 1830s the majority of their people rejoined their relatives in the west ("Agreement of Jacco, Ke-ke-quah or Hair Lip, Wa-pa-ga or Swan, Ke-she-wah or Bull, and Na-wa-pa-manda at St. Louis," United States Bureau of Indian Affairs 1972, roll 2; "Hairlip to William Clark 1830," United States Congress 1967, 245:116; Lykins 1830; "Abel Pepper to George Gibson, 1833," United States Congress 1967, 244:796–97; "J. H. Hook to William Clark, 1833," United States Congress 1967, 244:277). The few remaining Waayaahtanooki in Indiana incorporated themselves into Myaamia families and began to identify as Myaamiaki ("J. P. Simonton to George Gibson," United States Congress 1967, 244:900–901).

Between 1795 and 1840, the Myaamiaki signed eight treaties, each of which ceded further territory, to keep the peace with the United States and remain in their homelands. After years of the United States persistently pressuring the Miami Nation, its leaders finally agreed to their removal. Aging principal chief Pinšiwa was leading a National Council of mainly young, inexperienced leaders. The majority of National Council members had died between 1826 and1840, leading up to the death of Second Chief Palaanswa (Francois Godfroy) in May 1840 and culminating in Pinšiwa's death in August 1841. The 1840 treaty called for the Myaamiaki to give up their last communal reserve, the Great Miami Reserve, five hundred thousand acres in north-central Indiana, in exchange for a reservation that was to be approximately five hundred thousand acres in what would become the Kansas Territory (Kappler 1904, 531–34). Most significantly, the 1840 treaty contained provisions for the Myaamia people to remove to west of the Mississippi River within five years. They were the last tribal nation to be removed from Indiana. After watching the United States forcibly remove their friends and neighbors from their homes and because of the death of so many Myaamia leaders, those who remained may not have believed that they could continue to survive in Indiana, their homeland.

After their continued delays allowed the Myaamiaki to bypass the five-year deadline, the US government sent the army on September 26, 1846, to provide an incentive for the Myaamiaki to quietly leave their villages and be taken to Iihkipihsinonki (Peru, Indiana). They were held until they were forced to board canal boats on the Wabash and Erie Canal on October 6.

Some people managed to flee the soldiers, most notably families of the Waawiyaasita and Peepakicia (Flat Belly) bands, who fled north to the Pokagon Potawatomi in northern Indiana and southern Michigan ("Joseph Sinclair to William Medill, 1846," United States Office of Indian Affairs 1964, roll 418).

Witnesses describe seeing Myaamiaki taking handfuls of dirt from their ancestors' graves to take with them. A witness's memoir described the scene:

> One picture engraved on memory when I was perhaps about ten years old was the going away from their home so near of all the full blood Miami Indians. Government had bought their land and they were about to depart for new hunting grounds in Indian Territory. A company of blue coated soldiers had come to escort them and they were to depart on the several canal boats awaiting them. I was taken to see them on the eve of departure. We crossed—forded the river in a buggy—and the Indian camp was above and beyond the present cement bridge. There were tents and camp fires over which supper was cooking, and there was weeping among the squaws who

were mourning for their dead. They had put in sacks earth from the graves of their kin and tribe to carry with them to the strange country. My heart was made very tender by this weird scene, and has never lost sympathy with the wrongs which were wrought against our friendly predecessors. (Fetter 1980, 235)

Myaamiaki could not leave their homelands without taking even the smallest portion of it with them.

The canal boats took more than three hundred Myaamiaki through Fort Wayne to Junction City near Defiance, Ohio, where they transferred to the Miami and Erie Canal, which took them to Cincinnati (figure 9.4). The canal took them through familiar lands and passed places of historical and cultural significance. The Myaamiaki passed by Pinkwaawilenionki, an important village site in the 1700s. The canal often followed along the Ahseni Siipiiwi (Great Miami River), which had been a travel route to hunting grounds along the Kaanseenseepiiwi (Ohio River). The newspapers of the day remarked on seeing Myaamiaki walking through Cincinnati to the steamboat *Colorado* on the Kaanseenseepiiwi. Notices of daily receipts from the Miami Canal (figure 9.5) and of shipments on the *Colorado* show clearly that Myaamiaki people were viewed not as passengers on these boats but instead as cargo (figure 9.6).

The steamboat *Colorado* took the Myaamiaki down the Kaanseenseepiiwi and up the Mihsi-Siipiiwi to Bloody Island on the Illinois side of the Mihsi-Siipiiwi at St. Louis. On October 18 two days before arriving at St. Louis, the infant child of a woman from Waawiyaasita's band died. It is unknown why this woman did not flee with others from her village, but she was on the boat holding her dead baby for two days. On October 20 just before arrival in St. Louis, an elder man named Ottawa also died. The child and the elder were buried on Bloody Island, which today is directly across from the St. Louis Arch, the Gateway to the West (LaFontaine to Hamilton 1846).

Because the Peekamiiki Siipiiwi (Missouri River) is much shallower than the Kaanseenseepiiwi and Mihsi-Siipiiwi, the Myaamiaki waited three days on Bloody Island for a steamboat that could navigate the Peekamiiki Siipiiwi. They boarded the *Clermont No. 2* on October 23 and arrived at the Westport Landing on November 1. Also known as the Kanza Landing, the Westport Landing was a trading site at the town of Kansas, today's Kansas City, Missouri. "An Indian trader who accompanied the Miami during the removal commented on the widespread despair upon their landing in Kansas: 'I am ... unused to the melting mood, but when the young braves at my parting with them burst into tears and begged like children to be taken back to their old home, I could not help crying also'" (McCulloch 1888, 93–112).

From the Westport Landing, the Myaamiaki went overland south to Sugar Creek in what would become Kansas, which was to be their new home, for a while. The US government had not planned to house them, and they lived in tents until they could build

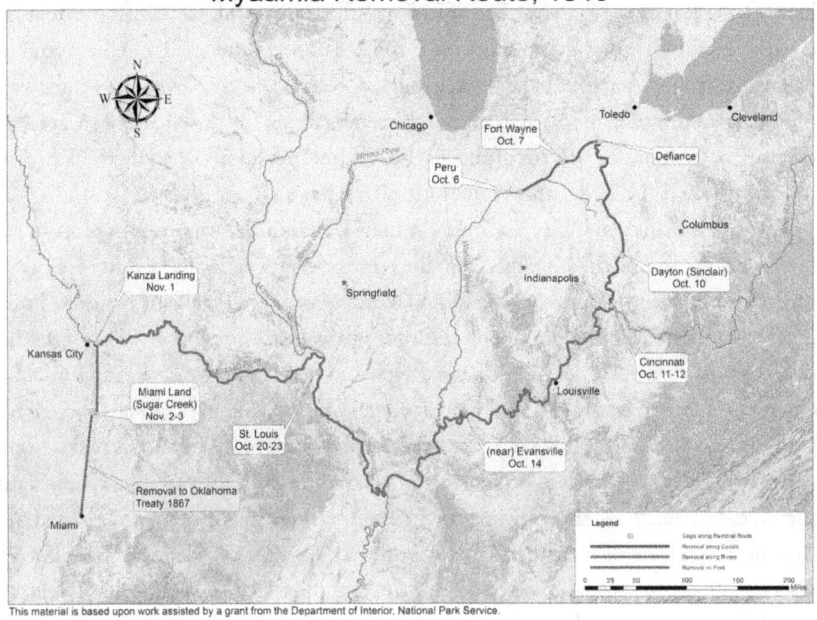

Figure 9.4. Myaamia removal. Map by Kristina Fox. Courtesy of Miami Tribe of Oklahoma Archive.

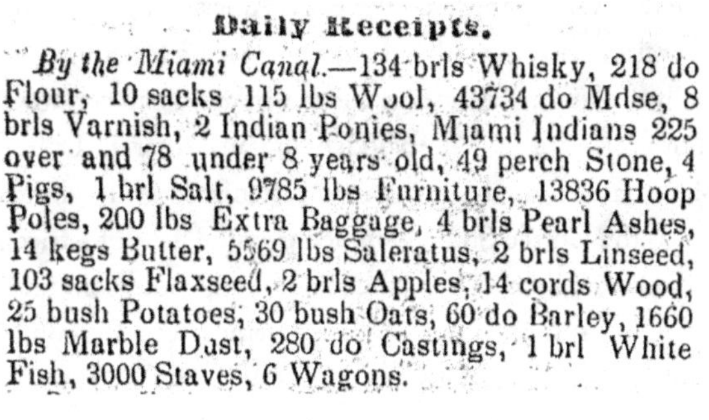

Daily Receipts.

By the Miami Canal.—134 brls Whisky, 218 do Flour, 10 sacks 115 lbs Wool, 43734 do Mdse, 8 brls Varnish, 2 Indian Ponies, Miami Indians 225 over and 78 under 8 years old, 49 perch Stone, 4 Pigs, 1 brl Salt, 9785 lbs Furniture, 13836 Hoop Poles, 200 lbs Extra Baggage, 4 brls Pearl Ashes, 14 kegs Butter, 5569 lbs Saleratus, 2 brls Linseed, 103 sacks Flaxseed, 2 brls Apples, 14 cords Wood, 25 bush Potatoes, 30 bush Oats, 60 do Barley, 1660 lbs Marble Dust, 280 do Castings, 1 brl White Fish, 3000 Staves, 6 Wagons.

Figure 9.5. "Daily Receipts. By the Miami Canal." *Cincinnati Gazette,* October 13, 1846, 3.

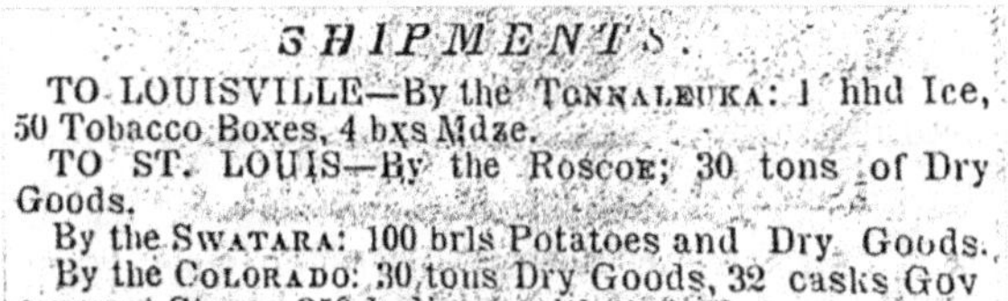

SHIPMENTS.

TO LOUISVILLE—By the TONNALEUKA: 1 hhd Ice, 50 Tobacco Boxes, 4 bxs Mdze.
TO ST. LOUIS—By the ROSCOE: 30 tons of Dry Goods.
By the SWATARA: 100 brls Potatoes and Dry Goods.
By the COLORADO: 30 tons Dry Goods, 32 casks Government Stores, 350 Indians, with their Baggage.

Figure 9.6. "Shipments. To St. Louis," *Cincinnati Gazette,* October 13, 1846, 3.

houses. They finished nineteen houses by late December ("Alfred Vaughn to Thomas Harvey, 1846," United States Office of Indian Affairs 1964, roll 643; "List of Miamis," United States Office of Indian Affairs 1964, roll 418). Six children and the elder Ottawa had died en route from Iihkipihsinonki to Sugar Creek. The early November winter was unusually cold, and many were sick from the removal trek. By the end of 1846, at least thirty people, about 10 percent of those who left Iihkipihsinonki, had died ("Vaughn to Harvey, 1846," United States Office of Indian Affairs 1964, roll 643).

Although Principal Chief Toohpia (Francis LaFontaine) was exempted from removal, he was among the Myaamiaki on the removal boats. A few weeks after arrival at the new reservation, he and other Myaamia leaders wrote to President James K. Polk expressing the emotions of his people: "Dear to us was that home of our children, still dearer to us were the ashes of our forefathers, and how could we expect to find anywhere else aught that would compensate for such a loss" ("Miami National Council to James Polk, 1846," United States Office of Indian Affairs 1964, roll 416). Still tied to their homelands, in March 1847 Toohpia and the majority of the National Council returned to Indiana to sell their privately owned reservations, but Toohpia did not survive that journey. He died en route in Waayaahtanonki. As soon as he left the Sugar Creek reservation, the Myaamiaki elected a new principal chief, Oonseentia, who had served as a village leader along the Nimacihsinwi (Mississinewa River) in Indiana ("Thomas Harvey to William Medill, 1846," United States Office of Indian Affairs 1964, roll 416).

In their new reservation, the Myaamia people began building houses, schools, and businesses to create a better life for their children, even reuniting with their Waayaahtanwa relatives whose reservation bordered theirs. As Americans illegally migrated onto the Miami Reservation, however, they began to disrupt Myaamia society. American squatters illegally took up residence on their reservation and cut down Myaamia timber, which was not as plentiful as in the woods of Indiana. After the United States established the State of Kansas in 1861, that government attempted to illegally tax Myaamia lands. Additionally, as the United States grappled over the issue of African slavery, Missourians, exemplified by William Quantrill, raided Indigenous communities across eastern Kansas in their pursuit of spreading slavery farther west. The combination of illegal American immigrants, power grabs by the State of Kansas, and proslavery Confederates placed increased pressure on Myaamia leaders to defend their people.

Following the American Civil War, federal officials sought to remove Native communities from Kansas to the Indian Territory (now Oklahoma). As Myaamia leaders, along with Peewaalia, Shawnee, and Wyandot delegations, traveled to Washington, D.C., to negotiate their potential removal, the Myaamia delegation passed through their homelands and stopped to visit their relatives in Indiana. Principal Chief Awansaapia's (John Bigleg) sister-in-law Kiilhsoohkwa (Margaret Owl Revarre) lived in Roanoke, Indiana, and he wished to visit with her. While in Indiana, Awansaapia became ill and could not continue the journey. He nominated Waapimaankwa (Thomas F. Richardville) to represent him to the federal government along with Second Chief Mihtohseenia (Thomas Miller). When they arrived in Washington in February 1867, they found that Lewis Body, the commissioner of Indian affairs, and the other delegations had commenced negotiations in their absence. By the time Waapimaankwa and Mihtohseenia arrived, the other Kansas tribes had negotiated their removal into the Indian Territory, freeing them from the issues they faced in Kansas, but they had not reserved any land for the Miami Nation.

Without any place remaining in the Indian Territory for the Myaamiaki, Lenipinšia (Baptiste Peoria), the principal chief of the Confederated Peoria Tribe, gave the Myaamia delegation the opportunity to unite with the Peoria on their reservation in the Indian Territory but required the Myaamiaki to confederate with the Peoria. Faced with two unappealing decisions, Waapimaankwa and Mihtohseenia agreed to confederate with the Peoria to secure their removal from Kansas. Although conflict within the Myaamia community led to the Senate striking their articles from the Treaty of 1867, the Miami and Peoria tribes in 1872 made an agreement to politically merge as long as the Miami tribe paid the Peoria for "an equal proportionate interest" in their reservation. Their contract also allowed the Myaamiaki to choose to become citizens of the United States if they wished to remain in Kansas ("Contract between the Miami and Peoria Tribes, 1872," United States Office of Indian Affairs 1964, roll 61). Although the Myaamiaki initially chose to confederate with the Peorias, US federal government delays prevented the Miami Nation from paying for its portion of the Peoria Reservation until after its contract with the Peoria had expired. After the contract expiration date, Myaamia people expressed their decision to "continue there [sic] chiefs after the consolidation with the Peorias and to hold the same Privlage [sic] as the Peorias" (Miami National Council 1874, roll 6).

This decision was pivotal. Without it, the Miami Tribe would not exist as a sovereign and distinct tribal nation. The Tribe reaffirmed that decision under the Oklahoma Indian Welfare Act of 1936 in which the Miami Tribe, under Chief Katakimaankwa (Harley Palmer), reorganized as a constitutional democracy, formally recognized by the United States as the Miami Tribe of Oklahoma. That same year the Peoria Tribe, which included descendants of the Wea, also ratified its constitution as the Peoria Tribe of Oklahoma. Today, the sovereign government of the Miami Tribe of Oklahoma is located in Ottawa County in northeastern Oklahoma. By its constitution, the governing body is the General Council, which consists of all Tribal citizens ages eighteen and older who attend the Annual Meeting, where they elect their Tribal leadership: chief, second chief, secretary-treasurer, and first and second councilpersons (figure 9.7).

Today, the Myaamiaki still feel the effect of the removals. They are a divided people, with citizens in nearly all fifty states. This separation of their people led to assimilation

Figure 9.7. Miami Tribe of Oklahoma elected leaders at the General Council meeting in 2022, Miami, Oklahoma. Photograph by Karen L. Baldwin. Courtesy of Miami Tribe of Oklahoma Archive.

Figure 9.8. Students and staff building the community web activity during the Miami Tribe of Oklahoma's Summer Youth Educational Experience in Fort Wayne, Indiana. This activity helps young Myaamiaki see how they are connected to one another. Photograph by Karen L. Baldwin. Courtesy of Miami Tribe of Oklahoma Archive.

Figure 9.9. Miami Tribe of Oklahoma's Summer Youth Educational Experience students and counselors participating in a Peekitahaminki (traditional lacrosse) game in Fort Wayne, Indiana. Photograph by Karen L. Baldwin. Courtesy of the Miami Tribe of Oklahoma Archive.

and a loss of much of their culture, including their language. The last native speakers of Myaamiaataweenki, the Miami language, died in the 1960s and 1970s. However, the 1990s saw the beginning of a cultural revitalization, Myaamiaki Eemamwiciki, picking up the thread of their cultural knowledge (figure 9.8).

They are again learning their history, culture, and language and are bringing what it means to be Myaamiaki into the twenty-first century. In Oklahoma, Indiana, and Kansas, tribal citizens tell traditional stories and play games that Myaamiaki have played since time immemorial (figure 9.9).

They are growing, learning, and developing as Myaamiaki. They value all that their ancestors have passed on to them and visit places in their ancestral homeland, including the Ouiatenon Preserve, which is located across the Wabash River from the original Wea village of Waayaahtahnonki. They are committed to protecting and revitalizing everything they have received from their ancestors. They are not a people of the past. They are a living people with a past.

ACKNOWLEDGMENTS

The author would like to acknowledge the assistance provided for this chapter by Dr. David Costa, Dr. John Bickers, and George Ironstrack.

REFERENCES

Carter, Clarence, ed. 1934. *Territorial Papers of the United States*, Vol. 17, *The Territory of Illinois 1814–1818, Continued*. Washington, DC: US Government Printing Office.

The Cincinnati Gazette. 1846a. "Daily Receipts. By the Miami Canal." October 13.

———. 1846b. "Shipments. To St. Louis." October 13.

Costa, David J. 2010. *Myaamia neehi peewaalia aacimoona neehi aalhsoohkaana: Myaamia and Peoria Narratives and Winter Stories*. Myaami Project, Oxford, Ohio.

Fetter, Ellen Cole. 1980. "The Memoirs of Ellen Cole Fetter 1837–1934." In *Miami County [Indiana] Encyclopedia, Vol. 1*, ed. Charles A. Wagner, 225–55. Peru, IN: Peru Public Library.

Hays, John. 1822. Letter to John Calhoun, May 15. Miami File, Great Lakes–Ohio Valley Indian Archives, Glen A. Black Laboratory of Archaeology, Indiana University, Bloomington.

Kappler, Charles Joseph. 1904. *Indian Affairs: Laws and Treaties*, Vol. 2, *Treaties*. Washington, DC: US Government Printing Office.

LaFontaine, Francis. 1846. Letter to Allen Hamilton, October 21, Fort Wayne, Indiana. Allen County–Fort Wayne Historical Society, History Center Digital Collections, box 26, folder 13. https://digital.library.in.gov/Record/IPFW_cc_acfwhs-1003.

Lykins, Johnston. 1830. Letter to Robert Simerwell, December 20. Simerwell Papers, Ms. 1125, box 2. Kansas Historical Society, Topeka.

McCulloch, Hugh. 1888. *Men and Measures of Half a Century: Sketches and Comments*. New York: Scribner. As quoted in Kate A. Berry and Melissa A. Rinehart, "A Legacy of Forced Migration: The Removal of the Miami Tribe in 1846," *International Journal of Population Geography* 9 (2003): 93–112.

Miami National Council. 1874. Communication to Hiram Jones, January 22. Quapaw Agency Records, roll 6. Oklahoma Historical Center, Tulsa, Oklahoma.

Parke, Benjamin. 1820. Communication to John Calhoun, August 15. Miami File, Great Lakes–Ohio Valley Indian Archives, Glen A. Black Laboratory of Archaeology, Indiana University, Bloomington.

Thwaites, Reuben Gold, ed. 1896. *The Jesuit Relations and Allied Documents: Travels and Explorations of the Jesuit Missionaries in New France, 1610–1791*. 73 vols. Cleveland, OH: Burrows Bros.

Trowbridge, Charles. 1938. *Meearmeear Traditions*. Ann Arbor: University of Michigan Press.

United States Bureau of Indian Affairs. 1972. *Records of the Central Superintendency of Indian Affairs, 1813–1878*. Washington, DC: National Records and Archives Service, General Services Administration.

United States Congress. 1832–1861. *American State Papers: Indian Affairs*. Washington, DC: Gales and Seaton.

———. 1967. *United States Congressional Serial Set*, Vols. 244–245. Washington, DC: US Government Printing Office.

United States Office of Indian Affairs. 1964. *Letters Sent to the Office of Indian Affairs, 1824–1882*. Washington, DC: National Records and Archives Service, General Services Administration.

The Western Sun. 1824. May 17.

10

THE FEAST OF THE HUNTERS' MOON

A Commemoration of the History of Indiana's First European Settlement

DAVID M. HOVDE, PROFESSOR EMERITUS,
PURDUE UNIVERSITY

INTRODUCTION

The Feast of the Hunters' Moon, an annual eighteenth-century historical reenactment, is one of the largest events of its type in North America. It is unique among such events in that it is not centered on a battle. Certainly, Fort Ouiatenon was the site of conflict between empires and an emerging nation, and these conflicts resulted in the upheaval of Native cultures. However, for the Tippecanoe County Historical Association (TCHA), the emphasis has always been a commemoration of a peaceful time of trade, feasting, and celebration between cultures as well as the history of the fort and its various occupants. This chapter provides a historical timeline of how the Feast grew and evolved over fifty years as the TCHA presented the history of the fort and the nations that passed through the Wabash Valley from 1717 to 1791 and met at Fort Ouiatenon.

THE BLOCKHOUSE, EARLY HISTORICAL REENACTMENTS, AND COMMEMORATIVE EVENTS: 1929–1957

In March 1929, the TCHA, along with the City of Lafayette, hosted a delegation of thirty French war heroes of the Association Amicale Croix de Guerre. Among them was Count de Pusy Dumortier de Lafayette, a direct descendant of the Revolutionary War hero in whose honor the city is named. The ceremonies, a parade, a luncheon, and a banquet were features of the visit. The TCHA held a pageant at what was thought to be the Fort Ouiatenon site, now the Fort Ouiatenon Park. The March 16 *Lafayette Journal and Courier* reported the event: "With the Daughters of the American Revolution monument as the scene of exercises, Boy Scouts, under Scout Executive E. L. Wheeler, provided an Indian dance, Prof. J. L. Cattell read in French a history of Ouiatenon prepared by Mrs. C. B. Kern, and characters portraying French traders and peasants, a priest and Indians of that early day were introduced. Members of the Red Men and Pocahontas lodges assisted" (*Lafayette Journal and Courier* 1929, 1, 13). This event may be the first recorded reenactment on the Fort Ouiatenon Park site.

During the early part of 1929, Dr. Richard B. Wetherill, the driving force in the creation of two earlier Tippecanoe County historical societies as well as the TCHA, took an overseas tour. One of the places he visited was the Bibliotheque Nationale de France. His goal was to locate original documents from the administrators of the fort during the French occupation. He did not complete the task but did hire a researcher to finish the work. Eventually, records concerning the fort from military and Jesuit sources found at the Bibliotheque Nationale as well as records at the National Archives in Washington and Jesuit records in Canada were copied.

Wetherill's dream of a reproduction fort on the site he believed to be the original location came into reality in the spring of 1930. This building is the present-day blockhouse located on the grounds of Fort Ouiatenon Park. According to Alameda McCollough, Wetherill and others, fully aware of their lack of knowledge of pre–Anglo-American pioneer architecture, proceeded with the knowledge they possessed (McCollough 1982–1983). A palisade was also planned but never built. The Monon Railroad donated sixteen carloads of pine logs (actually white cedar), and Clark Horlacher, who built a log cabin at the Cary Boy Scout Camp east of Lafayette, Indiana, was hired to do the work. The design was based on the work of Elmer Waters, the secretary of the TCHA. The blockhouse was dedicated on June 14, 1930 (figure 10.1), with music provided by the Old Gold and Black Orchestra. The Daughters of the American Revolution and local Boy Scouts performed a flag ceremony, raising the American, French, and British flags from poles while standing on the blockhouse roof (Tippecanoe County Historical Association 1930).

Figure 10.1. Dedication of the blockhouse in 1930. Courtesy of J. C. Allen and Son.

Over the years, the blockhouse was used for meetings and programs for the TCHA, Boy Scouts, Girl Scouts, the Indiana Historical Society, and other groups. It even served as a township polling station. In the 1940s, it was one of the sites visited annually by the Hoosier Historical Institutes sponsored by the state universities, the Indiana Historical Bureau, and other state agencies. Teachers could receive college credits for participating in the institute through the Indiana State Teachers College. The TCHA held open houses at the blockhouse every Sunday during the month of October into the 1960s. Generally, someone was on hand to talk about the history of the site. For the October 16, 1960, program, for example, Herbert H. Heimlich, editor of the *Lafayette Journal and Courier* newspaper and member of the board of the TCHA, gave a presentation at 3:00 p.m. (*Lafayette Journal and Courier* 1960).

THE FEAST OF THE HUNTERS' MOON: 1958–1966

Beginning in 1931, the TCHA published an annual program catalog that ran from the fall of that year to the beginning of summer the following year. In that first year the opening event was Ouiatenon Day, with Maude Leiter in charge. Such events did not occur annually.

In 1958, however, a fall members-only event called the Feast of the Hunters' Moon was first held. One source gives credit to Martha Robertson for coming up with the name (*Lafayette Journal and Courier* 1960). In that year, the TCHA program opened as follows:

FEAST OF THE HUNTERS' MOON

October 23, 1958, 6 P.M. Fort Ouiatenon Blockhouse Cook-out, Folk Music, Stories of Ouiatenon
    Mrs. Raymond M. Robertson, Chairman (Tippecanoe County Historical Association 1958a).

A ticket cost "five beaver skins," or one dollar (Tippecanoe County Historical Association 1958b; Schumpert 1977). Over the years few changes were made. Regular features of these events included readings such as the "hair-raising fictional tale" titled "Eve of the Crazy Moon" written by a Purdue student, Lydia Heim; music; and Boy Scouts demonstrations of Native American dances (figure 10.2).

Figure 10.2. The Feast of the Hunters' Moon of 1962. Feast publicity photo.
Courtesy of the Tippecanoe County Historical Association.

UNDERSTANDING THE MANY FACETS OF REENACTING AND ITS RELATIONSHIP TO THE FEAST OF THE HUNTERS' MOON

Reenacting in this country goes back at least to the American Civil War, when veterans returning from their service in the war reenacted battles for the folks back home. Later they continued to do this at veteran reunions such as the 1913 Veterans Reunion at Gettysburg (Schons 2022). In Tippecanoe County, where the Feast of the Hunters' Moon is held, the earliest was a fully costumed reenactment of the Battle of Tippecanoe in 1911, one hundred years after the actual event. Thirty thousand people witnessed the Purdue Corps of Cadets and the "Red Men" reenact the battle on the original site (*The Debris* 1912).

Modern reenacting began with the advent of the centennial of the Civil War. Over time, authenticity of uniforms and equipment, drill and troop movements, and national organizations developed. Various nonmilitary groups sprang up over time, with reenactors portraying civilians of the period and engaged in such things as Victorian balls. Magazines were created that catered to the reenactment community and private companies developed that made and sold uniforms, weapons, tinware, tents, and a host of other material culture needs of the reenactors. Many of these groups and companies have come and gone. Several private companies have been around for decades not only supplying reenactors also suppling to living history sites, museums, and the film industry military uniforms, civilian clothing, tents, weapons, and other goods. Some Civil War reenactments in past decades have had tens of thousands of participants. In the 1988 Battle of Gettysburg reenactment, for example, Hood's Texas Brigade had 125 more soldiers in its ranks than the original brigade in 1863. Estimates for the number of reenactors at the 135th anniversary of the Battle of Gettysburg stand at around 30,000. The American Bicentennial in 1975–1976 brought an interest in eighteenth-century military reenacting. Today, there are a host of communities that hold reenactments of battles from the Roman Legions to the Vietnam War.

From the earliest Feast of the Hunters' Moon to the present, another aspect of reenactments has been present. Many participants explore the material culture, activities, and civilian professions of earlier times, which includes everything from birchbark canoe making to blacksmithing, making clothing by hand, exploring foodways using period cookbooks and equipment, recovering heirloom seeds, and making the tools for all the above. Professional organizations related to this element of reenacting, generally referred to as living history, include the Midwest Open Air Museums Coordinating Council and the Association for Living History, Farm and Agricultural Museums, for example. Living history sites such as Conner Prairie, Colonial Williamsburg, Fortress Louisbourg, and Living History Farms all represent this element of reenacting, merging scholarly textual research, experimental archaeology, and role playing. The Feast represents the whole gamut: people who dress in eighteenth-century clothing once a year and work at the food booths and merchants who make their living catering to the reenacting community as well as museologists, academics, and dedicated hobbyists who attend many events a year and spend a great deal of time researching and improving their impression.

In the various eras representing the reenacting community, there are restricted events that are time- and event-specific and are by invitation only, with very strict clothing and accoutrements requirements. Other wide-ranging events include Renaissance fairs and Society of Creative Anachronism events. These later groups can range over long periods of time and go onto the realm of fantasy. One issue with which the Feast has had to contend are walk-ons who come dressed in fringed chrome tanned buckskin clothing, complete with deer antler or bison horn headdresses or squirrel tail capes, or full nonmilitary Highland Scot kits with kilts, broadswords, and shields. Their principal motivation seems to be getting their pictures taken.

The question could be asked whether the Feast is a reenactment, and if it isn't, what it is. If you compare it to a reenactment of the Battle of Shiloh, for example, they are quite different. First and foremost, the Feast does not reenact an actual historically documented event. At a reenactment of Shiloh, the participants would have period-correct uniforms, weaponry, tentage (or lack thereof), and organization. The Feast covers the time frame of the existence of the fort, and not all the military or civilian reenactors represent people who were there. Certainly, French, German, British, American, civilian Scottish Highlanders, and Native American people would not all have been there at the same time, and some never were. However, the TCHA's mission is collecting, preserving, researching and sharing the county's unique and diverse history. The Feast is part of its educational mission.

THE FEAST OF THE HUNTERS' MOON: 1967 – 2017

The first public Feast of the Hunters' came in 1967, when it consisted of a 5:00 p.m. dinner on Thursday, October 19. It remained a one-evening event in late October, and the cost remained "five beaver skins." In that year, Lydia Heim continued to entertain the audience with the song "Voyageur," and Mrs. E. A. Hopkins read an "imaginative story" about the fort titled "Father Jaunay's Bell" (*Lafayette Journal and Courier* 1967). It was advertised as a public event, not restricted to the TCHA members only. Guests were invited to bring camp stools or blankets for "listening to the harangue" (Tippecanoe County Historical Association 1967).

The first weekend the Feast was held in 1968, the year that most feasters look upon as the beginning of the tradition. On Saturday, October 12, from 10:00 a.m. to 9:00 p.m., the TCHA cosponsored the event with the Rossville Junior High History Club, led by history teacher Bill Baugh. The day featured Indian dances, French folk songs, a flea market, vendors selling fall produce such as pumpkins and Purdue apple cider, flintlock demonstrations, historical displays, and historical tours by the Rossville students. Members of the Indiana University archaeological crew, led by Dr. James H. Keller, who had recently undertaken excavations at the fort site, gave three twenty-minute slide shows titled "Rediscovering Ouiatenon."

The day began with the firing of the morning gun. Crafts demonstrated at the event included candle making, ink making, shingle riving, spinning, carding, weaving, and split hickory crafts. Lunch consisted of ham, bean soup, and cornbread. Various sources claim that from 800 to 1,200 visitors attended the event. At 7:00 p.m., the evening program started with a lighting of the fires, then a lecture on the French in the Wabash Valley, a flintlock rifle demonstration, and Indian dances. At 9:00 p.m. the event ended with the raking of the embers.

This first Feast began the tradition of it serving as the major source of funding for the TCHA over the years. Net profits for the 1968 Feast amounted to $509.73. Apparently, the staff could not believe the amount of money generated by the event and hardly knew what to do with their good fortune (*Lafayette Journal and Courier* 1968a, 1968b).

It should be noted that the Feast of the Hunters' Moon of 1968 was part of a larger movement in the United States to commemorate history. Numerous other festivals looking back on America's past were established at this time, the most significant being the Smithsonian Folklife Festival, which inspired similar state and local festivals across the nation. Many centered on music, dance, and local traditional crafts. Some, such as the Goschenhoppen Folk Festival, focused on preindustrial crafts and technologies. To make the festival and the craft sustainable, each craftsperson is required to have an apprentice at Goschenhoppen. Some of these events, such as the Goschenhoppen with its celebration of Pennsylvania Germans, commemorated other ethnic identities rather than the dominant Anglo-American culture. For example, the Nordic Fest in Decorah, Iowa, celebrates Scandinavian immigration. Also founded during this time was the famous *Foxfire* magazine and book series started by an English teacher and students of the Rabun Gap–Nacoochee School in Rabun Gap, Georgia, publications that have celebrated and preserved the culture of the region. These festivals and folk history–oriented efforts came about in part due to the national trauma of the Vietnam War, the youth movement, and the weakening of local identity due to an increasingly mobile and commercialized society (Encyclopedia.com 2019).

The Feast has inspired people to improve the program and broaden participation by the public. In 1968, Jim Smith and William Baugh created the Tippecanoe Ancient Fife & Drums Corps, which made its first appearance at the Feast in 1969 (Tippecanoe County Historical Association 1977, 4). At the time, it was the only fife and drum corps in the United States outside of New England. The founding of the Voyageurs Ancient Fife and Drum Corps followed in 1971. The Ouiatenon Brigade, the Habitants, and other organizations came into being as the event took hold of the community.

The 1969 Feast was again cosponsored by the Rossville Junior High History Club as a two-day event, starting a tradition that continues to this day. Also musically, the Dulcimer Society held its annual gathering jointly with the Feast in those early years. Saturday's events that year involved dancing to French songs with the periodic firing of "old guns." The evening's festivities included dances by the Kunieh Indian Dancers (a Boy Scout Order of the Arrow group) and the Tecumseh Lodge (an adult fraternal organization). Members of the Ottawa, Chippewa, and Miami tribes were also present and demonstrated tribal crafts and customs. A display of Native American artifacts, along with French and English trade items and "bits and fragments from the actual fort" were on display thanks to Larry Chowning and John Henry.[1]

The final act of this Feast on Sunday was the dedication of the blockhouse museum, which contained models, maps, tools, and artifacts from the site. The Sunday event was marred by both the British and French consuls general from Chicago failing to arrive for the festivities. The British were caught in a heavy downpour and were forced to turn back. The French had their vehicle heavily damaged by members of Students for a Democratic Society and apparently could not get other transportation (*Lafayette Journal and Courier* 1969a, 1969b).

The presence of the Tecumseh Lodge led the Native American participants to complain about its representation of Native peoples. Members of the public also complained. The lodge was not invited back. This was the first time this issue manifested itself at the Feast and similar events and reenactments across the country. Today, federally recognized tribes are becoming more vocal about this issue, and events are responding positively to their views. Fewer events allow nonnatives to portray Native Americans. Today at the Feast all of the Native American performers are from either state or federally recognized tribes (Leslie Martin Conwell, pers. comm., October 13, 2022).[2]

The 1969 Feast attracted eight thousand people despite the introduction of a small admission fee. The money was intended for the purchase of additional land and blockhouse restoration. Additional craftspeople, food, and a primitive camp hinted at a slow evolution of the event. Chiefs Ike Peters of the Ottawa Grand Rapids and Little Elk from the Match-E-Be-Nash-She-Wish Band of Potawatomi near Grand Rapids, Michigan, as well as family and friends came to demonstrate ceremonies, tell stories, and discuss tribal lifeways. Chief Mon-Gon-Zah (William Hale), chief of the Miamis living in Indiana, also talked about his people (DeAtley 1970). An encampment of costumed coureurs de bois also appeared as a feature of this Feast. Musket firing, dulcimer playing, pewter pouring, blacksmithing, weaving, butter churning, and many other crafts and activities were demonstrated.

The Feast is an event full of decades-old traditions. The opening and closing parades, flag raising, and lowering ceremonies, and the mass firing of a salute is one of those (figure 10.3). The parades and flag ceremonies are the most photographed and videoed parts of the Feast by any measure. To many the Feast would not be the Feast without them. In 1969, eight flagpoles were erected by the blockhouse. The flags represented the eight nations or groups that exercised control over Ouiatenon. These are central to those ceremonies.

At this event, one fixture at the Feast first appeared and represents volunteers who have a genuine knowledge of their craft that comes from generations in their families. On a lark, James and Dorothy Morré came. Among the small group of crafters, James, who came from a long line of blacksmiths who had served apprenticeships, encountered a Purdue student attempting to demonstrate blacksmithing; it was not going well. James asked if he could help, and the student thankfully accepted. The Morrés were asked to come back, and they led the Ouiatenon Blacksmiths for decades. The blacksmith shop on the east end of the Feast grounds has been a favorite for tens of thousands

Figure 10.3. This image of the 2016 opening ceremony is typical of the decades-long tradition. Courtesy of Angela Bruntlett, ABruntlett Design.

of visitors, and many blacksmiths who were trained and worked under James at the Feast have continued the tradition he started (Morré 2014, 37).

In 1970, the TCHA staff recognized that the event had become a tradition. Questions were asked about its future and whether it would survive. The staff concluded that standards needed to be established and that the quality of the historical interpretation and impression needed to be increased. Up to this time the Feast had operated without a budget, and planning started around Labor Day, about a month prior to the event. The director, William Baugh, traveled to other festivals and consulted with participants in order to improve the Feast.

The 1971 Feast attracted twelve thousand people. The Boy Scouts returned as a strong presence and continue to do so to this day. In the early days of the event, the Boy Scouts from the Harrison Trails Council extended the festivities by camping the following weekend. There they continued to sharpen the pioneer skills they learned from the demonstrators as well as furthered their exploration of history and period crafts (*Lafayette Journal and Courier* 1971).

A big decision for the TCHA staff was to determine that three portable toilets were not going to be enough. They made changes to the layout of the grounds, with particular attention to having vehicles parked farther away to improve the ambience. Eighty children made pottery using Native American techniques, with resulting pots being fired in a corn cob–fueled fire pit. At this Feast church services first appeared in the program, and both Roman Catholic and Protestant services took place. At 9:00 a.m. on Sunday, a Roman Catholic folk mass featured the Joyful Noise and Father Piquet. At 11:00 a.m., folk church services were held with the Mountain Dulcimer Society and a Reverend Wick. The 1971 Feast also featured the presence of voyageur canoes, a now iconic feature of the event. The arrival of the canoes in the mornings and the canoe races are regular features of the event.

Part of the development of events such as the Feast of the Hunters' Moon is a slow and steady evolution of the understanding of the past. During its early years, as many as sixty tepees and not-so-authentic clothing styles were present. It looked more like a Hollywood version of a nineteenth-century Western fur trade rendezvous west of the Mississippi River in many respects. Prairie dresses, leather hippie hats more appropriate for Woodstock, and fringed buckskins were in evidence in those days. The TCHA's mission is to both preserve the past and educate the public. To do so, the organization has had to educate itself and change what is permissible at the Feast. Certain types of clothing, tents, weapons, and goods for sale have been disallowed over the years as the understanding of the period became clearer. The classic Plains tepee, once predominant at the event, came no farther east than the Minneapolis–St. Paul region in the mid-nineteenth century, and canvas tepees only came into being during the post–Civil War reservation period (Laubin and Laubin 1980; Hovde 1982; Vestal

1980). Many dedicated researchers, from both the TCHA and the participants, have moved the quality of the event forward. This continuous process keeps the event fresh and interesting.

In 1971, period and regional costuming became the expected norm. The quality and authenticity of goods for sale also began to concern the Feast committee. One after-action report noted "Made in Japan" pottery being sold in one booth. A desire on the part of the TCHA to improve the authenticity of the event came with the publication of a booklet on period women's clothing (Tippecanoe County Historical Association 1977, 6).

In 1972 a "handicraft row" was introduced, with around seventeen crafts being demonstrated (Tippecanoe County Historical Association 1977, 7). The flea market fortunately was a thing of the past. This same year the TCHA began to keep careful records of the many volunteers and their skill sets. Clearly, the staff had come to realize that the Feast could not happen without the volunteers and their many contributions of time and talents. The first military reenactment units appeared in 1973. A grand total of five units and three tents made up the military encampment (Tippecanoe County Historical Association 1977, 8).[5] The number of craft demonstrations rose to twenty-four, and twenty-three blanket traders offered wares. For the first time, concessionaires sold buffalo stew to the public. It was also the first year for the creation of highly prized commemorative buttons. Thirty-six thousand visitors attended the event.

By 1974, as many as fifteen military units came to the Feast. Many were under the umbrella of the Officers Council of the West, one of a long line of reenacting organizations that have tried to organize and standardize the reenacting community as well as bring a level of authenticity and safety to reenactment events. Twenty-nine crafts booths demonstrated period technologies. Over thirty-six thousand visitors passed through the gate. For the first time, medallions were presented to a select group of participants who made an outstanding contribution to the event.

It was routine during the mid-1970s for the food booths to run out of their buffalo burgers, pork chops, potato soup, and fry bread even on Saturday. Many had to make trips into town on Saturday night to find more items for their grills and cooking pots.

The 1975 Feast received designation as an official Bicentennial event. Unfortunately, the weather consisted of bone-chilling wind, cold temperatures, and rain. Despite this, it was a year of continued expansion. Three thousand costumed participants set a record. Their efforts to make the event more like a living history community and the TCHA's continued push for authenticity inspired the first fashion show. The application form for that year came with detailed information for blanket traders, food booth workers, and Feast volunteers as well as camping and costume requirements, which helped to improve the event. Unfortunately, it still allowed tepees. The TCHA continued to look for ways to enhance the event such as inclusion of more craft demonstrations.

The number of military reenactment units that participated continued to increase, with groups such as the Virginia Regiment of the Continental, the 64th Regiment of Foot, the Fort Lernoult Militia, and the Frear's Regiment–Duchess County Militia. That year Thomas J. Griffin formed the 42nd Royal Highlanders of Lafayette for men interested in Scottish history and culture and portraying the unit during the American Revolution.

In the mid-1970s, the grounds expanded west across the road that forms the main entrance to the park. This expansion would not be the last, but it set the groundwork for a broadened interest in the event and its constant improvement. The 1976 Bicentennial heightened interest in America's past. Local history, reenacting, and rediscovering the preindustrial past became a passion for many. Twenty-five military reenactment units were represented that year, and thirty-eight crafts were demonstrated to forty-five thousand attendees (figure 10.4). A nonmilitary unit was the Elgin Brigade of Voyageurs formed from Boy Scout Troop 20 out of Elgin, Illinois. Fifteen voyageur canoes, including those of the Elgin Brigade, arrived Saturday morning.

Figure 10.4. Aerial photograph of the 1976 Feast of the Hunters' Moon.
Plains tepees were a common sight during this period. Feast publicity photo.
Courtesy of the Tippecanoe County Historical Association.

New musical groups appeared at the 1976 event. Locally, the Tecumseh Fiddlers, a fourteen-member group from the Tecumseh Junior High School, and the North Fork Rounders, a string band from Granville, Ohio, entertained Feast goers. The Colonial Fife and Drum Corps from Alton, Illinois, came for the first time, as did the 4th Continental Artillery Band of Musick from Milwaukee, Wisconsin. Its style of music is similar to chamber music, with oboes, clarinets, bassoons, and natural horns.

The 1977 Feast demonstrated that the event was getting national attention. Merchants, musicians, crafts persons, and reenactors came from Arizona, Colorado, Florida, Illinois, Indiana, Iowa, Kentucky, Michigan, Ohio, Tennessee, Texas, and Wisconsin. By 1979, the event offered thirty-five food booths with around 1,000 costumed participants helping to prepare and serve the food. The event also included 115 musicians, 50 dancers, 280 members of military units, 70 muzzleloaders, 40 booth traders, 75 traditional craftsmen, 100 blanket traders, and 100 other costumed participants engaged in other activities. Contest winners were honored. The top scorer in the tomahawk throw, for example, received a pipe tomahawk. Traffic had become an issue over the years. Rain or shine, people came in droves. Commercial buses helped relieve some of the congestion. Since then, traveling by bus from locations around the Lafayette/West Lafayette communities has become the best option for many due to the limited parking available on-site.

As the 1980s began, the Feast had over fifty craft booths. In addition to the requirement for costuming more appropriate to the period, the TCHA made efforts to improve visitors' experience by focusing on craft demonstrations specific to eighteenth-century French and Native Americans. The number of participants, reenactors, musicians, crafts people, vendors, and food booth staff was approaching five thousand. Music, another iconic feature of the event, steadily improved over the years as well. In the early days, a lone voice singing the "Indian Love Call" may have been the featured performance. In 1980 music became an essential element, and the highlight was the first massed fife and drum corps performance. Forfar bridies, Scottish handheld meat pies, made their first appearance at the 1980 Feast.

Planning for the event became increasingly complicated. In 1981, the event required 7 two-by-twos for each booth, 100 trash barrels, three-quarters of a mile of snow fencing, and 1,200 poles for the fencing. Over 145 booths needed tables, chairs, wood, trash barrels, matting, twine, and stakes.

For several years prior to 1980, quality control and authenticity issues were being extensively monitored. The TCHA annual files of rejected vendor applications continued to thicken. On-site reports from staff note anachronisms such as colored rabbits' feet, cowboy clothing, Civil War figures, and Guatemala bags as some of the items' vendors were asked to remove. The children's trade blanket was introduced in 1981, and in 1982 the Native American Woodland camp was established. At the 1982 festivities, the TCHA introduced a new book on French colonial dress to help participants. This publication is now considered out of date because research into period clothing has expanded understanding of the topic. For its time, it was a good faith effort so participants could improve the impression they made and help with the event's historical accuracy.

Periodically, groups have come to the Feast that liven things up a bit. In 1983, forty-seven Canadian Boy Scouts and historical interpreters from Fort William of Thunder Bay, Ontario, joined the festivities. The Scouts, from twelve to seventeen years of age, made their own period clothing and studied the period they portrayed (Moser 1983). During these years, the Feast attracted national attention. People came from all over the country, and other communities were asking the organizers how they put on such a successful event. Carol Waddell, one of the Feast planners from that period, believed that the success of the event was due to the location, the unique theme, the constant striving for authenticity, loyalty to the participants, and participants' dedication (Matter 1986). Over thirty years later, these elements remain. The evolution of what is "authentic" continues as new scholarship and interpretation of sources change. Further, generations of families, churches, civic groups, reenactment units, and scout troops have remained loyal participants for decades.

In 1983, the TCHA ran a survey of participants requesting ways to improve the event. Responses included the need for more food booths, sanctioned historical activities at night such as bagpipe contests, more seating, no green firewood, more space between booths, tighter control on food booth clothing, a participant-only day, less buckskin, more French clothing, and more portable toilets. With the ever-growing interest in the Feast, the grounds were expanded by an additional two and a half acres in 1983 by moving into what had been the participants' parking lot.

By the end of the decade attendance exceeded fifty thousand. Participants could see about seventy traditional craft presentations. These included craftspeople such as Jo Bartholomew making apple-head dolls, Viola Brenner weaving, Howard Cunningham cordwaining, the Girl Scouts spinning wool, Mike Goering making maple syrup, Chuck Leonard silversmithing, and Sally DeMar Music making fishnets. Fifty food booths were available to hungry feasters including applesauce by the Purdue Food Science Club; Brunswick stew by the West Lafayette Assembly No. 44, International Order of the Rainbow for Girls; crepes by the Northwest Labor Council; and pork chops by the Federated Roundtable of Mulberry. Performers included the Marion Barber Puppets, the Full Moon Folk Band, Great River Fife and Drum, the Pendragon Puppets, and the Madame Cadillac Dancers and Musicians from Detroit, elaborately costumed performers who gave a lively show of French colonial dances and music. Another new act, the Psaltery, provided traditional French Canadian folk songs and clogging.

The military remained a strong presence. Forty-five units are listed as present in 1988, including Rogers' Rangers, the Fort des Chartres Marines, the St. Francis Xavier Militia, Feldjagerkorps, and the Hamilton's Artillery.

In 1990 due to increased attendance, the grounds were expanded to twenty-four acres, which improved traffic flow and freed up space around the booths. The year ushered in an improvement in authenticity with the arrival of White Thunder, a group of Potawatomi and Iroquois singers and dancers who gave the Feast a more balanced program, given that the event was commemorating a meeting of European and Native Americans in peace.

The Feast of the Hunters' Moon has always been a family-oriented event. Making sure that the children are both entertained and educated, several 1990 booths offered programs especially for them. The long tradition of candle dipping continued as well as the Pendragon Puppet Theatre, pottery making, children's gifts at the blockhouse trading post, children's trade blankets, a costume try-on, the story tepee, and woodturning.

One of the many unsung heroes of the festivities for years was the Hospitality Committee. In the middle of the morning and afternoon, these wonderful people came to where craft demonstrations were under way and offered refreshments. Their appearance offered a welcome relief. On Saturday nights, they distributed sandwiches at the dance attended by the participants. A popular feature of their operation was the big caldron of popcorn stirred with a canoe paddle over a fire.

Sometime during the event's twenty-fifth year on Saturday in 1992, the one millionth Feast attendee walked onto the grounds. Another noteworthy occasion that year involved the Ouiatenon Brigade, the Kankakee Alliance, and the Southwest Brigade, who paddled 125 miles over the course of a week trying to live the life of the French voyageurs (*Lafayette Journal and Courier* 1992) and demonstrating how some of the groups go over and above the usual to get in the spirit of the occasion.

The 1994 celebrations were also memorable when two days of sunny weather brought a crowd so large that in places it was hard to move around or for visitors to see what was happening at demonstrations and at many booths. So, in 1995 the TCHA decided to expand the event's location by five acres on the western side of the grounds. A military drill area and a performance area at the voyageur encampment were added, giving visitors a more open feel to the increasingly crowded event. Again in 1998 five more acres were added to the Feast grounds in response to requests from visitors. A military drill area and more performance space helped ease the congestion (*Lafayette Journal and Courier* 1998a). The voyageur camp also expanded.

The weather was nearly perfect in 1996, and the crowds responded. That year, visitors and food vendors produced over fifty thousand pounds of trash. The ever-faithful Boy Scout troops were there to help in the removal. Not only were many locals involved, but craftspeople also came from New Hampshire, including Caleb Davis, a master canoe and paddle maker, while others came from Maryland, Pennsylvania, and many other states (*Lafayette Journal and Courier* 1998b). Over the years, in addition to booths that featured crafts people, vendors, and demonstrators, other displays and activities emerged. Fort Ouiatenon archaeological displays as well as ones of heirloom seeds offered educational experiences. Activities for children have always been an important feature of the event, and in 1997 the children's bead booth for making necklaces and bracelets appeared for the first time.

To further its educational mission, the organizers began offering school days prior to the weekend event. On Friday, October 1, 1999, 2,100 fourth graders came to learn about eighteenth-century life in Indiana (figure 10.5). It was the second year the TCHA added an extra day to the Feast solely for nine- and ten-year-old students who study Indiana history during the fourth grade. The students moved from station to station learning about food, music, Native American life, weapons, tools, and clothing.

Dave Edwards, cochair of the Feast, developed a new feature for 2000 with the addition of a fourth day: Thursday became Special Kids Day, a tradition that has continued. About 475 special needs students toured the grounds, allowing them to experience the same sights, smells, and sounds as the fourth graders receive on Fridays. For example, vision-impaired children could spend quality time handling items such as

Figure 10.5. One of the many booths educating children during school days. Feast publicity photo. Courtesy of the Tippecanoe County Historical Association.

the pottery of La Compagnie des Beaux Eaux, and students in wheelchairs who did not have to fight the crowds could enjoy watching the Ouiatenon blacksmiths up close. The TRW Commercial Steering Division of Lafayette and the Tree of Hope of Carmel sponsored this first Thursday event.

The reputation of the Feast continued to bring new vendors that year. Steve and Katie Freede of the Trunk Shoppe from Crawford, Colorado, came for the first time with their period reproduction trunks. The variety of foods continued to draw people to the event, and by this time many food-related traditions had been established. The Lafayette Junior Women's Club, for example, in 2000 participated for their twenty-eighth year of selling buffalo burgers. Many of these forty groups from churches, civic organizations, and scout troops by this time could point to families with two or more generations of participants in their operations.

For some commercial vendors who sell reproduction period goods, their attendance represents a culmination of a year-long process of preparation. For others, it is just one of many events. Going from one reenactment or festival to the next is how they make their living. They also sell their goods via the internet, and some have international reputations.

The majority of vendors moved into making and selling goods from their days of reenacting. They saw a need and developed a skill. They had a passion for authenticity and a love of history. They come to the Feast to offer trade silver brooches, tinware, pottery, ironwork, firearms, and clothing (figure 10.6). Theirs is a life of the love of history. They constantly research and improve their products, visiting museums and historical sites. Participating in events involves days of packing and unpacking at times while wet, long drives, and a dedication to their fellow reenactors who benefit from their work such as Jefferson Brown, a voyageur, who came from western Wyoming to participate in "one of the finest reenactments in the nation" (*Lafayette Journal and Courier* 2000).

One downside to being a vendor is not being able to enjoy many of the new features, music, magic and juggling acts, and food or see what other vendors are selling. Most of the performances are in fixed locations, and vendors can only hear the distant music above the crowd noise. For many years, two groups have taken their performance afoot. Peg Black and the Strolling Singers traveled the grounds singing period music, and Common Stock brought smiles and laughter in their wake with their puppets and shadow boxes.

The 2001 event began on a somber note. The nation was still in shock over the terrorist attack on the World Trade Center in New York and the Pentagon in Washington, D.C., in September of that year. Like many major events, the Feast saw heightened security. The National Guard had a highly visible presence along with uniformed and plainclothes police. The weather did not help the mood, and the 2001 Feast made history as the wettest on record. The TCHA staff and volunteers, vendors, and reenactors looked at the forecasts with dread. Several spaces were left empty, as some chose not to participate.

Figure 10.6. This tinsmith, plying his craft during the 1991 Feast, represents the dozens of demonstrators who participate each year. Feast publicity photo. Courtesy of the Tippecanoe County Historical Association.

On Thursday, despite the rain and mud, five hundred special needs children enjoyed the Wildlife Center's live animal exhibit, including a beaver, a skunk, and a woodchuck. Twenty-five vendors and demonstration booths braved the weather to give the students a hands-on experience after two weeks of learning about Native American and European frontier life in school before coming that day. Longtime participants David and Caroline Moses and others of the Dulcimer Gathering gave lessons on how to play the mountain dulcimer, much to the delight of the students and their teachers. Forty-seven schools sent fourth graders to the Feast grounds on Friday (*Lafayette Journal and Courier* 2001). New features added to the 2001 offerings included a colonial-style tavern, thanks to Mel Brutsman of Sarge Oaks Restaurant, and the Patin Glen Theatre for entertaining children. In addition, that year showcased the restored blockhouse, thanks to a grant from the Indiana Department of Natural Resources.

Unfortunately, the river hit flood stage late Friday evening. Jeff Schwab, chair of the Feast Committee, recalled that the river had yet to affect the festival grounds directly. He noted:

> We had started to make plans regarding the voyageur landing the next day as the river had reached an unsafe level for the traditional landing. About 6:30 Saturday morning, the river hit around 13½' and started to enter the lowest portions of the grounds which is the southwest corner of the near modern camping field and the southeast corner of the far camping field. At this point, we started the evacuation of modern camping. We also started to work on getting the artillery field pieces (along the river on low ground) moved out due to their weight and the soft conditions of the ground. Around mid-Saturday, the river had continued to rise above 14', and the low sections of the west grounds started to flood. In the area of what is now the Grande Arena, the merchant booths were under 2–4 inches of water. We relocated merchants from there as best we could, but several left. At this point, the parking lot adjacent to the grounds was also closed. Due to the mud and water, the tow trucks were ineffective at pulling many of the larger vehicles (trucks, motor homes) out. I believe Lee Brand helped organize several large farm tractors to pull the remaining vehicles out before they got into the water. That evening it appeared the river had crested, so after a brief meeting of the feast leadership it was decided to continue on with Sunday with as much program as we could. (Jeffery R. Schwab, email message to author, February 28, 2017)

From Thursday through Sunday some 4.3 inches of rain fell. The heavy National Guard vehicles in places created deep canals, but their presence was appreciated. Cars and buses had become stuck in parking lots. Along with the tractors, wreckers, and other vehicles, volunteers helped get vehicles out of the mud. The *Lafayette Journal and Courier* gave the 2001 event the name "Feast of the Hunters' Muck." No one would dispute that assessment. Still, many die-hard participants took it all in stride. It is an outdoor event, after all. Kids used the road below the bread oven as a slip n' slide; some adults just stayed in the tavern. The Boy Scouts and others spread a great deal of straw in the areas of heavy foot traffic. Despite the conditions and an attendance that was half from the previous year, some vendors reported sales at or better than in 2000.

Hurricane Lili was on the minds of everyone as the Feast weekend approached in 2002. A second year of heavy rain, mud, and an overflowing Wabash River would be devastating. The track of the storm pointed directly at Indiana. Although it was deadly in the Caribbean, it weakened as it hit the Gulf Coast and dissipated by the time it reached Tennessee. The TCHA was looking forward to a better year. Because the event is the organization's main fundraiser, 2001's mud fest caused painful cuts in staffing and programs. As a precaution, the TCHA took out a rain insurance policy for Saturday and Sunday between 8:00 a.m. and 2:00 p.m. in case of rain over a quarter of an inch. A rainy Friday, partly of Lili's remaining strength, served to settle the dust.

The newly restored blockhouse and the museum it held opened to the public for the first time in years. The tavern at the event was under new management, with the Lafayette Brewing Company featuring eighteenth-century home brewing demonstrations. They continue to carry on this adult feature of the event, which has included after-hours music by Hogeye Navvy, a Feast goer's favorite, and other groups.

The food booths as always were a hit. Boy Scout Troop 337 out of Rossville, Indiana, offered fry bread for the thirty-second year in a row. Boy Scout Troop 313 offered fried catfish, smelt, and "buffalo chips." The Rossville FFA offered up its grilled pork chops. This booth can easily go through one and a half to two tons of chops over the course of the weekend, and Central Catholic High School could make as many as five thousand apple dumplings. Volunteers such as Cathy Grafton of Pontiac, Illinois, a quilter, embroiderer, and thirty-two-year veteran of the Feast, demonstrated her craft, as did Glen Summers of Parke County, who carved wood bowls (*Lafayette Journal and Courier* 2002).

From the Feast of the Hunters' Moon's early days, dancers have been an attraction. In 2002 the Heritage Musick and Daunce Society of Milwaukee returned demonstrating French colonial dancing. Russell Smith and dancers represented the Iroquois Confederacy of Six Nations, as they had done for more than ten years. Smith, a member of the Seneca tribe, appreciated the large crowd of onlookers: "We spread the word of peace and community and love and equality. We share our culture with everyone so they better understand who we are" (Geller 2002).

Like the French and Native American dancing and the military tactical demonstrations, other popular fast-moving demonstrations draw large crowds. Lacrosse

Figure 10.7. The game of Lacrosse being demonstrated to members of the public. Feast publicity photo. Courtesy of the Tippecanoe County Historical Association.

demonstrations (figure 10.7) performed by the Green family of Niagara Falls, New York, who are descendants of the Tuscarora tribe, fascinated spectators. With little equipment and no rules, the fast-paced game in the past was so violent it was called the "little brother of war." Casualties were common in history but fortunately not at the Feast.

Besides sharing the sights, sounds, and flavors of the past, teaching how people of eighteenth century North America viewed the world serves as a major focus of the event. Steve Gerlach from Sparta, Illinois, brought period medical practices to life in 2003. At that time, doctors still used the "Wisdom of Greeks" to view the world of science. Gerlach discussed methods of keeping the "four humors" in balance by purging and bleeding; he also demonstrated the use of various instruments for amputation of limbs.

The 2003 Feast on September 13–14 was much earlier than usual. Eighty-degree temperatures cut down on hot food sales, and many of the participants shed their colorful outer garments. Campfires were few (Brouk 2003). The weather and ticket prices brought the total attendance to only 35,600.

The TCHA took to heart many suggestions from the public for the 2004 event. The association made changes to the arrangement of the grounds and added more booths. For the first time, ATMs were present on the site. There were also lower ticket prices, family passes, and larger buses, which helped the traffic flow. The St. James Lutheran School sold grilled venison ribs, and elk was also available. A notable addition to the event this year were the eight-members of the US Army's Third Infantry Regiment Old Guard based in Fort Myers, Virginia. This group serves as the official ceremonial unit and escort to the president and the oldest active-duty regiment in the army. Over the years, members of local fife and drum corps went on to join this unit, so the Feast and the Third Infantry Regiment have a long connection. A total of thirty-eight thousand people attended during Saturday and Sunday that year.

The TCHA staff and volunteers are always looking for new and fresh ways to educate the visitors, particularly children. In 2005 a featured activity simulated an archaeological site where Laura Black, a graduate student from Purdue, demonstrated archaeological techniques to children. The children could dig through the soil and find, clean, and examine artifacts as well as try to reconstruct a ceramic vessel. Unfortunately, the rain that brought back memories of 2001 kept numbers down. The 2006 Feast goers were greeted with perfect weather and fall colors. One thousand performers took to the three stages and the two arenas, much to the delight of the crowds. These included festival mainstays such as the Tippecanoe Ancient Fife and Drum Corps, Hogeye Navvy, the Voyageurs Ancient Fife and Drum Corps, Bittersweet and Briars, the 42nd Highlanders, Traveler's Dream, and the Madame Cadillac Dancers (figure 10.8). Other groups that year included the River Valley Colonial Fife and Drum Corps of Naperville, Illinois, and the Janesville Fife and Drum Corps of Janesville, Wisconsin. Nonmusical acts included Alex Kensington, aka Otto the Sword Swallower, who brought many gasps and laughter during the delightful weekend.

The weather for the fortieth Feast of the Hunters' Moon in 2007 made for another perfect weekend. Lows in the 40s and highs in the 70s meant that the food booths did well, and the reenactors stayed in their full attire. The TCHA leadership breathed a sigh of relief. It took approximately $300,000 in cash and in-kind contributions to put on the event during this time, and a rainy weekend had a significant impact on the organization's survival. Because it had become the major revenue stream for the TCHA, leadership has worked to lessen the impact of a bad year on its financial stability but has met with little success. That year, Willard Sharp of the Lenni Lenape, or Delaware Tribe and his wife Yvey Perez educated visitors in their home in the Living History Village on their Tribe's history and culture. Selling rosettes, Girl Scout Troop 425 was one of thirty nonprofit organizations that benefited by selling foods based on Native American, English, and French cuisine (figure 10.9). More than forty thousand visitors attended.

The 2009 Feast demonstrated continued expansion to meet the interests of the visitors. Seven stages were found throughout the grounds. Locating this many venues within that space was not an easy task. The staff spent a great deal of effort determining how far the sounds of performances carry so that one will not interfere with another. Saturday morning was a bit of a mud fest due to Friday's all-day rain. Attendance was slow at first, but the cool temperatures and the sunshine brought out a good crowd by midday. This was the fourth straight year without rain on Saturday or Sunday. The cool weather that ranged from the mid-30s to the 50s gave many a strong appetite.

Figure 10.8. Period music is a significant feature at the Feast. Feast publicity photo. Courtesy of the Tippecanoe County Historical Association.

Figure 10.9. One of the many food booths at the Feast staffed by area nonprofit organizations. Feast publicity photo. Courtesy of the Tippecanoe County Historical Association.

There was a no-burn ordinance in effect for the region due to dry conditions in 2010 (*Lafayette Journal and Courier* 2010); however, the festival was given an exemption. After all, what would people do without their smelt, Forfar bridies, and pork chops? The return of members of the US Army's Old Guard as well as attendance by six other fife and drum corps made it a special year. The opportunity for a massed band performance with such a distinguished and experienced collection of bands should never be missed, and on Saturday afternoon visitors and participants were not disappointed.

That year, over 175 vendors, demonstrators, and craftspeople provided period reproduction clothing, weaving, pottery, tinware, ironwork, and furniture as well as period-inspired foods. Many dedicated participants demonstrated various crafts to educate the many visitors about eighteenth-century lifeways, including sheep herding with border collies.

The 2012 Feast featured thirty-seven food booths, all run by nonprofits as usual. The Lafayette Church of the Brethren sold parched corn, Boy Scout Troop 303 sold smelt and catfish, the Ouiatenon bakers sold bread samples, the Rossville FFA sold pork chops, the Youth Service Bureau of Wabash County sold turkey noodle soup, the Tippecanoe Shrine Club sold ribeye sandwiches, the Sycamore Audubon Society sold turkey legs, and the Lions sold croquignoles.

During the Thursday and Friday school days of 2014, eighty-nine craft demonstrators, vendors, reenactor organizations, and musical groups were on hand to educate the students. However, it was a wet year. The La Grande Arena on the west side of the grounds flooded. As an example of the resilience of participants, impromptu canoe races were held, and in the evening residents on the shore partied, with the area lit by candle lanterns and campfires along their new lakefront property in true Feast style.

One hundred and eighty-six groups participated in 2015, including fifty-seven craft demonstrations by groups or individuals, with potters, blacksmiths, chair caners, coopers, gunsmiths, lace makers, natural dyers, period painters using period materials, rope makers, spinners, tinsmiths, and wooden bowl carvers participating. Thirty-three musical groups, Native cultural programs, story tellers, dance demonstrations, and reenactors such as the military units, habitants, and voyageurs entertained the crowds (figure 10.10). Among the many musicians and entertainers were Colonel Webb's Band of Musick, the Northland Voyageurs, Water Spider Drum, Travelers Dream, and Rodney the Younger, Conjurer. Those selling eighteenth-century reproduction goods included MT Forge, Romantically Bent; Wm. Booth, Draper; Jas. Townsend & Son, Inc.; the Smoke and Fire Company; Spring Valley Lodges, and Sheldon Pewter.

The highly anticipated fiftieth anniversary of the Feast of the Hunters' Moon and the three hundredth anniversary of the founding of Fort Ouiatenon in 2017 was magical. Many people came who had not attended in years, and many others visited for the first time. The fall weather proved exceptional, and some fifty-six thousand people

Figure 10.10. The landing of one of the voyageur canoes at the beginning of each day continues a long-held tradition at the Feast. Feast publicity photo. Courtesy of the Tippecanoe County Historical Association.

attended. Guillaume Lacroix, consul general of France in Chicago, attended as the special guest. The food booths and many vendors saw record sales. It was a time of remembrance of Feasts gone by and of the many original and early participants who had passed on. Some of the old feasters announced their retirement from the event. Thankfully, for some of those it was only talk.

The Feast of the Hunters' Moon remains one of the largest events of its type in North America. No one knows what it cost the TCHA to operated the one. It could not have been much, since the association was amazed at the $509.73 profit. Recent years have seen about $365,000 for pre-event expenditures. This amount, of course, does not include the expenses of the various participants including craftspeople, musicians, reenactors, and merchants.

The Feast of the Hunters' Moon is like Brigadoon. It appears every year with generations of families that have come, some for fifty years. Old friends who see each other for just two days a year get reacquainted. At times, gatherings mourn the death of old comrades who passed in the intervening months. Several weddings have taken place over the years, and genuine neighborhoods have been formed. Groups gather for their annual dinners, and thousands of visitors arrive to get their taste of specific foods as well as to support their favorite nonprofits. Some of these nonprofits make the bulk of their annual operating budget at the Feast. Many Boy Scouts have gone to the Philmont Scout

Ranch or the Boundary Waters for their High Adventure experience thanks to their grueling two-day rain-or-shine struggle providing food, wood, and ice for the masses or cleaning up the trash. For fifty years, the festival has endured horizontal freezing rain, snow, straight-line winds, flooding, ninety-degree temperatures with heavy dust clouds, and occasionally absolutely perfect fall weather.

Each year after the Boy Scouts collect the last of the trash, groups such as the Purdue Crew, the TCHA staff, the TCHA Board of Governors, and other volunteers come to clean up, take the booths down, and perform other chores. The TCHA is grateful to the Tippecanoe County Parks and Recreation Department, the Tippecanoe County Sheriff's Department, the Tippecanoe County Highway Department, the Tippecanoe Emergency Ambulance Service, the Wabash Township Fire Department, the Tippecanoe County Emergency Management Agency, volunteers from other agencies, and the numerous bus services that have worked over the years to make the event happen. The worn pathways are reseeded throughout the park, and the Feast Committee, led by Leslie Conwell and Jeffrey Schwab, takes a short break before beginning to plan for next year's Feast of the Hunters' Moon.

NOTES

1. Larry Chowning and John Henry are mentioned in chapter 1 concerning their investigations of the actual Fort Ouiatenon site in the 1970s.
2. Concerns over Euro-Americans portraying Native Americans are increasing. Paul René Tamburro's dissertation goes into some detail about this issue as well as the motivations of these reenactors (Tamburro 2006). See also Reese and Himler (2022) and Bardwell (2022).
3. Numbers of participants in the various military units, food booths, and other groups have never been accurately counted. Numbers were generally based on the number of buttons issued to each group. From the photographs over the years, military units, excluding pipe bands and fife and drum corps, could be as few as two or three members. These units would consolidate into larger units for parades and demonstrations.

REFERENCES

Bardwell, Neely. 2022. "Pretending to Be Native Was Not Pretty in My Hometown." *Native News Online*, July 24. https://nativenewsonline.net/opinion/pretending-to-be-native-is-not-pretty.

Brouk, Tim. 2003. "Blast from the Past." *Lafayette Journal and Courier*, September 12, TGIF 11.

DeAtley, Gertrude. 1970. "About Antiques." *Indianapolis Star*, November 1, 95.

The Debris. 1912. "The Battle of Tippecanoe." 181.

Encyclopedia.com. 2019. "Traditional Folk Music Festivals." https://www.encyclopedia.com/humanities/encyclopedias-almanacs-transcripts-and-maps/traditional-folk-music-festivals.

Geller, Marc B. 2002. "Sunshine Makes for Fine Feast." *Lafayette Journal and Courier*, October 7, C1.

Hovde, David M. 1982. "Stone Circles and the Ethnographic Record." *South Dakota Archaeology* 6: 33–46.

Lafayette Journal and Courier. 1929. "Visitors from France Leave City after Enjoyable Stay," March 16, 1, 13.

———. 1960. "Open House' Set at Fort Ouiatenon." October 14, 13.

———. 1967. "Feast Is Planned by History Buffs." October 18, 56.

———. 1968a. "Hunters' Moon Feast Recreates for 1,200." October 14, 17.

———. 1968b. "Hunters' Moon Feast Set at Ft. Ouiatenon." October 10, 20.

———. 1969a "Genuine Indians to Attend Festival at Ft. Ouiatenon." October 7, 11.

———. 1969b. "Rain, Skirmish Reduce Ouiatenon Officialdom." October 13, 32.

———. 1971. "A Great Feast." October 18, A-14.

———. 1992. "Fans of Feast Unfazed by Rain." September 27, A10.

———. 1998a. "Expanded 'Feast' Dubbed a Success." October 12, B1.

———. 1998b. "Feast Focuses on British Presence on the River." October 9, TGIF 9.

———. 2000. "Music Makes for a Merry Feast." October 15, C1.

———. 2001. "Fun Serves as Umbrella for Rainy Kid's Day at Feast." October 12, B1.

———. 2002. "This Year, Rain Not a Problem." October 5, A1, A8.

———. 2010. "Feasting on a Fall Tradition." October 1, TGIF 10.

Laubin, Reginald, and Gladys Laubin. 1980. *The Indian Tipi: Its History, Construction, and Use*. Norman: University of Oklahoma Press.

Matter, Kathy. 1986. "Authenticity Preserves Feast's Reputation." October Extra: Feast of the Hunters' Moon. *Lafayette Journal and Courier*, October 10, 2.

McCollough, Alameda. 1982–1983. Oral history interview, Alameda McCollough, September 1982 and June 1983. Accession 83.018. Tippecanoe County Historical Association, Lafayette, IN.

Morré, D. James. 2014. Oral history interview, Dr. D. James Morré, June 24. Purdue University Archives and Special Collections. Purdue University, West Lafayette, IN.

Moser, Heidi. 1983. "Savoring the Feast: Canadians Rendezvous for History." *Lafayette Journal and Courier*. October 9, B5.

Reese, Quincey, and Jeff Himler. 2022. "Concerns Voiced as Reenactors Replay Penn Township Battle of British, Native Americans." Trib Live, August 6. https://triblive.com/local/westmoreland/concerns-voiced-as-reenactors-replay-penn-township-battle-of-british-native-americans.

Schons, Mary. 2022. "The Past in the Present." Resource Library, *National Geographic*. https://education.nationalgeographic.org/resource/past-present.

Schumpert, Larry. 1977. "Blockhouse Dinners Inspired Feasts." *Lafayette Journal and Courier*, October 7, A-1.

Tamburro, Paul René. 2006. "Ohio Valley Native Americans Speak: Indigenous Discourse on the Continuity of Identity." PhD diss., Indiana University.

Tippecanoe County Historical Association. 1930. "Dedication of the Block House on the Site of Fort Ouiatanon." TCHA Scrap Book 1929–1930, 38. Tippecanoe County Historical Society, Lafayette, IN.

———. 1958a. "Tippecanoe County Historical Association Program 1958–59." Program Booklets, folder 52, box III A, Programs, yearly booklets, tours, etc. 1926–1986, 6. Tippecanoe County Historical Association, Lafayette, IN.

———. 1958b. "Heap Big Feast of the Hunters' Moon." Scrapbook 1956–1965, 50. Tippecanoe County Historical Association, Lafayette, IN.

———. 1967. "Feast of the Hunters' Moon. October 19, 1967." Scrapbook 1966–1970, 10. Tippecanoe County Historical Association. Lafayette, Lafayette, IN.

———. 1977. *Feast of the Hunters' Moon: A Look into the Past*. Lafayette IN: Tippecanoe County Historical Association.

Vestal, Stanley. 1980. "The History of the Tipi." In *The Indian Tipi: Its History, Construction, and Use,* ed. Reginald Laubin and Gladys Laubin, 3–13. Norman: University of Oklahoma Press.

11

CONNECTING THE SONG TO THE ARTIFACT AT THE FEAST OF THE HUNTERS' MOON

RONALD V. MORRIS, BALL STATE UNIVERSITY, AND LESLIE MARTIN CONWELL, TIPPECANOE COUNTY HISTORICAL ASSOCIATION

PARTICIPANTS IN THE FEAST OF THE HUNTERS' MOON EDUCATE AND ENtertain visitors from far and wide. The event represents the time of homecoming, feasting, dancing, and celebrating from the earliest days of historic Fort Ouiatenon. Eighteenth-century music, crafts, dance, and lifeways of the outpost's original inhabitants are presented to the public. Skilled interpreters, musicians, and artisans come into interactive contact with public and school audiences and engage the imagination while inspiring exploration of the music, cultures, and crafts of the past. Programming provides insight into the era's lifestyles, industries, and entertainment.[1]

Musicians prepare to entertain visitors who come from across the Midwest to listen to melodies that predate everything played on the radio on their drive to visit the Feast of the Hunters' Moon. One weekend in the fall people listen to traditional songs, chants, and instruments, hearing music they will wait an entire year to hear again. Every year thousands of people converge across four days to listen to music that was popular three hundred years ago. On the banks of the Wabash River at the Feast of the Hunters' Moon, visitors memorialize people and events at this place. Hearing the sounds and songs of long ago is a remembrance of ancestral heritage and recognition of others who shared the events of the time. The songs remind the musicians and the audience of the continuity of tradition and the memory of people who influenced the present generation.

But what is the trigger for these memories and memorialization? What is the evidence base for the music performed at the Feast of the Hunters' Moon, and how does that translate into interpretation at the Ouiatenon site? In this chapter the authors provide an opportunity to review the international musical tradition re-created every year near the site of Fort Ouiatenon, the archaeological evidence at the site for the re-created musical traditions, and the historic and geographical influences that intersect at the site. Examples of cultural influences from Native American, French, Scottish, Celtic, British, and Americana sources and historical musical instruments are discussed. Visitors encounter traditional tunes performed vocally, instrumentally, or vocally and instrumentally for a variety of purposes. Surprisingly, multiple generations of performers are featured on the live stages at Ouiatenon. Visitors explore world culture through the investigation of a mixture of Old World and New World music at the Feast of the Hunters' Moon.

HISTORICAL SOURCES

Archaeologists found multiple jaw harps at the site but no other evidence of music in the archaeological record (figure 11.1).[2]

While the archaeological record is thin in regard to music material culture, it does tell that like the rest of humanity these people enjoyed music, but for more details an examination of historically contemporary written sources is needed.

Sir William Johnson reveals the music and instrument during the mid to late eighteenth century on the frontier of a British colony. He was the British agent working to the south and east of the Great Lakes in the English frontier negotiating between the British crown and the Native Americans. His journals provide insight into relations between representatives of his majesty's government and Native Americans in the backcountry. Johnson recorded on June 20, 1770, that "with Us as there Will be no possibility of Doing Without, the Lad we have Intends to [words faded] I forgot to Mention Rid Strouds, Jews harps, [words faded] & a funnel or two. We would be Glad if You would Order [words faded] Inquire Whether Finn & Ellis Got the Boat we Left behind." (Johnson and Hamilton 1926, 756). The primary sources are parsimonious in what they reveal about music on the Great Lakes. Johnson tries to bring order to traders in his area with the intent to provide smooth relations with the Native Americans. On November 17, 1764, he established trade prices listing "Jews Harps 6 for a large raccoon" (Johnson and Hamilton 1926, 11:991). Established prices would make trade more

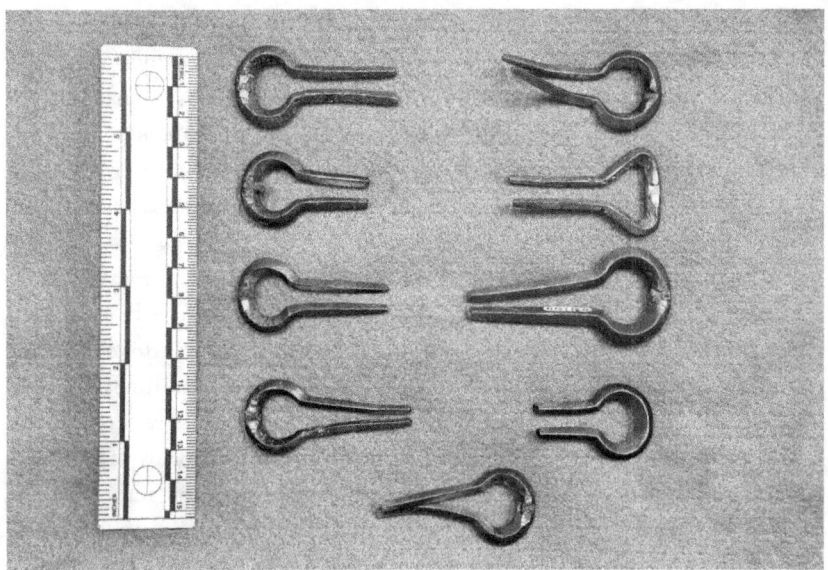

Figure 11.1. Bronze jaw harps found at the site of Fort Ouiatenon. Photograph by Brooke Sauter.

uniform, and some customers would therefore not think they had been taken advantage of by a trader at one post or another. The records do not tell everything about musical life on the frontier, but they do offer some clues.

However, Sir William Johnson goes to a great deal of effort to get jaw harps. He received a letter from Hugh Wallace of New York on January 7, 1771, that read, "I heartily thank you for your generous kind offer of 2000 Acres Lands adjoining my Land of Ledighquida, which I accept of with pleasure & shall get the Deed drawn as you desire. I sent to Ireland for the Jews Harps you ordered & expect they will be in in Spring" (Johnson and Hamilton 1926, 7:1072). Hugh had the power to trade on the New York wharf, other colonies, and England for Johnson's interests. He managed the orders, provided quality control, and had Johnson's financial confidence. On August 27 of that same year Hugh says, "I cannot think your plate Iron too thin it must be well painted both Sides & nailed very thick & I am convinced it will answer your purpose. I sent up the Jews Harps by Cap. Marseillis & told Mr. Phyn when he left this a few days ago to enquire for them & have them sent up to you" (Johnson and Hamilton 1926, 8:236). After ascertaining the durability of the product, it was a matter of waiting for the goods to come from Ireland. Once the jaw harps landed in New York, they came up the Hudson to Albany by another boat. Hugh writes yet again on September 19 that "your Jews Harps were sent up to Albany by Skipper Henry Marseiles the 15 June last, & we have his receipt for them. Mr. Phyn promised me he would enquire for them, & I hope he has succeeded. No News here. Our compl to all Friends at ye River" (Johnson and Hamilton 1926, 8:263–64). Hugh reported that the job was successfully completed, with the proper receipts filled. With the merchandise in hand, Johnson started using it in his capacity as royal agent. In June 1761 he signed for jaw harps to be given to Native Americans as presents at meetings (Johnson and Hamilton 1926, 10:279). He understood the importance of giving presents at any negotiation, and musical instruments made a novel gift in this setting.[3]

Sir William Johnson had access to a variety of instruments on the frontier, and he was either proficient or had people around him who were. He received a letter from Charles Lewis Reily stating "I send this letter to Captain Ross to forward to you. Goshen August 24th, 1749. I'll also if you please bring with me all my musical instruments Fiddle, German Flute, Hautboy & bagpipes" (Johnson and Hamilton 1926, 1:244–45). Having a variety of instruments on the frontier meant that he had the option of playing chamber music for amusement on long cold winter nights with friends or family members. Accomplished members of a household had musical instruction as part of their curriculum so that they could provide music in social settings. Music performance was the only option for melody prior to the much later invention of the phonograph.

Meanwhile, the French were also living with music on the frontier. The Jesuits in multiple reports from the North American continent documented the French and found an existing musical tradition in North America, in this instance among the Iroquois:

> Therefore, we invited all the Savages in our neighborhood to a grand feast, where we exerted our utmost skill and spared neither the drums nor the musical instruments, in order to lull them to sleep by an innocent charm.
>
> He who presided at the ceremony played his part with such skill and success that each one was bent on contributing to the public joy. They vied with one another in uttering piercing yells, now of war, now of glee; while, out of complaisance, the Savages sang and danced in the French manner, and the French in that of the Savages. To encourage them more and more in this fine game, presents were distributed to those who best played their parts, and who made the most noise for drowning that made outside by two-score of our men in transporting all our outfit. When the lading of the boats was entirely completed, the feast came to an end at the appointed time; the guests withdrew. (Thwaites 1898–1901, 44:177)

Native Americans used drums and a variety of percussion instruments as part of their feasting accompanied by music making and dancing. Similarly, Sir William Johnson wrote of the spectacle of the Native Americans moving between their seasonal homes. He wrote in his journal on the morning of September 17 that "the Caghnawagas being ready to depart assembled in the Summer house in the Garden, and 10 of their Warriors being naked, painted, and feather'd, (one of whom had a Drum on his back and made of a Cag covered with Skin) marched in Slow order in two Ranks, Singing their song accord, to the Ottawa Custom, Tom Wildman in the Rere Tank beating the Drum with one Stick, and the rest accompanying it with Notched Sticks which they Struck to good time on their Axes" (Johnson and Hamilton 1926, 10:852). Johnson was struck by the musical pageantry as the people passed from one seasonal home to another.

The French also adapted and shared their dancing and instruments to the North American continent with instruments brought from Europe. In 1636, a Native American ally presented to Monsieur du Plessis Bochart, commandant of the fleet, a young Iroquoian woman taken as hostage during recent warring:

> Monsieur the Commandant made known to him that he would cherish this present for the sake of the hand of his friends, whence it proceeded, and not for the Country from which it had come, which he hated like death; that, besides, they themselves could see clearly that if the French had followed them they would have deserted them, when the quarrels arose among themselves; and that, if we ever did go to war, we would go strong and powerful, and not return until we had destroyed entire villages. They received this answer with pleasure, begging that, as a sign of mutual rejoicing and love, some of our young people should dance to the sound of a hurdy-gurdy, that a little Frenchman held. (Thwaites 1898–1901, 9:269)

The much-maligned hurdy-gurdy was a relatively simple way to make music for a dance, and it was also forgiving of temperature and humidity fluctuations.

The French desire for music permeated the liturgical year and everyday life. Also, like the Native American musical traditions found in North America, when the French arrived vocal music with or without instrumental accompaniment:

> On the 8th [June 1662], the feast of Corpus Christi, there was a procession in the morning at 8 o'clock. As usual, it went to the storehouse, where there was a temporary altar, and then it ascended to the fort, where there was also an altar. The soldiers were drawn up in rank from the cannon mounted on the platform outside, with their backs to the gate of the fort [Quebec]; all knelt bareheaded, with The muzzles of their guns turned toward the ground. The 3rd altar was our Chapel. We sang at the 1st altar the *Dixit*, at the 2nd the *Exaudiat*, at the 3rd *Ecce panis*, and at the Parish church the *Tantum ergo* with musical accompaniment. Then high mass was sung, and afterward low mass at the same place, the parish church. Monseigneur bore the blessed Sacrament in the procession, but did not sing the high Mass; Monsieur de Bernieres sang it. On the octave, the same was done as last Year. The procession was Considered too short. (Thwaites 1899–1901, 47:283)

As part of the celebration of the Catholic mass, the French used traditional ecclesiastical music as part of the service. Choral works were used on both sides of the Great Lakes, as Johnson also speaks of the use of a cantata (Johnson and Hamilton 1926, 12:811). Written by composers such as the celebrated George Frideric Handel, cantatas had a tradition in England, and due to their religious nature they were tolerated by the Catholic Church at a time when opera and theater were considered decadent or banned. Instrumental music seems to have been a treat possibly being dependent on instruments or talent. However, the desire for instrumental music was certainly present almost from the beginning of French occupation. "During holy week, the *tenebræ* were sung and solemn service was held at the parish church, where the passion primum was chanted by three deacons. On Thursday we had benediction here, with Instrumental music, as in the morning for the *pange lingua; religua more solito*. On Friday we Began the office at 10 o'clock, *et hoc bene*" (Thwaites 1899–1901, 48:229). The Quebec church in March 1664 was an organizational force in arranging for music performance around mass, holy days, and the liturgical calendar. Instrumental music was specifically described as contributing to mass along with part singing. "The 1st stroke of the midnight mass rang at eleven o'clock, the 2nd, a little before the half-hour; and then they began to sing two airs—*Venez, mon Dieu*, etc., and *Chantons noc*, etc. Monsieur de la ferté sang the bass; St. martin played the violin; there was also a german flute, which proved to be out of tune when they came to the Church. We had finished a little before midnight; they nevertheless sang the *Te Deum*" (Thwaites 1898–1901, 27:113). Across the centuries, people have noted the changes of humidity and temperature being hard on instruments and pitch, more so for players who were not talented, especially given the variable nature of intonation from woodwinds and strings.

As a matter of trade, a jaw harp would be shiny if constructed all from silver, but that was not pragmatic. A silver jaw harp would not have enough spring to resonate and would in fact just bend, as silver is a soft metal. The uninspiring steel spring, while not visually thrilling, was the superior instrument. Other instruments were also ordered including a hautboy (arcane oboe), fiddle, and German flute (Johnson and Hamilton 1926, 1:244, 7:711). In 1770 Sir William Johnson received this communication at Johnson Hall in Albany: "Dr. Sir Your most obedt Servt, Hugh Wallace: I Ordered the Hautboy & Jews Harps for you from Dublin—& have recd them, they are sent up to Albany to the Care of Mr. Cartwright for you in a small Box directed—there is no Jews Harps made with Silver Tongues, they write us they would not sound so well as Steel tongues—Groce of Jews Harps cost Irish 1.17, the Haut Boy cost 1.4" (Johnson and Hamilton 1926, 7:711). Silver was more malleable and would bend; the steel would provide a stronger vibration from its spring. More correspondence explains that Johnson ordered his jaw harps from Dublin. Hugh and Alex Wallace provided this receipt: "Rec. from Sir William Johnson Four pounds twelve Shilings & Nine pence—being the Cost of two dozen of Jews Harps & a Hautboy, which we Imported from Dublin for him—New York 21st June 1770" (Johnson and Hamilton 1926, 7:760). The hautboy, a wooden oboe, may have been for himself or for trade since he seems to have had one earlier. He also received information about the price of a violin, and since he seemed to have one earlier than this mention it cannot be determined if it was to replace his or was for trade or for the purpose of playing in ensemble. On December 13, 1773, Francis Wade of Philadelphia mentions the price of a violin to be between five and ten shillings (Johnson and Hamilton 1926), 8:944, 947, 1020). Francis Wade could be a factor handling accounts out of Philadelphia for Sir William Johnson or a manufacturer of musical instruments in the largest city in the colonies at that time. While a violin was portable, the cello was less mobile on the frontier especially in being hauled by canoe or portaged between streams. The cello is an important instrument in providing a different range of tones in ensemble playing, and music for it as a solo or chamber instrument was plentiful. Johnson noted the availability of a cello on the East Coast (Johnson and Hamilton 1926, 13:632).

Instrument builders would be a welcome addition to a community as settlement progressed, though the service would probably be provided by hobbyists until the population of a place increased. Sir William Johnson refers to trading in guitar strings (Johnson and Hamilton 1926, 12:391). Obviously someone was playing, and someone was building guitars. They would have been more easily shipped than a cello and would have easily fit in a canoe. It was an instrument for singing ballads typical of the Celtic, French, and English traditions. The harp was another instrument easily transported and perfect for accompanying folk tunes and songs (Johnson and Hamilton 1926, 4:840, 5:733). Small handheld harps were good for families and even taverns, where there was a small space that could be filled with the sound. Gut strings common at the time also provided a more muted sound as opposed to the metal strings popular later that gave the harp a brighter sound.

Of course, by 1773 the French provincial capital had been captured earlier by the British toward the end of the Seven Years' War and now served as the capital of British Canada. Daniel Claus wrote in his journal in Quebec from July 28 to August 10, 1773, that "Miss gave a tune on the harpsichord. After all hands went to Mr. Hays Country Seat of a very elegant Taste the Band being there playing before Supper and it being served up out of doors being a very calm Moonlight Night it made a fine show for Canada" (Johnson and Hamilton 1926, 13:632). Bands at this time could be almost any conceivable instrumentation or size. In a settled area such as this there were accomplished individuals who performed in intimate spaces on the harpsicord, and there were multiple outdoor musicians. On February 19 of either 1749 or 1750, Johnson wrote to Samuel W. Baker for "an Historicall review of the Transactions of Europe from the Commencement of the War with Spain. The Whole proceedings in the House of Peers against the three Condemned Lords. Amaryllis a new Musical Design well Bound. A good French Horn with the Notes. A good Common Hunting Horn. A good loud Trumpett" (Johnson and Hamilton 1926, 1:265). A hunting horn would be a natural horn with no valves and a limited range of notes, while a the valved French horn has a full range of notes. A trumpet had a higher range of notes than the hunting horn and the natural horn.

While it is inconceivable that an organ would have come to such a remote and small site as Fort Ouiatenon, the French did love their organs and built an organ tradition of three hundred–plus years that is still visible today. At this time New York was a more provincial community compared to the large and relatively sophisticated Philadelphia. On February 2, 1773, Guy Johnson from New York wrote to Sir William Johnson that "I am much at a Loss about an Organ, especially as you Mention no price, there is not one to spare here, but I expect to hear [every] day from Philad. Concern it—the lowest price any that may be fitting would be 80 or 100 for a very small one" (Johnson and Hamilton 1926, 8:704). Organ music was popular in the great homes of the gentry and was performed by accomplished children. These organs had limited range and stops, thus combinations of pipes and moderate volume in keeping with a parlor instrument. On June 16, 1773, Hugh Wallace wrote from New York that "I am glad you got the 1000 sent by Capt. Stevenson—Gen. Haldimand is well and desires his respects will always be happy to hear from you. I am his old Acquaintance, & very happy in his Friendship—I have got a Man gone to Jersey for your Organ, & shall have it sent up as soon as it comes here" (Johnson and Hamilton 1926, 8:824). The effort to move such an instrument was difficult, but to move it without damage, the obstacles were prodigious. The price and trade arrangement for acquiring an organ were negotiable on the frontier. On November 25, 1773, Major General Haldimand sent Reverend Dr. Hindimand a note from Johnson Hall stating that "the adjacent Country is becoming populous, tho' not in any such proportion, for want of the same encouragement, all which people were without the benefits of Religion, till I built the Church at Johnstown, which is a handsome Stone building, near 90 feet in length with the Steeple and Chancel, to which I have lately added a neat Organ that cost me 100 Ster," (Johnson and Hamilton 1926, 8:927). Johnson was quite pleased with himself that he had made the sacrifice to get this instrument on the frontier.

Organ music would certainly have been an aspiration to accompany mass on the frontier and would certainly have been a part of larger French communities to the northeast and southwest. The journal of the Jesuit Fathers at Quebec in 1661 recorded for February that

> the 40 hours' devotion took place as last year. On Sunday, at the benediction, the *Ecce panis* was sung in plain-chant at the commencement, after Father Mercier had

incensed; Father Pijart then preached the short sermon. Monseigneur the Bishop thereupon donned the vestments, and the *pange lingua* was chanted with some verses of the litany of the name of Jesus. The *sub tuum præsidium* was forgotten. The organ played while the Blessed Sacrament was being taken down, and during the benediction. The whole concluded with the *Domine salvum fac regem*. (Thwaites 1899–1901, 46:163)

The organ performed a transitional function as important parts of the service transpired in musical interludes and background music for the benediction. The organ does not seem to be used in these passages as necessarily supporting congregational hymn singing as recorded in the journal of the Jesuit Fathers at Quebec in 1664:

> High mass was sung here with Musical accompaniment, at 7½ o'clock, without prejudice to the mass in the parish church which was sung at 9 o'clock. There was also high mass on tuesday, in honor of the blessed sacrament. It is good to have high Mass as often as possible on those Days; otherwise the morning devotions lack fervor. Benedictions and short exhortations as usual.
>
> The order of the music was as follows: 1st, a motet in honor of the blessed sacrament; then a short sermon; then the organ, while the rest of the candles were being lighted; then the above Anthem, and the *Dixit* of the vespers of the blessed sacrament; repetition of the Anthem; orisons; then the benediction of the virgin and a *Domine salvum fac regem. Sic aliis diebus* proportionately. (Thwaites 1899–1901, 48:227)

The organ was part of the celebration of the Counter-Reformation mass, with its solemnity and majesty. Organ music and motets, candles, processionals, and sacraments were all part of the religious experience of motivating the faithful to participate in church community life. Anthems and sermons helped the people celebrate religious and nationalistic traditions.

DEPICTIONS AT THE FEAST TODAY

Today the site of Fort Ouiatenon is a very quiet and contemplative space except when people visit during the four-day Feast of the Hunters' Moon and hear music from the past. Table 11.1 illustrates the musical genres found at the Feast in the last three years of the 2010s. Each group is contextualized by the genre it most likely performs: vocal acapella, instrumental, and instrumental and vocal. This is not a hard-and-fast rule, because musicians are versatile and extend their creativity in a variety of directions when they find new opportunities for their talents. Looking across the three years illustrated, it is remarkable how stable the performers are; they seem to regularly return year after year.

Table 11.2 illustrates the cultures represented at the Feast of the Hunters' Moon. There were multiple ethnic groups performing at the Feast, including Native Americans, French, Scottish, Celtic, British Colonial, and Americana. It is interesting that the representation of the groups has been equal, with no one group getting more time than other groups.

There were also multiple groups that performed with multiple generations including those under the age of eighteen. Table 11.3 shows the variety of multigenerational aspects of the Feast. For example, the Niagara River Iroquois include at least three generations and a variety of ages. Father, Son, and Friends contains three generations of performers, and Traveler's Dream contains multiple generations. It is very possible to share the stage with performers who cannot yet drive, such as the fiddlers who are in middle school and the youths from elementary through high school age the Voyageur Ancient Fife & Drum Corps.

To analyze the Feast of the Hunters' Moon today requires the division of the musical events into four categories: music heard, possible music heard, music probably not heard, and music not heard at the Fort Ouiatanon site. Musical events are grouped in these four categories to help illustrate the connection between what is heard at the Feast of the Hunters' Moon and the primary sources and sounds of the frontier. Some sounds would have been very familiar to the occupants of Fort Ouiatenon, some may or may not have been heard at the fort, and some would have been foreign to the ears of the people at the fort.

People at Fort Ouiatenon most likely heard and seen Native Americans singing, drumming, and dancing and may have watched or joined. They also heard the French inhabitants singing a capella voyageur songs at the fort or while the traders were at work. Chanting during the mass, a part of the church liturgy, was familiar to the French when a priest was in town. Later in the British period history of the site, people engaged in the singing of popular hymns. From time to time all the inhabitants of the fort formed small groups of people who sang with instruments.

Voyageurs sang these eighteenth-century songs on the rivers and at home, and these songs are still heard frequently at the Feast of the Hunters' Moon as songs or instrumental melodies. French musicians are careful not to introduce post–fort occupation songs into the musical offering at the Feast. The authors have witnessed an enthusiastic fifer who struck up "La Marseilles" only to be silenced by another musician with the explanation that it had not been written yet.

The song "C'est L'aviron" features a thirsty girl who enjoys libations and the company of her voyageur:

TABLE 11.1. FEAST MUSICAL GENRES

Genre	2017	2018	2019
Vocal	Common Stock Northland Voyageurs Strolling Singers Voyageur Camp Area	Common Stock Northland Voyageurs Strolling Singers Voyageur Camp Area	Common Stock Northland Voyageurs Strolling Singers Voyageur Camp Area
Instrumental	42nd Royal Highlanders Closing Ceremonies Colonel Webb's Band of Musick First Michigan Fife & Drum Corps Great River Fife & Drum Corps Heritage Musick & Daunce Society Janesville Fife & Drum Corps Madame Cadillac Dance Theatre Massed Field Music River Valley Fife & Drum Corps Theatiki Fife & Drum Corps Tim Schaiper Tippecanoe Ancient Fife & Drum Corps Truman/Sperreng Fiddlers Voyageur Ancient Fife & Drum Corps Whole Nine Yards	42nd Royal Highlanders Closing Ceremonies Colonel Webb's Band of Musick First Michigan Fife & Drum Corps Great River Fife & Drum Corps Heritage Musick & Daunce Society Janesville Fife & Drum Corps Madame Cadillac Dance Theatre Massed Field Music River Valley Fife & Drum Corps Theatiki Fife & Drum Corps Tim Schaiper Tippecanoe Ancient Fife & Drum Corps Truman/Sperreng Fiddlers Voyageur Ancient Fife & Drum Corps Whole Nine Yards	42nd Royal Highlanders Closing Ceremonies Colonel Webb's Band of Musick First Michigan Fife & Drum Corps Great River Fife & Drum Corps Heritage Musick & Daunce Society Janesville Fife & Drum Corps Madame Cadillac Dance Theatre Massed Field Music River Valley Fife & Drum Corps Theatiki Fife & Drum Corps Tim Schaiper Tippecanoe Ancient Fife & Drum Corps Truman/Sperreng Fiddlers Voyageur Ancient Fife & Drum Corps Whole Nine Yards

TABLE 11.1. CONTINUED

Vocal and Instrumental	Bush Family Native American Drum & Dance Dulcimer Gathering Father, Son, & Friends Hasty Puddin' Hogeye Navvy Jim's Red Pants Niagara River Iroquois Dancers Opening Ceremonies Rusty Musket SouthEastern Water Spider Drum Traveler's Dream	Bush Family Native American Drum & Dance Dulcimer Gathering Father, Son, & Friends Hogeye Navvy Jim's Red Pants Niagara River Iroquois Dancers Opening Ceremonies Rusty Musket SouthEastern Water Spider Drum	Bush Family Native American Drum & Dance Dulcimer Gathering Father, Son, & Friends Hogeye Navvy Jim's Red Pants Niagara River Iroquois Dancers Opening Ceremonies Rusty Musket SouthEastern Water Spider Drum

TABLE 11.2. CULTURES REPRESENTED AT THE FEAST OF THE HUNTERS' MOON

Ethnic Groups	2017	2018	2019
Americana	Common Stock Dulcimer Gathering Father, Son, and Friends Hasty Puddin' Hogeye Navvy Strolling Singers Truman/Sperreng Fiddlers	Common Stock Dulcimer Gathering Father, Son, and Friends Hogeye Navvy Strolling Singers Truman/Sperreng Fiddlers	Common Stock Dulcimer Gathering Father, Son, and Friends Hogeye Navvy Strolling Singers Truman/Sperreng Fiddlers
Celtic	Common Stock Father, Son, & Friends Hogeye Navvy Rusty Musket	Common Stock Father, Son, & Friends Hogeye Navvy Rusty Musket	Common Stock Father, Son, & Friends Hogeye Navvy Rusty Musket
Colonial	Colonel Webb's Band of Musick First Michigan Fife & Drum Corps Great River Fife and Drum Corps Heritage Musick and Daunce Society Janesville Fife and Drum Corps Jim's Red Pants River Valley Fife and Drum Corps Traveler's Dream Theatiki Fife & Drum Corps Tim Schaiper Truman/Sperreng Fiddlers	Colonel Webb's Band of Musick First Michigan Fife & Drum Corps Great River Fife and Drum Corps Heritage Musick and Daunce Society Janesville Fife and Drum Corps Jim's Red Pants River Valley Fife and Drum Corps Theatiki Fife & Drum Corps Tim Schaiper Truman/Sperreng Fiddlers	Colonel Webb's Band of Musick First Michigan Fife & Drum Corps Great River Fife and Drum Corps Heritage Musick and Daunce Society Janesville Fife and Drum Corps Jim's Red Pants River Valley Fife and Drum Corps Theatiki Fife & Drum Corps Tim Schaiper Truman/Sperreng Fiddlers

TABLE 11.2. CONTINUED

French	Madame Cadillac Dance Theatre Northland Voyageurs Tippecanoe Ancient Fife & Drum Corps Voyageur Ancient Fife & Drum Corps Voyageur Camp Area	Madame Cadillac Dance Theatre Northland Voyageurs Tippecanoe Ancient Fife & Drum Corps Voyageur Ancient Fife & Drum Corps Voyageur Camp Area	Madame Cadillac Dance Theatre Northland Voyageurs Tippecanoe Ancient Fife & Drum Corps Voyageur Ancient Fife & Drum Corps Voyageur Camp Area
Native Americans	Bush Family Native American Drum & Dance Niagara River Iroquois Dancers SouthEastern Water Spider Drum	Bush Family Native American Drum & Dance Niagara River Iroquois Dancers SouthEastern Water Spider Drum	Bush Family Native American Drum & Dance Niagara River Iroquois Dancers SouthEastern Water Spider Drum
Scottish	42nd Royal Highlanders Common Stock Whole Nine Yards	42nd Royal Highlanders Common Stock Whole Nine Yards	42nd Royal Highlanders Common Stock Whole Nine Yards

TABLE 11.3. GROUPS THAT INCLUDED PEOPLE UNDER THE AGE OF EIGHTEEN

	2017	2018	2019
Americana	Truman/Sperreng Fiddlers	Truman/Sperreng Fiddlers	Truman/Sperreng Fiddlers
Celtic	Father, Son, & Friends	Father, Son, & Friends	Father, Son, & Friends
Colonial	Traveler's Dream, multiple generations		
French	Closing Ceremonies Massed Field Music Opening Ceremonies Voyageur Ancient Fife & Drum Corps	Closing Ceremonies Massed Field Music Opening Ceremonies Voyageur Ancient Fife & Drum Corps	Closing Ceremonies Massed Field Music Opening Ceremonies Voyageur Ancient Fife & Drum Corps
Native American	Bush Family Native American Drum & Dance Niagara River Iroquois Dancers	Bush Family Native American Drum & Dance Niagara River Iroquois Dancers	Bush Family Native American Drum & Dance Niagara River Iroquois Dancers
Scottish	Whole Nine Yards	Whole Nine Yards	Whole Nine Yards

Riding along the road to Rochelle City,
Riding along the road to Rochelle City,
I met three girls, and all of them were pretty
[LINE BREAK]
Chorus:
Pull on the oars as we glide along together,
Pull on the oars as we glide along.
[LINE BREAK]
By chance I chose the one who was the beauty,
By chance I chose the one who was the beauty,
Lifted her up so she could ride beside me.
[LINE BREAK]
With never a word we rode along together,
With never a word we rode along together,
After a while, she said, "I'd like a drink, sir."
[LINE BREAK]

> *Quickly I found a spring from out the mountain,*
> *Quickly I found a spring from out the mountain,*
> *But she'd not drink the water from the fountain.*
> *[LINE BREAK]*
> *On then we went to find her home and father,*
> *On then we went to find her home and father,*
> *When we got there, she drank . . . but not of water.*
> *[LINE BREAK]*
> *Many a toast she drank to her dear mother,*
> *Many a toast she drank to her dear mother,*
> *Toasted again her sister and her brother.*
> *[LINE BREAK]*
> *When she had drunk to sister and to brother,*
> *When she had drunk to sister and to brother,*
> *Turning to me, she toasted her own lover. (Waltz 2008b)*

With an allusion to traveling by river and multiple toasts to all the relatives she could think of, this felicitous song delights present audiences as it did voyagers of the past.

Another authentic playful song, "Ah! Si Mon Moine Voulait Danser!," conjures images of a dancing frier. The singer is willing to give a variety of gifts of clothing and a songbook for this pleasure including a rosary—giving up faith—for a moment and at the end yielding a kiss in exchange for a wedding ring. Exploring the idea of the dancing monk more reveals that another name for a top is a monk, so the double meaning is a not too subtle flirtatious child's game.

> *Oh, if my monk would dance with me!*
> *Oh, if my monk would dance with me!*
> *A hooded coat I will give to thee,*
> *A hooded coat I will give to thee.*
> *[LINE BREAK]*
> *Chorus:*
> *Dance, dance, my monk, yes dance,*
> *Together let us dance now,*
> *With you I want to dance now,*
> *Together let us dance today.*
> *[LINE BREAK]*
> *Oh, if my monk would dance with me,*
> *A shining belt I will give to thee.*
> *[LINE BREAK]*

Oh, if my monk would dance with me,
A rosary I will give to thee.
[LINE BREAK]
Oh, if my monk would dance with me,
A homespun coat I will give to thee.
[LINE BREAK]
Oh, if my monk would dance with me,
A fine songbook I will give to thee.
[LINE BREAK]
And if you'll give a kiss to me,
A ring of gold I will give to thee. (Waltz 2008a)

While children originally enjoyed this song, adult listeners and performers enjoy it enough to keep it alive at the Feast. Folk music performers and enthusiasts recognize these songs, but visitors who return to the Feast year after year also recognize them.

People at Fort Ouiatenon might have heard a variety of instruments. The bagpipes of the Scottish Highlands could have arrived with an exodus of refugees from the Jacobite Revolution, and the smaller Celtic pipes could have come from France. The violin and viola were possible on the frontier, with the cello and double bass still possible but logistically more difficult. These would never have been massed like the orchestras popular in the twenty-first century but instead would have been more in the style of small ensembles. Later in the history of the fort military bands with natural horns, double reeds, and serpents were possible. The archaic serpent was a wood instrument with keys, not valves, played with a metallic horn mouthpiece that wound around the body of a player roughly similar to a sousaphone to provide a solid bass foundation to ensemble playing. Again, these would have been played in chamber music–style performances.

Fort Ouiatenon might not have heard massed dulcimer music. There may not have been that many dulcimers in the entire Great Lakes watershed at the time prior to Pontiac's Rebellion. As popular as the fife and drum corps are today, it is unlikely that large numbers of people were ever gathered at the fort at one time for a military music performance. Residents at the fort might have heard a couple of fifes and a couple of drums during most of the history of Fort Ouiatenon. Regardless, this would have still been thrilling if a small body of soldiers were marching to the music.

Most likely no one at Fort Ouiatenon ever heard the massed military numbers in the opening and closing ceremonies at the Feast, with a higher number of instruments in one day than were probably ever present at the fort. The groups playing today might also have attained a proficiency that former part-time musicians on the frontier did not have the time to achieve. Also, the musical literacy of modern performers allows them to read a variety of music that military performers needed to learn by ear.

Without being able to read musical notation, military performers would have had to learn tunes from other performers. At a remote frontier post, getting exposure to new musical ideas would be difficult.

Just as the Feast has some overrepresentation, it probably also has some underrepresentation. The hurdy-gurdy is not often seen on the grounds of the Feast, and it does not always play nicely with other instruments because of intonation issues. The organ is logistically difficult to bring onto the Feast grounds and is not gracious when wet. The harpsicord is easy to transport but is also not a happy instrument in wet weather. It has the added disadvantage of not being heard beyond the stage, and background noise can easily drown its sound. The harp is also not easily heard without electronic enhancement and in audio competitions tends to lose. Ironically, the jaw harp, the only musical instrument found in the archaeological record, is not found frequently on the grounds due to its atonality and lack of power. It was lost and recovered as an archaeological artifact on the site and is presently not used in modern reenactments.

TRADITION AND REMEMBRANCE

Other people have also studied spaces where people learn historic music. Scottish Gaelic cultural heritage and song are imperiled due to the nature of oral transmission. However, Indigenous people have preserved and sustained this music by Gaelic singers from generation to generation within family discourse and in the Native American community. Scottish musicians have been interviewed to determine how higher education could support revival and interest in the nonliterary tradition through practices, values, traits, and issues (Sheridan, MacDonald, and Byrne 2011). The members of the community remained committed to the preservation of Gaelic singing and traditional music passed on through oral transmission into a performance experience. Celtic musical traditions memorialize ancestral ties and cultural practices.

Learning Celtic music happens in a family environment where individuals observe and listen to Irish and traditional Celtic music and Irish musicians. Waldron (2007) calls for a more holistic instruction whereby musical notation is a memory aid, not the primary vehicle of teaching. Modeling familial sounds and traditions connects one generation with another through music.

The role of music making in the lives of students depended on listening to families and examining the social and emotional role it played in the life of the family. Parents talked about past, present, and future desires for music in their families. Koops (2018) described that parents played roles in their child's musical experiences through control, coordinating, encouraging, participating, providing, and satisfaction. Students described their beliefs and perceptions about their current musicianship and a disconnect between musical experiences in and out of school among students between the ages of eight and twelve. They also discussed their aspirations for future musical involvement.

Adult interactions with young learners during family visits to informal learning environments provide opportunities for meaning making (Riedinger 2012). Informal learning events include music festivals, concerts, reenactments, and museums where people meet and exchange information. Informal learning events are places to learn without a didactic structure or formalized curriculum such as school. Young learners share conversations with their parents when they learn and relate together through interactive experiences. Parents guide young learners and need to engage in conversations to interpret exhibits and program content. Those conversations maximize learning and engage children in coconstructing understanding.

Rather than individual performance and output learning, music for an orthodox church is a communal process (Brashier 2016). Knowing and performing music requires internalization and imitation in a social cultural context. Music is learned in a socially constructed space where everyone needs to collaborate to create traditional music.

Community festivals provide a sense of place where people meet in a common area with dedicated experts. A social festival defines the community and allows the community to participate in education. Students investigate and engage in research activities as they gather information, key contacts, and local resources to share with classroom peers. As the students learn from people of multiple ages who transmit their culture, student research directly connects to their community as they observe diverse people within their community (Morris 2008, 2012). People learn and demonstrate proficiency in an informal social space at a community festival. As such, community festivals meet the criteria for a musical informal learning environment where people of mixed ages learn together.

CONCLUSION

The memorialization of Fort Ouiatenon is in good health, as the annual celebration is observed auditorily as a sensual pleasure equal to the Feast of food, the riot of color, the pattern and design in historic clothing, and the smells of living around a fire. Furthermore, traditional music is in good health, with the audience interested in hearing, a group of musicians eager to perform it and the next generation of youths willing to learn it. Moreover, a variety of musical traditions reflect the backgrounds and preferences of the performers on the grounds. A rich mixture of melodious interchange occurs between performers who gather to socialize and learn more from their musical community. The interaction between performers and the audience opens new areas of music to visitors who are interested in traditional music.

A surprisingly large number of youths are participating in events or onstage with the performers at the Feast. This multigenerational mentoring of talent bodes well for both the learning of history and the learning of traditional music. A couple of groups are composed entirely of students, and three events are for performers regardless of age. A more interesting phenomenon is the multiple-generational performers, usually extended families that include all members regardless of age. It is easy to see that children who mature as performers at the Feast will carry on the tradition with their families in the future.

It is also surprising that no one is capturing the musical accomplishments at the Feast for larger distribution across the Midwest and that a series of radio performances from the Feast has not been undertaken while the performers are all in the area. Live performances coupled with studio performances and interviews would all be important to archive. Likewise, PBS-style television documentaries have not been created about the musical accomplishments of individual performers or large military ensembles. Some of the performers are more mature, and some were at the first Feast of the Hunters' Moon. Capturing their histories, their musical traditions, and the hobby of reenacting through traditional music all seems to be important stories to preserve. A living history platform serves to invite more curiosity, involvement, questions, and discussion and helps children and adults alike compare and contrast the lifestyles, politics, and heritage arts of the past with what is now relevant in their own lives.

NOTES

1. For a history of the Feast of the Hunters' Moon, see chapter 10 in this volume.
2. We use the term "jaw harp," which is another name for the Jew's harp. "According to Webster's New World Dictionary, Third College Edition, 1988, jew's harps were earlier called jew's trumps, a more direct translation of the French trompe. The Dutch term jeugdtromp, or child's or youth trumpet, became confused in English with the Middle English term for Jew, Judeu." "Trompe" is the French term for Jew's harp found in the eighteenth-century trade invoices and military inventories in New France (Jackson 2005, 419).
3. The following are all mentions of jaw harps by Johnson not already included in the chapter. Johnson 1926, 2:616; 7:711, 756, 760, 780, 782, 844, 885, 1072; 8:236, 263; 9:562; 10:279; 11:991; and 13:474, 647–48.

REFERENCES

Brashier, Rachel. 2016. "'Just Keep Going, Stay Together, and Sing OUT': Learning Byzantine Music in an Informal and Situated Community of Practice." *Action, Criticism, and Theory for Music Education* 15: 67–85.

Jackson, Misty M. 2005. "Classifications by Historical Archaeologists and Eighteenth Century Montreal Merchants and Military Personnel in New France: Emic and Etic Approaches." PhD diss., Michigan State University.

Johnson, William, and Milton W. Hamilton. 1926. *The Papers of Sir William Johnson*. 14 vols. Albany: University of the State of New York. https://catalog.hathitrust.org/Record/000622241.

Koops, Lisa H. 2018. "Musical Tweens: Child and Parent Views on Musical Engagement in Middle Childhood." *Music Education Research* 20: 412–26.

Morris, Ronald V. 2008. "Learning from a Community Festival or Reenactment." *International Journal of Social Education* 23, no. 2 (Fall/Winter): 61–78.

———. 2012. *History and Imagination: Reenactments for Elementary Social Studies*. New York: Rowman and Littlefield.

Rath, Richard Cullen. 2005. *How Early America Sounded*. Ithaca, NY: Cornell University Press.

Riedinger, Kelly. 2012. "Family Connections: Family Conversations in Informal Learning Environments." *Childhood Education* 88: 125–27.

Sheridan, Mark, Iona MacDonald, and Charles G. Byrne. 2011. "Gaelic Singing and Oral Tradition." *International Journal of Music Education* 29: 172–90.

Thwaites, Reuben G., ed. 1896–1901. *The Jesuit Relations and Allied Documents: Travels and Explorations of the Jesuit Missionaries in New France, 1610–1791; the Original French, Latin, and Italian Texts, with English Translations and Notes*. 73 vols. Cleveland: Burrows Brothers. http://moses.creighton.edu/kripke/jesuitrelations/.

Waldron, Janice. 2007. "Once the Beat Gets Going It Really Grooves: Informal Music Learning as Experience by Two Irish Traditional Musicians." *International Journal of Community Music* 1: 89–103.

Waltz, Robert B, ed. 2008a. "Ah! Si Mon Moine Voulait Danser!" In *The Minnesota Heritage Songbook*. https://mnheritagesongbook.net/the-songs/foreign-language-songs/french-ah-si-mon-moine-voulait-danser/.

———. 2008b. "C'est L'aviron." In *The Minnesota Heritage Songbook*. https://mnheritagesongbook.net/the-songs/foreign-language-songs/cest-laviron/.

12

PRESERVING THE PAST FOR THE FUTURE

Sustainable and Responsible Curation of Colonial Archaeological Collections in the Midwest

ERIKA K. HARTLEY, FORT ST. JOSEPH CURATORIAL FELLOW, CHRISTINA H. ARSENEAU, DIRECTOR, NILES HISTORY CENTER, AND MICHAEL S. NASSANEY, PROFESSOR EMERITUS, WESTERN MICHIGAN UNIVERSITY

REPOSITORIES, LARGE AND SMALL, STRUGGLE WITH COLLECTION MANagement due to limited resources for secure storage space, routine care and updates, and full-time curatorial staff (Allen, Ford, and Kennedy 2019; Brin, McManamon, and Niven 2013; Buck and Gilmore 2007; Childs and Benden 2017; Kersel 2015a, 2015b; Sullivan and Childs 2003). Coupled with the challenge of burgeoning collection size, the management problem—better known as the curation crisis—becomes unimaginably overwhelming. To make matters worse, aspects of collection management are often deprioritized in favor of more pressing needs identified by museum and repository personnel, such as building improvements and public outreach initiatives (Buck and Gilmore 2007).

Despite the curation crisis, repositories of all sizes and types are charged with organizing, managing, and enforcing preservation standards to meet ethical responsibilities (Buck and Gilmore 2007; Johnson 2003; Kersel 2015a, 2015b; Sullivan and Childs 2003). Without proper preservation and documentation, the value of a collection is severely diminished. Curators, archivists, and museum professionals argue that "good curation practice requires more than just improving the storage and environmental conditions. Collections need to be well-organized, documented, and stored in such a way as to promote preservation and security, while also making collections accessible for research and educational purposes" (Morehouse 2019, 3). Those who use collections for research can appreciate this point and recognize the importance of collection management.

Curatorial practices such as regular inventories, accessioning, cataloging, and conservation ensure the longevity of a collection. Accessible collections allow researchers to ask new questions, make comparisons to other sites, and implement advanced technologies for analysis, all of which lead to a better understanding of the past (Allen and Ford 2019). Extant collections can provide data for masters theses and dissertations (Allen and Ford 2019). A collection that lacks integrity due to poor preservation and improper collection management procedures limits the possibility of future archaeological inquiries.

Educators and museum personnel can also benefit from a well-managed collection by using the materials to engage students and the public. For instance, students can refine their critical thinking skills and obtain hands-on experience in the classroom by identifying and examining artifacts. This type of educational promotion can heighten interest in a collection and encourage students to become more involved in archaeological endeavors, sign up for a field school, and conduct independent research. Students also learn the importance of curation and collection management by working with collections and encountering curatorial challenges such as unsuitable packaging materials, illegible paperwork, and unorganized boxes (Williams and Ridgway 2019).

Outreach initiatives remind the public about the significance of archaeological sites, their research potential, and, more broadly, the importance of archaeology and history in constructing our national heritage. Collections are crucial to attaining these goals and presenting modern interpretations of historical sites. For example, artifacts on display allow the public to observe authentic objects from the past and use them as a vehicle to travel back in time and imagine the types of clothes people wore, the houses they lived in, and the activities they conducted on a daily basis. Public interest in historic places, museums, and archaeological projects often stems from and is maintained through effective exhibits and programs. Without well-managed collections, these types of outreach endeavors are difficult to develop (Morehouse 2019).

For more than a century there has been considerable interest in examining material evidence of seventeenth- and eighteenth-century French and later British activities in the western Great Lakes region. In the late nineteenth century, avocational archaeologists, local collectors, and historians recovered artifacts from colonial sites with an understanding that these items could assist them in learning about the past and were critical in efforts to commemorate and interpret historic places (Nassaney 2008, 2009). In the absence of relevant historical documents, archaeology contributes to our knowledge of these sites, their occupants' identities, and their daily activities (Nassaney 2009). Many people in the colonial Midwest were illiterate, and others who could read and write did not record prosaic activities. Thus, through archaeology and the examination of collections at sites such as Forts Michilimackinac, Ouiatenon, and St. Joseph, information about European exploration and settlements can be gleaned, particularly in regard to architecture, trade, subsistence practices, and social relationships especially with the surrounding Native Americans (Nassaney 2009).

At Fort Ouiatenon, archaeological excavations began in 1968 after surface evidence of eighteenth-century artifacts found a year earlier ended the search to relocate the fort (Noble 2018). Various scholars, groups, and institutions have conducted site investigations. As a result, artifacts recovered from the fort have not been curated as one large collection, leading to inconsistent management practices over the years. The variation in excavation and curation standards has impacted the collection's research potential and accessibility. Today, the Tippecanoe County Historical Association (TCHA) recognizes these challenges and is working to implement better collection management and preservation policies and practices.

The Fort Michilimackinac artifact collection is a result of over sixty years of archaeological work at the site. Initial excavations began in 1959, motivated by the desire for a reconstruction of the fort and public interpretation of the site (Evans 2013; Nassaney 2009). Since then, much of Fort Michilimackinac has been subject to archaeological investigation, providing information that has been used to reconstruct fifteen buildings, many of which include interpretive exhibits (Evans 2013). The site employs living history interpreters during the summer months, when visitors can also view ongoing excavations (Nassaney 2009). Items within the collection, now housed permanently at the Petersen Center in Mackinaw City, Michigan, have been instrumental in interpretation, reconstruction, and public engagement (Lynn Evans, pers. comm., 2021). The many curatorial improvements implemented on the collection over the years have aided these initiatives and provide examples of attainable preservation practices.

Artifact collection at Fort St. Joseph began in the late nineteenth century as avocational historians recovered several thousand artifacts from the vicinity of the fort (figure 12.1); the area was eventually marked by a commemorative boulder (Nassaney 2008). Recognizing the importance of this history, the collectors retained the artifacts, which lacked detailed provenience information, and later donated them to the Fort St. Joseph Museum (now the Niles History Center). Nearly a century later in 1998, archaeologists from Western Michigan University (WMU) led by Michael Nassaney surveyed the same area, identified material evidence of the fort, and initiated the Fort St. Joseph Archaeological Project (Nassaney, 1999). Excavation continues at the site today, and all artifacts recovered are stored and curated at the Niles History Center. However, the artifact collection has been subject to different curation practices, moved between buildings, placed on loan, and sometimes separated from assigned catalog numbers. To rectify these management inconsistencies, the Niles History Center and the Fort St. Joseph Archaeological Project developed the Fort St. Joseph curatorial fellowship. The goal of this position is to identify common preservation challenges and best curation practices, address the problems facing the Fort St. Joseph collection, and create a sustainable collections management plan. In hopes of assisting other institutions facing similar collection conundrums, we aim to develop, outline, and implement best practices here.

The collections of Forts Michilimackinac, Ouiatenon, and St. Joseph are a result of research projects and the interests of local collectors. While each face their own preservation challenges from packaging to accessibility to funding for a full-time conservator, the collections are all important to the study of the colonial Midwest. The discrepancy in curatorial practices is a result of varying acquisition, preservation, and management procedures at each site as well as the diverse capacities and expertise of the agencies that have managed the collections since they were formed. Here, we examine the management of each collection in detail and suggest attainable plans for the sustainable curation of colonial archaeological collections in Midwest repositories and beyond.

Figure 12.1 Members of the Miami Cross Society combed local agricultural fields in search of evidence of Fort St. Joseph. Courtesy of the Niles History Center.

CURATING OUIATENON

Fort Ouiatenon—the focus of this volume—was one link in the great chain of fortified trading posts that served religious, military and commercial functions in the eighteenth-century French and British efforts to secure the interior of the continent (Noble 2018). Located near a strategic portage connecting the *pays d'en haut* and the Illinois Country, the fort played a role in the events that culminated in American control over the region that came to be known as the Old Northwest. From 1717 to 1791, soldiers, priests, fur traders and their families, and occupational specialists such as blacksmiths lived adjacent to a large population of Wea and related Native American groups, leaving behind a significant archaeological record of their activities. After a long search to relocate the fort in the twentieth century, surface evidence of colonial artifacts led to archaeological excavations beginning in 1968 that prompted interest in the material legacy of the site (Noble 2018).

Several authors have summarized the history of investigations at the fort (e.g., chapter 2, this volume; Noble 1991, 2018). These overviews reveal how varying research designs, collection methods, and spatial controls have led to the absence of a consistent protocol for recording and curating archaeological data from the site. In his assessment of the importance of these data in the early 1980s, Noble (1982, 40) opined that "the Ouiatenon artifact assemblage has grown to one of the largest curated collections of eighteenth-century European archaeological specimens in North America. The value of this collection to future researchers concerned with the colonial frontier is immeasurable." Of course, the value of any archaeological collection is dependent upon not only the degree of preservation and integrity of the deposits but also the development and implementation of a plan for its curation. An overview of the archaeological collection and curation practices at Ouiatenon exposes some limitations that should be mitigated to maximize the use of the collection in the future.

Different individuals and groups have worked at Fort Ouiatenon and bequeathed us collections that have been moved on several occasions and subjected to irregular curatorial practices, with implications for their research potential. Table 1 summarizes the Ouiatenon site investigations and the curated collections. The investigations can be grouped into three periods based on the goals of the investigators: exploratory (1968–1973), intensive survey (1974–1979), and extensive survey (1986–present) (cf. Noble 1991, 76).

The exploratory period began after a concentration of eighteenth-century artifacts was discovered in 1967 and the TCHA invited James H. Kellar, then director of the Glenn A. Black Laboratory of Archaeology (GBL) at Indiana University–Bloomington, to conduct archaeological field school investigations at the presumed site in the summers of 1968 and 1969 (chapter 1, this volume; Kellar 1970; chapter 2, this volume).

TABLE 12.1 SUMMARY OF OUIATENON SITE INVESTIGATIONS AND CURATED COLLECTIONS

Year	Field Activity	Principal Investigator	Methods and Areas of Investigation	Curation Repository	Collection Condition and Accessibility	Related Publications and Reports
1968–1969	Site identification: archaeological field school	James Kellar, Indiana University–Bloomington	Central excavation block along north palisade wall	Glenn A. Black Laboratory (1968–present)	Cataloged, unanalyzed, accessible	Kellar (1970); Jackson (2005); Myers (2019); Noble (1991); Pope-Pfingston and Justice (1993)
1971	Site identification: avocational excavation confined to the plow zone	Larry Chowning, Tippecanoe County Historical Association	Northeast interior of the post	Tippecanoe County Historical Association	Cataloged, unanalyzed, accessible	Myers (2019); Noble (1991)
1972	Site identification: avocational excavation confined to the plow zone	Claude White, Tippecanoe County Historical Association	Unknown	Tippecanoe County Historical Association	Cataloged, unanalyzed, accessible	Myers (2019)
1973	Site identification: avocational excavation in and below the plow zone	Larry Chowning, Tippecanoe County Historical Association	Southwestern portion of the site	Tippecanoe County Historical Association	Cataloged, unanalyzed, accessible	Myers (2019); Noble (1991)

TABLE 12.1 CONTINUED

1974–1975	Site evaluation: geophysical survey	Geosciences Department, Purdue University	Unknown	On file, Purdue University	Limited accessibility	von Frese (1978, 1984); von Frese and Noble (1984)
1974–1976	Site evaluation/ data recovery: dissertation research	Judith Tordoff, Michigan State University	Exploratory trenching to determine site limits and ground-truthing geophysical survey results	Michigan State University (1974–2000); Tippecanoe County Historical Association (2000–present)	Limited analysis, cataloged, accessible	Jackson (2005); Martin (1986); Tordoff (1980, 1983); von Frese (1978, 1984); von Frese and Noble (1984)
1977–1979	Site evaluation/ data recovery: dissertation research	Vergil Noble, Michigan State University	Systematic sampling of the north half of the site and limited block excavations in areas of interest	Michigan State University (1977–2000); Tippecanoe County Historical Association (2000–present)	Limited analysis, cataloged, accessible	Jackson (2005); Martin (1986); Noble (1978, 1979, 1980, 1982, 1983); Sauer et al. (1988); von Frese (1978, 1984); von Frese and Noble (1984)
1986–1988	Extensive survey to locate and investigate Native American sites	Neal Trubowitz and James R. Jones III, University of Indiana–Indianapolis	Sites in the vicinity of Ouiatenon	Glenn A. Black Laboratory (1986–present)	Limited analysis, cataloged, accessible	Jones (1988); Trubowitz (1992)

TABLE 12.1 CONTINUED

2009	Geophysical survey	Michael Strezewski, University of Southern Indiana, and Robert G. McCullough, Indiana University, Purdue University, Fort Wayne	Large-scale survey in and around the fort	University of Southern Indiana	Soon to be uploaded to the Digital Archaeological Record	Strezewski and McCollough (2010)
2012–2013	Data recovery: archaeological field school	Michael Strezewski, University of Southern Indiana	Tested magnetic anomalies outside western palisade; excavated Native American built structure	Tippecanoe County Historical Association	Artifacts washed and cataloged; comprehensive report completed	Strezewski (2014)
2016–2017	Geophysical survey	Michael Strezewski, University of Southern Indiana	Large-scale survey in and around the fort	University of Southern Indiana	Soon to be uploaded to the Digital Archaeological Record	Strezewski and McCollough (2017)

From 1971 to 1973, the TCHA sponsored continued exploratory work by local volunteers under the direction of Larry Chowning and Claude White, archaeology students at Purdue University. Those teams confined their efforts to screening for materials located in the plow zone, with some limited excavations below the plow zone in the southwest area of the site in 1973. These investigations resulted in the accumulation of numerous artifacts and accelerated local interest in the study of Ouiatenon, leading the TCHA to acquire the site from private landowners in 1972.

The large artifact assemblage derived from the 1968–1969 excavations, still curated at the GBL, has never been fully analyzed and reported in detail, though a management study was later prepared (Pope-Pfingston and Justice 1993). In the 1980s Neal Trubowitz, then at Indiana University–Indianapolis, acquired a loan of the pre-1974 Fort Ouiatenon artifacts, still stored in their original paper field bags at the GBL. Trubowitz directed students and volunteers in cleaning, rebagging, and preparing a preliminary inventory of these collections and conducted research on selected artifact classes leading to brief summary reports and unpublished student research papers (Noble 1991, 75; Trubowitz 1989a, 1989b, 1990, 1991; Trubowitz, pers. comm., 2021). The 1968–1969 collections were returned to the GBL in 1990 (Pope-Pfingston and Justice 1993), whereas those from the 1971–1973 excavations were subsequently curated by the TCHA. Prior to their return to the TCHA, a more detailed inventory and photographic record was completed under the direction of Noel Justice at the GBL, and all of the early excavated collections up to and including the 1971 field season were cataloged (Pope-Pfingston and Justice 1993). This project consumed two years of work and amassed a collection amounting to sixty-five cubic feet of storage. The 1972 and 1973 collections including soil samples and fine-screened materials remained uncataloged. The GBL currently curates over 9,900 catalog numbers, and those materials are accessible for study (Glenn A. Black Laboratory of Archaeology 2020). All but the 1968–1969 collections and associated notes from Ouiatenon are currently housed in the basement of the TCHA's History Center.

The period of intensive survey began when the TCHA invited Charles E. Cleland from Michigan State University (MSU) to conduct site excavations under two three-year agreements. Judith Tordoff directed the fieldwork for her dissertation at MSU from 1974 to 1976, while Vergil Noble served in the same capacity from 1977 to 1979 (Noble 1983; Tordoff 1983). In 1974 and 1975, Purdue University conducted a geophysical survey to identify anomalies of possible cultural significance (von Frese 1978, 1984; von Frese and Noble 1984). These geophysical data remain at Purdue University (Ralph von Frese, pers. comm., 2021). In the six years of intensive study by MSU, student crews determined that the site of Fort Ouiatenon was largely intact. The wide variety of cultural features beneath the plow zone, coupled with exceptional preservation, demonstrated that Ouiatenon can be used to address important anthropological and historical questions related to colonialism and the fur trade. Be that as it may, these excavations led to the creation of a very large collection of field notes, artifacts, animal remains, and other archaeological materials that were processed (i.e., washed, labeled, cataloged) by MSU archaeologists. The majority of these collections were transferred to the TCHA in 2000, though MSU may retain some of the records associated with the collection (Kelly Lippie, pers. comm., 2021).

Trubowitz and James R. Jones III began investigating related sites associated with Euro-American and Native American interaction in the Lafayette area of Tippecanoe County in 1986, ushering in a period of extensive survey (Jones 1988; Trubowitz 1992). All the collections they made from the sites surrounding Fort Ouiatenon (e.g., the Wea village site) are curated at the GLB with the exception of several large maps and 4x5-inch black and white photo negatives that remain in Trubowitz's possession (pers. comm., 2021).

After a considerable hiatus, work on predominantly Native American components in proximity to the fort resumed. Michael Strezewski (University of Southern Indiana) conducted large geophysical surveys in 2009 and 2016–2017 in and around the fort site to document the presence of subsurface anomalies in some of the surrounding Indigenous village areas (Strezewski and McCullough 2010, 2017). No artifacts were collected. In 2013 he excavated a portion of a Native American house that had been identified through magnetometry near the western wall of the fort. All of the associated artifacts were washed and cataloged, and a report was submitted to the TCHA, which now curates the collection (Strezewski 2014).

With a few exceptions, all of the Ouiatenon archaeological collections are curated by the GBL and the TCHA. Materials from both of these repositories are accessible to researchers. Ideally, all these materials should be stored in one place; this may be possible if a suitable facility can be located in proximity to the fort. April Sievert, the current director of the GBL, indicates that its collections are now part of the new Indiana University Museum of Archaeology and Anthropology. The old repository is undergoing complete renovation, and all collections have been moved to temporary quarters. The archives are still accessible, though they are more difficult to search at present. Sievert (pers. comm., 2021) stated that the administrators of the new museum consider the collections highly significant. They want to encourage research and exhibits on Ouiatenon and are working to consolidate extant information from Ouiatenon and related sites.

The TCHA collections are equally sizable and significant. Because collection space is limited in the basement of the TCHA's History Center where the Ouiatenon artifacts and associated records are stored (figure 12.2), efforts are under way to identify a new storage space to accommodate the artifacts, records, offices, and possibly exhibits. Kelly Lippie, the current curator of collections, monitors the temperature and humidity of the current space on a regular basis. Cameras and an alarm system ensure that the collection is secure. The handwritten field forms and notes are being digitized, a tedious and time-consuming process. While some of the artifacts are stored in ziplock bags, others are kept in open storage in boxes and cabinets and lack proper labels, thereby jeopardizing contextual information (figure 12.3). No comprehensive catalog exists for the entire TCHA collection, thereby making it difficult to locate and determine the context of individual specimens.

TCHA staff and volunteers have been working to organize the collections and make them more accessible for study. They have observed that some artifacts in the collection from the Chowning excavations have become intermingled with those collected by MSU when materials were used repeatedly to create displays for public viewing at the blockhouse (Rick Conwell, pers. comm., 2021). There is no way of knowing if all the Chowning materials are represented in the collection because there is limited documentation (e.g., unit excavation forms, complete inventory) from these excavations. Fortunately, the Chowning materials can be distinguished from those collected by MSU archaeologists because the latter employed a consistent numbering system and took care to conserve many of the objects. Kelly Lippie (pers. comm., 2021) indicates

Figure 12.2. Storage space for collections is limited in the basement of the Tippecanoe County Historical Association's History Center. Photo by Brooke Sauter.

Figure 12.3. Open storage boxes can lead to comingling of artifacts and loss of provenience data. Photo courtesy of Leslie Martin Conwell.

that it is difficult to locate specific artifacts in the collection and relate them to the records. Moreover, the open storage of many artifact types has potentially conflated their provenience, thereby compromising their research potential. Efforts are currently under way to reorganize the materials, link them to the records, verify their provenience, and make them more accessible for research.

Noble (1991, 70) rightly noted that artifact inventories from the early investigations (pre-1974) were "superficial by today's standards." This condition also extends to the inventories provided in the reports submitted by MSU to the TCHA (e.g., Noble 1980, appendix C). Noble (1991, 73–74) indicated that the Tordoff and Noble dissertations contain a comprehensive catalog of the artifacts recovered from the site by MSU field crews. These are highly generalized descriptions; quantifications lack detailed attribute information (e.g., 88 bottle glass, 7 brown glazed redware), and the items are not widely accessible. Indeed, publication brings data on the collections to the light of day; both Noble (1991) and Myers (2019, 275) have remarked on the "paucity of published information on the archaeology" conducted at the site, dissertations notwithstanding (e.g., Noble 1983; Tordoff 1983). Consequently, further research on Ouiatenon is dependent on consulting the original collections, though dissertations such as Terrance Martin's (1986) analysis of the Ouiatenon animal remains and Misty Jackson's (2005) study of the folk and scientific classifications of the artifacts in the collections are notable exceptions.

In sum, the artifact collection from Fort Ouiatenon is similar to collections curated by many small municipal and county museums and historical societies throughout the Midwest, including the Fort St. Joseph collection before the Niles History Center and the Fort St. Joseph Archaeological Project began prioritizing curation in the past few years. Such entities often expend great effort in identifying and recovering archaeological materials, whereas considerably less attention is paid to preserving, recording, and organizing materials for long-term care and easy access. It comes as no surprise that state- and federal-level organizations often have more resources for professional personnel and facilities that approach and meet the standards needed to sustain archaeological collections for future use. One such state agency is Mackinac State Historic Parks (MSHP). We now turn to the work the agency has done and continues to do at Fort Michilimackinac.

SIXTY YEARS OF COLLECTING AT FORT MICHILIMACKINAC

Located at the Straits of Mackinac in northern Michigan, Fort Michilimackinac was established in 1715 and became a main fur trading center in the Great Lakes region (Evans 2013; Nassaney 2009; Stone 1974a). Jesuit missionaries were initially drawn to the area in the second half of the seventeenth century due to a large Native American presence at this strategic location (Evans 2013; Miller and Stone 1970). The missionaries first settled on Mackinac Island in the 1670s but a year later moved to St. Ignace north of the straits, where land was more suitable for agriculture (Evans 2013; Miller and Stone 1970). Shortly afterward fur traders arrived, and Fort de Buade was established in 1690 when the crown realized the economic and political importance of this area (Evans 2013). Seven years later the fort was abandoned; Fort Michilimackinac was built in 1715 on the south side of the straits (Evans 2013). The growth and development of this fortified trading center is demonstrated by its expansion in the mid-1730s and several later building and palisade improvements (Evans 2013; Heldman 1976; Miller and Stone 1970, 14). French occupation of the fort ended in 1761 when the British took control as a result of the Seven Years' War (Evans 2013; Heldman 1976). Soon after, British soldiers and traders inhabited the fort along with French civilians. Occupation of Fort Michilimackinac ended in 1781 when the population moved to Mackinac Island and the fort was abandoned and destroyed (Evans 2013).

Fort Michilimackinac and a portion of the eighteenth-century village just outside of the palisade wall were preserved as a municipal park in 1857 by land speculators (Lynn Evans, pers. comm., 2021; Miller and Stone 1970). In 1904 the site was acquired by the State of Michigan and placed under the control of the Mackinac Island State Park Commission (MISPC) (Mackinac State Historic Parks n.d.a; Miller and Stone 1970). Archaeological work was first conducted in 1932 by Chris Schneider, the park superintendent, resulting in the location and reconstruction of the 1760 palisade (Miller and Stone 1970).

Approximately twenty-five years later excavations resumed, motivated by the desire for a complete reconstruction of the fort and public interpretation of the site (Miller and Stone 1970). The MISPC and MSU's Department of Anthropology and Museum agreed to form an archaeological program; the MISPC sponsored the work, while MSU Museum personnel directed the excavations (Miller and Stone 1970). The museum also analyzed, cataloged, and housed the material remains recovered from the site, apart from those on display at the fort (Miller and Stone 1970). The museum's curator of anthropology was responsible for the program (Moreau S. Maxwell, 1959–1964; Charles E. Cleland, 1965–1969), and fieldwork was directed by a number of prominent archaeologists including Moreau S. Maxwell, Lewis R. Binford, Carl Jantzen, Ronald Vanderwall, Lyle M. Stone, and James A. Brown (Miller and Stone 1970, 19). The field crew consisted of prisoners from the Michigan Corrections Department's Pellston Corrections Camp until 1966, when an archaeology training program for MSU anthropology students was developed at the site (Miller and Stone 1970).

In 1969 the partnership with MSU ended, and the MISPC took ownership of the collection, moving it to the MISPC facility in Lansing (Mackinac State Historic Parks 2009). After the archaeology season was completed each year, staff members cataloged and analyzed the artifacts before they were stored in Lansing (Lynn Evans, pers. comm., 2021). The MISPC Lansing facility included a storage and conservation area as well as a research library (Mackinac State Historic Parks 2009). During this time, the MISPC staffed a curator of archaeology (Lyle M. Stone, 1969–1974; Donald P. Heldman, 1975–1995) and a collections conservator (William Fritz, 1983–2007).

Over the next twenty years, the need for a year-round facility at Fort Michilimackinac was realized, especially as the number of staff increased (Lynn Evans, pers. comm., 2021). In 1994 MSHP, the parks program of the MISPC, hired its first registrar, Linnea Aukee, to oversee collection management and preservation. Lynn Evans became the curator of archaeology in 1996 after excavating at the site and working with the collection for seven years prior. In 2001, the Eugene and Marian Petersen Archaeology and History Center in Mackinaw City was designed and built with space for the collection, a conservation lab, and a research library, the same facilities included in the Lansing building (Lynn Evans, pers. comm., 2021). This move was part of a larger plan to improve management of the collection, which included some one million archaeologically recovered artifacts and twenty thousand historical components (archival documents and artifacts that were collected and donated) (Mackinac State Historic Parks n.d.b). Several collection improvements were identified, including additional collection staff members, a collection database system, data entry of collection records, exhibit upgrades, annual inventories, a conservation plan, and a revised collection policy (Mackinac State Historic Parks 2009). Brian Jaeschke (pers. comm., 2019), the current registrar, was added to the staff in 2006 to assist in managing the collection. In 2008, Jennifer Lis became the collections conservator; however, after she left in 2011, MSHP began to rely on contract conservators. Once all the items related to the collection were housed in the Petersen Center, staff members aimed to address "inventory and control issues, including discrepancies in artifact numbering" (Mackinac State Historic Parks 2009).

Monetary resources to manage the collection have been and continue to be acquired from admission fees to Fort Michilimackinac (later known as Colonial Michilimackinac), membership dues, donors, and grants (Mackinac State Historic Parks 2009). Like many other historic places, additional resources and support are also provided by volunteers and the local community. Nevertheless, additional funding was needed to drastically enhance the management of the collection's archaeological components, and in 2009 MSHP applied for the Museums for America Grant (Mackinac State Historic Parks 2009). A physical inventory of the more than 122,000 archaeological artifacts or groups of artifacts recovered from the site was the main goal, as this task had not been completed since excavations began (Lynn Evans, pers. comm., 2021). During this process, MSHP was able to resolve cataloging discrepancies by ensuring that the artifact number and location written in the original catalog matches the information in the Argus collection database, the artifact container, and the storage box (Lynn Evans, pers. comm., 2021). The completion of this project allowed MSHP greater intellectual control so that staff members and outside researchers could better utilize the collection.

The collection is a result of over sixty years of archaeological investigation at Fort Michilimackinac. The items within the collection contribute to MSHP's public education and engagement programs as well as the reconstruction of the fort (Mackinac State Historic Parks 2009) (figure 12.4). The many curatorial improvements implemented for the collection over the last thirty years have facilitated these efforts. Although MSHP does not have unlimited resources to achieve its top curatorial desires (e.g., a full-time conservator), the agency provides a model for achievable preservation practices that repositories should seek to emulate. The Niles History Center, charged with preserving the Fort St. Joseph collection, is one repository that has prioritized the development of better curatorial practices by examining the standards of others such as the Fort Michilimackinac collection.

Figure 12.4. Currently on display in the Powder Magazine exhibit, these artifacts recovered from excavations at the fort assist in its interpretation. Courtesy of Mackinac State Historic Parks.

AVOCATIONAL AND PROFESSIONAL COLLECTIONS FROM FORT ST. JOSEPH

Fort St. Joseph, built by the French in 1691, was a mission, trading post, and garrison complex located in present-day Niles, Michigan (Nassaney 2019). Control of the fort fell to the British following the Seven Years' War (1756–1763), with short periods of both Native American and Spanish rule. Artifacts collected at Fort St. Joseph fall roughly into two categories: (1) items collected by Niles residents during the late nineteenth and early twentieth centuries and donated to the local Museum and (2) items recovered by the Fort St. Joseph Archaeological Project, which began with a locational survey in 1998 and continues to the present.

To discuss the challenges of curating the avocational and professional collections from Fort St. Joseph, it is necessary to examine the history of collecting and museums in the Niles area. The organization known today as the Niles History Center consists of the Fort St. Joseph Museum and the Historic Chapin Mansion. The museum is located in the former boiler and carriage houses of the Chapin Mansion (figure 12.5). The mansion was built as a private residence by prominent Niles citizens Henry and Ruby Chapin in 1882. Their grandchildren sold the home to the City of Niles in 1932 for the sum of $300 with the stipulation that the buildings be used for "civic purposes." The mansion itself served as the Niles City Hall from 1933 until 2012. The once separate carriage and boiler houses, located behind the main house, were physically connected through a 1939 Works Progress Administration project and became the Fort St. Joseph Museum. After 2012, city administration offices were relocated, and the Niles History Center was formed to interpret the historic home as well as continue operation of the Fort St. Joseph Museum.

Figure 12.5. The 2016 Western Michigan University archaeological field school at the Fort St. Joseph Museum. Photo by Genevieve Padley.

Long before the Fort St. Joseph Museum was established, Niles residents collected and exhibited their finds. The first notable "exhibition" originates from an 1842 display of natural history specimens owned by Clement Barron, who began his collection in England during the 1830s. He immigrated to America in 1837 and found his way to Niles. After Barron's death his grandson, Clement Weatherby, continued displaying his grandfather's materials around town. By this time, it had grown to include taxidermic birds, reptiles, fish, and other animals, along with "arrowheads" (likely an assortment of projectile points and other stone tools). No complete inventory of the original Barron collection is known to exist. Some of the specimens can still be found at the Fernwood Botanical Garden and Nature Preserve and the Niles History Center.

While Barron's museum was gaining notoriety, it seems that the old fort was largely ignored. According to Niles historian Ralph Ballard (1948, 35), no one thought much of "Indian relics" and fort materials in the early days (though he notes that Barron was an exception). This changed in the 1890s when a group of four men (L. H. Beeson, E. H. Crane, E. D. Lombard, and W. Hillis Smith) began speculating about the old fort. The men—calling themselves the Miami Cross Society—scoured the agricultural fields where Fort St. Joseph was believed to be located, finding copper kettle parts, weapons, animal bones, beads, and other objects associated with the fort (Nassaney 2008, 99) (see figure 12.1). Many of their discoveries would find their way to the forthcoming Fort St. Joseph Museum. Thanks to their efforts, the fort became a point of pride for the community, leading to the eponymous Fort St. Joseph Historical Association (FSJHA) and the Fort St. Joseph Museum.

The "official" Niles Museum traces its history to 1932 with the organization of the FSJHA, whose mission was to "collect, preserve and exhibit [historical artifacts]." The building that housed the local newspaper, the *Niles Daily Star*, provided space for these exhibits. In 1939, the FSJHA opened the Fort St. Joseph Museum at its present location in the former Chapin Mansion carriage and boiler house. From 1939 until 1978, the FSJHA served as the governing authority of the museum and operated as a nonprofit organization. A curator was hired and later a director. During the 1970s, several other historical groups merged with the FSJHA. In 1978, the Niles City Council created the Niles Historical Commission, placing the museum under the authority of the commission. Governance of the Fort St. Joseph Museum passed to the City of Niles. By 1993 the Niles Historical Commission was defunct, and control passed to the Niles City Council as the trustee.

Records for the collection exist dating from 1932, and several describe items collected from the area of the old fort. Details vary greatly; often donations are simply noted as "stone or iron tools" with no record of a precise count. Locations of the finds, if provided at all, are never specific. Many records merely ascribe the specimens to "the vicinity of the fort." George I. Quimby (University of Michigan Museum of

Anthropology) and Glenn A. Black (Indiana Historical Society) studied the materials attributed to the fort in 1937 when they were examining eighteenth-century sites and collections in order to establish a chronology for the western Great Lakes region (Nassaney 2008, 101). Quimby reasoned that these objects were good chronological markers for postcontact Native American sites, and he used them to define his middle historic period (1670–1760). In October 1974, Lyle M. Stone (1974b) examined many of these materials, verified their authenticity, and confirmed their derivation from eighteenth-century French and English occupations. However, because many of the early local collectors also traveled "out west" to procure items, one cannot assume that all materials attributed to Fort St. Joseph actually derived from the fort.

During the 1970s and 1980s some efforts were made by the museum's curators to organize the collection, which may have been spurred by Stone's (1974b) recommendation to prioritize the preservation of the collection above all else (e.g., research and reconstruction). Per Stone's suggestion, many of the "Fort" artifacts were cleaned, roughly sorted by function and type, and placed into acid-free boxes. A numbering system was created, though it is not the standard three-part number system used today by most museums, and many artifacts were not labeled. Charles Hulse (1977) completed the most comprehensive inventory for his master's thesis, and his work serves as a finding aid for artifacts in the collection.

In the 1990s, Fort St. Joseph Museum staff sought additional information about how to better manage the museum and its collections. An institutional assessment (MAP I) was conducted in September 1996 by the Museum Assessment Program of the American Association of Museums (Carr 1996). The MAP I surveyor, Joseph D. Carr, spent a day at the museum in order to tour the collection's storage room and meet with the museum director and city administrator. In his report, Carr pointed out the need for long-term planning, efficient environmental control, better lighting, engaging exhibits, and additional staff. Though Carr's assessment was not fully enacted upon, the museum staff remained committed to discovering the fort's history and using the collection to base their inferences.

Professional investigation of the site began in 1998 when a group of Niles history enthusiasts called Support the Fort, Inc., reached out to archaeologists at WMU. Support the Fort, Inc., was organized in 1992 with the goal of reconstructing Fort St. Joseph based on the discovery of physical remains. The fort's exact location was confirmed, and the Fort St. Joseph Archaeological Project was established (Nassaney 1999; Nassaney and Cremin 2002). This rediscovery was made largely possible by Joseph L. Peyser, who, through extensive documentary research in the 1970s and 1980s, ascertained that the location of the fort was likely on the east bank of the St. Joseph River in Niles. Subsequent excavations by WMU archaeologists, working with field school students, have led to the recovery of more than three hundred thousand artifacts. After excavation each season, project staff and students produce an inventory of the artifacts in Microsoft Excel and prepare the artifacts for storage at the Fort St. Joseph Museum. The associated documents (field notes, artifact inventories, photographs, maps, field reports and summaries, published articles, and conference papers) largely remain at WMU.

In 2005 a second survey and assessment was performed, specifically on the collection management of the Fort St. Joseph Archaeological Project (Fritz 2005). William Fritz, collections conservator for the MSHP, lent his professional services as part of an "angel project" from the Michigan Alliance for the Conservation of Cultural Heritage. His study was limited to the management and storage of the archaeological artifacts held in the WMU Department of Anthropology lab space and the Fort St. Joseph Museum. Again, several suggestions were made, most of which pertain specifically to the treatment, storage, and long-term curation of artifacts that alerted project personnel to the importance of proper procedures. Fritz also recommended the implementation of an emergency management plan.

A classification system for organizing the items was developed by Amanda Brooks (2010), who reorganized the artifacts recovered through excavation by raw material followed by function (e.g., iron, nail; glass, container). In tandem, Erin Claussen (2010) developed an artifact lexicon to standardize classification when entering artifact information into the collection management database PastPerfect. Claussen chose PastPerfect because the program was already being used by the Fort St. Joseph Museum, meaning that the data could be shared between the two institutions. Afterward a paid intern, usually a WMU graduate or senior-level anthropology student, was appointed each semester to enter the information into PastPerfect and to integrate the new items into the collection according to Brooks's and Claussen's protocols.

As the recovered artifacts began to number in the tens of thousands, storage space became an issue. A back room at the museum, roughly 250 square feet, was designated for archaeological storage. When the collection outgrew this space, the artifacts were moved to a basement room at the Chapin Mansion. Though the space was larger, basements are never ideal for storage, as they are prone to flooding and excessive dampness. Almost as soon as these artifacts were settled into their new home, the basement did indeed experience a flood from a burst boiler pipe. No artifacts were harmed, but the decision was made to move the items immediately to a room on the first floor, where they remain today. In a few years the collection will outgrow this space as well, prompting staff members to begin considering an alternative storage location.

In addition to limited physical space, environmental control has also been a concern at the Niles History Center. A steam boiler provided heat, and window air-conditioning units cooled the historical buildings. Once the artifacts were moved to their current location in the Chapin Mansion, a dehumidifier was added to help control humidity levels. To further improve the space, a new HVAC system was planned in 2018 and installed in 2020. This major upgrade has already aided in the collection's preservation.

Another problem has been inconsistent skill level and training of people handling the collections. Since the 1930s, the skill levels of the museum's curators and directors have varied greatly. At times, volunteers were left to catalog as well. Once the Fort St. Joseph Archaeological Project began, much of the work with the new finds were left to the WMU student intern. A new intern began each school year, sometimes each semester, and faced a steep learning curve. The student intern only had a few hours each week to learn the collection organizational chart and Niles History Center's storage system. At times, items were "misfiled" within the collection's storage area (i.e., placed in the wrong box) due to either a lack of understanding or haste. The storage location for the items housed at the Niles History Center was also not recorded in PastPerfect, making them even more difficult to access for research. In 2011, Nassaney applied for a small grant from the Digital Archaeological Record, a Mellon Foundation–supported initiative designed to store archaeological data from around the world for ready access to researchers (Nassaney 2012). Two graduate students spent the better part of a summer entering artifact inventories, images, and other archaeological data into the Digital Archaeological Record. Unfortunately, after the grant was over, the project and Niles History Center did not have the personnel or expertise to continue uploading data each field season, so we were unable to continue the process. The project continued to upload data into PastPerfect until 2018, when data stored at WMU was lost in the process of computer updates, and files had not been shared with the Niles History Center or backed up on the project's external hard drive.

Misplaced artifacts were not entirely the fault of staff and students. Within a few years, it became clear that the classification system was not working. The system called for sorting items first by material and then by function. With little variance, researchers study items by function and then consider material. Over the past twenty years, graduate and honor's theses have been published on architectural elements, gun parts, and lead seals, among other items (Davis 2014; Jones 2019; Loveland 2017). Fulfilling research requests meant sorting through various boxes to gather items made from stone, lead, copper alloy, etc., which is time-consuming and leaves open the possibility that materials/specimens might be returned to the wrong box.

Though the Niles History Center staff was able to improve the physical and environmental space, overhauling the collections system was a daunting task. A dedicated professional familiar with colonial artifacts was needed to implement best curation practices and develop a functional classification system for organizing the collections. A supporter of the Fort St. Joseph Archaeological Project was moved by the urgency of the "curation crisis" as presented by Arseneau, the Niles History Center director, and Nassaney, the project's then principal investigator, and offered to help us create and fund the Fort St.

Joseph Curatorial Fellowship. After this donor's initial financial gift, other donations followed. Erika Hartley, who had five years of experience as a teaching assistant, an assistant field director, and now director of the project, was selected as the curatorial fellow.

The first stage of the fellowship required familiarity with proper curation practices. Hartley traveled to two different repositories, MSHP and the Michigan Office of the State Archaeologist, to speak with their collections staff. Once she was back in Niles, a written plan was created. Hartley is currently in the process of implementing this plan.

Among the first improvements was the purchase of new boxes. Much of the Fort St. Joseph Archaeological Project artifacts were stored in square cardboard boxes divided into compartments to hold individual items. Working with an archival company, custom boxes were designed and fabricated from acid-free materials (figure 12.6). LED lights were installed in the storage room, which are safe for the artifacts and provide bright working light. A new artifact typology was developed and is being tested to organize the items primarily by function. The next phase will involve moving the three hundred thousand items into new boxes as well as integrating approximately one hundred thousand "pre-Project" items. This will allow for artifacts to be retrieved more easily for research and will provide better-organized storage space. Other recent acquisitions include a high-quality digital camera and a photo box that allow for professional-quality images as well as a digital monitoring system to store data about the collection room's environmental conditions.

Figure 12.6. Flat acid-free boxes were purchased to make finding artifacts in storage much easier. Reorganizing the items by function instead of material will also help. Here, we have begun separating the iron hardware (e.g., hinges, locks, and pintles) from the iron tools (e.g., awls, axes, files, and hoes). Courtesy of the Niles History Center.

With improvements to storage come better opportunities for research, public programs, and exhibits that will lead to greater public knowledge of this important historic place. More than one thousand artifacts have already been added to the museum's exhibits on Fort St. Joseph. New topical panels that highlight the fort's history (e.g., the role of the fur trade, military, and religion at the fort) now have illustrative artifacts. The Niles History Center's mission is to connect the past, present, and future. By ensuring the longevity of the Fort St. Joseph collection, Niles will have preserved an important vestige of its colonial past.

LESSONS LEARNED AND NEXT STEPS

The preservation practices and institutional resources differ for each of the collections presented in this chapter. As we have shown, various data collection strategies have been employed at colonial archaeological sites in the Midwest, leading to different curation challenges and opportunities. The types of artifacts found at these three eighteenth-century colonial sites are very similar, yet the excavation techniques, data recordation, and collection management procedures are markedly different. At Fort Ouiatenon, the archaeological techniques varied among the researchers excavating at the site over the years. Changing goals, procedures, and ownership can and often does lead to many unforeseen problems, especially regarding a collection's care and research potential. While most of the artifacts in the collections have been recovered through archaeological excavation at Forts Michilimackinac, Ouiatenon, and St. Joseph, many objects were also donated by local historians and collectors who may or may not have understood the importance of recording provenience. Thus, the acquisition methods for each collection can present their own challenges outside of the regular upkeep and required maintenance.

The approaches to collections from historic places such as Fort Michilimackinac have aided us in identifying ways to plan for the sustainable curation of the Fort St. Joseph collection. The steps taken and lessons learned can serve as a model for other repositories housing colonial archaeological collections such as those from Ouiatenon. During the first stage of the fellowship, we recognized that it was important for repository staff to understand what types of artifacts are in the collection, how and when they were acquired, and what purpose they will serve in the future (research material, exhibit displays, etc.).

At this step, it was also crucial for us to take time and identify the current issues and limitations of the Fort St. Joseph collection while envisioning the best possible outcomes of our curatorial improvements. As mentioned, the packaging, organization, climate, and lighting were immediate concerns. While some of these improvements were implemented, the reorganization of the collection has been a work in progress. To accompany this process, a comprehensive physical inventory is also under way. The accession and catalog numbers for some of the pre-Project items have become disassociated from the artifacts, highlighting the need to realize that not all of the pieces to this collection's puzzle may be found. Still, as the collection becomes better organized and manageable, we will be able to digitize records, catalog the items in PastPerfect, and ultimately increase the collection's accessibility for researchers and the public.

In the Fort Ouiatenon collection, a similar experience and undertaking has begun. Some of the artifacts recovered by the GBL at Indiana University–Bloomington and MSU have been found to lack records of their spatial provenience, decreasing their research potential. However, Kory Cooper along with undergraduate and graduate students at Purdue University have been and hope to continue linking spatial information from the excavations with these artifacts in the collection (Cooper, pers. comm., 2022). This requires considerable effort that will not go unrewarded if it will allow for further research that provides greater insights into the fort and its occupants. It is the authors' hopes that the practices employed in organizing and inventorying these collections can serve as models to assist other curators in developing a long-term plan and forestall expedient and ill-advised decisions.

As repositories continue to work toward better curation practices, the potential for what we can learn from and do with the artifacts in collections drastically increases. Unfortunately, it is not enough to ensure a collection's preservation for the future. A further step must be taken to promote the collection and access to it for those in academia and for the general public. Better collection management allows for more public outreach initiatives such as programs and exhibits. Together, the preservation efforts, the information gleaned from research, and the resulting outreach efforts at Forts Michilimackinac, Ouiatenon, and St. Joseph remind people about the significance of historic places, museums, and archaeological collections as we preserve the past for the future.

ACKNOWLEDGMENTS

The authors would like to thank a number of individuals and organizations for information that contributed to the completion of this paper, including Kelsey Grimm, Melody Pope, and April Sievert (Indiana University Museum of Archaeology and Anthropology); Lynn Evans and Brian Jaeschke (Mackinac State Historic Parks); Leslie Martin Conwell, Rick Conwell, and Kelly Lippie (Tippecanoe County Historical Association); and Kory Cooper, Terrance Martin, Vergil Noble, Michael Strezewski, and Neal Trubowitz.

REFERENCES

Allen, Rebecca, and Ben Ford, eds. 2019. *New Life for Archaeological Collections*. Lincoln: University of Nebraska Press.

Allen, Rebecca, Ben Ford, and J. Ryan Kennedy. 2019. "Introduction: Reclaiming the Research Potential of Archaeological Collections." In *New Life for Archaeological Collections*, ed. Rebecca Allen and Ben Ford, xiii–xxxix. Lincoln: University of Nebraska Press.

Ballard, Ralph. 1948. *Tales of Early Niles*. Niles, MI: Niles Printing Co.

Brin, Adam, Francis P. McManamon, and Kieron Niven, eds. 2013. *Caring for Digital Data in Archaeology: A Guide to Good Practice*. Oxford, UK: Oxbow Books.

Brooks, Amanda. 2010. "Collections Management Internship at the Michigan Office of the State Archaeologist and Its Application for the Fort St. Joseph Archaeological Project." MA internship report, Department of Anthropology, Western Michigan University, Kalamazoo.

Buck, Rebecca A., and Jean Allman Gilmore. 2007. *Collection Conundrums: Solving Collections Management Mysteries*. Washington, DC: American Association of Museums.

Carr, Joseph D. 1996. MAP I: Fort St. Joseph Museum. Unpublished institutional assessment, American Association of Museums, Washington DC.

Childs, S. Terry, and Danielle M. Benden. 2017. "A Checklist for Sustainable Management of Archaeological Collections." *Advances in Archaeological Practice* 5, no. 1: 12–25.

Claussen, Erin. 2010. "Fort St. Joseph 1.0: Creating a Comprehensive Information Management Scheme for the Fort St. Joseph Archaeological Project." Master's thesis, Western Michigan University.

Davis, Cathrine M. 2014. "Lead Seals from Colonial Fort St. Joseph (20BE23)." Honors thesis, Western Michigan University.

Evans, Lynn L. 2013. "Michilimackinac, a Civilian Fort." In *The Archaeology of French and Indian War Frontier Forts*, 216–28. Gainesville: University Press of Florida.

Fritz, William H. B. 2005. "Fort St. Joseph Collection Management Survey and Assessment." Unpublished report, Michigan Alliance for the Conservation of Cultural Heritage, Lansing. On file in the History Center, Niles, MI.

Glenn A. Black Laboratory of Archaeology. 2020. "GBL Collections Descriptions." https://iumaa.iu.edu/collections/archaeological-collections.

Heldman, Donald P. 1976. *Fort Michilimackinac Archeological Investigations 1974 and 1975*. Technical Preservation Services Division, Office of Archeology and Historic Preservation, National Park Service, Department of the Interior.

Hulse, Charles. 1977. "An Archaeological Evaluation of Fort St. Joseph: An Eighteenth-Century Military Post and Settlement in Berrien County, Michigan." Master's thesis, Michigan State University.

Jackson, Misty M. 2005. "Classifications by Historical Archaeologists and Eighteenth-Century Montreal Merchants and Military Personnel in New France: Emic and Etic Approaches." PhD diss., Michigan State University.

Johnson, Eileen. 2003. "An Archaeological Curation Dilemma with an Approach to a Solution: The Texas-Based Accreditation Program for Curatorial Facilities." *Plains Anthropologist* 48, no. 186: 151–64.

Jones, James R., III. 1988. "Degrees of Acculturation at Two Eighteenth Century Aboriginal Villages Near Lafayette, Tippecanoe County, Indiana: Ethnohistoric and Archaeological Perspectives." PhD diss., Indiana University.

Jones, Kevin P. 2019. "An Examination of Flintlock Musket Components at Fort St. Joseph (20B23), Niles Michigan." Master's thesis, Western Michigan University.

Kellar, James H. 1970. "The Search for Ouiatenon." *Indiana Historical Bulletin* 47: 123–33.

Kersel, Morag M. 2015a. "An Issue of Ethics? Curation and the Obligations of Archaeology." *Journal of Eastern Mediterranean Archaeology & Heritage Studies* 3, no. 1: 77–79.

———. 2015b. "Storage Wars: Solving the Archaeological Curation Crisis?" *Journal of Eastern Mediterranean Archaeology & Eastern Heritage Studies* 3, no. 1: 42–54.

Loveland, Erika K. 2017. "Archaeological Evidence of Architectural Remains at Fort St. Joseph (20BE23), Niles, MI." Master's thesis, Western Michigan University.

Mackinac State Historic Parks. 2009. "Proposal to the Institute for Museum and Library Services for Museums of America." Copy provided to the authors by the organization.

———. 2020a. "History: Organizational History." https://www.mackinacparks.com/more info/history/.

———. 2020b. "Research and Collections." https://www.mackinacparks.com/more-info/research-collections/.

Martin, Terrance J. 1986. "A Faunal Analysis of Fort Ouiatenon, an Eighteenth-Century Trading Post in the Wabash Valley." PhD diss., Michigan State University.

Miller, J. Jefferson, and Lyle M. Stone. 1970. *Eighteenth-Century Ceramics from Fort Michilimackinac: A study in Historical Archeology.* Smithsonian Studies in History and Technology No. 4. Washington DC: Smithsonian Institution Press.

Morehouse, Rebecca J. 2019. "Yes! You Can Have Access to That! Increasing and Promoting the Accessibility of Maryland's Archaeological Collections." In *New Life for Archaeological Collections*, ed. Rebecca Allen and Ben Ford, 3–12. Lincoln: University of Nebraska Press.

Myers, Kelsey Noack. 2019. "Reconstructing Site Provenience at Ouiatenon, Indiana." In *New Life for Archaeological Collections*, ed. Rebecca Allen and Ben Ford, 272–88. Lincoln: University of Nebraska Press.

Nassaney, Michael S., ed. 1999. "An Archaeological Reconnaissance Survey to Locate Remains of Fort St. Joseph (20BE23) in Niles, Michigan." Archaeological Report No. 22. Department of Anthropology, Western Michigan University, Kalamazoo.

―――, ed. 2019. *Fort St. Joseph Revealed: The Historical Archaeology of a Fur Trading Post.* Gainesville: University Press of Florida.

―――. 2008. "Commemorating French Heritage at Fort St. Joseph, an Eighteenth-Century Mission, Garrison, and Trading Post Complex in Niles, Michigan." In *Dreams of the Americas: Overview of New France Archaeology,* ed. Christian Roy and Hélène Côté, 96–111. *Archéologiques,* Collection Hors Série 2. Québec: Association des Archéologiques du Québec.

―――. 2009. "European Exploration and Early Settlements." In *Archaeology in America: An Encyclopedia,* Vol. 2, *Midwest and Great Plains/Rocky Mountains,* F. McManamon, general ed., 45–52. Westport, CT: Greenwood.

―――. 2012. "The Benefits of tDAR for the Fort St. Joseph Archaeological Project." Paper presented in the forum Using the Digital Archaeological Record (tDAR) for Management, Research, and Education, organized by Joshua Watts at the 77th annual meeting of the Society for American Archaeology, Memphis, TN.

Nassaney, Michael S., and William M. Cremin. 2002. "Fort St. Joseph Is Found!" *Michigan History* 86, no. 5: 18–27.

Noble, Vergil E., Jr. 1978. "Excavations at Fort Ouiatenon 1977 Field Season: Preliminary Report." Submitted to the Tippecanoe County Historical Association and Office of Historic Preservation. Michigan State University, East Lansing.

―――. 1979. "Excavations at Fort Ouiatenon 1978 Field Season: Preliminary Report." Submitted to the Tippecanoe County Historical Association and Office of Historic Preservation. Michigan State University, East Lansing.

―――. 1980. "Excavations at Fort Ouiatenon 1979 Field Season: Preliminary Report." Submitted to the Tippecanoe County Historical Association and Office of Historic Preservation. Michigan State University, East Lansing.

―――. 1982. "Excavations at Fort Ouiatenon 1979 Field Season: Supplementary Report." Submitted to the Tippecanoe County Historical Association, Lafayette, Indiana. Michigan State University, East Lansing.

―――. 1983. "Functional Classification and Intra-Site Analysis in Historical Archaeology: A Case Study from Fort Ouiatenon." PhD diss., Michigan State University.

―――. 1991. "Ouiatenon on the Ouabache: Archaeological Investigations at a Fur Trading Post on the Wabash River." In *French Colonial Archaeology: The Illinois Country and the Western Great Lakes,* ed. John A. Walthall, 65–77. Urbana: University of Illinois Press.

―――. 2018. "National Historic Landmark Nomination (Draft): Fort Ouiatenon Archeological District." Submitted to the US Department of the Interior, National Park Service, National Historical Landmarks Program, Washington, DC.

Pope-Pfingston, Jodi, and Noel D. Justice. 1993. "Fort Ouiatenon: A French and Indian Occupation along the Wabash River in Tippecanoe County, Indiana: A Collections Management Report." Glenn A. Black Laboratory of Archaeology, Indiana University, Bloomington.

Sauer, Norman J., Samuel S. Dunlap, and Lawrence R. Simson. 1988. "Medicolegal Investigation of an Eighteenth-Century Homicide." *American Journal of Forensic Medicine and Pathology* 9, no. 1: 66–73.

Stone, Lyle M. 1974a. "Fort Michilimackinac, 1715–1781: An Archaeological Perspective on the Revolutionary Frontier." East Lansing: Michigan State University Museum.

———. 1974b. "A Review of the Fort St. Joseph Artifact Collections: Niles, Michigan and South Bend, Indiana." On file at the Niles District Library, Michigan.

Strezewski, Michael. 2014. "Fur Trade Archeology in the Fort Ouiatenon Vicinity: The 2012/2013 Investigations." Reports of Investigations 13-03. University of Southern Indiana, Archaeology Laboratory, Evansville.

Strezewski, Michael, and Robert G. McCullough. 2010. "Report of the 2009 Archaeological Investigations at Three Fur Trade–Era Sites in Tippecanoe County, Indiana: Kethtippecanunk (12-T-59), Fort Ouiatenon (12-T-9), and a Kickapoo-Mascouten Village (12-T-335)." Reports of Investigations 903. Indiana University–Purdue University Fort Wayne Archaeological Survey, Fort Wayne.

———. 2017. "Fur Trade Archaeology at the Ouiatenon Preserve: The 2016/2017 Geophysical Investigations." Report of Investigations 16-03. University of Southern Indiana, Archaeology Laboratory, Evansville.

Sullivan, Lynne P., and S. Terry Childs. 2003. *Curating Archaeological Collections: From the Field to the Repository*. Lanham, MD: AltaMira.

Tordoff, Judith D. 1980. "Excavations at Fort Ouiatenon, 1974–76 Seasons: Preliminary Report." Submitted to the Tippecanoe County Historical Association and Office of Historic Preservation. Michigan State University, East Lansing.

———. 1983. "An Archaeological Perspective on the Organization of the Fur Trade in Eighteenth-Century New France." PhD diss., Michigan State University.

Trubowitz, Neal L. 1989a. "Historical Archaeology Research by IU-Indianapolis, 1987." In *Current Research in Indiana Archaeology and Prehistory: 1987 & 1988*, ed. Christopher S. Peebles, 29–30. Glenn A. Black Laboratory of Archaeology Research Reports No. 10. Bloomington: Indiana University.

———. 1989b. "Historical Archaeology Research by IU-Indianapolis, 1988." In *Current Research in Indiana Archaeology and Prehistory: 1987 & 1988*, ed. Christopher S. Peebles, 50–51. Glenn A. Black Laboratory of Archaeology Research Reports No. 10. Bloomington: Indiana University.

———. 1990. "Inventory and Analyses of Fort Ouiatenon (12T9) Collections, 1987–1990." Paper presented at the Indiana Historical Society Conference, Indianapolis.

———. 1991. "Inventory and Analysis of Fort Ouiatenon (12T9) Collections, 1987–1990." In *Current Research in Indiana Archaeology and Prehistory: 1990*, ed. C. S. Peebles, 24. Glenn A. Black Laboratory of Archaeology Research Reports No. 12. Bloomington: Indiana University.

———. 1992. "Native Americans and French on the Central Wabash." In *Calumet & Fleur-de-Lys: Archaeology of Indian and French Contact in the Midcontinent*, ed. John A. Walthall and Thomas E. Emerson, 241–64. Washington, DC: Smithsonian Institution Press.

von Frese, Ralph R. B. 1978. "Magnetic Exploration of Historical Midwestern Archaeological Sites as Exemplified by a Survey of Fort Ouiatenon." Master's thesis, Purdue University.

———. 1984. "Archaeological Anomalies of Midcontinental North American Archaeological Sites." *Historical Archaeology* 18, no. 2: 4–19.

von Frese, Ralph R. B., and Vergil E. Noble. 1984. "Magnetometry for Archaeological Exploration of Historical Sites." *Historical Archaeology* 18, no. 2: 38–53.

Williams, Emily, and Katherine Ridgway. 2019. "Balancing Access, Research, and Preservation: Conservation Concerns for Old Collections." In *New Life for Archaeological Collections*, ed. Rebecca Allen and Ben Ford, 115–41. Lincoln: University of Nebraska Press.

13

AT THE EDGE OF FOREVER

Preserving Fort Ouiatenon and the
Creation of the Ouiatenon Preserve, a
Roy Whistler Foundation Project

J. COLBY BARTLETT, DIRECTOR,
OUIATENON PRESERVE INC.

IN THE LATE NINETEENTH CENTURY, CURIOSITY ABOUT THE HISTORY AND location of the old French settlement of Ouiatenon, the first of three forts built by France in the early eighteenth century in what would become Indiana, led several individuals to search for it. Over the years numerous eighteenth-century artifacts and several graves had been encountered over a several mile stretch along the Wabash River in western Tippecanoe County. These early efforts to locate the site were hindered by a lack of archaeological methods and the false assumption that Fort Ouiatenon must have been located on an elevation high enough to avoid the seasonal flooding of the Wabash River. Some historic artifacts had been found on a high ridge near the Sand Ridge Church and Cemetery, and an elderly resident of the area had recollections from her youth of there being remnants of an old structure there. Despite the scant evidence, a spot was designated and became generally accepted as what must have been the location of Fort Ouiatenon. By 1930, Lafayette physician and Tippecanoe County Historical Association (TCHA) founder Dr. Richard Wetherill had purchased the property and constructed an early nineteenth-century English-style log blockhouse as a monument on the site and donated the property to the TCHA. In the late 1960s, the TCHA deeded the property to the newly formed Tippecanoe County Parks

Department, and the site became its first county park. For those several decades, this was accepted as being the location of Ouiatenon.

By order of the governor of New France in 1717, Ouiatenon was established to protect France's interests in the fur trade from England and cement its relationship with the Weas, a group of the Miami people who had settled in several villages along the Wabash following the seventeenth-century Beaver War. Ouiatenon was constructed along the Wabash River on the opposite bank from the Weas' principal village. The fort's geographic location was also of importance. Ouiatenon was the southernmost outpost of the French colony of Canada, with everything farther south including the slightly later established settlement of Vincennes, being under the dominion of the French colony Louisiana. French control of the Wabash was of significant value, as it was a segment of the only direct inland water route connecting its two largest colonies in North America.

Ouiatenon existed during several important formative periods in the history of North America, which included the competition of colonial empire between France and England that eventually resulted in the French and Indian War, the American Revolution, and the birth and expansion of the United States of America.

By the mid-1960s several area individuals, unconvinced of the legitimacy of the blockhouse as the location of the fort, began researching and searching for the site. In April 1966 Joseph "Del" Bartlett (the author's father), a native of Tippecanoe County and at the time a student at Purdue University, located a dense surface scatter of eighteenth-century artifacts on a sandy ridge in a plowed field approximately one mile west of the blockhouse. On a later visit to the site he encountered Larry Chowning and John Henry, who were also interested in locating the site. In early December 1967, Bartlett conducted a small informal test excavation (approximately 1 m by 1 m) down to sterile sand at a depth of approximately 48 inches and discovered that there were extensive subsurface deposits, artifacts, and features that he interpreted as being consistent with a substantial eighteenth-century European habitation site. The location of this test unit is believed to have been near what was later determined to be the southwestern corner of the stockade (Bartlett 1966–1976, 18–19). Having brought the location of this site and the artifacts recovered to the attention of the TCHA, Bartlett and representatives of the TCHA and the Indiana Historical Society met with Dr. James Kellar of Indiana University, and an agreement was made for the university to conduct an archaeological field school in the summer of 1968 to investigate the site.

Early that spring, Bartlett discovered that the tenant farmer had plowed the field with a new plow and tractor, which was more powerful and plowed deeper than any previously used. This brought several inches of formerly undisturbed archaeological deposits to the surface. These included numerous hearths and large stones believed to be from either foundations or fireplaces that seemed to be oriented on two parallel north-south lines. A rough sketch and photographs were made of these (Bartlett 1966–1976, 34–35) (figure 13.1). While the disturbance was unfortunate, Bartlett realized that the circumstances might present an ideal opportunity for aerial photography of the location to see if any outlines or features could be identified. A plane and a pilot were rented, and the results were extraordinary (figure 13.2). A clearly defined rectangle of ashy deposits representing the interior area of the stockade and numerous features, both inside and outside of the stockade, could be observed. It was further convincing evidence that the site of Ouiatenon had been found. These photographs were shared with Dr. Kellar and were used to locate the excavation units for the field school later that summer.

Encouraged by the results of the 1968 field season, Kellar again conducted a field school at the site in the summer of 1969. The two summers produced a wealth of artifactual material as well as features, and this led to the conclusion that the site of Ouiatenon (12T9) had now been identified. Further excavations did not continue due to Kellar's commitments to projects at Angel Mounds and overseeing the construction of the new Glenn Black Laboratory of Archaeology at Indiana University. Unfortunately, aside from a few brief articles in the Indiana Historical Society's bulletin, detailed reports of the excavations, the results of analysis, and interpretations of the findings were never completed.

One of the unique aspects of Ouiatenon is that unlike most other similar eighteenth-century sites, later nineteenth- and twentieth-century settlement and urban development did not occur at its location. Aside from agricultural activity, it remained largely undisturbed and is considered among the best archaeologically preserved sites of its type. Ouiatenon is an especially valuable research resource in that it provides an opportunity to study the processes and patterns of acculturation between the Native American and French inhabitants as both adopted certain practices and material culture from one another. There are opportunities to study, compare, and contrast data from both Native Americans and Europeans living side by side during this period, the study of which can not only give us insight to this period of history but also the universal human condition and the ways human culture works.

In 1972, the TCHA was able to negotiate with the landowner and raised the funds necessary to purchase a small twenty-acre tract of the field that included the stockaded portion of Fort Ouiatenon and its immediate surroundings (Schumpert 1972). An agreement was also reached with Michigan State University to assume the archaeological investigations of the site. From 1974 to 1979, excavations took place each summer under the direction of Dr. Charles Cleland. This work greatly added to our understanding of Ouiatenon, resulting in several PhD dissertations and creating one of the largest scientifically excavated archaeological collections of eighteenth-century fur trade material in the United States. However, all combined, the excavations by the Indiana University and Michigan State University only account for less than 15 percent of the area within the stockade, leaving significant opportunities for future archaeological research (Strezewski and McCollough 2019).

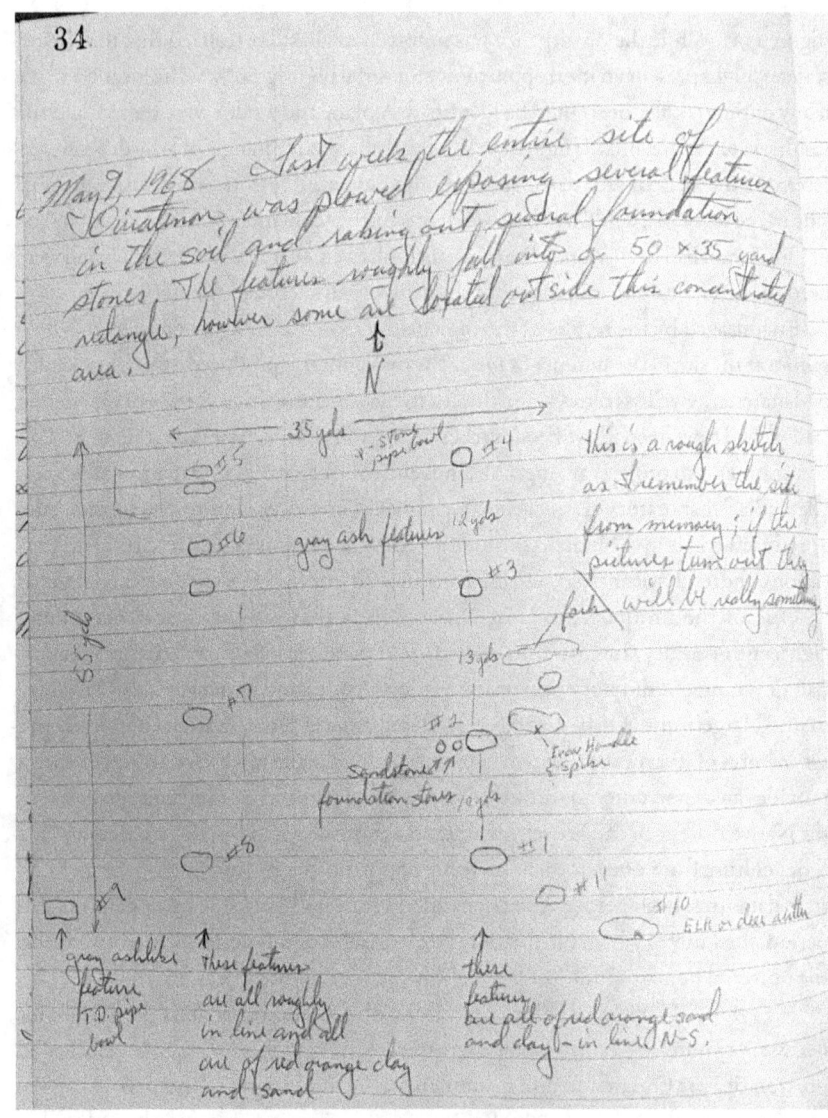

Figure 13.1. Joseph "Del" Bartlett's journal with sketch map of hearths exposed by deep plowing, May 1968. Courtesy of Joseph "Del" Bartlett.

During the 1980s, Dr. James R. Jones III (who later served as Indiana's state archaeologist for over two decades) and Dr. Neil Trubowitz with Indiana University–Purdue University Indianapolis conducted surface surveys in the fields surrounding the twenty-acre TCHA tract, identifying numerous additional eighteenth-century sites including large sites thought to represent the Kickapoo and Mascouten villages that

Figure 13.2. Aerial photograph of the Fort Ouiatenon site (12T9) taken in the spring of 1968 by Joseph "Del" Bartlett. Courtesy of Joseph "Del" Bartlett.

were described in historic documents as having been established near the Fort in the early 1730s. In 1986 I participated in those surveys, and it planted a seed in my mind for the need for additional expanded preservation of the area.

Over twenty-five years later in the early spring of 2013 while I was serving as president of the TCHA, we became aware that the two adjoining parcels to the north of the site might go to tax sale. These tracts contained several significant eighteenth-century archaeological sites related to Ouiatenon, including significant portions of those thought to represent the Kickapoo and/or Mascouten villages. It was then that the idea and opportunity for an effort to expand the preservation of Ouiatenon began to take shape. While the idea was grand, unfortunately, like most county-based historical associations, the TCHA did not have the financial resources necessary to pursue this on its own.

We initiated contact with the Archaeological Conservancy (TAC), and its midwestern director, Paul Gardner, came to visit the site and meet with us. TAC was formed in 1980 and modeled after the Nature Conservancy but with the mission to acquire, preserve, and manage archaeological sites with significant research value throughout the United States. TAC now own and protect over five hundred such sites and is well respected as a leading expert in the acquisition, protection, and management of archaeological resources. We knew the TAC's experience and expertise would be of great value to the project. After a review of the situation, TAC's board of directors agreed to become involved and joined our effort to acquire and protect these sites surrounding the fort.

Conversations with the landowners of other adjacent parcels to the east and west also indicated a potential opportunity for acquisition. In the late summer of 2013, a meeting was held with potential local and state stakeholders including representatives from the TCHA, TAC, the Indiana Department of Natural Resources Division of Historic Preservation (DHPA), Indiana State Museum, the Indiana Heritage Trust (IHT), and others to discuss the idea of acquiring the properties surrounding the fort and to investigate potential sources for support. During that meeting we were briefed on the newly introduced Indiana Bicentennial Nature Trust (IBNT) program. In essence, the program was developed under then Indiana governor Mitch Daniels as a present to the State of Indiana and its citizens in conjunction with Indiana's 2016 bicentennial. The program provided $20 million from the state, with an additional $10 million from the Lilly Foundation, to create a 1:1 matching grant program for locally based projects to acquire and protect lands considered important to the state because of their natural, environmental, recreational, cultural, archaeological, or historic significance. In return for funding, properties acquired under the program would be subject to a preservation easement and some degree of public access. Initial feedback on the project from IBNT administrators was very positive, and they felt that it was an ideal fit and a very worthy project. If successfully funded, the IBNT program would cover half of the cost of acquisitions; however, this still left a significant amount to be raised in order to be able to match this grant program.

Knowing of the situation and appreciating the value of the project, representatives of the IHT indicated that they could likely contribute half of this needed match. But this still left over $100,000 to be raised by the TCHA and TAC. TAC committed to half of this, and it was up to the TCHA to find the remainder.

Nearly simultaneously, a chance encounter (or providence) brought us into contact with a board member of the Roy Whistler Foundation (RWF). This resulted in an invitation to present the project to the RWF board and a request for funding. Professor Roy Whistler of Purdue University had been a founder and leading expert in the area of carbohydrate chemistry research. In addition, he was highly respected for his business acumen and served on many large corporate boards. He was also an avid naturalist and sportsman. Prior to his death, Professor Whistler created a foundation with the mission of supporting the preservation and restoration of natural lands in and around Tippecanoe County. The RWF has become a major force in preservation efforts in this region. The foundation committed $80,000 to the project and indicated that it would be willing to support additional acquisitions and encouraged us to move forward.

In June 2014, the project to acquire the two parcels to the north and one to the east of the fort site, consisting of approximately 105 acres total, was presented to the IBNT board and resulted in an awarded of $216,514, with an additional $108,227 from the IHT. With the balance funded from TAC and the RWF, the process to acquire the properties commenced. Unfortunately, the two parcels to the north went to tax sale prior to the time that funds could be made available from the IBNT and the IHT. Thankfully, the RWF board stepped in with an emergency loan and made it possible for the TCHA and TAC to purchase the tax liens at auction. A little over a year later, we were able to redeem those and perfect title to the properties. The RWF also loaned the funds necessary to proceed with the purchase of the property to the east while the IBNT and IHT funding was in process.

In 2015, we were finally able to reach an agreement with the owner of the 80-acre tract to the west that contained the western portion of the Fort Ouiatenon(12T9) site itself, along with large portions of the sites thought to represent the Kickapoo and Mascouten villages. A second IBNT grant application was submitted and approved for $188,000. The RWF provided the matching $188,000 required for this. Pending receipt of the IBNT funding, the RWF again loaned the TCHA and TAC the funds necessary to close on the property in 2016 to ensure acquisition.

During Indiana's 2016 bicentennial, with nearly two hundred acres of newly acquired and protected property containing approximately twenty archaeological sites, the TCHA, TAC, and the RWF were able to publicly announce the creation of the Ouiatenon Preserve. A project nearly fifty years in the making had come to fruition. The property that comprises the preserve is protected by not only state archaeological protection laws but by conservation and preservation easements held by the Indiana Department of Natural Resources and TAC. The co-ownership of the properties, with full rights of survivorship, by the TCHA and TAC provides redundant protection should anything ever happen to one of these organizations that prevents it from fulfilling its role and responsibilities as owners and stewards of the preserve. The Ouiatenon Preserve is the largest archaeological preserve in Indiana and one of the largest east of the Mississippi in TAC's network of national holdings.

Thanks to a Historic Preservation Fund grant administered by the DHPA, Dr. Michael Strezewski of the University of Southern Indiana and Dr. Robert McCullough were able to complete geophysical surveys in 2016 and 2017 of high probability areas in the newly acquired properties. These surveys were successful in identifying several previously unknown structures, features, and possible activity areas and will be important in guiding future research and the management of the preserve (Strezewski and McCullough 2017).

In 2017 the RWF funded an additional 3.14-acre acquisition along the wooded bluff overlooking the preserve, allowing it to be protected and preventing its development. While this area has not been archaeologically surveyed, its location on the bluff overlooking the site has a high probability of containing cultural deposits.

Also in 2017 with funding from the RWF, the TCHA was able to develop a public overlook and interpretation area. This property had been donated to the TCHA in

2009 by Mr. Lee Brand, a longtime farmer and property owner of the area, and it was one of the last undeveloped yet developable areas that overlooks the site of Ouiatenon. The overlook was developed as a public access point and interpretive area. In the future, we hope that it will serve as a trail head and perhaps someday even as the site of a museum or interpretive center for Ouiatenon.

In the spring of 2017 a group of computer graphics technology students with Purdue University's Polytechnic Institute completed a capstone project that combined the few brief eighteenth-century descriptions of Ouiatenon found in historic documents along with archaeological results to create a digital reconstruction of what Fort Ouiatenon might have actually looked like (figure 13.3). The results have been very useful in interpreting the site for the public.

The year 2018 was a big one for the Ouiatenon Preserve. In April at the statewide historic preservation conference, the DHPA honored the TCHA, TAC, and the RWF with the Indiana Archaeology Award for their efforts in creating the Ouiatenon Preserve (figure 13.4). In May, a ceremony was held at the overlook by the TCHA to formally dedicate the preserve. Honored guests and speakers included representatives from TAC, the RWF, the Miami Tribe of Oklahoma, the Indiana Department of Natural Resources, Indiana's state legislature, Tippecanoe County, the City of Lafayette, and the City of West Lafayette. Performances were conducted by the Tippecanoe Ancient Fife and Drum Corps and the 42nd Royal Highlanders Band of Music. Consul General of France Guillaume Lacroix sent a special letter of congratulations, which was read, and Diane Hunter of the Miami Tribe of Oklahoma cut the ceremonial ribbon.

In late 2018, a new 501c3 was created, Ouiatenon Preserve Inc. (OPI), to serve as the operating entity for the preserve. OPI was tasked with the environmental restoration, development of public access and interpretation, operation, and maintenance of the preserve. OPI's board consists of representatives from the TCHA, TAC, and the RWF.

In 2019, 105 acres of former agricultural fields were enrolled in the US Department of Agriculture's Conservation Reserve Enhancement Program and planted with a mixture of flood-tolerant native grasses and pollinators specifically designed for the preserve. The selected mixture avoided deep tap root species usually used in such applications in order to avoid damage to subsurface archaeological deposits. Employees with the Tippecanoe County Soil and Water Conservation District provided invaluable technical and material assistance in this project. The US Fish and Wildlife Service provided $10,000 of assistance to improve the seed mixture to support at-risk pollinator species such as bees and Monarch butterflies. This was the first Conservation Reserve Enhancement Program installation in the state of Indiana to receive Fish and Wildlife Service augmentation.

In 2020, an additional eighty acres were enrolled in the Conservation Reserve Enhancement Program and planted, which completed the restoration of all the former

Figure 13.3. Digital reconstruction of Fort Ouiatenon by Purdue University students as it may have looked based on historic descriptions and the results of archaeological investigations. Courtesy of the Tippecanoe County Historical Association.

Figure 13.4. Left to right: Colby Bartlett, Tippecanoe County Historical Association; Amy Johnson, Indiana Department of Natural Resources Division of Historic Preservation; Michael Reckowsky, Roy Whistler Foundation; and Paul Gardner, the Archaeological Conservancy. Presentation of the 2018 Indiana Archaeology Award for the creation of the Ouiatenon Preserve. Photograph by J. Colby Bartlett.

agricultural fields in the preserve native to a lowland prairie. These areas will require intensive ongoing maintenance to monitor and cull invasive species and to prevent volunteer trees from growing that might damage archaeological deposits. By removing these areas from agricultural use and establishing a prairie cover, the archaeological resources are protected from mechanical damage as well as erosion caused by seasonal flooding. This restoration also benefits the environmental health of the Wabash River and provides habitat for wildlife, including migratory birds that use the Wabash as a flyway and other at-risk riverine species. The restoration also improves water quality by reducing runoff of agricultural chemicals into the Wabash.

Also in 2020, the RWF again provided a large grant that allowed the TCHA to purchase the property and house west of and adjacent to the overlook. This has provided a base of operations for the preserve that allows for equipment storage, access to shelter, utilities, and office space and is also being used to help support archaeological field schools and environmental research.

On January 13, 2021, the US Secretary of the Interior designated the Ouiatenon Preserve as a National Historic Landmark Archaeological District. This included not only the site of Fort Ouiatenon but also over a dozen other historic sites related to it, including those believed to represent the Kickapoo and Mascouten villages. National Historic Landmark status is the highest level of recognition given to historic sites by the federal government and is reserved only for those sites that are deemed of significant importance to the history of the United States and possess a high degree of integrity, preservation, or both. According to National Park Service National Historic Landmark Program staff, Ouiatenon is the first National Historic Landmark to include Native American habitation sites from this period of history. The National Historic Landmark application was initiated in 2016 by Dr. Vergil Noble, who was preparing for retirement as an archaeologist after more than thirty years with the National Park Service Midwest Archeological Center. Dr. Noble had directed the excavations at Ouiatenon in 1977–1979 while completing his dissertation on the site at Michigan State University. Seeing Ouiatenon receive National Historic Landmark status brought a major aspect of his archaeological career full circle.

The designation of Ouiatenon as a National Historic Landmark caught the attention of the Ambassador of France to the United States, Philippe Étienne, who while on a diplomatic visit to Indiana in May 2021 along with Consul General Lacroix toured the Preserve. Members of the Miami Tribe of Oklahoma made the journey to welcome Ambassador Étienne to their ancestral homeland and presented him with gifts including a traditional welcoming of wrapping him in a blanket (figure 13.5).

We are currently working toward the development and installation of a series of interpretive panels at the preserve overlook to provide information about the history and archaeology of Ouiatenon as well as the ecosystem, flora, and fauna of the preserve. OPI is actively consulting with representatives of the Miami Tribe of Oklahoma and is grateful for its assistance in helping us to improve public interpretation at the Ouiatenon Preserve and gain their insight to assist us with better understanding and interpreting its history and archaeology.

Figure 13.5. Diane Hunter, tribal historic preservation officer of the Miami Tribe of Oklahoma, welcomes ambassador of France to the United States Philippe Étienne. Courtesy of Brooke Sauter.

In terms of the future, we are investigating how a future extension of the Wabash Heritage Trail could connect with an ADA-accessible pedestrian interpretive trail loop going from the overlook down through the preserve to the site of the fort and back (figure 13.6). This would allow for increased public access and allow for additional enjoyment and interpretation for visitors. This would also improve the security of the sites in the preserve. For most of the twentieth century, the strategy had been to keep the locations of such archaeological sites confidential in an effort to prevent unauthorized collecting and looting. Unfortunately, this has proved rather unsuccessful. Over the last several decades, TAC and state and federal agencies have begun to embrace a strategy of putting sites "in the public view" and encouraging visitation as a way to help protect them. We hope to follow that model by ensuring that visitors know what the preserve area is and that it is an important and legally protected area. OPI patrols the preserve on a regular basis to ensure the protection of its cultural and natural resources. Until such time that a pedestrian trail is developed to allow for at-will visitation, OPI conducts guided tours for groups on request and hosts public tour days periodically. It has been the vision and hope of many over the last fifty or more years that a museum and interpretive center might be developed in which the extensive collection of artifacts and an enhanced interpretation of this history could be shared with the public.

Figure 13.6. A view from the overlook of the site of For Ouiatenon and the Ouiatenon Preserve. Photograph by J. Colby Bartlett.

Undoubtedly, this is only the beginning of the story of the Ouiatenon Preserve. It is a gift from our generation to those in the future who can continue to learn from the archaeological resources it contains and benefit from its restored natural habitat.

REFERENCES

Bartlett, Joseph D. 1966–1976. Personal unpublished journal. Private collection.

Schumpert, Larry. 1972. "Historical Society Buys Original Ouiatenon Land." *Journal and Courier*, August 18.

Strezewski, Michael, and Robert G. McCullough. 2017. *Fur Trade Archaeology at the Ouiatenon Preserve: The 2016/2017 Geophysical Investigations.* University of Southern Indiana Archaeology Laboratory Reports of Investigations 16-03.

———. 2019. "Fort Ouiatenon, 1717–2019: 300+ Years of Indiana History." *Indiana Archaeology* 14, no. 1: 54–88.

ACKNOWLEDGMENTS

THE EDITORS OF THIS VOLUME WOULD LIKE TO EXPRESS THEIR GRATItude to those who helped make it possible. Starting with the 2017 Midwest Historic Archaeology Conference, the presentations from which served as the basis of this volume, we wish to thank the following for providing financial, logistical, and moral support: the Tippecanoe County Historical Association; at Purdue University, the Office of the Executive Vice President for Research, the College of Liberal Arts, the Department of Anthropology, the Department of History, and the School of Foreign Languages and Cultures; the Peyser Endowment for the Study of New France; and the Archaeological Conservancy. Dr. Michael Nassaney provided invaluable advice in both the planning of the original conference and the publication of this book. The editors would also like to recognize the support of Dr. Melissa Remis (head) and the Purdue University Department of Anthropology, the College of Liberal Arts, and the Office of the Executive Vice President for Research and Partnerships for funding the indexing of this book through the CLA Publication Subvention Program. We also would like to extend our thanks to the staff at the Tippecanoe County Historical Association, Leslie Martin Conwell and Kelly Lippie, who kindly assisted in providing access to collections, and Brooke Sauter, who provided photographs for the book cover and various chapters. Thanks also to the staff at Purdue University Press, especially Justin Race, Andrea Gapsch, Christopher Brannan, and Katherine Purple.

CONTRIBUTORS

CHRISTINA H. ARSENEAU has a BA in classics from the University of Illinois, an MA in classics, and a graduate certificate in museum studies from New York University. She has worked in museums for more than twenty years as an educator, curator, and director. Since 2015 she has held the position of director of the Niles History Center. Arseneau also serves on the Michigan Museum Association's board of directors.

J. COLBY BARTLETT has a BA in anthropology from Purdue University. He has served on the board of governors for the Tippecanoe County Historical Association for over a decade, including five years as president during which he led the effort to create the Ouiatenon Preserve, a Roy Whistler Foundation Project. Bartlett serves as the director for Ouiatenon Preserve Inc., which is charged with the operation and development of the Ouiatenon Preserve. Over the last thirty years he has served in various capacities including field supervisor, analyst, coauthor, and research associate on dozens of archaeological projects throughout the United States, including positions with the University of the New Mexico, Office of Contract Archaeology, and the University of Texas, Texas Archaeological Research Laboratory, as well as several private firms.

H. KORY COOPER is an associate professor of anthropology at Purdue University. As an archaeometallurgist, he uses both anthropology and materials science methods to investigate the ancient and historic use and innovation of metals. Cooper has published on native copper use among hunter-gatherer societies in the Arctic, Subarctic, and Northwest Coast regions of North America; the use of copper alloys in the Byzantine Near East; and the electronic waste problem. He has worked in Alaska, California, Jordan, Sudan, and Indiana and is currently studying metallurgy at historic fur trade sites in the Midwest and Alaska. In the summer of 2022 Cooper codirected (with Dr. Michael Strezewski) an archaeological field school in the Ouiatenon Preserve.

ERIKA K. HARTLEY is the director of the Fort St. Joseph Archaeological Project, Fort St. Joseph curatorial fellow through the Niles History Center, and part-time instructor at Western Michigan University. She earned her MA in anthropology from Western Michigan University in 2017, where she focused on historical archaeology and the architectural elements of Fort St. Joseph. Hartley's interests include historical archaeology, public archaeology, colonialism, the fur trade, identity, and material analysis.

DAVID M. HOVDE, professor emeritus, retired in 2017 after serving in the Purdue University Libraries since 1989. Most recently he was the research and instruction librarian in the Virginia Kelly Karnes Archives and Special Collections. Hovde has authored or coauthored more than seventy books, book chapters, scholarly articles, conference proceedings, occasional papers, monographs, and scholarly web publications in the areas of archaeology, ethnohistory, history, and library and information science. He has worked in an editorial capacity on four professional journals, a professional newsletter, and a book series. He also serves on the board of the Tippecanoe County Historical Association.

DIANE HUNTER is the Tribal Historic Preservation Officer (ret.) for the Miami Tribe of Oklahoma (ret.) and a citizen of the tribe. She is a descendant of the Miami family of Seekaahkweeta and Palaanswa through their son Waapanaakikaapwa. After many years as a librarian, Hunter came to work for the Miami Tribe of Oklahoma in 2015, when the tribe opened its Cultural Resources Extension Office in Fort Wayne, Indiana. Her work as tribal historic preservation officer involves preserving and protecting historic sites and resources, providing education about the presence and history of the Miami Tribe, and serving over seven hundred tribal citizens in Indiana. Hunter has a bachelor's degree from Indiana University and master's degrees from Ball State University and Georgetown University.

MISTY M. JACKSON received her PhD from the Department of Anthropology at Michigan State University in 2005. Her dissertation utilized archaeological collections from Fort Ouiatenon in combination with archival documents. Jackson was an adjunct professor at Central Michigan University in 2006 and 2007 and is currently the principal investigator with Arbre Croche Cultural Resources, based in Leslie, Michigan, which she founded in 2007. She currently serves on the boards for the Center for French Colonial Studies and the Center for Maritime and Underwater Resource Management and previously served on Michigan's State Historic Preservation Review Board. Jackson's work has included providing expert witness for a Native American treaty case in 2014–2015 and coediting and contributing to a forthcoming book on Upper Greats Lake historical archaeology.

KEVIN JONES earned his MA in anthropology in 2019 from Western Michigan University and wrote his thesis on the topic of flintlock weapons at Fort St. Joseph, Niles, Michigan. As an undergraduate at Purdue University, he volunteered at the Tippecanoe County Historical Association organizing Fort Ouiatenon archaeological documents and artifacts while working on his honor's thesis in anthropology on Fort Ouiatenon. Jones currently works in cultural resource management and is employed by Stantec in Indianapolis.

TERRANCE J. MARTIN earned his BS from Grand Valley State University, his MS from Western Michigan University, and his PhD from Michigan State University. He is currently emeritus curator of anthropology at the Illinois State Museum in Springfield, Illinois, and an adjunct professor of anthropology at Michigan State University. Martin specializes in zooarchaeology and is the author or coauthor of numerous publications and technical reports concerning the use of animals at late precontact, early contact, colonial period, and late historic sites in the Midwest. He participated in Michigan State University's excavations at the Fort Ouiatenon site in 1979, and Fort Ouiatenon was the subject of his PhD dissertation.

LESLIE MARTIN CONWELL has served in many roles during her more than forty years as staff for the Tippecanoe County Historical Association, including executive director, Feast of the Hunters' Moon event manager, and program director. She is an anthropologist who double-minored in history and French at Purdue University and began her passion for serving Tippecanoe County Historical Association in 1974 at her first Feast of the Hunters' Moon. Martin Cornwell has also worked as a consultant for the National Muzzle Loading Rifle Association, serving as museum, library, archives, and American history coordinator; coordinated the 200th Battle of Tippecanoe Commemoration; owns with her husband Rick the largest living history show east of the Mississippi, the Kalamazoo Living History show; and recently retired as the executive director of The Farm at Prophetstown.

RONALD V. MORRIS, PhD, is a professor of history at Ball State University, where he teaches interpretive media courses for public history students. Morris is the author of *Bringing History to Life: First Person Presentations in Elementary and Middle School Social Studies*; *The Field Trip Book: Study Travel Experience in Social Studies*; *History and Imagination: Reenactments for Elementary Social Studies*; and *Yountsville: The Rise and Decline of an Indiana Mill Town*. In 2012 Indiana Landmarks presented him with the Servaas Memorial Award for outstanding achievement in historic preservation. In 2014 the Indiana Historical Society bestowed the Dorothy Rikker Hoosier Historian Award for his work in the historical community. In addition to being active in the community with a variety of local causes, Morris has restored an 1830s row house and is presently restoring the former home of American Civil War governor Oliver P. Morton when he is not hiking on the Appalachian Trail.

KELSEY NOACK MYERS, RPA, PhD, is an archaeologist and the district tribal liaison for the US Army Corps of Engineers Rock Island District of the Mississippi River Division. She has participated in archaeological projects across the mid-Atlantic, Southeast, Midwest, and northern Great Plains of the United States in the private, academic, and government sectors. As a coconvener for the Digital Data Interest Group of the Society for American Archaeology, Myers facilitates technological capacity building and open-source ethics in professional development and practice. Her interests include zooarchaeological analysis, culture contact and colonialism, and cooperative research combining archaeological methods with traditional Indigenous knowledge. She also maintains a strong interest in public archaeology education, legacy collections, and 3D data applications in archaeology. Myers holds degrees from Southern Illinois University Carbondale (BA), the College of William & Mary (MA), and Indiana University Bloomington (MA, PhD).

MICHAEL S. NASSANEY is emeritus professor of anthropology at Western Michigan University. His research interests include the archaeology of colonialism, the fur trade, material analysis, public archaeology, and ethnohistory. From 1998 to 2020, Nassaney served as the principal investigator of the Fort St. Joseph Archaeological Project, an interdisciplinary program in community service-learning that focuses on the site of Fort St. Joseph in Niles, Michigan. He has published numerous works on the archaeology of the eastern United States including *The Archaeology of the North American Fur Trade* (2015, University Press of Florida) and *Fort St. Joseph Revealed* (University Press of Florida, 2019).

VERGIL E. NOBLE received a 1983 doctorate in anthropology at Michigan State University, where he also did a year of postdoctoral study in history. He served briefly as an assistant professor and administrator at Illinois State University and then joined the National Park Service in 1987 and began conducting field investigations for the service's units throughout the Midwest. Assigned to the National Historic Landmarks program in the latter part of his career, Noble retired in 2019 after thirty-two years. He is a past president of the Society for Historical Archaeology.

LINA C. PATINO, originally from Colombia, received her BS (1990), MS (1993), and PhD (1997) in geological sciences from Rutgers University. Lina is a senior program director in the Office of the Assistant Director for Geosciences at the National Science

Foundation (NSF), overseeing a broad portfolio that includes education and diversity, international activities, and innovation. Most of her tenure at the NSF has been in the Division of Earth Sciences (2005 to 2020), where she was division director, section head, and program director. Prior to joining the NSF, Lina was an associate professor at Michigan State University, where she conducted research in the origin and evolution of volcanic rocks from Central America and led the MSU ICP-MS laboratory.

MICHAEL STREZEWSKI, PhD, is an associate professor of anthropology at the University of Southern Indiana and since 2005 has conducted research on a number of fur trade–era sites in Indiana, including the town of Kethtippecanunk, Fort Miamis, and Fort Ouiatenon. He has presented nineteen conference papers on French colonial archaeology and has authored two peer-reviewed publications on the topic, the most recent being a long-form summary of the history of Fort Ouiatenon and the archaeological fieldwork conducted there as part of the 300th anniversary of the fort's founding, both coauthored with Robert G. McCullough: "Report of the 2009 Archaeological Investigations at Three Fur Trade–Era Sites in Tippecanoe County, Indiana" (2010) and "Fort Ouiatenon, 1717–2019: 300+ Years of Indiana History" (2019).

DAVE W. SZYMANSKI, PhD, is a geologist at Bentley University with research interests ranging from the chemical evolution of magmas to environmental impacts of human and natural processes on surface waters. He is also a forensic scientist and court-qualified expert witness specializing in the examination of glass as trace evidence. After earning a doctorate in geology and a master's degree in forensic chemistry at Michigan State University, he served as a Congressional Science Fellow and policy adviser for US senator Jon Tester (D-MT). Szymanski now involves students in research for nonpartisan policy development on issues of energy, climate, and natural resources. As a science communicator and science educator, he conducts pedagogical research on the integration of STEM and business curricula, applying scientific understanding to real-world problems of sustainability.

INDEX

Page numbers in *italics* indicate figures, tables, or photos.

Abbott, Edward, 11, 91–92
Abbott, Raymond Barrington, 26, *27*
acculturation, 313; European supremacy and, xiv–xvii
Aciipihkahkionki, 218–19; French colonial history and, 89–92
"Ah! Si Mon Moine Voulait Danser!" (song), 276–77
Allen, R., 47
Allison, Harold, 97–98
Alvord, Clarence Walworth, 10–11
American Association of Museums, 300
American Battlefield Protection Program, 44
American Civil War, 24, 226, 237
American period: American settlement period, 15–17; economy during, 12–13; Fort Ouiatenon and, 12–17; Myaamiaki during, 222–25; Native Americans during, 12–17
American Revolution, 11–12, 312; military reenactment of, 244; Myaamiaki and, 221
amphibians, 108–9, *114*, 127, *128*
Andrássy I Mine, 183
animal use: aquatic habitats and, 108–9; artifacts and, 69, 131–32, *133*, 140; biomass percentage and, 110, 137–39, *138, 139*; birds and, *112–14*, 124–27; bone or antler projectile points, 131–32, *133*; cancellous bone paint applicator and, *133*; changes over time, 134–36; data on, 110, 111; environmental setting and, 106–9, 139–40; features versus sheet midden contexts, 132–34; fishes and, *114–15*, 127–30; at Fort de Chartres, 136–38; at Fort Miamis, 136; at Fort Michilimackinac, 134–36; at Fort Ouiatenon, 105–40; at Fort St. Joseph, 117, *118*, 136–38; fur trade and, 106, 122–23, 134–40; intersite comparisons of, 136–39; livestock and, 108, 120–21, 122, 137; mammals and, *111–12*, 116–24; miscellaneous modified animal specimens, 131–32; MNI and, 110, 132–34; mollusks and, *115*, 130–31, *131*; NISP and, 110, 132–35; particular contexts at Fort Ouiatenon site, 132–36; reptiles and amphibians, 108–9, *114*, 127, *128*; species composition of animal remains from Fort Ouiatenon site, 1974-1979, *111–16*; zooarchaeology methods, 109–10; zooarchaeology overview, 111–32. *See also* fur trade
anomaly 14, 69–71
anthropology, 39, 292, 295, 301
antlers, *119*; projectile points of, 131–32, *133*
aquatic habitats, 108–9
Archaeological Conservancy (TAC), 315–16
archivists, 283–84. *See also* collections management
Arion (legend), 161–63, *162*
Arion on the Dolphin (Boucher), *162*, 162–63

INDEX

artifact collecting, 18–19; from charcoal, 69, 71; collections management and, 284–86; at Fort Michilimackinac, 285, 294–97; at Fort St. Joseph, 285–86, *286*, 294, 297–304; historical sources and, 262–69; misplaced artifacts and, 302; music and, 262–69; pipes and, 71. *See also* collections management

artifacts, 25; animal use and, 69, 131–32, *133*, 140; "double crosses," 19, *22*; at Fort Miamis, *88*; at Fort Wayne, 87–88; at Locomotive Museum, 23; from 1971-1973 excavations, 49; pipes and, 71; rings, 151–68; screws and screwdrivers, 207, *208*; slag fragments and, 71; storage space for, 291–93, *293*, 302, 303, *303*; superpositioning of, 73; trade silver disc, *20*, *21*. *See also* buckles; flintlocks

artifact studies, xviii
Austria, 9

badgers, 109, 123
bagpipes, 277
Baker, Samuel W.., 267–68
Baldwin, Karen L., *228*
Ballard, Ralph, 299
Barron, Clement, 299
Bartlett, Colby, *319*
Bartlett, Joseph "Del," 26–28, 37–38, 312–13; aerial photography by, *315*; journal of, *314*
Battle Ground, Indiana, 16
Battle of Fallen Timbers, 15–16, 221–22
Battle of Gettysburg, 237
Battle of Shiloh, 238
Battle of the Wabash (St. Clair's Defeat), 221
Battle of Tippecanoe, 16, 237
Baugh, William, 239, 240, 242
bear, 108–9, 121–22, *122*
Beaugrand, Jean de, 163, *164*
beaver, 123
Beaver Wars, 221
Beckwith, Judge, 19
beer brewing, 252
Belcher, Jonathan, 178
Bellestre, Marie-François Picoté de, 164

Bellin, Jacques Nicolas, 6, *7*
Belue, Ted Franklin, 108
Biggs, William, 61
biomass percentage, 110, 137–39, *138*, *139*
birds: environmental setting and, 108–9; use of, *112–14*, 124–27
bison, 107–8, 120–21, 137
Bissot, Francois-Marie, xiii, 4; Post Vincennes and, xii, *xiii*, 89–92; Vincennes forts and, 81–82, 92–98, *93*
Bissot, Jean Baptiste, 82
Bitting, Arvill Wayne, 19, 22–28
Black, Glenn A., 299–300
blacksmith area, 42
blockhouse: Feast of the Hunters' Moon and, 234–35, *235*, *241*, 252; Fort Ouiatenon, 19–25, 26, 234–35, *235*, *241*, 252, 312; legitimacy of, 312
Bochart, Monsieur du Plessis, 265
Bodley, John, 75n3
Bodley, Thomas, 14–15, 22, 62
Body, Lewis, 227
bone projectile points, 131–32, *133*
Bonnecamps, Jean de, 84
botanical samples, 49
Boucher, Francois, *162*, 162–63
Boy Scouts, 234–35, 242, 246, 252, 257–58
brass, 186
Brehm, Detrich, 14
British conflict: American Revolution and, 11–12, 221, 244, 312; in British period, 10–12; Canada and, 9; Fort Miamis and, 85–86; Fort Ouiatenon and, 7–12; French colonial history and, 85–86, 89, 91, 221; in French period, 7–9
British period: in Canada, 10; Fort Ouiatenon and, 10–12; fur trade during, 10–12, 134
Brooks, Amanda, 301
Brown, Jefferson, 249
Brown, Samuel R., 15
Bruntlett, Angela, *241*
Brutsman, Mel, 251
buckles: composition of, 176–85, *179*, *184*, *185*; discussion and conclusions about, 185–86;

eighteenth-century, 176–80; elemental analysis of, 180–89, *184, 185*; ethnicity and, 186–88; from Fort Ouiatenon, 173–89, *175*; Fort Ouiatenon people and, 188–89; gender and, 176–77, 179; jewelry and, 177–78; LA-ICP-MS technique on, 173, *175*, 180–85; military, 187–89; MMR and, 174, 176–80, *179*, 188–89; of Native Americans, 186–88; by quantity, price, and year, *179*; semiquantitative compositional analysis of, 180–85; sixteen variables of, 176–77; social status and, 177–78, 186–88; TCHA and, 173–74, *175*; women's, 176–77, 179
building construction, 45–46; of Fort Miamis, 83–84; of Fort Michilimackinac, 295; of Fort Wayne, Indiana, 83–84
Buntin, Robert, 93
burned villages, 45–46
Burroughs, Ruby, 19, *23*, 25
Butler, Amos W., 22, 26–28
Butler, John, 14, 85
butt plates, *210, 211*

camping, 242
Canada: British conflict and, 9; British period in, 10; New France and, 3–4, 7–9; Public Archives of, 176
"Canadian Archives," 20–21, 24–25
cancellous bone paint applicator, *133*
canid remains, 123
canoes, 242, 244, 247–48, *257*
Carr, Doug, *120*
Carr, Joseph D., 300
Carte du Cours de l'Ohio ou de la Belle Riviere (Bellin), 6, *7*
Carter, Clarence Edwin, 10–11
Cary, John, 4, *5*
Catholicism, 160, 266, 269
cats, 124
cattle, 120–21, 137
cello, 267
Celtic music, 277, 278
"C'est L'aviron" (song), 270, 276
Chapin Mansion, 299, 301–2
charcoal remains, 69, 71

Charles I (King), 163
Charles Scott Campaign, 44–45
children, 90, 226; at Feast of the Hunters' Moon, 234–35, 246–49, *248,* 252–54, *253,* 257–58; music and, 276–80; Special Kids Day for, 248–49. *See also* youth
Chinese mining archaeology, 43
Chowning, Larry, 26–28, 40–41, 151–52, 240, 293, 312
Cincinnati, Ohio, 224
Cincinnati Gazette, 225
citizenship, 227
Clark, George Rogers, 11–12, 12–13, 92
classification systems, 301, 302; folk classification, 174
Claus, Daniel, 267
Claussen, Erin, 301
Cleland, Charles E., 41–42, 134, 291, 313
Clermont No. 2 (boat), 224
clothing, 242–43, 245–46
Cold Foot (Le Pied Froid), 84, 85
Cold Foot Village, 85
Cole, Edward, 11
collections management: artifact collecting and, 284–86; classification systems and, 301, 302; curation and, 283–84, 286, 287–94; curatorial practices and, xix, 284, 302–3; digitizing records and, 293; environmental control and, 301–2, 303; at Fort Michilimackinac, 285, 294–97; at Fort Ouiatenon, 285, 287–94, 305; at Fort St. Joseph, 285–86, *286,* 294, 297–304; GBL and, 287, 291–92; improvements to, 303–4; lessons learned and next steps for, 304–5; materials for, 303, *303*; misplaced artifacts and, 302; monetary resources for, 296–97; organization and, 293–94, 300, 302, 304–5; outreach initiatives and, 284; PastPerfect and, 301; preservation and, 284, 305; public engagement and, 284; storage space and, 291–93, *293,* 302, 303, *303*; summary of Ouiatenon site investigations and curated collections, *288–90*; TCHA and, 287, 291–94; training and, 302

Collett, John, 17
Colonial Fife and Drum Corps, 245
Colorado (steamboat), 224
commandants, 163–68, *166–67*
community, xviii; involvement and public outreach, xix, 284; public engagement and, 284; public suggestions for Feast of the Hunters' Moon and, 253–54
community-based archaeology, 39–41
Compagnies Franches de la Marine, 6
composite map, of Fort Ouiatenon excavations, *48*
conservation: Fort Ouiatenon archaeology and, 315–18; Ouiatenon Preserve and, 315–22; Wabash Heritage Trail and, 321; of Wabash River, 319–20
Conservation Reserve Enhancement Program, 318–20
Conwell, Leslie Martin, *133*, 258
Cooper, Harold Kory, 28, 305
copper, 180–86, *184, 185*
copper alloy, 181–82, 186
costume jewelry, 178
costumes, 243
Cox, Sanford C., 17, 36–37
Craddock, Paul, 177, 186
craft demonstrations, 239, 241–43, 245–47, *250*, 251, 256
Craig, Oscar J., *5*, 19, 23, 26, 28
Crawfordsville Journal, 24
Croghan, George, 10–11, 60–61, 86, 107–8
cultural representation, at Feast of the Hunters' Moon, 270, *273–74*
Cuppy farm, 19
curation, 283–84, 286; at Fort Ouiatenon, 287–94; practices, xix, 284, 302–3. *See also* collections management

Daily Receipts *(Cincinnati Gazette)*, 225
dances, 239, 240, 247, 252; music and, 265
Daniels, Mitch, 316
data: on animal use, 110, 111; on eighteenth-century buckles, 176–80; on flintlocks, 194–97; spatial, 46–49, *48*; synthesizing, 46–49

dating, 95, 189; with dendrochronology, 70
d'Auger, Pierre-Alexandre, 164
Daughters of the American Revolution, 25, 234; Fort Ouiatenon Society and, 37
Dauphin of France, 163–65, *164*, 168
Davis, Caleb, 247–48
de Bellerive, Louis Groston de Saint-Ange et, 90
de Bienville, Jean-Baptiste Le Moyne, 60
deer, 108–9, 116–20, *120*; antlers, *119*, 131–32, *133*; skeletal portions at Fort Ouiatenon and Fort St. Joseph sites, *118*
Dehaître, Antoine, 194
DeHart, Richard Patten, 16–17, 19, 20–22, 24–25
dendrochronology, 70
Denny, Ebenezer, 86
diamonds, 161
Dictionaire Universel (Savary), 179
digitizing records, 293
Dillon, John B., 19
disease, 8–9, 221
Dobbs, Clark, 39
dogs, 123
dolphin symbol, 152, 161–63; Dauphin of France, 163–65, *164*, 168
"double crosses," 19, *22*
driftwood, 75n3
drums, 264–65
Dubuisson, Louis-Jacques-Charles, 82
Dulcimer Gathering, 251
Dunn, Jacob Piatt, 11, 19–20

economy: during American period, 12–13; during British period, 10–12
Edwards, Dave, 248
Eel River, 15, 17
Eel River Indians, 62–63
eighteenth-century buckles, 176–80
11-Lo-8 (Rhoads site), 73–74
Elgin Brigade of Voyageurs, 244
Elkhart River, 219–20
Embarras River, 218–19
English origin flintlocks, 199, *200*, 206, *206*
environmental control, for collections, 301–3

INDEX

environmental setting, 106–9, 139–40
epidemics, 8–8–9, 221
ethnicity, 186–88
Étienne, Philippe, 320
European contact, 58
European material culture, xiv–xvii
European supremacy, xiv–xvii
Evans, Lynn, 296
excavation grid, 52–53

"Farmer 1747" lockplate, 209–10
farmers, 12–13, 209–10, 312–13
faunal remains. *See* animal use;
   zooarchaeology
Feast of the Hunters' Moon, xix, 28, 37; from 1929-1957, 234–35; from 1958-1966, 236–38; from 1967-2017, 238–58; authenticity and quality control at, 243, 245–46; blockhouse and, 234–35, *235, 241,* 252; canoes at, 242, 244, 247–48, *257;* children and youth at, 234–35, 246–49, *248,* 252–54, *253,* 257–58; clothing at, 242–43, 245–46; commemorative events at, 234–35; commercial vendors at, 249; cost to operate, 257; costumes at, 243; craft demonstrations at, 239, 241–43, 245–47, *250,* 251, 256; cultural representation at, 270, *273–74;* dances at, 239, 240, 247, 252; depictions at the Feast today, 269–78; early historical reenactments and, 234–35, 237–38, 258nn2–3; educational mission at, 248–49, 254; expansion of, 247–48; Feast on Sunday at, 240; fiftieth anniversary of, 256–57; floods at, 251–52, 256; food at, 239, 243, 249, 251, *255,* 256; grounds, 242–43; handicraft row at, 243; historical sources for, 262–69; Hospitality Committee, 247; introduction to, 233; military reenactments at, 237–38, 243–44, 247; musical genres at, 269–70, *271–72;* musical groups including people under eighteen, 270, *275;* music at, 245, 247, 252, 254, *255,* 256, 261–80; national attention to, 245; photos of, *235, 236, 241, 244, 248, 250, 253, 255, 257;* planning for, 242, 245–49, 253–54, 258; public suggestions

for, 253–54; Rossville Junior High History Club and, 239, 240; security at, 249; Special Kids Day at, 248–49; sponsors of, 239, 240; traditions at, 241–42, 278–79; traffic and parking at, 245; weddings and receptions at, 257–58
Feature 4, Fort St. Joseph: artifact age in, 204, *206;* artifact origin in, 204, 206, *206;* damage and breakage in, 204; flintlocks, 201–8; most numerous flintlock artifact types found in, 204; number of artifacts by artifact type within and outside of, *203;* proportion of artifacts by artifact type within and outside of, *203;* summary of artifacts, by type and damage, *205;* weapon types in, 207, *207*
Fernwood Botanical Garden and Nature Preserve, 299
Fetter, Ellen Cole, 223–24
field methods, xviii
field notes, 18
fire-cracked rock, 49
fishes: environmental setting and, 108; use of, *114–15,* 127–30
flintlocks: archaeological data on, 194–97; artifact ages and origins, 200–201; artifact details, 197–200; artifacts, by determined age, *198;* artifact summary by ages and origins, *199,* 199–201, *200;* artifact summary by type, damage, and raw material, 195–97, *196;* butt plates, *210, 211;* discussion on, 208–9; by English origin, 199, *200,* 206, *206;* Feature 4, 201–8; flintlock musket components, *195;* at Fort Ouiatenon, 209–13; at Fort St. Joseph, 193–210; by French origin, 199, *199,* 206, *206,* 209–10; frequency of gunsmithing repairs and, *195;* historical review of, 193–94; screws and screwdrivers, 207, *208;* sideplates, *212;* weapon types and, 201, *202–3,* 207, *207*
floods, 14, 46; evidence of ongoing, 64; at Feast of the Hunters' Moon, 251–52, 256; restoration, conservation, and, 319–20; seasonal flooding and, 75n3

folk classification, 174
food: beer brewing and, 252; at Feast of the Hunters' Moon, 239, 243, 249, 251, *255*, 256; foodways and, xviii; livestock for, 108, 120–21, 122, 137
Ford, B., 47
Fort de Baude, 295
Fort de Chartres, 90, 136–38
Fort Des Chartres, 10–11
Fort Detroit, 10
Fort Duquesne, 9
Fort Harmar treaties of 1789, 12–13
Fort Harrison, 15
Fort Knox, 92, *93*
Fort Miamis, xii, *xiii*, 8; abandonment of, 86; animal use at, 136; British conflict and, 85–86; construction of, 83–84; French colonial history and, 81–86, 97; fur trade and, 84–86; map of artifacts at, *88*; occupation of, 13–14
Fort Michilimackinac, xii, 44; animal use at, 134–36; artifact collecting at, 285, 294–97; construction of, 295; fur trade and, 295; Jesuits at, 294–95; location of, 294–95; MISPC and, 295–96; rings at, 163–64
Fort Niagara's 1737 inventory, 159–60
Fort Ouiatenon: American period and, 12–17; American settlement and, 15–17; animal use at, 105–40; archaeological investigations outside of, 63–75; blacksmith area of, 42; blockhouse, 19–25, 26, 234–35, *235, 241*, 252, 312; British conflict and, 7–12; British period and, 10–12; buckles from, 173–89, *175*; collections management and curation at, 285, 287–94, 305; commandants at, 163–68, *166–67*; decline of, 10–12; destruction of, 12–13, 73; digital reconstruction of, *319*; disappearance of, 13–15; doubts and rediscovery of, 26–28; driftwood and other debris on, 75n3; environmental setting and resource potential at, 106–9, 139–40; establishment of, 3–9; flintlocks at, 209–13; French abandonment of, 12; French period and, 3–9; fur trade and, 14–15; geographical location of, 6, 311–13;

history of investigations at, 287, 291; Kickapoo and, 60–63, 69, 74–75, 314–15; magnetometry survey of, 64–73, *65–68*; maps of, xii, *xv–xvi, 5, 7*; Mascouten and, 60–63, 314–15; music at, 262–69; Myaamiaki and, 221; naming of, 221; Native American villages and, 1690-1834, 58–63; Ouiatenon area and, 58–75; Ouiatenon Preserve, xix, 229, 311–12, 317–22, *322*; Ouiatenon term use and spelling, xi, 15; rings at, 151, 152–56, *153*, 163–68; search for location of, 17–26, 311–13; site 12-T-9, 44–46, 313, *315*; site 12-T-499, 64; storehouse, 42–43; summary of site investigations and curated collections, *288–90*; three symbols of, 6, *7*; weapons at, 209–13; years of existence, 6; zooarchaeology at, 109–32. *See also specific topics*
Fort Ouiatenon archaeology: 1969 excavation student summaries, 49–52; 1971-1973 excavations and, 39–41, 49; 1974-1976 excavations and, 42–43; 1977-1979 excavations and, 43–44; community-based archaeology and, 39–41; composite map of Fort Ouiatenon excavations, *48*; conservation and, 315–18; definition of excavation grid and site placement, 52–53; funding for, 42–44, 49, 313, 316–18; history of, 35–53; investigations, outside Fort Ouiatenon, 63–75; Kellar and, 35, 38–43, 46–47, 49–53, 106, 132–34, 287, 312–13; material culture and, 49–52, 69, 71–72, 313; by Michigan State University, 41–44, 69–70, 105–6, 110, 291–92; more recent fieldwork at 12-T-9 site, 44–46; RWF and, 28, 316–17, 318, 320; spatial data and mapping excavation sites, 46–49, *48*; synthesizing previous archaeological research and data, 46–49; TCHA and, 37–43, 49, 287, 291, 311–12, 315–16; Tordoff and, 41–44, *48*, 51, 53, 70
Fort Ouiatenon Park, 19, 25, 234. *See also* Feast of the Hunters' Moon
Fort Ouiatenon Society, 37
Fortress Louisbourg, 9

INDEX   337

Fort Sackville, 91–93, *93*

Fort St. Joseph, xii, *xvi*, 8; animal use at, 117, *118*, 136–38; artifact collecting at, 285–86, *286*, 294, 297–304; avocational and professional collections from, 297–304; Chapin Mansion and, 299, 301–2; control of, 297–98; Feature 4 at, 201–8; flintlocks at, 193–210; location of, 299, 300–301; Miami Cross Society and, *286*, 299; Niles History Center and, 285–86, 294, 297–304; professional investigation of, 300–301; Seven Years' War and, 297–98; skeletal portions at, *118*

Fort St. Joseph Archaeological Project, 294, 301–2

Fort St. Joseph Curatorial Fellowship, 302–3

Fort St. Joseph Historical Association (FSJHA), 299

Fort St. Joseph Museum, 300–304

Fort Viattanow, 14

Fort Wayne, Indiana (Kekionga), 8, 13; artifacts at, 87–88; construction of, 83–84; French colonial history and French forts at, 81, 86–88; fur trade in, 87; Guldlin Park, 83, *83*, 86–87; Kiihkayonki and, 82–86; map of, *83*; West Superior Street, 87

Fox, Kristina, *225*

Fox Wars, 8–9

Franz, Philip J., *119, 122, 125, 128, 131, 133*

Fraser, Alexander, 11

Frazer, Darius, 26

Freede, Steve and Katie, 249

French and Indian War, 9, 85, 90–91, 106, 221, 312

French citizens, 163–68

French Colonial Archaeology (Walthall), 44

French colonial history: Aciipihkahkionki and, 89–92; British conflict and, 85–86, 89, 91, 221; environmental setting and, 107–8; Fort de Chartres and, 90, 136–38; Fort Miamis and, 81–86, 97; Fort Wayne and, 81, 86–88; fur trade and, 84–86, 89–91, 97, 106, 134; Myaamiaki and, 221–23; Post Vincennes and, 89–92; Queen Anne's War and, 89; Vincennes forts and, 92–98

French officers, 163–68, *166–67*

French origin flintlocks, 199, *199*, 206, *206*, 209–10

French period: British conflict in, 7–9; Fort Ouiatenon and, 3–9; fur trade in, 6–9; music in, 265–68; New France in, 3–9

Fritz, William, 301

FSJHA. *See* Fort St. Joseph Historical Association

funding, 42–44, 49, 313, 316–18

fur trade, xviii; animal use and, 106, 122–23, 134–40; during British period, 10–12, 134; early documentation of, 63–64; Fort Miamis and, 84–86; Fort Michilimackinac and, 295; Fort Ouiatenon and, 14–15; in Fort Wayne, 87; Fox Wars and, 8–9; French colonial history and, 84–86, 89–91, 97, 106, 134; in French period, 6–9; Maumee-Wabash trade route and, 8–9, 11–12; at Post Vincennes, 89–91; river mammals and, 122–23; seal rings and, 159–60

Gardner, Paul, *319*

garnets, 154, 156

GBL. *See* Glenn Black Laboratory of Archaeology

gemstones, 152, 154, 156, 158–59, 161

gender, 176–77, 179

"General Haldimand's documents," 20–21, 24–25

The Gentleman's Magazine, 187

geographic information systems (GIS), 46, 47–49

geography, 6, 106–7, 312

George Rogers Clark National Historic Park, 92–97, *93, 95*

Gerin-Lajoie, Marie, 176

Gerlach, Steve, 253

GIS. *See* geographic information systems

glass, 156, 158–59

Glenn Black Laboratory of Archaeology (GBL), xix, 38–40; collections management and, 287, 291–92; student summaries from, 49–52

Godfroy, Francois, 223
Goschenhoppen Folk Festival, 239
Gravier, Jacques, 160
Great Lakes, 4, 129, 300
Great Miami Reserve, 223
Greek legend, 161–63
Greene, George E., 94
Griffin, Thomas J., 244
Griswold, B. J., 87–88
Guldlin Park, 83, *83*, 86–87
Gunsmithing exhibit, *297*
gunsmithing repairs, *195*

Hamilton, Henry, 11–12, 86, 97
Hamtramck, John, 13
Hancock, R. G. V., 186
Handel, George Frideric, 266
handicraft row, 243
Harmar, Josiah, 12–13
harps: jaw, 262–67, *263*, 278, 280n2; music and, 262–67, 278, 280n2; strings for, 267
Harrison, William Henry, 63
Hartley, Erika, 303
Hatcher, Robert, 18–19, 23–25
Hawkins, Hubert, 28
hawks, 126
Heacox, Vivianne, 50
Heim, Lydia, 238
Heimlich, Herbert H., 235
Henry, John, 26–28, 240, 312
Hipskind, Scott, 45
historical festivals, 239. *See also* Feast of the Hunters' Moon
historical reenactments: Feast of the Hunters' Moon and, 234–35, 237–38, 258nn2–3; history of, 237; military reenactments and, 237–38, 243–44, 247; music and, 245, *255*; understanding many facets of, 237–38
Historical Society of Tippecanoe County. *See* Tippecanoe County Historical Association
historical sources, 262–69
Holmes, Robert, 85
Hood's Texas Brigade, 237

Hopkins, E. A., 238
horses, 121
"How I Found Ouiatenon" (Smith, B. W.), 19
human condition, 313
human remains, 23–24, 223–24; Native American Graves Protection and Repatriation Act and, 18; reburial of, 18; repatriation and, 18
Hunter, Diane, *321*
hunting, 108, 116–17, 134. *See also* fur trade
Hurricane Lili, 252
Hutchins, Thomas, xii, *xv–xvi*, 14, 91, 107–8

IBNT. *See* Indiana Bicentennial Nature Trust
IHT. *See* Indiana Heritage Trust
illegal immigration, 226
Illinois Country, 12
Illinois State Museum, 110
Indiana. *See specific locations*
Indiana Academy of Science, 24
Indiana Bicentennial Nature Trust (IBNT), 316–17
Indiana Geological and Water Survey, 49
Indiana Heritage Trust (IHT), 316, 317
Indiana Historical Bureau, 12
Indiana Historical Society, xi, 25, 38–39, 312
Indiana University, xi, xix
Indian Creek, 22–23
instrumental neutron activation analysis, 186
instrument builders, musical, 267
Integrated Taxonomic Information System, 110
invoices and inventories: Fort Niagara's 1737 inventory, 159–60; music prices and invoices, 262–63; other rings in, 160–61; receipts and, *225*; seal rings in, 159–60
iron, 180–86, *184, 185*
Iroquois, 264–65; raids, 58, 221
Iroquois Confederacy, 221, 252

Jackson, Misty May, 44, *153, 212*
Jacobite Revolution, 277
jaw harps, 262–67, *263*, 278, 280n2
Jenkins, Edward, 10

The Jesuit Relations (Thwaites), 160, 221, 265
Jesuits, 234, 264–65, 268–69; at Fort
    Michilimackinac, 294–95; Jesuit rings, 160
jewelry: buckles and, 177–78; composition
    of, 179–80; costume, 178; gemstones and,
    152, 154, 156, 158–59, 161; making, 156–
    58; rings, 151, 152–56, *153*, 163–68; strass,
    156–58
Jews Harps. *See* jaw harps
Johnson, Amy, 319
Johnson, William, 262–69
Jones, James R., xiii–xiv, 45–46, 64, 292,
    314–15
Jones, Kevin P., *212*

Kankakee River, 82
Kansas Territory, 223, 226–27
Kaskaskia, 222
Keene, David, 137
Kekionga. *See* Fort Wayne, Indiana
Kellar, James, xi, 28, 106, 132, 287, 312–13;
    Feast of the Hunters' Moon and, 239;
    Fort Ouiatenon archaeology and, 35,
    38–43, 46–47, 49–53, 106, 132–34, 287,
    312–13
Kentucky Pioneer Memorial State Park, 26
Kessler, Jeff, 152–56
Kethtippecanunk, 14, 61–63
Kickapoo, 60–63, 69, 74–75, 314–15
Kickapoo-Mascouten villages, 45, 57, 60–63
Kiihkayonki, 82–86, 220
King, Frances, 107
King George's War, 9
Klippel, Walter E., 131–32
Koops, Lisa H., 278
Krauskopf, Frances, xi, 6, 163–64

La Belle shipwreck, 160
Lacrosse, 252–53, *253*
Lafayette Brewing Company, 252
Lafayette Journal and Courier, 235–36, 238, 252
LA-ICP-MS technique, 173, *175*, 180–85
land acquisition, 247–48, 316, 317
land speculation, 295
language, Miami, 227, 229

Late Woodland period, 46, 50
leaded glass, 156, 158
Le Moyne, Charles, 9
Lenape, Lenni, 254
Le Pied Froid (Cold Foot), 84, 85
Levering, John, 19, 24
Lilly Foundation, 316
Lippie, Kelly, 292–94
Lis, Jennifer, 296
livestock, 108, 120–21, 122, 137
living history sites, 237–38, 254. *See also* Feast
    of the Hunters' Moon
Locomotive Museum, 23
Lonergan, Thomas, 21
Louisiane, 3–4, 7–8, 9
Louis XIII (King), 164
Louis XIV (King), 164
Louis XV (King), 158, 162–63
Louis XVI (King), 164

Mackinac Island State Park Commission
    (MISPC), 295–96
Mackinac State Historic Parks (MSHP), 294,
    296–97, 303
MacLeod, Normand, 86
magnetometry survey: of Fort Ouiatenon,
    64–73, *65–68*; of Wea village, 64–65, *65*
mammals: antlers from, *119*, 131–32, *133*; badgers, 109, 123; bear, 108–9, 121–22, *122*; bison, 107–8, 120–21, 137; cats, 124; deer,
    108–9, 116–20, *118*, *119*, *120*, 131–32, *133*;
    dogs and canid, 123; environmental setting and, 107–9; horses, 121; pigs, 122;
    racoons, 122–23; river, 122–23; small, 124;
    use of, *111–12*, 116–24; wapiti, 108–9, 121
MAP I assessment, 300
maps: composite map of Fort Ouiatenon excavations, *48*; of Fort Miamis artifacts
    at, *88*; of Fort Ouiatenon, xii, *xv–xvi*, *5*, *7*;
    of Fort Wayne, *83*; of Myaamia Removal
    Route, 1846, *225*; of Ouiatenon area, 58–
    59, *59*; Sanborn Fire Insurance 1892 map
    of Vincennes, *93*; spatial data and mapping excavation sites, 46–49, *48*; of vegetation zones, *59*

Marseiles, Skipper Henry, 263–64
Martin, Terrance J., 44, 58
Mascouten: Fort Ouiatenon and, 60–63, 314–15; Kickapoo-Mascouten villages, 45, 57, 60–63
Mason, Carol, 160
material culture, 49–52, 69, 71–72, 313
Maumee River, 4
Maumee-Wabash corridor, 8–9; during British period, 10–11
Maumee-Wabash trade route, 8–9, 11–12
McCollough, Alameda, 26, 28
McCullough, Robert, 44–45, 317
medical practices, 253
Meehcikilita, 218
Meehkwaakonanka, 222
Miami Cross Society, *286*, 299
Miami Nation, 223, 227
Miami National Council, 222, 223, 226
Miami people. *See* Myaamiaki
Miami Reservation, 226–27
Miami Tribe of Oklahoma, 217–19, *218–20, 225*, 227–29, *228, 229*, 320
Michigan Alliance for the Conservation of Cultural Heritage, 301
Michigan State University, xi, xvii–xviii; Fort Ouiatenon archaeology and, 41–44, 69–70, 105–6, 110, 291–92
middens, 132–34
"middle ground," xiv
Midwest Historical Archaeology Conference, xi–xii, 28
migration: illegal immigration and, 226; of Myaamiaki, 218–24, 226
Mihtohseenia, 226–27
Mihtohseeniaki, 218
military buckles, 187–89
military music, 277–78, 280
military reenactments, 237–38, 243–44, 247
militia, 12–13, 61–62
Miller, Thomas, 226–27
Mineralogical Research Company, 183
minimum number of individuals (MNI), 110, 132–34
mining, 43, 183

Minnesota Historical Society, 176
MISCP. *See* Mackinac Island State Park Commission
misplaced artifacts, 302
MMR. *See* Montreal Merchant Records
MNI. *See* minimum number of individuals
mollusks, *115*, 130–31, *131*
Molnar, Peter, 183
Moniere, Alexis, Sr., 176
monograms, 158–59
Montreal Merchant Records (MMR), 160, 174, 176–80, *179*, 188–89
Moore, Elijah, 16
Moreau, J. F., 186
Morris, Thomas, 10
Moses, David and Caroline, 251
MSHP. *See* Mackinac State Historic Parks
Mulvey, Robert Raymond, 26–28, 38, 63–64
music: in "Ah! Si Mon Moine Voulait Danser!" song, 276–77; artifact collecting and, 262–69; bagpipes and, 277; cello and, 267; Celtic, 277, 278; in "C'est L'aviron" song, 270, 276; children and, 276–80; cultural representation and, 270, *273–74*; dance and, 265; drums and, 264–65; Feast musical genres, 269–70, *271–72*; at Feast of the Hunters' Moon, 245, 247, 252, 254, *255*, 256, 261–80; at Fort Ouiatenon, 262–69; in French period, 265–68; harp and, 262–67, 278, 280n2; historical sources for, 262–69; instrument builders and, 267; Johnson, W., and, 262–69; military, 277–78, 280; musical depictions today, 269–78; musical groups including people under eighteen, 270, *275*; organ and, 268–69, 278; prices and invoices, 262–63; religion and, 269; remembrance and, 278–79; Scottish, 277, 278; tradition and, 278–79
mussels, 130–31
Myaamiaki (Miami people), xviii–xix; during American period, 222–25; American Revolution and, 221; cultural revitalization of, 227–29; Fort Ouiatenon and, 221; French and Indian War and,

INDEX

221; French colonial history and, 221–23; history of, 217–25; leadership of, 220, 222, 226–27; map of villages and territories of, *219, 220*; Miami language and, 227, 229; Miami National Council and, 222, 223, 226; Miami Nation and, 223, 227; Miami Reservation and, 226–27; Miami Tribe of Oklahoma and, 217–19, *218–20, 225,* 227–29, *228, 229,* 320; migration of, 218–24, 226; Oklahoma Indian Welfare Act and, 227; organization of, 220; Ouiatenon Preserve and, 229; Peoria Tribe of Oklahoma and, 219, 227–29; politics and, 220, 222; removal of, 222–27, *225*; treaties and, 221–23, 226–27; Wabash River and, 218–20
Myaamia Removal Route, 1846, *225*
Myaamia reservation land, 36
Myers, Kelsey Noack, 47, *48*

National Historic Landmark Archaeological District, 320
Native American Graves Protection and Repatriation Act (1990), 18
Native Americans: during American period, 12–17; buckles of, 186–88; Euro-Americans portraying, 258n2; European contact with, 58; farmers and, 12–13; military victories by, 62; New France and, 6–8; recognizing tribes of, 240; removal of, 35–36, 222–27, *225*; villages in Ouiatenon area, 1690-1834, 58–63. *See also specific topics*
Nature Conservancy, 315
neenawihtoowaki (war leaders), 222
Neff, Lucianne, 38, 49–52
New France: administration of, 4; in French period, 3–9; Native Americans and, 6–9; Washington, G., and, 9
New Life for Archaeological Collections (Allen and Ford), 47
A New Map of the Western Parts of Virginia, Pennsylvania, Maryland and North Carolina (Hutchins), *xvi*
Nickel, Robert K., 96–97

Niles Daily Star (newspaper), 299
Niles History Center, 285–86, 294, 297–304
NISP. *See* number of identified specimens
Noble, Vergil, 43–44, *48,* 106, 294; National Historic Landmark application and, 320
Nordic Fest, 239
North Fork Rounders, 245
Northwest Ordinance of 1787, 13
Northwest Territory, 13, 15–16, 221–23
number of identified specimens (NISP), 110, 132–35

Ohio Country, 9, 12
Ohio River, 4
Ohio River valley, 89, 97–98
Oklahoma Indian Welfare Act (1936), 227
Old Fort Harrod, 26
"Old Settlers" (Cox), 36–37
organ music, 268–69, 278
Ouiatanon Documents (Krauskopf), xii
Ouiatenon area: archaeological investigations, outside Fort Ouiatenon, 63–75; environmental setting of, 106–9, 139–40; map of, 58–59, *59*; Native American villages in, 1690-1834, 58–63; upland areas, 58–59; vegetation zones in, *59*
Ouiatenon Brigade, 240
Ouiatenon Club of Crawfordsville, 24, 25
Ouiatenon Preserve, xix; accomplishments and expansion of, 317–19; conservation and, 315–22; Conservation Reserve Enhancement Program and, 318–20; creating, 311–12; land acquisition for, 317; Myaamiaki and, 229; National Historic Landmark Archaeological District and, 320; overlook and interpretation area, 317–18, *322*; view from overlook of, *322*; Wabash Heritage Trail and, 321
outreach initiatives, xix, 284

Padley, Genevieve, *298*
Palaanswa (Second Chief), 223
Pallier, Joseph, 11
Panchrestographie (Beaugrand), 163, *164*
Parmalee, Paul W., 131–32

Pascaud (merchant), 177–79
Pasquier, Jacques Jean, 163
paste stones, 178; figures depicted on, 161–63; history of, 156–58
PastPerfect, 301
Pays d'en Haut, xii, xiv
Peepakicia family, 223–24
Peewaaliaki, 219
Peeyankihšiaki, 222
Peoria Tribe of Oklahoma, 219, 227–29
Perez, Yvey, 254
periods: American, 12–17, 222–25; British, 10–12, 134; French, 3–9, 265–68; Late Woodland, 46, 50
Petersen Center, 285
Piankashaw Tribe, 8, 62–63, 89
Pickawillany, 60
pigs, 122
pinchbeck, 177–80, 182, 186, 188
Pinšiwa, 218, 223
pioneer skills, 242
pipes, 71
politics, 220, 222
Pontiac's Rebellion, 10, 51, 85–86, 134, 277
postholes, 67, 69
Post Vincennes, xii, *xiii*; French colonial history and, 89–92
Potawatomi, xii–xiii, *xiii*, 16; land of, 36; structures of, 72
Potawatomi Trail of Death, 36
poteaux-en-terre structure, 69–70, 96
Powder Magazine exhibit, *297*
prairie, 16, 17
preservation, 284, 305; of tribal land, 35–36. *See also* collections management
projectile points, 131–32, *133*
Prophetstown, 63
Public Archives of Canada, 176
public engagement: collections management and, 284; public outreach and, xix, 284; suggestions and, 253–54
Purdue Exponent (newspaper), 22–23
Purdue University, 22–24, 26, 42

Quantrill, William, 226

Queen Anne's War, 89
Quimby, George Irving, 50, 299–300

racoons, 122–23
raids, 12–13
Ravenscroft, George, 156, 158
Raymond, Charles de, 84–85
Raymond, Chevalier de, 165
Reaume, Simon, 163–64
receipts, *225*
Reckowsky, Michael, *319*
Recollections of the Early Settlement of the Wabash Valley (Cox), 17
Reily, Charles Lewis, 264
Reitz, Elizabeth J., 110
religion: Catholicism and, 160, 266, 269; music and, 269
remembrance, 278–79
remote sensing, xviii
removal, of Native Americans, 35–36, 222–27, *225*
repatriation, 18
reptiles, 108–9, *114*, 127, *128*
resource potential, 106–9, 139–40
Rhoads site (11-Lo-8), 73–74
Richardville, Thomas F., 226–27
Rigaud, Phillipe de, 6, 7–8
rings: at Fort Michilimackinac, 163–64; at Fort Ouiatenon, 151, 152–56, *153*, 163–68; Jesuit, 160; other, 160–61; seal, 159–61; signet, 151, 152–59, 161–63
rivercraft: canoes and, 242, 244, 247–48, *257*; on Wabash River, 14–15
river mammals, 122–23
Rogers, Robert, 13–14
Rosasco, Betsy, 162
Ross, Harvey Lee, 72
Rossville Junior High History Club, 239, 240
Royal Highlanders of Lafayette, 91, 97, 244
Roy Whistler Foundation (RWF), 28, 316–17, 318, 320
Rumsey, John, 91, 97–98
RWF. *See* Roy Whistler Foundation

Saakiiweeyonki, 217–20

INDEX

Sabrevois, Jacques-Charles de, 107–8
Saint-Aubin, Augustin, 163
St. Clair, Arthur, 13
St. Clair's Defeat (Battle of the Wabash), 221
St. Marys treaties, 15–16
Šako, 222
Sanborn Fire Insurance 1892 map of Vincennes, *93*
Sand Ridge Cemetery, 19
Sand Ridge Church, 19, 22
Sauter, Brooke, *153*
Savary, des Brûlons, Jacques, 179, 182–83
Scarry, C. Margaret, 110
Schoolcraft, Henry R., 16
Schwab, Jeff, 251, 258
Scott, Charles, 44–45, 61–62, 73
Scott, John, 14
Scottish music, 277, 278
screwdrivers, 207, *208*
screws, 207, *208*
seal rings, 159–61
seasonal flooding, 75n3
settlement, during American period, 15–17
Seven Years' War, 267, 297–98
Sharp, Willard, 254
Shawnee brothers, 63
Shawnee Prophet's movement, 63
sheet midden contexts, 132–34
Shipments *(Cincinnati Gazette), 225*
Sholty, Bill, 26–28, 38
sideplates, *212*
Sievert, April, 292
signet ring: composition of, 152–56, *155, 157*; description of, 152; at Fort Ouiatenon, 151, 152–56, *153*, 163–68; history of, 158–59; symbolism in, 151, 152, 161–63
Šiikwia, 222
similor, 161, 177–80, 182, 186
site placement, Fort Ouiatenon, 52–53
slag fragments, 71
slavery, 226
small mammals, 124
Smith, Benjamin Wilson, 18–22, 25
Smith, Bruce, 124–25
Smith, Jim, 240

Smith, Russell, 252
Smithsonian Folklife Festival, 239
snails, *115*, 130–31, *131*
snakes, 127
social status, 177–78, 186–88
Spain, 7
spatial data, 46–49, *48*
Special Kids Day, 248–49
Spoon River valley, 72
Stadler, Alphonso, 49–50, 53
Ste. Genevieve, Missouri, 96
stockade trench, 51
Stone, Lyle, 174, 300
storage space, for artifacts, 291–93, *293*, 302, 303, *303*
storehouse, 42–43
Strass, Georges-Frédéric, 158
strass jewelry, 156–58
Strezewski, Michael, *xiii*, 44–46, *48*, 51, *166–67*, 292, 317
structural forms, 71–74
Sunderland, Francis, 19
Sunderland family, 19
superpositioning, of features, 73
symbolism: of Dauphin of France, 163–65, *164*, 168; in signet rings, 151, 152, 161–63

TAC. *See* Archaeological Conservancy
Tamburro, Paul René, 258n2
tarnish, 178–79
taxes, 226
Taylor, J. N., 25
TCHA. *See* Tippecanoe County Historical Association
Tecumseh Fiddlers, 245
Tecumseh Lodge, 240
tepees, 242–43
Terre Haute, 15, 63
Thomas, David, 15, 108
Thomas, Julian, 52
Thwaites, Reuben Gold, 7–8, 160, 221, 265
tinsmith, *250*
Tippecanoe Ancient Fife & Drums Corps, 240
Tippecanoe County, 16; environmental setting and resource potential in, 106–9, 139–40

Tippecanoe County Historical Association (TCHA), xi, xix, 28, *293*; buckles and, 173–74, *175*; butt plates and, *210, 211*; collections management and, 287, 291–94; community-based archaeology and, 39–41; Fort Ouiatenon archaeology and, 37–43, 49, 287, 291, 311–12, 315–16; founding of, 18–19, 25–26; RWF and, 316–17, 318, 320; search for Fort Ouiatenon by, 17–26; stakeholders of, 316. *See also* Feast of the Hunters' Moon

Tippecanoe County Park Department, 37

Tomak, Curtis H., 94, *95,* 96

tombac, 177–80, 181–88, *184, 185*

Toohpia, 226

Tordoff, Judith D., xiii, 106, 132–34; collections management and, 291, 294; Fort Ouiatenon archaeology and, 41–44, *48,* 51, 53, 70

A Tour from Fort Cumberland North Westward Round Part of the Lakes Erie, Huron, and Michigan, Including Part of the Rivers St. Joseph, the Wabach, and Miamis, with a Sketch of the Road from Thence to the Lower Shawnoe Town to Fort Pitt (Hutchins), *xv*

trade goods, 173–74, 177–80. *See also* buckles; fur trade

trade silver disc, *20, 21*

trading posts, 51–52

traditions: at Feast of the Hunters' Moon, 241–42, 278–79; music and, 278–79; remembrance and, 278–79

treaties, 10, 35–36, 62; Myaamiaki and, 221–23, 226–27; St. Marys treaties, 15–16; Treaty of 1867, 227; Treaty of Fort Harmar, 12–13; Treaty of Greenville of 1795, 15–16, 222; Treaty of Paris, 9, 221; Treaty of Stanwix, 12

trees, 16

trenches, 51, 67–69, *68*; function of, 69–70; at Vincennes forts, 94–96

tribal land preservation, 35–36

"Tri-County Historical Itinerary" (pamphlet), 36

Trowbridge, C. C., 218

Trubowitz, Neal, 45–46, 49, 64, 107, 292, 314–15

turkey, 108–9, 124–25, *125*

Turner, Jocelyn, 49

turtles, 108–9, 127, *128*

Ulrich et al., 58

University of Southern Indiana, 67

upland areas, 58–59

van Frese, Ralph, 132

vegetation zones, *59*

Vermillion River, 63

Vietnam War, 239

Vincennes forts: archaeology of, 81–82, 92–98; Post Vincennes and, 89–92; Sanborn Fire Insurance 1892 map of Vincennes, *93*

Voyageurs Ancient Fife and Drum Corps, 240

Waapimaankwa, 226–27

Waawiyaasita family, 223–24

Waayaahtanooki, xviii–xix, 217–19, 221–23. *See also* Wea people

Wabash College, 24

Wabash Heritage Trail, 321

Wabash River, 4, 106–7; American settlement and, 15–17; conservation of, 319–20; fishes in, 128–30; flooding of, 46; mollusks in, 130–31; Myaamiaki and, 218–20; rivercraft on, 14–15; Wea people and, 58–63, 218–19

Waddell, Carol, 246

Wade, Francis, 267

Wade, John, 14–15

Wagner, Mark J., 73–74

Waldron, Janice, 278

Wallace, Hugh, 263–64, 266–67

wall trenches, 51, 67–70, *68*; at Vincennes forts, 94–96

Walthall, John A., 44, 160

wapiti, 108–9, 121

war heroes, 234

war leaders (neenawihtoowaki), 222

War of 1812, 92, 222
War of Austrian Succession, 9
War of Spanish Succession, 7
Washington, George, 9
Washington, Martha, 178
water craft, 4
waterfowl, 125–26
Wayne, Anthony, 14–16
Wea Creek, 16, 20, 25
Wea people, xi–xiii, 60–61, 75n1, 106; Wabash River and, 58–63, 218–19
Wea Plains, 58–59, 106–7
weapons, 193–94; in Feature 4, 207, *207*; at Fort Ouiatenon, 209–13; frequency of gunsmithing repairs and, *195*; in Gunsmithing exhibit, *297*; gunsmithing repairs and, *195*; types of, 201, *202–3*, 207, *207*. *See also* flintlocks
Weatherby, Clement, 299
Weaver, Peter, 16
Wea village, 45, 52, 57, 58; magnetometry survey of, 64–65, *65*
weddings, 257–58
The Western Gazetteer (Brown, Samuel R.), 15
West Superior Street, 87
Wetherill, Richard B., 18–19, *19*, 26, *27*, 234, 312
Whalen, Michael, 50
Whetherhill, Richard B., 37

White, Claude, 40
White, Richard, xiv
white-tailed deer. *See* deer
White Thunder, 247
Widder, Keith R., 14
wigwams, 71–72, 74
Wildman, Tom, 265
Wilkinson, James, 13, 14, 62
women's buckles, 176–77, 179
wood, 69; driftwood and, 75n3

youth, 90, 226, *228, 229*; Boy Scouts and, 234–35, 242, 246, 252, 257–58; at Feast of the Hunters' Moon, 234–35, 246–49, *248*, 252–54, *253*, 257–58; music and, 276–80; Rossville Junior High History Club and, 239, 240

zinc, 180–86, *184, 185*
zinc alloy, 181–82
zooarchaeology: birds and, *112–14*, 124–27; fishes and, *114–15*, 127–30; at Fort Ouiatenon, 109–32; Integrated Taxonomic Information System and, 110; mammal use and, *111–12*, 116–24; methods, 109–10; miscellaneous modified animal specimens, 131–32; mollusks and, *115*, 130–31, *131*; overview of, 111–32; reptiles and amphibians and, *114*, 127, *128*